ELECTIONS, PARTIES, AND COALITIONS IN INDIA

Eswaran Sridharan

ELECTIONS, PARTIES, AND COALITIONS IN INDIA

Theory and Recent History

permanent black

Published by
PERMANENT BLACK
'Himalayana', Mall Road, Ranikhet Cantt,
Ranikhet 263645
perblack@gmail.com

Distributed by
ORIENT BLACKSWAN PRIVATE LTD
Bangalore Bhopal Bhubaneshwar Chandigarh Chennai
Ernakulam Guwahati Hyderabad Jaipur Kolkata
Lucknow Mumbai New Delhi Patna
www.orientblackswan.com

ISBN 978-81-7824-673-4

Typeset in Adobe Garamond Pro
by Guru Typograph Technology, Crossings Republic, Ghaziabad

Printed and bound by Manipal Technologies Limited, Manipal

Contents

Preface and Acknowledgements

THIS SELECTION of ten of my papers – earlier published in a range of academic journals and edited volumes – covers two broad areas: elections and voting behaviour, and political parties and coalition politics. My objective in collecting them within a single volume is to present the evolution of key elections and shifts in voting patterns in the post-1989 period of post-Congress dominance. Read collectively, the essays show the rise or decline of parties, a reshaping of the party system, developments in the patterns of coalition politics, the emergence of the era of coalition and/or minority governments, and the rise of the Bharatiya Janata Party (BJP). They also show, conversely, how coalition politics has enabled the rise of the BJP and regional parties, and a temporary revival of the Congress from 2004 to 2014, and how this has affected elections and the party system in reverse.

All the papers undertake empirical analysis of the electoral system – including one on its origins and one on the evolution of political finance, elections, party behaviour – or coalition patterns situated in relevant theorising. Read as a body they show interconnected historical, conceptual, theoretical, and empirical points in the study of recent Indian politics of value for scholars and students in this broad area of scholarship.

Let me briefly explain what these papers are essentially about and why they are important for the study of Indian politics.

The first cluster is of four papers on "The Electoral System and Voting Behaviour in Key Elections". Here, the first paper, "The Origins of the Electoral System: Electoral Rules, Representation and Power-sharing in India's Democracy", is the only piece of research, to my knowledge, on how India debated and chose its first-past-the-post electoral system in the Constituent Assembly debates. The important questions it asks are whether possible alternative systems were considered and systematically debated, how the choice was made, and what modifications were adopted. This paper is relevant to both electoral studies and contemporary history.

The second paper, "Understanding Voting Patterns by Class in the 2019 Indian Election", is an analysis of voting patterns by class and caste as well as an analysis of the extent of spread of anti-minority attitudes based on CSDS/Lokniti post-election survey questions on nationalism and minorities. A key finding in it is that anti-minority attitudes were less prevalent than is widely believed.

The third paper, "Class Voting in the 2014 Lok Sabha Elections: The Growing Size and Importance of the Middle Classes", is an analysis of voting patterns by class based on CSDS/Lokniti post-election survey data. It shows that the votes of the rising middle classes were very important to the BJP victory but also that anti-minority attitudes are less prevalent than might appear.

The fourth paper in this cluster is "Electoral Coalitions in the 2004 General Elections: Theory and Evidence". It reveals the impact of pre-electoral alliances, state by state, for the 2004 election, which resulted in a revival of the Congress party for a decade. It is relevant both for understanding the role of electoral alliances in India as well as a key past election which resulted in a change of power for the next ten years.

In the second cluster of papers, on "Political Parties and Coalition Politics in India's Federal Polity" – the fifth paper in this volume and the first in its cluster (co-authored with Adnan Farooqui) – "Can Umbrella Parties Survive? The Decline of the Indian National Congress" – is an empirical and theoretical analysis of the decline of Congress as a historically dominant umbrella party. Against a backdrop of the sharpening of social cleavages based on caste and religion and the rise of regional assertions over the decades, the paper discusses why Congress is still the second largest political party in India today.

The sixth paper, also co-authored with Adnan Farooqui, "Incumbency, Internal Processes and Renomination in Indian Parties", is the only available empirical analysis set in comparative context of how candidates for elections are nominated/renominated by major Indian parties. It covers five national parties – Congress, BJP, CPI (M), Samajwadi Party, and Bahujan Samaj Party.

The seventh paper, "Coalition Strategies and the BJP's Expansion, 1989–2004", is an analysis of the key role played by pre-electoral alliances, state by state, in the crucial build-up and consolidation phase of the BJP from 1989 to 2004, when it went from 11 per cent vote share in 1989 to 25 per cent in 1998 to 19 per cent in 2004. In addition to its ideological spread, skilful formation and management of alliances enabled the BJP to successfully contest ever-larger numbers of seats in more and more states over this growth phase in its history. Coalitions as an enabler of the BJP's growth are often neglected in the literature.

The eighth paper, "Coalition Congruence in India's Federal System", is both a contribution to the fourth-generation coalition theory literature – that is, the interaction between coalition politics, including pre-electoral alliances, at the state level with the national level – as well as an explanation of the evolution of the Indian party system over time based on the evolution of coalitions at both levels.

The ninth paper, "Why are Multi-party Minority Governments Viable in India? Theory and Comparison", is an analysis of the period of minority and/or coalition governments in India, post-1989, in theoretical and comparative context. It explains why and how India, counterintuitively, had several stable minority and coalition governments under Prime Ministers Rao, 1991–6, Vajpayee, 1999–2004, and Singh, 2004–14.

The tenth and last paper in this selection, co-authored with Milan Vaishnav, "Political Finance in a Developing Democracy: The Case of India", is an analytical and historical account of the evolution of the little-studied issue of political finance in India – how parties fund themselves for elections and inter-election needs, and the evolution of the regulatory framework set in the context of the evolving political economy since Independence. These issues are necessary to understand party functioning, hidden constraints on policy, and political outcomes. The subject of this essay remains under-researched despite its crucial relevance.

I would like to acknowledge the original publishers of these essays and thank them for permission to republish them in this volume.

Permanent Black for "The Origins of the Electoral System: Electoral Rules, Representation and Power-sharing in India's Democracy", which first appeared in Zoya Hasan, E. Sridharan and R. Sudarshan, eds, *India's Living Constitution: Ideas, Practices, Controversies*, New Delhi: Permanent Black, 2002, and London: Anthem Press, 2005.

Taylor and Francis for permission to publish the following papers which first appeared in the UK-based Routledge journal *Commonwealth and Comparative Politics*: (with Adnan Farooqui), "Can Umbrella Parties Survive? The Decline of the Indian National Congress", *Commonwealth and Comparative Politics*, vol. 54, no. 3, July 2016; (with Adnan Farooqui) "Incumbency, Internal Processes and Renomination in Indian Parties", *Commonwealth and Comparative Politics*, vol. 52, no. 1, January 2014; "Coalition Strategies and the BJP's Expansion, 1989–2004", *Commonwealth and Comparative Politics*, vol. 43, no. 2, July 2005, 194–221; "Why are Multi-party Minority Governments Viable in India? Theory and Comparison", *Commonwealth and Comparative Politics*, vol. 50, no. 3, July 2012.

The *Economic and Political Weekly* for permission to publish two papers from their Special Articles series: "Class Voting in the 2014 Lok Sabha Elections: The Growing Size and Importance of the Middle Classes", *Economic and Political Weekly*, vol. XLIX, no. 39, 27 September 2014, 72–6; and "Electoral Coalitions in the 2004 General Elections: Theory and Evidence", *Economic and Political Weekly*, vol. XXXIX, no. 51, 18–24 December 2004, 5418–25.

The Policy Studies Organization of Washington D.C. for permission to publish "Understanding Voting Patterns by Class in the 2019 Indian Election", *Indian Politics and Policy*, vol. 3, no. 1, Spring 2020.

Springer Nature for permission to publish "Coalition Congruence in India's Federal System" in Adrian Albala and Josep Maria Reniu, eds, *Coalition Politics and Federalism*, Cham, Switzerland: Springer, 2018.

Oxford University Press for permission to publish "Political Finance in a Developing Democracy: The Case of India", in Devesh Kapur and Milan Vaishnav, eds, *Costs of Democracy: Political Finance in India*, New Delhi: Oxford University Press, 2018.

I specially thank Adnan Farooqui for his consent to include two of our co-authored papers, and Milan Vaishnav to include one co-authored paper.

I acknowledge the support of the Ford Foundation for two multi-year projects between 2000 and 2015 on India's Constitution, which resulted in an edited volume, and on coalition politics in India, which resulted in two edited volumes; and that of Mahindra & Mahindra and the Japan Foundation for the latter project. Some of the papers here were the outcome of these projects, either directly or as spin-offs.

I would like to thank the Center for the Advanced Study of India, University of Pennsylvania, particularly Francine Frankel and Devesh Kapur in earlier years, and the Governing Council of the University of Pennsylvania Institute for the Advanced Study of India (UPIASI) for broad-based, long-term support.

I thank Anuradha Bhasin for careful reformatting of the papers and Tishya Sethi and Paridhi Chhatwal of UPIASI for reformatting the many tables in Excel; and the UPIASI staff, Ruchika Ahuja and Jacqueline Massey.

Last but not least I express my gratitude to Divya Raina and Tarini Sridharan for their affection and patience for which no words are adequate.

New Delhi, April 2023

1

The Origins of the Electoral System

Rules, Representation, and Power-sharing in India's Democracy

Democratic Constitutions as Power-sharing Devices

DEMOCRATIC CONSTITUTIONS pertain primarily to means rather than to ends. They lay down the ground rules of government and politics, usually undergirded by certain foundational principles, including fundamental rights, the rule of law, an implicit or explicit concept of justice, and the like. However, constitutions can also be interpreted as a historic social compact reflecting the state of a nation or nation-in-the-making at a specific historical moment, their subsequent career reflecting the evolution of the nation and the state. Constitutions can also, usually secondarily and indirectly, prescribe ends or outcomes, such as national unity, stability, integration, development and distributive justice, and the like. From both these perspectives, constitutions are effective in nation-building if they conduce to power-sharing in such a way that all sections of the nation or nation-in-the-making feel that the constitution embodies justice, protects their core interests, and gives them a fair share of representation in the structures of power, and a stake in the order created. This paper makes a preliminary attempt to view the

Indian constitution as a device for power sharing, and hence for building a united India in which all citizens can feel they have a share in power and a stake. The focus will be on *one particular aspect of the rules of the game of politics that is key to representation and hence to power sharing, viz., the electoral system*, and the evolution of debates about it. The electoral system will be viewed in the context of other features such as federalism and fundamental rights, including their sub-sets, minority rights, and reservations for historically disadvantaged groups, which crucially impinge on representation and, hence, power-sharing.

The paper deviates from the theme of constitutional ideas and political practices since it is more about a debate that did not take place, a blind spot rather than an explicit debate about the merits of alternative electoral systems for representation and power-sharing in a society plural along multiple axes – religious, linguistic, regional, caste, tribal, etc. However, the blind spots in the history of constitutional and political debate are often instructive. An underlying premise is that power sharing of a kind that is felt to be fair by all groups in society, including minorities and historically disadvantaged groups, is *a necessary condition for voluntary loyalty and national integration in the long run in a multiply-diverse society with a history of conflicts.* This does not mean that we judge an electoral system by the yardstick on how perfectly it represents all the groups in the population. Exact proportionality in representation may be impossible. Yet a purposive nation-building effort, or even just a society and a leadership aware of the interests of all of its members, has to continually review its system of representation to ensure that the entire citizenry feel that their interests are recognised in the system and opportunities created for them to find fulfilment.

We develop the paper as follows in the next four sections. In the second section, after outlining the existing electoral system, we outline the evolution of the Indian party system, particularly the period since 1989 when it took off on a trajectory that it was never intended to do by the electoral system chosen after independence. That is, it became a multi-party system characterised by large and unwieldy coalition governments, in a society increasingly politicised along communal, caste, and regional lines. In the third section, we then outline the various proposals for electoral-systemic reform that have been mooted in public discourse since the late 1990s in response to the emergence of such a party system and such governments, and such perceived politicisation of social cleavages. In the fourth section, we go back to the origins to investigate how the electoral system was originally chosen, that is, whether its merits were debated in comparison to possible alternative systems, what effects it was intended to produce or avoid, whether its current effects half a century later were ever anticipated, and whether any alternatives were seriously considered and why they were rejected and the existing system adopted. Finally, in the fifth and concluding section, we pull together the threads. The paper focuses on the importance of the electoral system for representation and power-sharing, both in the context of the various reform proposals at the beginning of the twenty-first century, and when it goes back to examine its origins and evolution and the debate, or lack of it, around it.

The Emergence of a Multi-Party System, Coalition Governments, and Politicisation of Social Cleavages

The Indian electoral system is a single-member district, simple-plurality system in which voters (over the age of eighteen since 1989) cast a single ballot to choose a single representative to the lower house of parliament (Lok Sabha) or the state legislative assembly, the candidate with the largest number of votes, even if only a plurality, getting elected to represent that constituency. There are 543 constituencies that send a single member each to the Lok Sabha (two members are nominated). This first-past-the-post (FPTP) system, in common parlance, was adopted shortly after independence, following debates in the Constituent Assembly (1946–9) and parliament (1950–1) just before the adoption of the Representation of the People Act, 1950 and 1951, and the first general elections of 1952. At that time, there were a significant number of two-member constituencies, and some three-member constituencies, in which one or two seats were reserved for Scheduled Castes or Scheduled Tribes, but in which the electoral formula remained the FPTP one, candidates getting elected in order of the number of votes cast. However, in these constituencies, voters had two or three ballots and had to cast them for different candidates. Multi-member constituencies were abolished in 1961, following which the electoral system has been the single-member, FPTP system.

This electoral system produced a party system, in the elections from 1952 to 1984, in which the single largest party won only a plurality of the votes but got a majority of the seats, and formed a single-party majority government. In all elections from 1952 to 1984, the single largest party which formed a majority government was the Congress party, except for 1977 when it was the Janata party formed by almost the entire non-Communist opposition. The single largest party never got a simple majority, the maximum percentage of votes received being 48 per cent by the Congress in 1984, but always got a majority, several times a two-thirds or (in 1984) even a three-fourths majority.

However, the party system changed from 1989. The past five general elections in India, in 1989, 1991, 1996, 1998, and 1999, have resulted in hung parliaments and, as a consequence, minority and/or coalition governments. Even the Congress government of 1991–6 was a minority government for the first two-and-a-half years of its term. The other post-1989 governments – those of the Janata Dal-led National Front minority coalition of prime minister V.P. Singh, dependent on the support of both the right-wing Bharatiya Janata Party (BJP) and the Left Front, the Janata Dal splinter group led by Prime Minister Chandra Shekhar with a tenth of the Lok Sabha (Lower House) supported by the much larger Congress party, the two United Front minority coalition governments of prime ministers Deve Gowda and I.K. Gujral, dependent on the support of both the Congress and most of the Left Front – did not last a full term, indeed less than a year each. The National Front and the two United Front governments were large coalitions (five to ten governing parties) which were dependent for their parliamentary majority on supporting parties. The BJP-led coalitions governing since March 1998, and again since October 1999, the latter formally called the National Democratic Alliance, were even larger coalitions. These coalitions have been some of the largest in the world in terms of the number of governing parties.

The decline of the Congress vote to below the critical (varying) threshold at which a vote plurality translated to a seat majority led to hung parliaments and coalition politics. The long-term reasons for this were: the desertion of the Congress by sections of its erstwhile base, including rich peasants, Scheduled Castes, and Muslims, in large parts of the country; the inability of the Congress to incorporate newly mobilised groups such as farmers and intermediate castes; in turn, at least partly because of the decline of the internally democratic and grand-coalitional character of the party following the Congress split of 1969 and centralisation under Indira Gandhi.

Second, another significant trend over the past decade in Indian politics is the rise of identity politics, including Hindu majoritarianism manifested in the rise of the BJP, and the like-minded Shiv Sena in Maharashtra. Identity politics is also represented by the Kashmiri Muslim secessionist insurgency since 1989, and regional parties with an ethno-cultural platform in several states, including the Dravidian parties in Tamil Nadu, the Akali Dal in Punjab, the Telugu Desam in Andhra Pradesh, and the Asom Gana Parishad in Assam, besides continuing secessionist insurgencies in Assam, Nagaland, and Manipur, and movements within some states to secede and form new states in parts of existing large states. The latter movements have led to the formation of three new states in November 2000 – Uttarakhand, Jharkhand, and Chhattisgarh – carved out of Uttar Pradesh (U.P.), Bihar, and Madhya Pradesh (M.P.), respectively. The rise of caste-based parties like the Bahujan Samaj Party (BSP), and to a lesser extent the Samajwadi Party in U.P. and the Rashtriya Janata Dal (RJD) in Bihar, also reflects the rise of identity politics.

The main points we wish to make are that *both the traditional justifications for the FPTP system,* in general and in India, including in the Constituent Assembly debates which we will discuss shortly, *viz., that it produces stable single-party majority governments, and that its aggregative imperative leads to national integration as against splitting of the party system along "ethnic" (broadly defined, including religio-communal, caste, regional-ethnic, cultural, etc.) lines,* have been belied in practice for a decade now.

Two questions arise: first, are coalitions unstable and short-lived due to the logic of the FPTP electoral system? We have argued in detail elsewhere that this is in fact the case, though emphasising that coalitions have the plus point of being more broadly representative.[1] The main reason is that the seat–vote disproportionality of the FPTP systems induces instability between the parties of the ruling coalition and the opposition on the one hand, and tensions between the coalition partners on the other. This is because even a small swing in votes can effect a much larger swing in seats. Therefore, power can shift between opposing coalitions quite dramatically, and coalition-making parties have an incentive to try to split the opposing coalition by every means, the payoff being potentially high. Likewise, a small swing in popularity leading to even a small swing in votes between coalition partners can lead to a large swing in seats, potentially decimating some parties while boosting others, dramatically altering their bargaining power. This is unlike under the proportional

[1] Sridharan, "Principles, Power and Coalition Politics in India", 270–90.

representation (PR) system, where vote swings, which are rarely dramatic, lead to only roughly proportional swings in seats. This leads to the question: would a shift to some form of proportional representation lead to more stable coalition governments? In short, could PR usher in a shift from majoritarian democracy to what Arend Lijphart has called a consensus democracy?[2] Or would it lead to even greater fragmentation of the party system? If the former, then there is a possible rationale for a shift to proportional representation of some kind, like the shift towards the German-style mixed FPTP-list PR system that Japan and New Zealand effected in the first half of the 1990s in their own variants.

And second, is the rise of such "ethnic" – communal, caste-based, regional nationalist/separatist – political parties and movements, and the social and psychological cost in terms of the fears of majority domination, political marginalisation, and cultural submergence, and the furies they unleash, ultimately rooted, at least in part, in the majoritarian character of the FPTP electoral system? We argue elsewhere that it is substantially the case.[3] The argument, in a nutshell, is that groups so distributed as to be in a minority in most parliamentary or state assembly constituencies would find it hard to win party nominations and get elected so long as ascriptive criteria influence, and are seen by party managers to influence, voting behaviour, which is substantially the case. Minority groups would then tend to be systematically under-represented, and deprived of a proportionate share in power, perhaps even to the extent that preservation of their minimum material interests and cultural identity is felt to be threatened, while "ethnic" majorities or pluralities would tend to be magnified in elected legislatures and executives. If this is the case, is there again a possible rationale for considering a whole or partial switch to

[2] Lijphart, *Democracies: Patterns of Majoritarian and Consensus Government.*

[3] See Sridharan, "Does India Need to Switch to Proportional Representation?"

proportional representation? It could reduce the magnification of pluralities to steamroller majorities.

All of the possible minorities are vulnerable to steamroller majoritarianism at the national and/or state levels if polarisation along the relevant majority-minority fault lines takes place, with all the consequences that such developments can unleash – suspicion, fear, perceived powerlessness, fury, violence, backlash, instability, chaos, and even national disintegration. This points to the need to qualify the political system's majoritarian tendencies in the interest of long-term social and political stability.

One way, without changing the electoral system, is to define the fundamental rights more precisely, especially as regards the extension of individual rights to derivative group rights, with special attention to religion, places of worship, cultural heritage sites and structures, place names, language, script, educational rights, particularly medium of instruction and optional language facilities, second-official-language status in the states, and the like. Such an extension of individual fundamental to derivative group rights and freedoms can be intellectually justified.[4] This would qualify majoritarianism by limiting the range and extent of basic policies and institutions which can be altered by legislative majorities or by executive fiat.

A second way, and one which is not a policy option but a development that has to come about in the natural course of political evolution if it is to happen at all, is the reconstruction of an umbrella party like the Congress party was in its heyday, with coalition politics being played out within the party, and electoral politics not being played out along lines of social cleavage.

A third way, not in contradiction to at least the first, is to change the electoral system to some variant of PR, or to introduce multi-member constituencies even if still following the first-past-the-post formula (as in Japan's multi-member plurality

[4] See Rajan, "Multiculturalism, Group Rights and Identity Politics", 1699–701.

system over 1950–93). This would ensure better representation of minorities, especially the minorities most vulnerable to under-representation, and simultaneously ensure that coalition and/or minority governments are more faithfully representative of the popular vote as well as more stable, and hence, coherent in terms of policy and governance. There would be a need here to simultaneously ensure that PR's tendency towards extreme fragmentation of the party system by undermining the FPTP system's incentive to aggregate votes, and hence, to build social coalitions, is checked.

Recent Proposals for Electoral-Systemic Reform

There have been a slew of proposals for electoral reform in the past few years. We mention here only those few which go beyond reforming the existing single-member district, FPTP system, technically, the single-member district, single non-transferable vote, simple plurality system, to consideration of features of alternative electoral systems, particularly, proportional representation (PR).[5] Most of these proposals have been motivated by concern about

[5] The debate on this in India has only just begun with the Working Paper, "Reform of Electoral Laws", of the Law Commission of India, discussed at a public symposium in New Delhi on 23-24 January 1999. The Working Paper (9–17) recommends increasing the number of seats in the Lok Sabha by 25 per cent (of the maximum of 550) to 138, these seats to be allotted to candidates of political parties on the basis of their pre-declared list (the list system) according to the parties' vote share in states, some smaller states being lumped together in territorial constituencies. For example, Andhra Pradesh with 42 Lok Sabha seats would have 11 extra seats to be filled on a party vote share basis going down the party list. A more recent set of proposals are those contained in the two Consultation Papers, issued as interim output of the NCRWC – "Review of the Working of Political Parties Specially in Relation to Elections and Reform Options", and "Review of Election Law, Processes and Reform Options".

the prospects of effective governance as well as of power-sharing which derived from the experience of the post-1989 hung parliaments and coalition and/or minority governments, political instability, and especially since 1996 perceived disproportionate or pivotal power of small and/or regional parties in coalition governments. Some of these proposals had also been motivated by the possible fresh delimitation of constituencies after the end of the constitutional freeze on delimitation after the 2001 census. Fresh delimitation could lead to changes in the share of seats in the Lok Sabha of several states, and at a minimum, would lead to redrawing the boundaries of existing constituencies.[6] Although the Ninety-first Constitution Amendment, passed by parliament in August 2001, extends the freeze of the inter-state allocation of seats in the Lok Sabha for another twenty-five years, until 2026, it is an open question how politically sustainable this amendment is, quite apart from the question of its desirability, which is debatable. It is quite possible that it may come under challenge after the 2011 census if not earlier.

The two major proposals which have been discussed in the Law Commission of India's Working Paper, "Reform of Electoral Laws" (January 1999) are: first, the introduction of a mixed FPTP-cum-PR system akin to the German model, consisting of the introduction of a list system in addition to the FPTP system based on single-member territorial constituencies, and, second, a two-ballot majority runoff system.[7] The mixed system would consist

[6] The government decided on 31 August 2000 to continue the freeze on the number of seats in the Lok Sabha and state legislative assemblies until 2026 but to set up a Delimitation Commission to refix the number of seats reserved for Scheduled Castes and Scheduled Tribes and to readjust and rationalise parliamentary and state legislative assembly constituencies. See McMillan, "Delimitation, Democracy and End of Constitutional Freeze", for projections of seats lost or gained by states in the event of inter-state reallocation of seats on the bases of the 1991 and projected 2001 censuses. The latter projection shows that Tamil Nadu (6) and Kerala (3) will lose 9 seats, the southern states 11 seats, while the Hindi-speaking states will gain 15 seats, U.P. alone gaining 7.

[7] Law Commission of India, "Reform of Electoral Laws", 1999.

of an increase of 25 per cent, or 138 seats, in the permitted maximum of 550 seats in the Lok Sabha, taking the new total number of seats to be 688. These additional seats would be filled on the basis of List PR, wherein parties would publish a list of nominees before the election. There would be no need for a second ballot since the allotment of seats would be on the basis of vote share. However, both the additional PR seats allotted and the vote share that would be taken into account to fill these seats would be at the state level, with additional PR seats allotted proportional to states' population shares, with small adjacent states being clubbed together, and likewise vote shares in such states. Only recognised parties, national and state, would be eligible for the additional PR seats.

The second system discussed but not recommended by the Commission is a majority runoff system where only candidates polling over 50 per cent of the votes cast get elected from single-member territorial constituencies under the existing FPTP system. If no candidates get a simple majority, a runoff election is held in which only the first two candidates of the first round contest, the winner of these being elected. An important provision is that negative votes are allowed, which will be counted as valid votes cast. This runoff system finds support in both of the Consultation papers of the National Commission to Review the Working of the Constitution, released in early 2001, except that they do not endorse the negative vote, and by some eminent persons including former President of India R. Venkataraman, and Chief Election Commissioner M.S. Gill.[8]

The justification given for considering these changes and for recommending the first of them, is that very often the winning candidate gets only 30–35 per cent of the votes cast, resulting in the wastage of the remaining 65–70 per cent of the votes, or the will of the majority going unrepresented, the seat-vote disproportionality

[8] NCRWC, "Review of the Working of Political Parties Specially in Relation to Elections and Reform Options", and "Review of Election Law, Processes and Reform Options". See also, Election Commission of India, "Electoral Reforms (Views and Proposal)".

being very great. Therefore, the introduction of mixed FPTP-list PR will make the system less disproportional. However, the part of the proposal that restricts the allocation of additional list PR seats only to recognised parties narrows the menu of choice and in effect, makes the system more proportional only among the existing established parties at the national and state levels, slanting it against the emergence of new and small parties. Furthermore, the Commission rejects a total switch over to list PR.

There are two main justifications given for the runoff system. First, "to cut down, or at any rate, to curtail the significance and role played by caste factor in the electoral process. There is hardly any constituency in the country where any one particular caste can command more than 50 per cent of the votes. This means that a candidate has to carry with him several castes and communities, to succeed."[9] Second, "the negative vote is intended to put moral pressure on political parties not to put forward candidates with undesirable record . . ."[10] The NCRWC's consultation paper argues that the "multiplicity of political parties, combined with our Westminster-based first-past-the-post system results in a majority of legislators and parliamentarians getting elected on a minority vote."[11] This is said to undermine the representative character of elected legislators, although this point was never raised in public debate or in party positions during the years of a Congress plurality in vote share resulting in substantial majorities in parliament, even though the system then was also characterised by precisely the fact of substantial numbers of legislators and parliamentarians getting elected on a minority vote. The paper recommends the runoff system for two reasons. First, that the runoff system would result in legislators who have a simple majority of the vote, thus resolving the problem of representative character. Second, "it also makes

[9] Ibid., 34.

[10] Ibid.

[11] NCRWC, "Review of Election Law, Processes and Reform Options", 33.

it in the self-interest of various political parties to widen their appeal to the electorate."[12]

The Election Commission of India also seriously considers for the first time a possible change of the present electoral system to majoritarian (runoff) system/ list system/mixed system or any other system, albeit cautiously, saying that the "need is to start a national debate so as to have a broad national consensus on this very fundamental subject."[13]

If we examine these justifications, we find that the argument for partial PR and the implied or explicit critique of the FPTP system is nothing new, being the same arguments advanced and debated decades ago the world over, including in the Constituent Assembly debates. *Then why has it become salient today?* The reason is clearly the fact that, for a decade since 1989, the FPTP system has resulted in hung parliaments and minority and/or coalition governments with their attendant instabilities rather than parliamentary majorities and stable one-party governments. In fact, the thrust is not on proportionality so much as stabilising the existing major parties by reducing the disproportionalities among them. Similarly, the runoff system strengthens the two biggest parties at the constituency level, being actually *less* proportional compared to the choices expressed by the electorate in the first round of voting in which voters choose from an unconstrained menu of options, unlike in the run-off round when the supporters of third and more parties have to vote for one or the other of the two run-off candidates. It actually reduces the menu of choice by forcing an artificial lumping of political options into two major alliances. The majority that it produces for the elected legislators is a *manufactured* majority, in which vote–seat disproportionality is greater than under FPTP elections. This system has not been used for parliamentary elections anywhere in the world and is used only

[12] Ibid., 37.

[13] Election Commission of India, "Electoral Reforms (Views and Proposal)", 1998.

for presidential elections in France, Portugal, and Algeria.[14] As for the ostensible reason given of being conducive to reducing caste conflict, it could well result in bipolar caste conflicts, say between Forwards and Backwards, with Scheduled Castes and minorities playing a balancing role. In addition, it would do nothing to reduce the other viciously divisive politics that has grown over the past decade, viz., minority-baiting communalism; indeed, it may create conditions favourable to communal polarisation – that may result in a totally majoritarian politics in which minorities which are not locally concentrated may be virtually excluded from representation.

Political parties have not taken explicit positions on electoral-systemic reform, although it should be noted that the Bharatiya Jana Sangh in the 1950s and 1960s supported PR. It was under-represented in terms of seats in relation to its vote share. However, the BJP is now a beneficiary of the FPTP system, getting one-third of the seats in 1999 with under a quarter of the votes, while the Congress with a greater (28 per cent) but more thinly spread vote share won only 21 per cent of the seats. The BJP no longer makes any mention of PR. Another noteworthy point is that all the reform options recently mooted, whether the runoff system or the mixed FPTP–PR system with relatively high cut-off points for representation in the second tier, favour the large parties and discriminate against the small parties, despite the justification for such proposals being the supposedly unrepresentative character of legislators elected on only a plurality vote or the disproportionality effect of the FPTP system.

Going Back from the Present to Examine the Origins

In light of the fragmentation of the national party system, particularly its increasing coincidence with social cleavages, the

[14] Lijphart, *Electoral Systems and Party Systems,* 18–19.

possible redistribution of the states' shares of seats in the Lok Sabha at some point in the future after 2001, and the demands for greater representation by reservation of seats for women, following that for Scheduled Castes and Scheduled Tribes, and within that a quota for Other Backward Classes, all reflecting the present electoral system's disproportionalities, and the proposals for electoral-systemic reforms, it would be interesting to look back to the Constituent Assembly and early parliamentary debates on the electoral system to examine whether the FPTP system's implications for representation and power-sharing were thoroughly debated, and whether its possible consequences were anticipated.

The Constituent Assembly was extremely aware of India's heterogeneity and sensitised to the issues of representation of various groups in legislatures, cabinets, and public employment. These issues cropped up in debates over the fundamental rights, minority rights, and the articles of the Draft Constitution, including of provincial governments. However, these debates centred on the then four-decade-old issue of joint versus separate electorates, and representation, including reservations, for minorities and Scheduled Castes and tribals. Explicit debate on the merits of alternative electoral systems did not take place except in the context of amendments moved, almost entirely by members of the Assembly belonging to the Muslim minority. Hence, *the debate on alternative electoral systems and their dynamics and implications for representation and, hence, power-sharing over time, was a debate that did not really take place*. Even to the extent that it did, it did not reveal a deep understanding of the dynamics of either the FPTP system or of various PR formulae. Rather, there was a pronounced tendency to assume as somehow natural the familiar Anglo-Saxon FPTP system.

This tendency was there in the Draft Constitution prepared by the Constitutional Adviser, B.N. Rau, placed before the Drafting Committee on 27 October 1947, based on the reports of various committees of the Constituent Assembly which submitted their reports between April and August 1947. The Draft Constitution tended to assume the single-member constituency and FPTP system, but also had multi-member constituencies to be filled by a multiple-ballot, distributive-vote quota system, at least for reserved constituencies (at that time reservation for religious minorities was also accepted).[15] That is, referring to the Fourth Schedule, point 34, "Where at an election in a territorial constituency, a poll is taken for the purpose of filling more than one seat, a voter shall have as many votes as there are seats to be filled on the poll, but shall not be entitled to give more than one vote to any candidate."[16] Thus the distributive vote meant that in a multiple-ballot system voters could not "cumulate" their ballots on a single candidate, called the cumulative vote. The cumulative vote system would tend to help minority groups to get at least some candidates elected by voters casting two or more, or all their votes for their favoured candidate. Rau was strongly influenced in favour of the FPTP system despite studying various PR systems, during his travels to several Western countries in October 1947, though he concedes that there was "general agreement even among the critics of proportional representation that the application of the system is a necessity in the case of countries with self-conscious racial or communal minorities."[17]

Prior to his preparing the Draft Constitution based on the reports of the various committees of the Assembly, he circulated a questionnaire at the first meeting of the Union Constitution Committee on 5 May 1947, and another questionnaire to the Provincial Constitution Committee, also at its first meeting on the same date. Question 23 asked: what should be the (a) composition; (b) franchise; (c) electorate; (d) constituencies; (e) method of election. The only response to the first questionnaire that touched

[15] Shiva Rao, *The Framing of India's Constitution,* 119–20.

[16] Ibid., 120.

[17] Rau, *India's Constitution in the Making,* 327. See ch. 17, "Systems of Representation" (315–70), for a flavour of his strong inclination towards FPTP and antipathy to PR.

upon (d) and (e) was that of Syama Prasad Mookerjee, who favoured equal electoral districts and single-member constituencies, but multi-member constituencies where seats were intended to be reserved (at that time for religious minorities too).[18]

Likewise, responses to the same question from members of the Provincial Constitution Committee, were as follows. Of the five who responded, Rajkumari Amrit Kaur suggested PR with multi-member constituencies, P. Subbarayan and B.G. Kher suggested FPTP in single-member constituencies with PR in reserved multi-member constituencies, and Brijlal Biyani FPTP with single-member constituencies.[19] What this implies is that though there was an assumption of continuity of the FPTP system, the issue was not decided and that some members did suggest PR and multi-member constituencies if only for reserved constituencies. However, the underlying assumption of the carry-forward of the FPTP system was very strong.

This assumption appears to have been implicitly accepted by most members of the Constituent Assembly, as indicated by the absence of a systematic and focused debate on the effects of various electoral systems on the pattern of representation. The only references to it were in debates that focused largely on minorities and the issue of the electoral system, questioning the merits of FPTP, were raised mainly by members belonging to minority communities. We give below illustrative snatches from the scattered debate on the electoral system to be adopted.

In the debate on the Draft Constitution, Z.H. Lari (U.P., Muslim) advocated PR by single transferable vote (STV) or cumulative voting.[20] He cited Ireland, which had then had fifteen years of rule by one party despite PR supposedly favouring a multiplicity of parties, and France having a plethora of parties despite FPTP. He also argued for an elected, not appointed, cabinet on the Swiss model, making it easier for minorities to get represented in the

[18] Shiva Rao, *The Framing of India's Constitution*, 531–2.

[19] Ibid., 628.

[20] Constituent Assembly Debates, vol. VII, 299–300.

cabinet, and recommended minority reservation in legislatures and public services though not in the cabinet.

Hussain Imam (Bihar, Muslim), in the same debate, recommended PR with large (10–12 member) multi-member constituencies, one or two per administrative district, on the grounds that effective opposition would be possible only under PR, citing the under-representation in seats compared to votes and hence, ineffectiveness of the Socialists in U.P.[21] This was a justification of PR on explicitly party-political grounds rather than concerning representation of minorities. The only other such justification was one in an earlier debate (Debate on Report on Minority Rights) in which D.H. Chandrasekharaiya (Mysore State) moved an amendment for the PR system in all elections by single transferable vote (STV) preferably, or if not, by single non-transferable vote (SNTV) on the grounds that the FPTP system over-represents the majority or plurality party, and also to ensure better minority representation.[22]

An indirect critique of FPTP was made in the debate on the legislative assembly in the larger debate on the Principles of a Model Provincial Constitution. Saiyid Mohammed Saadulla (Assam, Muslim) moved an amendment to raise the scale of representation from one representative per lakh of population to one per two lakhs.[23] Omeo Kumar Das (Assam, General) said in the debate on the amendment moved by Saadulla that the scale of representation should be lowered from 1 per 100,000 to 1 per 75,000, in Assam because "there are many backward communities and these communities have no chance of getting elected in bigger constituencies."[24] Rev. J.J.M. Nichols-Roy (Assam, General) supported this for better representation of hill tribes which inhabit large, low-density territories, citing the North Cachar Hills as an example.[25]

[21] Ibid., 303–4.
[22] Constituent Assembly Debates, vol. v, 273–4.
[23] Constituent Assembly Debates, vol. iv, 660–1.
[24] Ibid., 662–3.
[25] Ibid., 663–4.

This was supported by Gopinath Bordoloi (Assam, General) for the Assam tribes, and Lakshminarayan Sahu (Orissa, General), citing tribes in Orissa, and Jaipal Singh (Bihar, General), citing tribes in the Jharkhand region.[26] They were all keenly aware that smaller constituencies in the FPTP system would better enable small-population communities to be more proportionately represented, especially if territorially concentrated.

The closest the Assembly came to an explicit debate on FPTP versus PR was on 4 January 1949 (before the dropping of reservation of seats for religious minorities in May 1949) when Kazi Syed Karimuddin (C.P. and Berar: Muslim) moved an amendment (no. 1415) to clause 5 of Draft Art. 67 on the composition of parliament, in which he recommended PR by cumulative voting and attacked FPTP and single-member districts for promoting the tyranny of the majority and for the wasted votes of the collective majority of voters unrepresented in governments formed by a plurality victory.[27] He raised the issue of PR versus reservations for minorities, and attacked religion-based reservations of seats, then still under consideration, indeed, broadly accepted under Draft Art. 292, because such members elected under joint electorates would not be true representatives of their communities. *He favoured abolition of reservation if PR was introduced but not if it was not.* He made an explicit linkage between PR and abolition of reservation, the crucial issue being the representation of minorities and their assured share in power. He was supported by K.T. Shah (Bihar, General) who moved an amendment proposing PR by STV for political, not communal, reasons, and recommended states as constituencies, that is, very large, multi-member constituencies lending themselves to highly proportional outcomes.[28]

Mahboob Ali Baig Sahib Bahadur (Madras, Muslim) supported PR by STV, again for political reasons, for its favouring a strong

[26] Ibid., 666–7, 664–5, and 672–3, respectively.

[27] Constituent Assembly Debates, vol. VII, 1233–5.

[28] Ibid., 1236–8.

opposition, citing Pandit H.N. Kunzru on supporting PR and STV for the Upper House.[29] Sardar Hukam Singh (East Punjab, Sikh) also favoured PR rather than reservation for minorities as it did not violate individualist principles. He argued: "My position is that if separate electorates are detestable and if reservation of seats is objectionable, then some method has to be devised by which the rights of minorities can be safeguarded and this is the only method suggested in the amendments that can be considered."[30]

Interestingly, Ambedkar opposed PR on the grounds that it presupposes literacy, and also *because it does not ensure a share of representation and power as do reservations*. In his words: "I submit that PR is really taking away by the back door what has already been granted to the minorities by this agreement [he had in the earlier part of his speech favoured a majority-minority deal on joint electorates in exchange for reservations], because PR will not give to the minorities what they wanted, viz., *a definite quota*. It might give them a voice in the election of their representatives . . ."[31]

What comes across in the very sketchy and fragmented debate on the choice of an electoral system is that while the issues of representation and power-sharing were keenly felt by all, the main trade-off contemplated (and accepted until the turnaround in May 1949) was the abolition of separate electorates and the introduction of joint electorates under an FPTP system of voting, more assumed than seriously debated, in exchange for reservation of seats in the legislature for minorities (and for Scheduled Castes). In other words, the majoritarian character of the FPTP system was sought to be tempered by the introduction of an essentially *consociational* feature such as reservations. This was a mixture of opposites since what later came to be called consociationalism recognised explicit group rights in a way essentially at odds with the individualist premises of the FPTP system. The option of a

[29] Ibid., 1244–5.

[30] Ibid., 1250.

[31] Ibid., 1263. Emphasis added.

non-consociational system of representation based on liberal individualist premises such as the PR system, which tends to better represent minorities and small parties without having to resort to reservations, was never seriously debated or even understood.[32] Nor was the multi-member single-ballot plurality system of the Japanese type (1950–93), or other PR alternatives such as the Single Non-Transferable Vote (SNTV) system, both of which are more proportional than FPTP but are operable in an illiterate electorate.

The early parliamentary debates on the Representation of the People Bills of 1950 and 1951 did not reveal any informed and detailed discussion on the consequences of possible alternative electoral systems for the pattern of representation and, by implication, power-sharing. In fact, the members were not even clear whether the constituencies were going to be single- or multi-member and whether the electoral formula was to be FPTP or some other. This is revealed by interventions such as those of Hussain Imam (Bihar, Muslim):

> In this Bill no provision has been made as to how the constituencies are to be delimited. Do we want to have single-seated constituencies or multi-seated constituencies? Nor has it been mentioned here whether we are going to have proportional representation or the distributive voting or cumulative voting . . . Do we wish to have the anomaly of the British electoral system by means of which minorities in a three-cornered contest can get a larger number of seats in the House than the voting recorded at elections? . . . I wish that there should be a Select Committee to ascertain the wishes of the House as to how we wish to be represented.[33]

Ajit Prasad Jain (U.P., General), in the same debate, also criticised the vagueness of the Bill on constituency size (number of

[32] Even a scholar like Ambedkar did not seem to understand the workings of PR, as revealed by his remark that PR was not compatible with parliamentary democracy (Constituent Assembly Debates, vol. VII, 1261–3)!

[33] *Parliamentary Debates (Part II – Proceedings Other than Questions and Answers) Official Report*, vol. IV, 1950 (1 April 1950 to 20 April 1950), 3046.

members) and electoral formula, and whether, if there was to be a multi-member constituency, there was to be cumulative or distributive voting.[34] He endorsed single-member constituencies except for the reserved seats. The same criticism of vagueness about constituency size and electoral formula in the Bill was echoed by M.A. Ayyangar (Madras, General), leading Ambedkar to promise that there will be a Bill that will deal with these two issues.[35]

As a result of these interventions, the Representation of the People Act of 1950, as originally enacted, spelt out a system of both single-member general constituencies and multi-member constituencies, the latter by implication being for those constituencies in which some seats were to be reserved for Scheduled Castes and Scheduled Tribes. However, it did not make explicit the plurality formula (FPTP), this being assumed.

The fact of the electoral formula being FPTP and general seats being single-member and reserved seats multi-member, comes out only in the RPA 1951, Section 63 on Method of Voting: "In plural member constituencies other than Council constituencies every elector shall have as many votes as there are members to be elected, but no elector shall give more than one vote to any one candidate."[36] This also brings out the distributive voting rule for such constituencies. That the FPTP or plurality-rule formula is implied comes out in Ambedkar's remark, referring to the Constituent Assembly's resolution endorsing distributive voting (with reference to Art. 332 (5) on tribal constituencies), thus implying multi-member constituencies in which an SC or ST seat is reserved rather than reserved constituencies in which only an SC or ST candidate can contest.[37] If the latter, Ambedkar said, then there is no need

[34] Ibid.

[35] Ibid., 3068–9.

[36] Representation of the People Act 1951, Section 63.

[37] *Parliamentary Debates (Part II – Proceedings Other than Questions and Answers) Official Report*, vol. XI, 1951 (21 April 1951 to 14 May 1951), 8349–51.

to refer to distributive voting (which implied at least two ballots); it would have been one-man, one-vote (the implied default FPTP system). The FPTP formula is also implied in Section 65 of the Act on Equality of Votes: "If after counting of the votes is completed, an equality of votes is found to exist between any candidates, and the addition of one vote will entitle any of those candidates to be declared elected, the Returning Officer shall forthwith decide between those candidates by lot . . ."[38]

Lastly, the FPTP formula or plurality rule *for both single-member general and multi-member reserved constituencies* is clearly spelt out in the Representation of the People (Conduct of Elections and Election Petitions) Rules 1951, Rule 48 on Declaration of candidates elected, for both: "the Returning Officer shall . . . forthwith declare the candidate or candidates to whom the largest number of valid votes has been given, to be elected."[39]

However, what is interesting is that by this time, just before the first general elections of 1952, there was hardly any debate on either constituency size or the related issue of electoral formula, as regards their effect on representation of small parties or minorities. The SC and ST representation issue was resolved by reservation under joint electorates and plurality-rule multi-member constituencies. The debate did not veer in the direction of either changing the formula towards some form of PR, which would have benefited small parties and minorities, especially territorially dispersed minorities, nor moving towards larger, multi-member constituencies under the existing plurality formula (as in Japan's multi-member plurality-rule electoral system, 1955–93), which would have ensured better representation for both small parties and minorities, including perhaps assuring SC and ST representation without recourse to reservation.

[38] Ibid., section 65.

[39] Representation of the People (Conduct of Elections and Election Petitions), Rules 1951, Rule 48, 203.

The next and most illuminating debate on the electoral system as regards representation took place during the Two-Member Constituencies (Abolition) Bill in 1961. The move to abolish two-member (and the few three-member) reserved constituencies for SCs and STs originated in the demand for such abolition by some SC members, on the administrative grounds of size, multi-member constituencies being very large in area and population and difficult to cover in an election campaign without incurring inordinate costs, and more importantly, on the ground that SC and ST members in such constituencies felt that they would gain in importance in single-member reserved constituencies.

Thus, as A.K. Sen described it: "The Scheduled Caste and Scheduled Tribe members have been pleading for a long time that the system which would give reservation in their favour and give the best possible effect is one which would enable them to stand from single-member constituencies and which thus prevent the possibility of Scheduled Caste and Scheduled Tribe members being tacked on with members standing for general constituencies."[40]

There was opposition to the abolition from general constituency members who feared the possible reservation of their constituencies for SCs and STs. As Mahavir Tyagi (U.P.) put it: "This Bill goes against the interests of the Scheduled Castes . . . my submission is that the representative character will deteriorate to a great extent if single-member cosntituencies are created . . . As soon as you reserve a constituency for Scheduled Castes, 80 percent of the population of that constituency will feel frustrated because their sons cannot offer themselves as candidates from their home constituency."[41] There were also objections raised on the administrative grounds of the complications necessarily arising from the bifurcation of the assembly constituencies in each double-member parliamentary constituency, and further, the double-member

[40] *Parliamentary Debates, Second Series*, vol. L, 1961 (Thirteenth Session), 344–5.

[41] Ibid., 356–8.

assembly constituencies within such parliamentary constituencies. Opposition members also feared that opposition strength constituencies would be declared single-member constituencies reserved for SCs or STs.[42]

Mahavir Tyagi (somewhat prophetically, and presaging the criticisms of the Bahujan Samaj Party over three decades later) also raised the fear of Scheduled Caste members unrepresentative of their community because they would be dependent on a majority of non-SC voters to be elected.[43] The Bill, however, went through. After this debate the electoral system for the Lok Sabha has not undergone any basic change as regards constituency or electoral formula, and hence, the electoral system's effects on the representation of small parties and minorities, and hence further, its effects on power-sharing.

Conclusion

Looking back in the light of the changes since 1989, it is interesting to note how deeply entrenched the assumption of the first-past-the-post system was in the Constituent Assembly debates, the early parliamentary debates and Lok Sabha debates up to 1961 on the electoral system. In particular, in the debate on the Two-Member Constituencies (Abolition) Bill, 1961, *the debate never went in the direction of achieving greater proportionality of outcomes, or reducing the effective threshold of representation, even by adopting larger, multi-member constituencies (with or without multiple ballots) while retaining the plurality-rule formula*, leave alone moving towards any form of PR.

Essentially, there were three broad types of electoral system available for choosing, given a largely illiterate and politically poorly informed electorate (thus ruling out systems which assume considerable political information such as the single transferable vote among PR systems or the alternative vote among plurality systems).

[42] Ibid., 421, intervention by B.C. Kamble.

[43] Ibid., 863–4, intervention by Mahavir Tyagi.

These are plurality systems, PR systems, and semi-proportional systems. The latter include the single non-transferable vote and the cumulative vote. In India just after independence, the British FPTP system was the default system and, as we have shown, adopted mainly by default without a discriminating and informed debate on alternatives. Plurality systems like the single-member constituency FPTP system favoured the largest parties and tended to under-represent political and other minorities. PR systems, while being proportional in outcomes, especially in large, multi-member constituencies, and enabling better representation of small parties and minorities, would run the risk of not only fragmented legislatures but also the fragmentation of the party system along religious, caste, linguistic, regional, and tribal lines over time.

However, it was also within the realm of possibility to adopt semi-proportional systems which were operable by an illiterate electorate. Two variants possible were the single non-transferable vote (SNTV) system and the cumulative vote system. In the SNTV system, voters in multi-member constituencies using the plurality rule, have only one vote. Candidates are selected by the plurality rule. In a four-member constituency, for example, the top four candidates by votes received get elected. This system is more proportional in outcomes than simple plurality. Another variant which enables small parties and minorities to get their candidates more easily elected is the cumulative vote system, a special case of the limited vote system. In this, voters in multi-member constituencies using the plurality rule for election, have more than one vote but fewer than the number of candidates (hence limited vote). If they are allowed to "cumulate" their votes on only one candidate, this becomes the cumulative vote system, while if they have to cast not more than one vote per candidate, it is called the distributive vote system. The two-member and three-member constituencies that existed until 1961 were, in embryonic form, distributive vote systems. Both the SNTV system and the two limited vote systems, cumulative and distributive, are special cases of the multi-member plurality rule system. These systems, particularly SNTV and the cumulative vote system, enable political and other minorities to have a better chance of electing their preferred candidate, and while inducing greater competition for votes among two or more candidates belonging to the same party in a multi-member constituency, and hence weakening parties to some extent, not exerting as much centrifugal pressure on parties as PR systems. More proportional outcomes under PR and semi-PR systems are due to the fact that such systems, even semi-proportional systems based on the plurality rule, lower the effective thresholds of representation.

Contemporary research on comparative electoral systems has shown that there are *effective thresholds of representation* determined by the combination of electoral formula and district magnitude, especially the latter, which are a barrier to small party representation. The issue of effective thresholds and proportionality is complicated by the fact that the effective threshold is a range rather than a fixed percentage, and can be conceived of as having an upper and a lower bound. The upper bound is the threshold of exclusion, or the maximum percentage of the vote under the most unfavourable conditions, that may be insufficient for a party to win a seat. Anything over this guarantees a seat. The lower bound or threshold of representation (or inclusion) is the minimum percentage of the vote, under the most favourable conditions, that can win a party a seat. The exact effective threshold in any particular system would lie somewhere between these upper and lower bounds and would be determined by district magnitude, the electoral formula and the number of competing parties.

Lijphart arrives at an average upper threshold of 100 per cent/M+1 vote percentage, where M is the district magnitude.[44] That is, for a party to win a seat, it would in a 10-seat district have to win at least 9 per cent of the vote, in a 5-seat district, at least 17 per cent

[44] See Lijphart, *Electoral Systems and Party Systems*, 26.

of the vote. These are much lower percentages than anything conceivable under FPTP. For example, in a small (for PR systems) district of 5 seats, one-sixth of the votes would be sufficient for winning a seat but not one-tenth, whereas in a 10-member district, one-eleventh would be sufficient. Compare these cases with an average effective threshold of 35 per cent of the vote under FPTP in an Indian single-member constituency for general elections from 1952 to 1984, and likewise for post-war elections in the UK, Canada, Australia, New Zealand, and USA (Congressional).[45] Lijphart has, with Taagepera, modified his formula for effective threshold to 75 per cent/(M+1), which yields even lower effective thresholds for every district magnitude. By this formula, the effective threshold under FPTP is 37.5 per cent, while for a 5-seat district it falls from one-sixth to 12.5 per cent or one-eighth.[46]

It never appeared to strike anyone in the Constituent Assembly and early parliamentary debates on the electoral system that multi-member plurality systems, falling in-between FPTP and PR, would reduce the effective threshold of representation radically, thus enabling SCs, STs, smaller caste groups, and religious minorities to be more proportionately represented *without* the device of reservation, not to speak of more proportionate representation for smaller parties. A multi-member plurality system would also be as easy to implement in a largely illiterate population. In retrospect, reservation of constituencies for SCs and STs, especially the single-member constituencies since 1961, and especially the ending of rotation of reserved constituencies since 1976, has led to precisely what Mahavir Tyagi warned against (although he was not motivated by concern for SC representation) that SC members would be dependent on non-SC voters, and hence would be unrepresentative of their community's interests and, in turn, defeat the purpose of reservation. This criticism finds an echo in the

[45] Ibid., 17, Table 2.1.

[46] Ibid., 182–3, note 29.

dissatisfaction with SC MPs of existing parties manifested in the rise of the Bahujan Samaj Party in the 1990s despite four decades of reservation. Furthermore, reservation as a device to ensure representation can lead to snowballing demands for reservation for more and more groups and sub-groups as, for example, in the demand for women's reservation, the further demand for reservation for Other Backward Class women within any women's quota, and the demands by some Muslim groups for reservation for Muslims.[47]

To sum up, this paper has attempted to uncover the debate on the origins and adoption of India's electoral system. The single-member constituency FPTP system was adopted in the Constituent Assembly and early parliamentary debates, not so much from a focused debate on the merits of alternative electoral systems as regards their effects on the representation of parties and social groups, but from a default assumption of the FPTP system being somehow natural, carried forward largely unconsciously from British and British colonial practice since 1935. There was an awareness that this system would tend to under-represent territorially dispersed groups like the Scheduled Castes and Muslims, but that was sought to be remedied by the device of reservation, guaranteeing representation, rather than by electoral-systemic engineering. If the recent proposals on electoral-systemic reforms mentioned earlier in this paper are any indication, the state of knowledge and debate on the effects of alternative electoral systems remains extremely rudimentary.

Acknowledgements

I thank S.K. Mendiratta of the Election Commission of India for his help with historical records and data, and Yogendra Yadav

[47] See the paragraphs, "On Reservation in Public Employment, Legislature, etc.", in the Comprehensive Resolution on National and International Questions adopted by the Markazi Majlis-e-Mushawarat of the All India Muslim Majlis-e-Mushawarat, on 27 January 2001, *Muslim India*, March 2001, 128–9.

and Zoya Hasan for comments on an earlier draft. The usual disclaimer applies.

Bibliography

Election Commission of India, "Electoral Reforms (Views and Proposal)", 1998.

Government of India, "Constituent Assembly Debates, vol. IV", 18 July 1947.

Government of India, "Constituent Assembly Debates, vol. V", 28 August 1947.

Government of India, "Constituent Assembly Debates, vol. VII", 4 January 1949.

Government of India, *Parliamentary Debates (Part II – Proceedings Other than Questions and Answers) Official Report*, vol. IV, 1950 (1 April 1950 to 20 April 1950).

Government of India, *Parliamentary Debates (Part II – Proceedings Other than Questions and Answers) Official Report*, vol. XI, 1951 (21 April 1951 to 14 May 1951).

Government of India, *Parliamentary Debates, Second Series*, vol. L, 1961 (Thirteenth Session).

Law Commission of India, "Reform of Electoral Laws", Working Paper, January 1999.

Lijphart, Arend, *Democracies: Patterns of Majoritarian and Consensus Government in Twenty-one Countries* (New Haven: Yale University Press, 1984).

Lijphart, Arend, *Electoral Systems and Party Systems: A Study of Twenty-seven Democracies 1945–1990* (Oxford: Oxford University Press, 1994).

McMillan, Alistair, "Delimitation, Democracy and End of Constitutional Freeze", *Economic and Political Weekly*, vol. XXXV, no. 15, 8 April 2000.

National Commission to Review the Working of the Constitution (NCRWC), Consultation Paper, "Review of Election Law, Processes and Reform Options", January 2001, 33.

National Commission to Review the Working of the Constitution (NCRWC), "Review of the Working of Political Parties Specially in Relation to Elections and Reform Options" and "Review of Election Law, Processes and Reform Options", Reserve Bank of India.

Rajan, Nalini, "Multiculturalism, Group Rights and Identity Politics", *Economic and Political Weekly*, vol. xxxiii, no. 27, 4 July 1998, 1699–1701.

Rau, B.N., *India's Constitution in the Making*, second edition (Bombay: Allied Publishers, 1960).

Shiva Rao, B., *The Framing of India's Constitution: Select Documents*, vol. iii (New Delhi: Indian Institute of Public Administration; Bombay: N.M. Tripathi, 1967).

Sridharan, E., "Principles, Power and Coalition Politics in India: Lessons from Theory, Comparison and Recent History", in D.D. Khanna and Gert W. Kueck, eds, *Principles, Power and Politics* (New Delhi: Macmillan, 1999).

Sridharan, E., "Does India Need to Switch to Proportional Representation? The Pros and Cons", in Paul Flather, ed., *Recasting Indian Politics: Essays on a Working Democracy* (London: Palgrave, 2002).

2

Understanding Voting Patterns by Class in the 2019 Indian Election

Introduction

THIS PAPER ATTEMPTS to understand and explain patterns of voting by class in the 2019 Indian election based on the Centre for Study of Developing Societies (CSDS)/ Lokniti post-election survey data. The focus is on patterns of voting preference for the two major parties, the Bharatiya Janata Party (BJP) and the Indian National Congress (Congress). The thrust of the analysis is to try to explain why there is so little difference in voter preference across the four-class division in the Lokniti survey dataset. Unlike in 2014, where the higher turnout of upper and middle classes and their strong pro-BJP preference, particularly in the younger age groups and in metropolitan and urban areas, influenced the magnitude of the 12 per cent pro-BJP swing compared to 2009, this time, the further 6 per cent pro-BJP swing seems to have been fairly common across the classes and within classes by age group, rural-urban location, and caste/community disaggregation.

The paper proceeds as follows. Following a brief description of the Lokniti survey's classification of social classes and its comparison with 2014, the paper describes turnout and party preference across social classes, further disaggregated by breakdown by caste/community, age group, and rural-urban location. It next asks whether economic questions, including the government's many welfare schemes, affected voter preferences across classes. Coming to the conclusion that economic conditions as felt by the voters and the government's schemes did not produce major class differences in voter preferences toward parties, the question arises as to what explains the fairly uniform party preferences across classes. The paper then proceeds to look at broader questions of attitudes to leadership, nationalism, and minorities that might affect voting patterns in a way that produces relatively small differences across classes. Finally, bringing in findings from the comparative literature on why poor voters vote on the same lines as the better-off, and on recent patterns of class self-identification in India, at the end of the paper, I try to, somewhat speculatively, explain the above results from the dataset.

Defining Class in the Indian Electorate

The Lokniti survey groups 24,235 respondents into four classes – Rich, Middle, Lower, and Poor – based on a composite index of income, house type, occupation, and occupational level. This results in a breakdown by class of 13.6 per cent Rich, 22.1 per cent Middle, 34.1 per cent Lower, and 30.2 per cent Poor (Table 1). Compared to 2014, the Rich slightly increased from 11 per cent to 14 per cent, the Middle Class shrank considerably from

Table 1. Economic Class of Voters in 2019

Economic Class	*Figures (%)*
Poor	30
Lower	34
Middle	22
Rich	14
Total	100

Source: National Election Study (NES) (2019).

36 per cent to 22 per cent, the Lower class is about the same at about one-third, and the Poor increased from 20 per cent to 30 per cent, much higher than those below the official poverty line in 2011 (22 per cent).[1] Since in a poor country of approximately $2000 per capita GDP, 14 per cent of the population of over 1300 million would give us a huge figure of about 182 million people or more, only a small fraction would be recognisably rich in a serious sense, even by Indian standards, let alone world standards. Another perhaps more meaningful way of looking at the breakdown is to lump the Rich and Middle classes together as Upper-Middle and Middle class. In this case, we get a combined Upper-Middle and Middle class of 36 per cent, much lower than the corresponding 47 per cent of 2014, despite presumed upward mobility due to five years of 6–7 per cent growth and a Poor class of 30 per cent compared to 20 per cent in 2014. This does not fit well with the latest income-cum-occupational estimate of India's Middle class (28.1 per cent in 2012, according to Aslany, with a Rich class of only 0.8 per cent).[2] Hence, the 2014 and 2019 breakdowns, to say nothing of 2009, are not comparable except very roughly in terms of relativities, but not even then. So we will consider 2019 on its own without attempting class voting comparisons with 2014 except minimally and for some possible explanations of outcomes based in the literature. We turn to the scant theorising about Indian class voting behaviour at the end of the paper in an attempt to explain the findings.

Outcomes: Turnout and Party Preference

Class turnout ranged from 66.1 per cent for the Poor to 69.6 per cent for the Middle class (Table 2).The overall inter-class differential was small, and the overall turnout of 66.8 per cent was largely

[1] Asian Development Bank, "Poverty Data: India", https://www.adb.org/countries/india/poverty.

[2] Aslany, "The Indian Middle Class", 196–213.

Table 2. Economic Class*
Turnout 2019

Economic Class	*Turnout (%)*
Poor	66
Lower	66
Middle	70
Rich	67

Source: National Election Study (NES) (2019).

determined by rural locations (actual turnout calculated by CSDS from Election Commission data was 67 per cent). Differentiating by location, rural (73 per cent of respondents) turnout was 68.6 per cent, with the rural Middle class at 71.6 per cent; town (16 per cent of the respondents) turnout was a low 59.8 per cent, with the Rich at a very low 52 per cent; and city (11 per cent of the respondents) turnout was 65 per cent, with the Rich at 69.6 per cent and the Poor at a low 54.8 per cent (Table 3). There is no discernible reason for lower turnout in towns compared to cities and rural areas. Perhaps campaigning and campaign organisation was stronger in both cities and rural areas.

Table 3. Economic Class* Turnout* 2019
Locality

(figures in %)

	Locality		
Economic Class	*Rural*	*Town*	*City*
Poor	68	63	55
Lower	67	58	66
Middle	72	59	68
Rich	69	52	70
Total	69	60	65

Source: National Election Study (NES) (2019).

Class party preferences were as follows (Table 4). The BJP got 37.4 per cent of the votes of respondents, and Congress got 19.5 per cent, exactly matching their national vote shares. The four classes voted for the BJP as follows: Rich at 44 per cent, Middle at 38 per cent, Lower at 36 per cent, and Poor at 36 per cent, showing the by now well known but still only slight bias toward the BJP compared to the national average by the two upper classes and a surprisingly high pro-BJP vote from the Poor, but a spread of only 8 per cent between the highest vote for the BJP and the lowest across the four classes. For Congress, the classes voted as follows: Rich at 20 per cent, Middle at 21 per cent, Lower at 21 per cent, and Poor at 17 per cent. Overall, the poll shows fairly narrow class differences in party preference around the national average for each of the two major parties, with the Poor voting for the BJP twice as much as for Congress, roughly matching the overall pattern. The spread in BJP preferences between Rich and Poor is only 8 per cent.

Differentiating the vote for the BJP and Congress by caste/community, there is a much higher spread in caste/community voting patterns than in class voting patterns, even if we omit Muslims (Table 5).

While overall, 52 per cent of Upper Castes voted for BJP and 12 per cent for Congress, only 8 per cent of Muslims voted for BJP,

Table 4. Economic Class* Party Voted for Lok Sabha 2019

(figures in %)

Economic Class	*Party Voted for Lok Sabha 2019*						
	Congress	*Congress Allies*	*BJP*	*BJP Allies*	*BSP+*	*Left*	*Others*
Poor	17	6	36	7	7	2	26
Lower	21	8	36	7	7	2	21
Middle	21	8	38	8	6	3	17
Rich	20	7	44	7	4	2	16
Total	20	7	37	7	6	2	21

Source: National Election Study (NES) (2019).

Table 5. Caste Community AMONG* Party Voted for Lok Sabha 2019* Economic Class Cross-Tabulation

(figures in %)

Economic	*Class*	*Party Voted for Lok Sabha 2019* Congress	*Congress Allies*	*BJP*	*BJP Allies*	*BSP+*	*Left*	*Others*
Upper Caste	Poor	9	5	49	8	2	2	25
	Lower	12	5	49	9	2	1	21
	Middle	14	7	52	6	2	4	17
	Rich	12	5	58	6	1	1	17
	Total	12	5	52	7	2	2	19
OBC	Poor	12	5	46	10	4	1	22
	Lower	16	8	42	10	5	1	18
	Middle	18	8	42	12	4	2	14
	Rich	17	9	46	9	4	1	14
	Total	15	7	44	10	5	1	18
SC	Poor	14	3	34	8	14	3	24
	Lower	23	6	34	6	10	2	20
	Middle	24	7	30	6	10	2	19
	Rich	26	18	35	4	2	1	16
	Total	20	6	34	7	11	2	21
ST	Poor	27	5	44	2	1	2	19
	Lower	36	6	40	2	2	1	13
	Middle	30	5	48	2	4	2	9
	Rich	35	6	47	1	3	1	7
	Total	31	6	44	2	2	2	14
Muslims	Poor	30	11	8	1	14	4	33
	Lower	35	12	8	1	17	3	24
	Middle	32	17	10	1	20	2	17
	Rich	33	10	9	1	25	4	20
	Total	33	12	8	1	17	3	25
Others	Poor	14	6	28	6	7	4	36
	Lower	20	6	26	7	5	3	33
	Middle	30	6	21	10	4	4	26
	Rich	34	6	21	10	3	4	22
	Total	23	6	25	8	5	4	31

Source: NES 2019.

while 33 per cent voted for Congress. The other three major castes/communities – the Other Backward Classes (defined by caste) (OBCs), Scheduled Castes (SCs), and Scheduled Tribes (STs) – voted as follows: 44 per cent of OBCs voted for BJP and 15 per cent for Congress; 34 per cent of SCs voted for BJP and 20 per cent for Congress; and 44 per cent of STs voted for BJP and 31 per cent for Congress. Overall, Hindu–Muslim polarisation (sharp differences in preferences) is observed when it comes to BJP versus Congress. There is also a kind of Hindu consolidation, if one wants to call it that, with Upper Castes, OBCs, SCs, and STs very broadly following the national vote-share pattern with the Upper Castes in particular voting highly pro-BJP, but even the SCs are broadly in line with the national pattern. However, the spread in BJP preference between Upper Castes and SCs is 18 per cent. Notably, the SC vote for the BJP has gone up from 24 per cent in 2014 to 34 per cent in 2019, a significant jump.

Breaking down class voting by caste/community, the Poor (who are probably highly correlated with the lower castes) voted 36 per cent BJP and 17 per cent Congress, in line with the national pattern. What emerges is that there is a much higher spread in caste/community voting patterns than in class voting patterns, even if we leave out the Muslims. The Upper Caste Poor voted 49 per cent BJP and 9 per cent Congress, in line with overall Upper Caste patterns, as did Poor OBCs and Poor STs; even Poor SCs voted 34 per cent BJP and 14 per cent Congress. Poor Muslims voted 8 per cent BJP and 30 per cent Congress. The same caste/community pattern of voting, broadly in line with the national pattern, is roughly observable for the Lower, Middle, and Rich classes, with a more pro-BJP pattern among the Upper Castes, progress among the Muslims, and relatively higher pro-Congress votes among the STs and SCs, although their vote too follows the broad national pattern.

The spread in BJP preference between Upper Caste Rich (58 per cent pro-BJP) and the SC Middle Class (30 per cent pro-BJP, the least pro-BJP class among the SCs) is 28 per cent and between the Upper Castes and SCs, it is 18 per cent; far greater than spreads by class (the Rich-Poor spread is only 8 per cent).

Differentiating the class vote for the BJP and Congress by location, we get the following picture (Table 6).

Overall, there seems to be no rural–urban polarisation in party preferences, with 35 per cent rural, 38 per cent town, and 36 per cent of city voters preferring the BJP, in line with the BJP national vote share, and 17 per cent, 16 per cent, and 23 per cent preferring Congress, the latter having a slight relative preference advantage in cities, going against the historical impression of the cities being more pro-BJP.

Table 6. Locality* Party Voted for Lok Sabha 2019* Economic Class Cross-Tabulation

(figures in %)

Economic	Class	*Party Voted for Lok Sabha 2019* Congress	Congress Allies	BJP	BJP Allies	BSP+	Left	Others
Rural	Poor	14	5	33	7	8	2	31
	Lower	18	8	34	8	8	2	24
	Middle	18	8	34	8	8	2	24
	Rich	20	6	41	8	6	2	19
	Total	17	7	35	8	8	2	24
Town	Poor	15	6	41	5	7	1	25
	Lower	17	8	36	6	7	1	25
	Middle	17	8	36	6	7	1	25
	Rich	16	3	47	4	4	2	24
	Total	16	6	38	6	7	1	25
City	Poor	25	6	26	4	6	0	33
	Lower	25	6	26	4	6	0	33
	Middle	27	3	30	5	9	0	26
	Rich	14	12	47	5	2	1	19
	Total	23	6	36	5	6	0	24

Source: NES 2019.

Breaking down the classes by locations, we get the following picture. While nothing goes against the broad national pattern, and in fact, all three location types follow the broad national pattern, there is some degree of class polarisation visible in urban areas between the Rich in the cities and towns (47 per cent BJP in both cities and towns, 14 per cent and 16 per cent Congress, respectively) and the Poor in the cities (25 per cent BJP, 25 per cent Congress), with a spread in BJP preference between Rich and Poor in urban areas of 22 per cent. But this class polarisation is within urban areas, not between urban and rural areas.

Differentiating the class vote for the BJP and Congress by age group, we get the following picture (Table 7).

The survey differentiated the electorate into six age groups (up to 22 or first-time eligible to vote, 23–25, 26–35, 36–45, 46–55, 56 and above). Overall, we get the highest pro-BJP preference in the two youngest cohorts (41 per cent) and the least in the oldest cohort (35 per cent), but the broad national pattern is visible across age groups without any category going against it.

Breaking down classes into age groups, we get the following picture. There are remarkably similar voting patterns across age groups within classes. The notable standouts are that there are higher BJP preferences across age groups among the Rich, particularly in the two youngest cohorts: 50 per cent of the youngest and 53 per cent of second youngest are pro-BJP.

Summing up the overall patterns of pro-BJP and pro-Congress preference by class, one observes that the degree of class polarisation in party preference seems muted. The pro-BJP swing – and the static vote of Congress, nationally – seems to be reflected across classes regardless of age groups, location, or caste/community composition except for a marked higher Upper Caste preference across classes for the BJP, a marked pro-Congress preference among Muslims, and a marked pro-BJP preference among the Rich across age groups. These might be expected from patterns in past surveys, particularly 2014. What is remarkable, however, is that

Table 7. Age Group-1st (Respondent)* Party Voted for Lok Sabha 2019* Economic Class Cross-Tabulation

(figures in %)

		Party Voted for Lok Sabha 2019						
Age		*1: Congress*	*2: Congress Allies*	*3: BJP*	*4: BJP Allies*	*5: BSP+*	*6: Left*	*7: Others*
1: 22 yrs	Poor	19	3	36	8	6	1	27
	Lower	19	5	41	6	5	2	23
	Middle	23	6	39	8	5	2	18
	Rich	22	5	50	4	3	2	14
	Total	20	5	41	7	5	2	21
2: 23–25 yrs	Poor	15	4	37	7	10	2	25
	Lower	19	5	42	8	8	2	18
	Middle	23	8	35	8	7	3	17
	Rich	20	5	53	6	3	1	12
	Total	19	5	41	7	8	2	19
3: 26–35 yrs	Poor	16	5	40	7	8	1	23
	Lower	20	7	37	6	9	1	20
	Middle	21	9	39	6	7	2	17
	Rich	20	9	43	6	6	1	15
	Total	19	7	39	7	8	1	19
4: 36–45 yrs	Poor	16	5	37	7	7	3	25
	Lower	22	8	34	7	6	1	21
	Middle	21	7	39	8	7	2	15
	Rich	21	6	43	8	4	2	16
	Total	20	7	37	7	7	2	20
5: 46–55 yrs	Poor	18	7	35	6	7	2	26
	Lower	22	8	34	8	7	2	20
	Middle	17	21	16	20	15	25	16
	Rich	18	8	41	6	5	2	20
	Total	20	8	36	7	6	2	21
6: 56 + yrs	Poor	16	7	32	7	6	3	29
	Lower	21	9	33	7	5	3	23
	Middle	21	7	38	8	5	4	18
	Rich	20	8	43	8	2	2	17
	Total	19	8	35	7	5	3	23

Source: NES 2019.

the pro-BJP swing is reflected among the Lower and Poor classes across locations (except cities), age groups, and castes/communities (except Muslims), with a 10 per cent increase in pro-BJP vote among SCs and a 12 per cent swing among the Poor from 2014 (although the Poor were differently defined then and amounted to only 20 per cent).

Economic Questions and Voting Patterns by Class

This raises the question as to how important economic questions were for voting patterns in 2019. On this issue, there is rich data in the survey. The findings are as follows (I sum up the findings of the tables in the text from this point onwards, as there are too many tables to fit in the space constraints.)

All economic issues taken together seem to have been the most important for only 43 per cent of the respondents, with 57 per cent indicating either Other issues were the most important (39 per cent) or giving no response (18 per cent). Only 11 per cent mentioned unemployment, 4 per cent inflation, and 3 per cent corruption; and economic issues were each under 3 per cent. However, 17 per cent mentioned growth or development and 26 per cent were fully satisfied and 39 per cent were somewhat satisfied with the performance of the BJP-led NDA government at the Centre, making 65 per cent at least somewhat satisfied, with only 18 per cent fully dissatisfied. These responses were remarkably similar across the four classes. These responses perhaps indicate why economic issues were the most important for only 43 per cent and the "negative" economic issues (unemployment, inflation, corruption, etc.) were most important for only 26 per cent, while growth and development mattered for 17 per cent.

One cannot infer from the fact of economic issues being the most important that this indicates dissatisfaction with the government's performance; it is quite possible that the mention of growth and development is an indicator of satisfaction with the government's performance. As many as 47 per cent thought that the Modi government should get a second chance compared to 35 per cent against, with the Rich endorsing a comeback by 55 per cent and even the Poor by 44 per cent.

In terms of receipt of government benefits, the findings are as follows. In the past month (this was a post-election survey), one-fifth of households had received some government money remarkably evenly across classes, with only one-sixth of the poor receiving money, and 37 per cent crediting the Centre and the state government. The housing scheme (Awas Yojana) benefited 21 per cent over the past five years, fairly uniformly across classes, with the Rich at 15 per cent, with half crediting the Centre and one-third the state government. Again, 21 per cent benefited from the Mahatma Gandhi Rural Employment Guarantee Act (MNREGA) employment guarantee scheme (begun by the Congress-led UPA government, but continued by the NDA-II), again uniformly across classes, except for the Rich at a surprising 16 per cent, for which half credited the Centre and one-third the state government. And 17 per cent had benefited over the past five years from free hospitalisation, again uniformly across classes, for which over half credited the Centre and 30 per cent the state government. Further, 25 per cent had over the past five years received old age, widows, or disabilities pensions, again uniformly across classes, for which under a third credited the Centre and over half the state government. As many as 44 per cent had benefited from the food subsidy (Public Distribution System) over the past five years, with the Rich at 31 per cent and the Poor at 50 per cent, for which 57 per cent across classes credited the state government and 27 per cent the Centre; 13 per cent had received benefits from income support schemes for farmers, with the Poor less at 10 per cent and the Rich at 16 per cent, for which 44 per cent across classes credited the Centre. Moreover, 13 per cent had benefited from loan waivers with the Poor at 10 per cent and the Rich at 16 per cent, with half crediting the state government and one-third the Centre. As many as 34 per cent had benefited from the Ujjwala Yojana, with roughly similar proportions across classes, and with 71 per cent crediting the Centre. Finally, 22 per cent across classes benefited from the Jan Dhan Yojana of bank accounts for the unbanked, with 71 per cent crediting the Centre.

What is noteworthy is that *one-fifth* of households had received some money over the past month, and that the *nine welfare programmes above had benefited 13–34 per cent of the respondents,* with a large proportion in each case crediting the Central government, and hence the BJP or Modi personally; of those who credited the state governments, a large number would have inevitably been BJP or BJP-allied governments, particularly in northern and western India. That is, the Modi government's welfare outreach was considerable and gained it credit from significant slices of the electorate. What is also remarkable is that in each of the nine welfare programmes, the proportion of beneficiaries is similar in each of the four classes with small differences; that is, they seem to be universal, not income-targeted programmes, although some like MNREGA are aimed at the poor.

Leadership, Nationalism, Minorities, and the Ecology of Attitudes that Might Affect Party Preference Across Class Cleavages

Finally, given that non-economic issues were the most important issues for 39 per cent of the respondents, how did these issues impact the public and who would have gained electorally? What were general orientations on questions such as leadership, nationalism, and minorities that have implications for party preferences? The key issue – given the positions taken and propagated explicitly or implicitly by the BJP at various levels – is whether there was a Hindu consolidation across caste and class cleavages based on attitudes to Muslims or minorities in general. A number of questions throw light on these. Our finding is that accommodative attitudes toward minorities enjoy a large majority, although this needs careful interpretation. We examine what the data says on these matters.

Modi's leadership and the perceived lack of a credible alternative leadership appear to have played a decisive role. As many as 47 per cent (Rich at 53 per cent, Poor at 44 per cent, with others in between) preferred Modi as the next prime minister (the post-election survey was done before the results were announced), with only 23 per cent preferring Rahul Gandhi. And as many as one-third of the voters who voted for the BJP would have voted for some other party were Modi not the prime ministerial candidate (in 2014, a quarter of NDA voters would have voted for some other party were Modi not the PM candidate). It would appear that Modi's leadership was crucial in what appeared to have become a semi-presidential election, even more crucial than in 2014.

This interpretation is buttressed by responses to another question in which 39 per cent fully agreed with the proposition that the country "should be governed by a strong leader who does not have to bother about winning elections," with Rich at 49 per cent, Poor at 32 per cent, and only 7 per cent fully disagreeing with this position.

On nationalism, let us look at the much-talked about Balakot airstrike on Pakistan in response to the terrorist attack in Pulwama, and its aftermath, often mentioned as a nationalist rallying point around the ruling party and Modi as a leader. As many as 76 per cent had heard of it, including 87 per cent of the Rich and 67 per cent of the Poor, a 20 per cent spread; 32 per cent credited the air force alone for the strike (35 per cent of the Rich, 27 per cent of the Poor, other classes in between) and 16 per cent credited the Modi government and 22 per cent both, showing a large degree of support (70 per cent) across classes for the action. However, it would be too much to infer that that one action in late February swung the election in favour of a decisive NDA victory.

Relatedly, on the question of "how nationalist" the Hindu and Muslim communities are, a tricky question since "nationalist" can be variously interpreted (sometimes quite erroneously as pro-government), 57 per cent (Rich 65 per cent, Poor 50 per cent) found Hindus to be highly nationalist, only 27 per cent thought Muslims to be so, fairly evenly across classes, and 11 per cent thought them to be "not nationalist at all".

On the polarising issue of the Babri Mosque, a narrow majority of 40 per cent to 32 per cent (with a large proportion of Can't Say or No Response) thought that the demolition of the Babri Mosque in Ayodhya in 1992 was not justified, with narrow spreads across classes in each of these responses, but with majority disapproval of the demolition in each class. However, the fact that almost a third justified the demolition indicates the spread of the de facto BJP position. Among those who had heard of the demolition, 37 per cent said that a temple should be built on the site of the demolished mosque, while those who said that a mosque should be built or that both a temple and a mosque should be built add up to 35 per cent. Class differences within these opinions are very narrow (spreads of less than 5 per cent). A considerable degree of Hindu consolidation across classes appears to have taken place on this particular issue.

On the question of whether in a democracy the "will of the majority community should prevail", 23 per cent fully agreed (19 per cent Poor, 27 per cent Rich, others in between) and 27 per cent somewhat agreed, while 30 per cent fully or somewhat disagreed (inter-class spreads are very narrow in each category of response). This is a tricky question to interpret, but only under a quarter fully agreed with the completely majoritarian position. It is also noteworthy that among those who fully disagreed (16 per cent), the Rich were 20 per cent and the Poor 13 per cent; perhaps indicating more liberal attitudes correlate with education and information.

On whether "the Muslim community has been victimised under Narendra Modi's government", opinion was divided, with 14 per cent (Rich 17 per cent) fully agreeing but 24 per cent (Rich 24 per cent) fully disagreeing.

The above questions seem to indicate both a premium on perceived effective leadership and some degree of majoritarian consolidation in explicit (Babri Mosque) or vague opposition to minorities.

However, and very importantly, on some other questions explicitly about attitudes to minorities, the majority of respondents seem to have attitudes in line with pluralism and accommodation of minorities.

Up to 76 per cent, with an inter-class spread of only 4 per cent, felt that India belongs to citizens of all religions equally, while only 15 per cent (5 per cent spread between classes) felt that India belongs to only Hindus.

On the question of whether the "government should treat minorities in the same way as it treats the majority", 39 per cent fully agreed (with an 8 per cent inter-class spread between Rich 42 per cent and Poor 34 per cent) and 24 per cent somewhat agreed with this position, with only 6 per cent fully disagreeing. This would seem to indicate egalitarian attitudes toward minorities, but this can be tricky to interpret. If respondents start with a conscious or unconscious prejudice that minorities are being pandered to, then seemingly egalitarian attitudes could conceal anti-minority attitudes (in that respondents who are for egalitarian treatment of minorities could actually be expecting the government to correct, from their point of view, a bias toward minorities).

However, on the question, "giving equal treatment to minorities is not enough, the government should give special treatment to minorities", 27 per cent fully and 25 per cent somewhat agreed and only 12 per cent fully disagreed, with small inter-class spreads in each category of response.

On the question, "Even if it is not liked by the majority, the government must protect the interests of the minorities", 37 per cent (40–41 per cent of the Rich and Middle class) fully agreed, 28 per cent somewhat agreed, and only 6 per cent fully disagreed, indicating a largely accommodative attitude to minorities, more so among the Rich and Middle class than the Lower and Poor.

On whether "minorities must adopt the customs of the majority community", only 13 per cent, with little inter-class difference, fully agreed, while 27 per cent (Rich 32 per cent, Poor 24 per cent) fully disagreed.

An important question is whether there are significant differences in responses to these questions across regions given the actual result in which the BJP swept most of the North (Hindi-speaking states plus Punjab and Jammu & Kashmir) and West, doing less well in the South and East.

The findings from regional disaggregation of the response are that accommodative and pluralist attitudes to minorities largely prevail in all regions, with the South being more accommodative/less majoritarian on most questions, but counterintuitively less so on some. Only 15 per cent in the South justified the demolition of the Babri Mosque, while 39 per cent (West, comprising Gujarat, Maharashtra, and Goa), 37 per cent (East, comprising West Bengal, Odisha, Bihar, Jharkhand, and Northeast), and 35 per cent (North, comprising the Hindi-belt except Bihar and Jharkhand, plus Punjab and Jammu & Kashmir) did so. Only 20 per cent in the South thought that only a temple should be built on the site, whereas 41–43 per cent in the other three regions thought so. The South (21 per cent) fully agreed with the statement that Muslims had been victimised by the Modi government, while 10–15 per cent in other regions did so, and more of the latter three (25–27 per cent compared to 16 per cent for the South) fully disagreed.

However, counterintuitively, 37 per cent of the South fully agreed that the "will of the majority community" should prevail in a democracy, compared to 16 per cent (North), 21 per cent (East), and 26 per cent (West). In the South, 49 per cent fully agreed that the "country should be governed by a strong leader who does not have to bother about winning elections", whereas only 33–39 per cent fully agreed with this proposition in the other three regions, and 18 per cent of the South fully agreed with the statement that minorities should adopt the customs of the majority community, while only 9–12 per cent of the other regions did so.

On whether the government should treat minorities in the same way it treats the majority, 48 per cent (South) fully agreed, whereas 35–38 per cent of the other regions did so, with another 20–30 per cent in all regions somewhat agreeing and less than 7 per cent in all regions fully disagreeing. Only 14 per cent or less, in all regions, fully disagreed with the government giving special treatment for minorities. The South is broadly in line with other regions in considering Muslims only about half as "highly nationalist" as Hindus. The South also fully agreed (46 per cent) that the government must protect the interests of minorities, even if the majority does not agree (other regions 32–37 per cent), with only 7 per cent or less in all regions fully disagreeing with the statement.

How do we interpret the above responses to questions on minorities? Reading the responses to these questions together, it seems that accommodative attitudes to minorities enjoy a large majority in 2019 with a majority – including in the North and West – fully agreeing or somewhat agreeing, and only a relatively small minority fully disagreeing, with (a) equal treatment of minorities, (b) special rights for minorities, (c) the government needing to protect minority interests even if the majority is against it, and (d) minorities not needing to adopt the customs of the majority community.

However, opinion is divided on whether Muslims are "highly nationalist," being rated as much less than Hindus; on whether Muslims have been victimised under the Modi government; and on the Babri Mosque demolition and what should be built there. While majority opinion can be interpreted as still largely accommodative in its attitudes to minorities, this is not as large as it was in 2014, thus indicating a spread of anti-minority sentiment over the past five years. It should be noted that except where I noted above, inter-class differences in each category of response to each of these questions are small, with spreads of 5–8 per cent between the widest-apart opinions. This indicates a remarkable lack of class polarisation in each of the "attitudinal ecology" questions regarding minorities, which have their implications for party preference, specifically for BJP preference. Also, one needs to add a caveat that at a popular level, attitudes do not reflect thought-out political or ideological positions, only gut feelings in response to a questionnaire that has to be answered without much thought, and people are entirely capable of entertaining contradictory or mixed positions on sets of issues.

Does majoritarian Hindu nationalism as promoted by the BJP lead to a cross-class Hindu consolidation of opinion on a range of issues, including economic questions, rendering class cleavages unimportant? In addition to this, what might explain the smallness of cross-class differences of opinion? Are there other reasons?

Some Theoretical Issues and Possible Explanations for Low Class Polarisation

This raises various theoretical questions. Why do the Lower and Poor classes vote on broadly the same lines as the Rich and Middle classes? Is it because the SCs, STs, and even OBCs, who are probably correlated (with the first two categories probably highly) with the Lower and Poor classes, voted along these lines due to Hindu consolidation in opposition to minorities? We saw above that pluralist/accommodative attitudes to minorities are still dominant despite the probable growth of anti-minority, primarily anti-Muslim, attitudes to an extent greater than in 2014. And to some questions, the Rich and Middle classes are slightly more minority-sympathetic than the Lower and Poor. So we need to look at the larger comparative literature on class voting to search for explanations as to why the working class and poor vote, at certain times, for parties traditionally based on better-off classes and whose core platform reflects the latter's interests. Right-wing populism, with its three components – anti-elite attitudes, nativism/ethno-nationalism, and authoritarianism[3] – comes to mind in these times, but space constraints do not allow further exploration.

There are two theoretical speculations that we can make, and right now the data only allow us to speculate; however, speculation could possibly lead to more definitive research. One possibly profitable line of inquiry to follow is the "poor voter paradox" – why do poor voters in many countries routinely vote for parties that represent the interests of the better off? As Sridharan sums it up, citing Thachil: "there are three explanations in the literature – programmatic redistributive shifts (like anti-poverty programmes) undertaken by elite parties, patronage distribution, and 'distracting' appeals of identity politics."[4] All three factors appear to be in place in the backdrop of the 2019 BJP campaign. If we look at the responses to the questions on the economy and welfare programmes, we see that one-fifth of respondents received some public funds just before the election and significant slices of the respondents (13–34 per cent) received some benefits from various welfare programmes over the first Modi term. These could dilute class polarisation and reinforce pro-Modi attitudes especially given the perception of strong and decisive leadership and the lack of a unified opposition coalition, and a certain degree of growth of anti-minority sentiment across classes that the questions on minorities pick up (despite majority opinion being pluralist overall).

Second, one needs to also look at patterns of class self-identification in India and see whether they follow patterns that have long been picked up in Organization for Economic Cooperation and Development (OECD) countries in the social stratification literature. There is very little data on this and none from 2019, but Kapur and Vaishnav showed that as high as 49 per cent of respondents in their large 2014 survey self-identified as middle class,

[3] Mudde, *Populist Radical Right Parties in Europe*.

[4] Sridharan, "Class Voting in the 2014 Lok Sabha Elections", 72–6; Thachil, "Elite Parties and Poor Voters".

whereas all socioeconomic estimates of the middle class put the figure at much less (see Aslany for estimates in the literature; her own estimate is 28 per cent).[5] The 49 per cent figure for self-identification as middle class is much closer to the majority self-identification as middle class in OECD countries than to Indian economic realities and relativities. Are we then seeing, along with and perhaps as a byproduct of three decades of sustained high growth post-1991, an "aspirational" middle class that while being below the economic and social middle class cut-offs, still identifies "upwardly" or "aspirationally" with the upper and middle classes, including in political and party preferences? My speculation, in the absence of hard data, is that the relative absence of significant class differences in party preference in 2019 in responses to most questions is the result of a complex interaction between growing Hindu identity politics, perceived strong and effective leadership, "upward" or "aspirational" class identification, and effectively implemented welfare programmes.

Bibliography

Asian Development Bank, "Poverty Data: India", retrieved from https://www.adb.org/countries/india/poverty.

Aslany, M., "The Indian Middle Class, Its Size, and Urban–Rural Variations", *Contemporary South Asia* 27 (2019).

Kapur, D., and M. Vaishnav, "Being Middle Class in India", *The Hindu*, 10 January 2015.

Mudde, C., *Populist Radical Right Parties in Europe* (New York: Cambridge University Press, 2007).

Sridharan, E., "Class Voting in the 2014 Lok Sabha Elections: The Growing Size and Importance of the Middle Classes", *Economic and Political Weekly*, XLIX (2014), 72–6.

Thachil, T., "Elite Parties and Poor Voters: Theory and Evidence from India", *American Political Science* Review, 108 (2014).

[5] Aslany, "The Indian Middle Class"; Kapur and Vaishnav, "Being Middle Class in India".

3

Class Voting in the 2014 Lok Sabha Elections

The Growing Size and Importance of the Middle Classes

How did middle- and upper-middle-class voters vote in the 2014 elections? Apart from purely numerical effects, the middle class is electorally more impactful relative to its size because of its human capital and opinion-shaping character. The pro-BJP swing among the middle classes, indicated by the Lokniti post-poll survey, cannot be attributed to an anti-minority shift in middle-class opinion nationally, nor to simple economic dissatisfaction, nor to a broader attitudinal shift towards economic liberalisation; we have to search for more complex explanations.

In this paper, I attempt to analyse how the middle class and the other classes voted in the 2014 elections. I focus on the voting for the Bharatiya Janata Party (BJP) and Indian National Congress (INC), vote preferences along the caste/community and age groups within classes to the extent relevant, and economic policy, particularly as concerns economic liberalisation. I also attempt to engage with certain theoretical formulations on the middle class, economic liberalisation, the BJP and party-system change. The growth of the middle classes with the growth of India's economy, rise in incomes, urbanisation, and white-collar occupations have changed the bipolar elite-mass social structure at independence into a roughly three-layered elite, middle-class, mass social structure. This has been characterised by a broadening middle class, however defined, since liberalisation and faster economic growth post the 1980s, and particularly after 1991. Hence, with growing numbers of this class it is important to analyse middle-class voting behaviour. Also, apart from purely numerical effects, the middle class is electorally more impactful relative to its size because of its human capital and opinion-shaping character.[1]

But first, how is the middle class defined? "Middle class" is a nebulous and variable term that can and has been used in various ways in the Indian and comparative literature. It is possible to define the middle class in economic terms by income cut-offs, consumption cut-offs, asset ownership, all three being related, or in sociological terms by occupation, education, or self-identification.[2] The Centre for the Study of Developing Societies (CSDS)–Lokniti post-poll survey categorises the middle class in a particular way, and, since I depend on this data set in this paper, I follow this definition, although I refer to other possible definitions where relevant. The definition used here is a composite class index consisting of a combination of economic (income and ownership of selected durable assets; in particular, the type of house) and sociological criteria (that is, occupation and occupational level), with assets and income adjusted for rural or urban location of the survey respondent.[3] This classification results in the survey respondents being divided into four classes in the following shares of the sample: upper class or upper-middle class (11 per cent), middle (36 per cent), lower (33 per cent), and poor (20 per cent). To say a word

[1] Kapur, "The Middle Class in India"; Deshpande, "The Centrality of the Middle Class".

[2] For a review of the literature on possible conceptualisations and definitions and estimates of the Indian middle classes, see Sridharan, "The Growth and Sectoral Composition of India's Middle Class"; Sridharan, "The Political Economy of the Middle Classes in Liberalising India", and Kapur, "The Middle Class in India".

[3] Class index developed by the CSDS Data Unit.

about this classification before moving on, the classification results in a very large upper strata of 11 per cent and a huge middle class of 36 per cent that roughly coincides with the income-based definition of Bijapurkar (2007) of the 30 per cent after the top 10 per cent (with 36 per cent and 34 per cent of national income, respectively), resulting in a combined upper and middle class of 47 per cent or nearly half the population, and a poor (20 per cent) that roughly coincides with the pre-Tendulkar Committee, old poverty line poor of 22 per cent in most recent times. This 47 per cent is not far from Bijapurkar's "consuming class" of 375 million, based on the National Council of Applied Economic Research (NCAER) data, or about 37 per cent of the population (2001 Census).

The present paper's definition differs from my own earlier estimates of the middle class at the start of the twenty-first century and around 2005–6 in that it is much broader.[4] My estimate based on 1998–9 income-cum-(non-manual) occupation criteria based on NCAER data was that of an elite middle class of about 6 per cent of the population, a broader middle class of 12 per cent and the broadest middle class of 26 per cent. The present upper class in the National Election Study (NES) survey data would be largely coincident with my broader middle class, with my understanding of the elite middle class constituting the top half of the upper class. The present middle class would extend to nearly double that of my estimated 26 per cent broadest middle class. My "internationally recognisable middle class" based on 2005–6 data would be about 6 per cent of the population and within the current upper class.[5] Also, upper castes, an electorally significant social category, would be disproportionately within the upper class. Hence, in this paper I choose to call the upper class the upper-middle class.

[4] Sridharan, "The Growth and Sectoral Composition of India's Middle Class"; Sridharan, "The Political Economy of the Middle Classes in Liberalising India".

[5] Sridharan, "The Political Economy of the Middle Classes in Liberalising India".

To call the top 12 per cent of a low-income country like India upper class, implying they are rich, is misleading by world standards. The sample would include only a very tiny number of truly rich persons by world standards, or even Indian standards. I look at both this upper-middle class and the (NES) middle-class voting patterns and their relationships with age, caste/community, the BJP, INC, and economic liberalisation questions. Hence, in this paper I focus on the upper-middle and middle classes' voting patterns and expressed opinions in response to electorally relevant questions.

Theoretical Formulations on the Middle Class

A question raised by the huge 12 per cent swing (from 19 per cent to 31 per cent vote share) for the BJP that has catapulted it into power with a majority on its own is about how its social base has expanded. Have a large section of the upper-middle and middle classes, which are disproportionately upper caste, swung behind the BJP, spanning metropolitan cities, other cities/towns, and rural areas, aided by higher turnout? And if so, why is this so? What are the changes in class attitudes and towards economic policy that are detectable? These questions also point to the relevance, not necessarily validity, of certain theorisations that I lay out below in brief before looking at the data.

As far back as 1999, in the aftermath of the BJP's rise since 1989, and against the backdrop of its emergence as the single largest party in 1996, 1998, and 1999, Yadav, Kumar, and Heath (1999) put forward the concept of a "new social bloc" – a loose coming together of groups united by relative economic and social privilege that were tending towards the BJP – urban rich and middle classes, upper castes, and rising landed peasant castes. As they put it, "a new social coalition of various groups, that now lays claim to political power" formed by "the convergence of traditional caste-community differences and class distinctions . . . defined by an overlap of social and economic privileges."[6] Desai (2004) makes a similar argument about the incorporation of the middle-caste agrarian capitalists into the BJP's fold either directly or via their regional parties as National Democratic Alliance (NDA) coalition partners of the BJP in many states.[7] It is worth looking at whether 2014 represents the coming to full fruition of this incipient "new social bloc" at least regionally over a vast swathe of India.

Also relevant here is the formulation by Iversen and Soskice,[8] based on a broad, comparative historical study of Western democracies, that majoritarian electoral systems (of which the Indian first-past-the-post is one) in economies where the labour force is not organised in a corporatist style and where the economy and business are relatively decentralised, engendering top-middle coalitions against redistributive pressures by the poor, whereas proportional representation systems in corporatist economies tend towards redistributivist middle-bottom coalitions. As they conclude, "the middle class, which tends to decide who governs, has an incentive to ally with the poor to exploit the rich, but also has an incentive to support the rich to avoid being exploited by the poor. In a majoritarian two-party system, the latter motive dominates because the middle-class cannot be sure that the poor will not set policies in a centre-left leadership party."[9]

Relevant to the BJP's domination over the INC even in the lower and poor classes, in both urban and rural areas (and also, the INC's historical dominance for decades), is the issue, much debated globally, of the "poor voter paradox" – why do poor voters in many countries routinely vote for parties that represent the policy

[6] Yadav, Kumar, and Heath, "The BJP's New Social Bloc".

[7] Desai, *Slouching Towards Ayodhya*, particularly the first essay, "A Field Guide to Rough Beasts: The Right Politics to Come".

[8] Iversen and Soskice, "Electoral Institutions and the Politics of Coalitions", 178.

[9] Ibid.

interests of the wealthy. Thachil (2014) points out that there are three explanations in the literature – programmatic redistributive shifts (like anti-poverty programmes) undertaken by elite parties, patronage distribution, and the "distracting" appeals of identity politics.[10] He argues in favour of a fourth explanation as regards poorer voters voting for the BJP – private provision of local public goods by party-affiliated organisations of the Sangh Parivar – but this is outside the scope of this paper. What is relevant here is whether there has been a shift in attitudes to economic liberalisation, particularly to flagship anti-poverty and employment programmes, among various classes of voters, and whether this adds up to an attitude shift towards economic liberalisation that underpins the BJP victory.

Related to the above formulation, the question arises as to whether this election has seen the party system moving towards a western-style left-right axis ranging from social-democratic redistributivist policies on the Left to free-market-oriented policies on the Right, with right-of-centre policies supported by a top-middle, business-middle-class alliance? Is the growing middle class the social base for capitalism that Kohli (1989) had argued a quarter-century ago with reference to the 1980s and Rajiv Gandhi's initial moves towards deregulation of the economy?[11]

How Did the Upper-Middle Class and Middle Class Vote?

A significant difference between 2009 and 2014 was upper middle- and middle-class turnout, both in terms of the higher proportion of the population and hence the total vote constituted by these two classes (47 per cent from 26 per cent in 2009, Table 1) and in terms of overall turnout increase from 58 per cent to 68 per cent (Table 2).

[10] Thachil, "Elite Parties and Poor Voters".

[11] Kohli, "The Politics of Economic Liberalisation in India".

Table 1. Class Composition, 2014 and 2009 (NES 2014, 2009)

Class	*2009*	*2014*
Poor	41	20
Lower	33	33
Middle	20	36
Upper	6	11

Table 2. Class-wise Turnout, 2014 and 2009 (NES 2014, 2009)

Class	*Voter Turnout*	
	2009	*2014*
Poor	57	60
Lower	59	68
Middle	60	69
Upper	57	67
Total	58	67

This is partly due to the definitional effect of the cut-offs for class definitions remaining the same and hence for a much larger percentage of the sample falling in these two classes. Turnout by the poor at 60 per cent is significantly less than the 68 per cent turnout by the two richer classes (Table 2), this pattern resembling the pattern in Western countries where the better-off and more educated turn out at higher rates than the poor. Turnout by the upper-middle and middle classes is equal to that by the lower class and much higher than the poor class regardless of rural, town/city, or metropolitan location (Table 4) except for the upper-middle class in towns/cities compared to the lower class (but still higher than the poor).

Also, a larger proportion of metropolitan votes compared to 2009 were accounted by the upper-middle and middle class due to their higher turnout and higher proportion. Higher turnout

Table 3. Class-wise Party Preference (2014 and 2009)

Class	*Congress*		*BJP*	
	2009	*2014*	*2009*	*2014*
Poor	27	20	16	24
Lower	29	19	19	31
Middle	29	20	22	32
Upper	29	17	25	38
Total	29	19	19	31

by the upper-middle and middle classes in metros could be a sign of things to come in the future as India urbanises rapidly and as the middle classes, holding cut-offs constant, grow in relative size. Since the upper-middle and middle classes are disproportionately upper caste we would expect mutual reinforcement in terms of pro-BJP party preference – (36 per cent and 25 per cent, respectively) of the upper-middle- and middle-class voters were upper caste, 27 per cent of upper middle+middle classes taken together, compared to 22 per cent of all voters, from Table 6. Of the total pro-BJP vote, 52 per cent came from the top two classes (Table 3).

The age group within classes does not seem to have made a big difference overall but it is noteworthy that first-time voters (40 per cent

Table 4. Class-wise Voter Turnout in Rural-Urban Locations

Class	*Village*		*Town/City*		*Metro*	
	2009	*2014*	*2009*	*2014*	*2009*	*2014*
Poor	58	63	56	57	44	50
Lower	60	70	60	64	50	56
Middle	61	71	59	66	52	57
Upper	59	71	53	59	57	69
Total	59	69	58	63	49	57

Table 5. Party Preference of Voters by Different Class and Age Groups

	Poor		*Lower*		*Middle*		*Upper*	
Age Group	*Congress*	*BJP*	*Congress*	*BJP*	*Congress*	*BJP*	*Congress*	*BJP*
18–22	23	24	18	35	17	40	11	44
23–25	24	25	18	34	21	32	16	43
26–35	19	27	21	33	19	33	17	40
36–45	18	24	17	30	20	32	15	36
46–55	19	22	21	31	20	31	20	35
56 and above	20	22	18	28	23	29	21	35
Total	20	24	19	31	20	32	17	38

Table 6. Party Preference of Voters by Different Classes and Caste/Community

Caste/	*Poor*		*Lower*		*Middle*		*Upper*	
Community	*Congress*	*BJP*	*Congress*	*BJP*	*Congress*	*BJP*	*Congress*	*BJP*
Upper caste	13	37	11	48	15	46	13	55
OBC	15	28	15	37	16	33	14	37
SC	17	22	18	22	20	27	17	25
ST	28	33	31	36	25	39	26	53
Muslims	41	4	34	10	42	11	27	7
Others	19	17	23	18	22	24	31	16
Total	20	24	19	31	20	32	17	38

Source: CSDS Data Unit, Delhi.

pro-BJP in middle class) and under-35 age groups in upper middle class (Table 5) were disproportionately pro-BJP. This younger age group's relatively greater orientation towards the BJP could possibly be a sign of things to come in the future as this generation rises and the older generations fade out.

The upper-middle- and middle-class preference for the BJP (38 per cent and 32 per cent, respectively) was more marked than that of the rest of the sample, being 31 per cent for lower and only

24 per cent for the poor (Table 3), and this is still more marked in the case of the upper-caste component of these two classes (46 per cent middle and 55 per cent upper middle pro-BJP, Table 6). While in 2009 the BJP led the Congress only among the upper castes (36 per cent to 26 per cent, Table 6), in 2014 it led the Congress in all castes/communities except Muslims and Christians but most particularly among the upper castes (Table 6).

Therefore, the data shows a strong affinity for the BJP among the upper-middle and middle classes, and among the upper castes who have a disproportionately high share in these classes, as well as the younger age groups among the upper-middle and middle. Among the upper-middle class in the metros, there is a seeming emergence of the loose "new social bloc" of economic and social privilege after fifteen years of high growth, rising incomes, and greater urbanisation by historical standards.[12] This also seems to fit with the top-middle affinity postulated by Iversen and Soskice for majoritarian electoral systems without a corporatist organisation of the economy.

Explaining the Upper/Middle Shift Towards the BJP

But why did the upper-middle and middle class vote for the BJP disproportionately in 2014? After all this was not the pattern after five years of high growth under United Progressive Alliance (UPA)-I in 2009. So it cannot be assumed that the growth of the upper-middle and middle classes automatically translates into pro-BJP preferences. Was it due to an anti-minority sentiment promoted, as an undercurrent, by the BJP campaign, at least in certain states like Uttar Pradesh? Or was it due to a rightward shift in views among the population on economic policy issues? Or was it due to the upper-middle and middle classes' dissatisfaction with their economic

[12] Yadav, Kumar, and Heath, "The BJP's New Social Bloc".

condition and, implicitly, with the Congress-led UPA government's policies?

Was the upper-middle and middle-class shift towards the BJP part of a Hindu consolidation on an anti-minority platform? The responses to questions on equal treatment of minorities, and on special provisions for minorities indicate that it was not an anti-minority shift since an above-average solid majority of the upper-middle (68 per cent) and middle (62 per cent) classes strongly or somewhat agree on equal treatment of minorities, and only 16 per cent strongly or somewhat disagree, and an above-average majority of the upper-middle (61 per cent) and middle (58 per cent) classes strongly or somewhat agree on special provisions for minorities, and only 19 per cent strongly or somewhat disagree.[13] Although in response to a question on whether in a democracy the majority community's will should prevail, a majority agree, with a large percentage of "Don't Know/Can't Say" this cannot automatically be interpreted as anti-minority.[14] However, we do not have responses segregated regionally. It is just possible though not at all probable from the solid overall majorities nationally that are not anti-minority, with under 20 per cent who strongly or somewhat disagree on the acceptability of equal treatment and special provisions for minorities, that in the Hindi-belt and western states swept by the BJP with 61 per cent of the population, attitudes might be anti-minority as a whole. However, it is quite possible that attitudes on minorities might be somewhat less favourable in the pro-BJP regions than the overall average indicates.

Was the pro-BJP swing in response to dissatisfaction with the country's, or the respondents' household economic condition over the past five years? The responses indicate that there was no marked

[13] The questions were, respectively: "The government/state should treat minorities in the same way as it treats the majority?" and "The government should make special provisions to accommodate minorities?"

[14] The question was: "In a democracy, the will of the majority community should prevail?"

dissatisfaction with the country's economic condition or respondents' household's economic condition over the past five years. The responses indicate that there was no marked dissatisfaction with the country's economic condition or respondents' household economic condition over the past five years.[15] Of the upper-middle class, 38 per cent say India is better or much better off compared to 34 per cent worse or much worse off with 23 per cent the same in response to the question on the nation's economy; of the middle class, 44 per cent say better or much better off, 25 per cent worse or much worse off, with 23 per cent the same. In response to the question on their household's economic condition, more say their households were better off than worse off. On a more specific issue, electricity supply, more of the upper-middle and middle classes felt it had improved rather than deteriorated. Of the upper-middle class, 33 per cent felt it had improved, 28 per cent deteriorated, with 33 per cent the same. Of the middle class, 34 per cent felt it had improved, 25 per cent deteriorated, and 32 per cent the same.[16] However, on whether employment opportunities have improved, more people in the middle and upper-middle classes felt that they had deteriorated rather than improved.[17] Of the upper-middle class, 38 per cent felt they had deteriorated compared to 21 per cent improved, with 34 per cent saying they remained the same. Of the middle class, 34 per cent felt they had deteriorated, 20 per cent improved, and 35 per cent the same. However, taking responses to economic conditions

[15] The questions were, respectively: "As compared to five years ago, would you say the economic condition of India has become much better, better, remained same, become worse or much worse?" and "As compared to five years ago, how is the economic condition of your household today – would you say it has become much better, better, remained same, become worse or much worse?"

[16] The question was: "During the last five years please tell me whether supply of electricity have improved or deteriorated?"

[17] The question was: "During the last five years please tell me whether employment opportunities have improved or deteriorated?"

questions as a whole, simple economic dissatisfaction with the government does not explain the pro-BJP swing.

Was there an attitudinal shift towards economic liberalisation on the whole? This is not indicated by the pro-worker attitudes of all classes in response to a question on whether employers should be responsible for their workers even if their business is doing badly, or the evenly balanced attitudes on strikes in response to another question on whether the government should curb workers' strikes, or ambivalent attitudes to liberalisation of foreign direct investment.[18]

However, a distinct shift in attitudes is indicated by the responses to a question on whether the government should spend more on infrastructure than on subsidising the poor, in which all classes, most of all the upper-middle and middle, are in favour of government spending on infrastructure rather than on subsidies for the poor, something that seems to better fit the implicit message of the BJP/Modi campaign than the Congress one.[19] Whatever the reasons (which are not clear) behind this preference it gives us a clue that the Congress's anti-poverty programmes and employment guarantee programmes did not catch the popular imagination as they apparently did in 2009.

From the above analysis, it seems neither Hindu majoritarianism nor a dissatisfaction with the movement in their economic condition over the past five years explains the pro-BJP swing. One can only speculate that there was a general dissatisfaction with their current economic condition compared to what seem to be heightened expectations/aspirations. BJP/Modi campaign seemed to

[18] The questions were, respectively: "Employers should be responsible for taking care of their workers even when their business is not doing well?"; "Government should strongly curb strikes by workers and employees?"; "Government should allow foreign companies to freely invest in India without too many restrictions?"

[19] The question was: "Government should spend more on infrastructure than subsidising the poor?"

credibly promise the latter as compared to the lacklustre Congress campaign. The low ratings for the Congress leadership compared to Modi in response to questions on whom respondents prefer as prime minister, picked up by Lokniti and other tracker polls since Modi was projected as the BJP's candidate for prime minister since September 2013, back this up. For the Modi factor there is some support in that as many as 23 per cent of the upper-middle and middle classes said they would have voted for a different party than the one they voted for if Modi had not been the candidate, although this is not limited to pro-BJP/NDA voters. Also, this might have been much more the case in the states swept by the BJP, but for this we have to look at the regionally disaggregated data.[20]

Conclusions

Overall, one can say that in 2014 the class-wise gradation of pro-BJP responses, with pro-BJP sentiment rising as we go up the class hierarchy, as well as the caste hierarchy, indicate support for the emergence of a loose, not compact, "new social bloc" of class and caste privilege. This supports the Iversen-Soskice (2006) finding that majoritarian electoral systems tend towards a top-middle alliance in the absence of a corporatist economic structure.

However, on economic policy issues, particularly about liberalisation and the role of the state, the responses are much more mixed. As I have argued earlier,[21] the Indian middle classes' attitudes towards liberalisation are complex and contradictory because a large fraction of the middle class, though declining gradually over time with the growth of the private sector and also as we go up the class

[20] The question was: "Let us assume that in this election Narendra Modi was not the PM candidate of the BJP/NDA. In such a situation, would you have voted for some other party instead of the party you have voted for or this would have made no difference on your decision?"

[21] Sridharan, "The Growth and Sectoral Composition of India's Middle Class"; Sridharan, "The Political Economy of the Middle Classes in Liberalising India".

hierarchy, are public employees broadly defined. Thus, an estimated 58 per cent–75 per cent of the broadest middle class of 26 per cent of the population as of the turn of the century were either public employees or (publicly subsidised) rich peasants,[22] and even of the elite middle class of 6 per cent as of 2005–6 as many as 30 per cent belonged to these segments.[23]

Even those of the middle classes who are self-employed persons or private employees are, like public employees or rich peasants, the beneficiaries of a range of state subsidies including water, electricity, fertiliser, credit, fuel, higher education, public transport, and even food (which is supposed to go to the truly poor). In India, subsidies are not simply benefits paid to the poor out of taxes paid by the rich, as the debate is framed in developed democracies, particularly by the Right. The upper and middle classes as defined in the NES account for 48 per cent of the population in 2014, who cannot all be counted as part of a privileged group. Economic liberalisation that rolls back the role of the state would threaten the jobs of both public and private employees, subsidy-dependent rich peasants, and other members of the middle classes – and that is why one can expect to see the ambivalence or complexity of the responses to liberalisation noted above.

Hence, one can expect the middle classes' political alignments to be complexly determined by competition for patronage interwoven with identity politics, party loyalties, and ideology. Besides, the poorer classes and lower castes have also voted more for BJP than Congress or any other party in this election, a factor that needs explanation, and one that cannot be explained in terms of redistributive programmes or patronage politics except perhaps in the limited number of BJP-ruled states. Class is therefore only one of several axes of polarisation in India in 2014, and class politics

[22] Sridharan, "The Growth and Sectoral Composition of India's Middle Class".

[23] Sridharan, "The Political Economy of the Middle Classes in Liberalising India".

in the sense of developed democracies, particularly in Europe, or left-right axis on economic policy as in those countries, is still not the norm in India.

Overall, given the extremely regionally skewed nature of the BJP victory, with 244 seats of its 282 coming from the Hindi-belt states and western India, accounting for only 61 per cent of the population, we need to have regionally disaggregatable survey data to be able to fully comprehend the voting trends by class, caste/community and age groups within each region, as well as the attitudes towards minorities and majoritarianism, and towards economic policy questions – which we do not have as of now.

To sum up, it is too early to be able to confidently project the trends in this election into the future. We will need to observe a couple of more elections to see whether these trends hold.

Bibliography

Bijapurkar, R., *We Are Like That Only: Understanding the Logic of Consumer India* (New Delhi: Penguin, 2007).

Desai, Radhika, *Slouching Towards Ayodhya* (New Delhi: Three Essays, 2004).

Deshpande, Satish, "The Centrality of the Middle Class", in idem, *Contemporary India: A Sociological View* (New Delhi: Penguin, 2003), 125–50.

Iversen, Torben, and David Soskice, "Electoral Institutions and the Politics of Coalitions: Why Some Democracies Redistribute More Than Others", *American Political Science Review*, vol. 100, no. 2, May 2006, 165–81.

Kapur, Devesh, "The Middle Class in India: A Social Formation or a Political Actor?" *Political Power and Social Theory*, vol. 21, 2010, 215–40.

Kohli, Atul, "The Politics of Economic Liberalisation in India", *World Development*, vol. 17, no. 3, March 1989, 305–28.

Sridharan, E., "The Growth and Sectoral Composition of India's Middle Class: Its Impact on the Politics of Economic Liberalisation", *India Review*, vol. 3, no. 4, October 2004, 405–28.

Sridharan, E., "The Political Economy of the Middle Classes in Liberalising India", ISAS Working Paper No. 49, 2008, retrieved from www.isas.nus.edu.sg/Publica-tionbyCategory.aspx.

Thachil, Tariq, "Elite Parties and Poor Voters: Theory and Evidence from India", *American Political Science Review*, vol. 108, no. 2, May 2014, 454.

Yadav, Yogendra, Sanjay Kumar, and Oliver Heath, "The BJP's New Social Bloc", *Frontline*, vol. 16, issue 23, November 1999, 6–19.

4

Electoral Coalitions in the 2004 General Elections

Theory and Evidence

THE 2004 GENERAL elections saw, for the first time, a contest at the national level between two serious coalitions, the National Democratic Alliance (NDA) and the United Progressive Alliance (UPA), though the latter was named only after the elections (Tables 1 and 2 for their members in 2004 and 1999). The Congress Party, for the first time, put together a broad pre-election coalition covering several major states to take on the NDA coalition.

How important were coalitions in the unexpected verdict, compared to economic factors and anti-incumbency?[1] Without getting into the state-by-state debate on the latter issues, it has been clearly demonstrated that coalitions were of prime importance in the Congress alliance's victory, just as they were in the BJP's victory in the 1998 and 1999 elections. This paper examines the importance of coalitions, or lack of them, in Election 2004. I begin by attempting to situate electoral coalitions in India in a theoretical perspective.

[1] Virmani, "The Simple Economics of Election 2004"; Ramachandran, "Will There Be Inclusive Space and Depth?"

Table 1. All-India Lok Sabha Results 2004

Party	*Seats Contested*	*Seats Won*	*Change from 1999*	*Vote (per cent)*	*Change from 1999*
Congress allies	**535**	**222**	**69**	**36.53**	**–0.39**
Congress	414	145	31	26.44	–1.85
TRS	6	5	5	0.60	0.60
IND (Congress)	6	1	1	0.16	0.16
RJD	28	24	17	2.39	–0.38
LJNS	11	4	4	0.66	0.66
NCP	22	9	2	1.78	–0.36
JMM	7	4	4	0.41	0.20
PDP	3	1	1	0.07	0.07
MUL	2	1	–1	0.19	–0.03
KCM	1	0	0	0.05	–0.04
JDS	1	0	–1	0.05	–0.03
RPI	2	0	0	0.04	–0.09
RPI(A)	1	1	0	0.09	–0.04
PRBP	1	0	0	0.06	0.06
DMK	16	16	4	1.81	0.08
MDMK	4	4	0	0.43	–0.01
PMK	6	6	1	0.56	–0.10
PDS	2	0	0	0.02	0.02
AC	1	0	0	0.62	0.60
NDA	**543**	**189**	**–89**	**35.88**	**–2.39**
BJP	364	138	–44	22.16	–1.59
TDP	33	5	–24	3.04	–0.61
JD(U)	33	8	–13	1.94	–0.99
IND(BJP)	1	1	1	0.18	0.18
IFDP	1	1	1	0.07	0.07
SHS	22	12	–3	1.77	0.24
BJD	12	11	1	1.30	0.10
SAD	10	8	6	0.90	0.21
AIADMK	33	0	–10	2.19	0.27
TRMC	31	2	–6	2.06	–0.51
MNF	1	1	1	0.05	0.05
SDF	1	1	0	0.04	0.01
NPF	1	1	1	0.18	0.18

Table 1 (*Contd.*)

Table 1 (*Contd.*)

Party	*Seats Contested*	*Seats Won*	*Change from 1999*	*Vote (per cent)*	*Change from 1999*
Left	**112**	**61**	**18**	**8.01**	**0.13**
CPI	33	9	5	1.32	–0.16
CPI(M)	69	43	10	5.66	0.26
JDS(Left)	1	1	1	0.09	0.09
KEC	1	1	0	0.09	–0.01
IND(Left)	1	1	1	0.08	–0.07
RSP	4	3	0	0.43	0.01
FBL	3	3	1	0.35	0.01
BSP	**435**	**19**	**5**	**5.33**	**1.16**
SP +	**247**	**39**	**11**	**4.93**	**0.79**
SP	237	36	10	4.31	0.55
RLD	10	3	1	0.61	0.24
Others	3563	13	–14	9.32	0.69

Table 2. Net Effect of Change in Alliances

	Congress Alliance (UPA)		*National Democratic Alliance*	
	Seats	*Vote (Per Cent)*	*Seats*	*Vote (Per Cent)*
New allies added in 2004	49	6.32	4	2.53
Alliances of 1999 dropped	3	2.8	31	3.96
Net Gain/Loss (+/-)	+46	3.52	–27	–1.43

Notes: New allies of the Congress are: NCP, TRS, DMK, MDMK, PMK, LJNP, PDP, and JMM. Old Congress allies now dropped include: RLD and AIADMK. New allies of the NDA are: AIADMK, SDF, MNF, IFDP and NPF. Old NDA allies now dropped include: DMK, MDMK, PMK, INLD and LJNP. LJNP (Lok Janshakti Party) was formed after the 1999 Lok Sabha Elections and in 1999 it was a part of the JD (U) [Janata Dal (United)].

Source: CSDS Data tables.

State-level Electoral Coalitions: Expectations from Theory

What can we expect of coalitions in India, particularly electoral coalitions, and particularly state-level electoral coalitions, from theory and comparative experience?[2] India does not neatly fit theories of coalition politics that have been developed on the basis of the European experience of parliamentary democracy in mostly unitary states with less ethnic heterogeneity, and using proportional representation or mixed electoral systems. First, India's polity is not characterised by a single Left–Right ideological axis but multiple cross-cutting axes, e.g. secular–communal, centralist–regional autonomist, and a variety of caste-bloc-based axes, varying statewise.

Second, party identification in India is relatively weak both among politicians and voters, and parties tend to be clientelistic, lacking well-defined social bases as compared to most Western democracies. Defections and splits that are common in Indian parties would be most unusual in most European parties because of well-defined party ideologies, policy orientations, and relatively stable social constituencies. This is all the more the case in the post-1989 period of considerable electoral volatility with seismic shifts in the formerly stable Congress-dominated party system.

Third, and most important for my argument in this article, are the different implications of proportional representation (PR) and the plurality-rule or single-member district, simple plurality (SMSP) electoral systems. In SMSP electoral systems, parties have to get a plurality of votes in a constituency to win a seat, and derivatively, a plurality to win a majority of seats at the state and national levels (although this is not always the case; there have been cases in which

[2] For an account of the evolution of coalition politics in India, and expectations derived for state-level coalition politics from the logic of the SMSP system in a federal polity, see Sridharan "The Fragmentation of the Indian Party System 1952–1999", 475–503.

a party getting more votes gets less seats, e.g. the Congress in 1996, 1998, and 1999 at the national levels and a few examples at the state level, depending on the spatial distribution of votes at the state or national level). However, in general parties have a strong incentive to aggregate votes through the formation of alliances, based on sharing the total number of contested seats so as not to split but to pool votes. This is because a small addition of votes has the potential to hugely increase or alternatively decimate a party or coalition in terms of seats. Since electoral coalitions, unlike post-election coalitions, are formed under conditions of uncertainty about which party will get how many votes and win how many seats, there are even greater incentives to add on partners to increase the chances of victory, so as not to take any chance of losing, without being too particular about ideological and programmatic compatibility, except in conditions of extreme incompatibility. Thus the SMSP system would tend to give incentives to politicians to form ideologically indiscriminate pre-election coalitions, or even "seat adjustments" for pooling of votes or avoiding splitting of votes, which are only partial, not true, coalitions.[3]

Even if a single party majority results from a pre-election coalition in an SMSP system, the seat majority of the dominant partner in a surplus majority coalition depends on the vote transfer of the supporters of the minor partners to the major partner in seat-sharing, i.e. vote-pooling arrangements, though their seats may not be critical in the legislature elected, e.g. the CPI(M) in West Bengal in all governments between 1977 and 2001. This gives an incentive for the dominant party to continue the alliance in the longer term and to accommodate its smaller allies.

Fourth, where politics is substantially about access to state resources, as in a political economy of rent-seeking and patronage, the possibility of being electorally wiped out would matter much

[3] Laver and Schofield, *Multiparty Government,* 25–6, 204–6; Sridharan "Principles, Power, and Coalition Politics in India", 280–1.

more. Thus, indiscriminate power-seeking coalition formation, in which ideology and policy compatibility take a back seat, is due to incentives created by a structural characteristic of such systems, not cultural factors. Viewing political behaviour in terms of the motivations of politicians, one can make a broad distinction between opportunistic or office-seeking politics (in which power is sought for its own sake) and partisan or policy-seeking politics (in which power is sought to influence policy).[4] This distinction also tends to correspond with societies without or with, respectively, the kind of clear socio-political and ideological spectrum that each is associated with. While the Indian situation in the past decade has been a mixture of opportunistic and partisan politics, the stronger tendency has been to correspond to a particularly corrupt form of opportunistic politics with all that that implies for the likely behaviour of coalitions.

Fifth, however, there has also been growing ideological polarisation since 1989 on the issue of secularism between the BJP and the rest, even its NDA allies, to the extent that the NDA agenda was possible only after the BJP agreed to shelve its controversial Hindutva issues, because the BJP was seen to a degree as an "anti-system" party in conflict with the democratic and constitutional consensus. There have also been regionally varying and complex polarisations on a caste-bloc basis, even while there appears to be developing a growing inter-party consensus on the broad direction of economic policy, if not on specifics, with even the Left parties adjusting, in practice, to the economic reform programme. On the whole, however, Indian politics would appear to be more opportunistic than partisan, unlike the predominant pattern in Western democracies.

Sixth, such imperatives towards indiscriminate aggregation in electoral coalitions are accentuated in a federal system with several

[4] See Budge and Keman, *Parties and Democracy*, 10–19, and Laver and Schofield, *Multiparty Government*, 36–61, for discussions of office-seeking and policy-seeking motivations.

explicitly regional or effectively state-based parties. National, i.e. multi-state parties, if they are to win enough seats to stand a fair chance of forming a government at the centre either on their own or in a coalition, would tend to form electoral coalitions, or partial "seat adjustment" alliances with state-based parties in a number of states. These would very often be a trade-off of parliamentary seats for the national party in exchange for state assembly seats in state assembly elections for the regional/state-based party. The alliance between the Congress Party and the AIADMK in Tamil Nadu was the longest-lasting example of such a trade-off. There are inherent tensions in such alliances because national parties cannot retain their status as national parties if they cede state-level power to regional/state-based parties beyond a point. Furthermore, in the era of hung parliaments since 1989, regional/state-based parties may be less inclined to make such deals. They may want to increase their presence in parliament to increase their prospects of sharing power in a national coalition government.

Thus, the SMSP system in a federal polity sharply differentiates coalition formation and behaviour in the Indian case from cases based on PR systems, and provides powerful support to the extension of coalition theory to "party competition as a whole, looking at the impact of elections on the politics of coalition and on future elections, as well as at the impact of the politics of coalitions on elections and future government formations."[5]

Seventh, to understand the coalition formation process in Election 2004, it is important to understand the incentives to form coalitions at the state level. The imperative to aggregate votes there can be no alliance between the two major parties competing nationally even in a context where one or both is a third/minor party in a state. Conversely, third parties at the state level can be expected to be highly "coalitionable", and therefore wooed by the two major parties at the state level (whichever they may be) to

[5] Laver, *Private Desires, Political Action*, 137.

win seats leads to the following incentives for coalition formation at the state level for parliamentary elections. In a situation where most states have bipolarised party systems, i.e. either two parties or two coalitions or a leading party versus a coalition of two or more parties, there is an incentive for both the first and second party or coalition in a state to seek an alliance with a minor/emerging third or fourth party in the state to mop up additional votes and strengthen its electoral chances.[6] This is so particularly if the third or fourth party has pockets of concentrated strength that could make the difference at the constituency level. Thus one can expect to see both first and second parties in a state competing nationally to form coalitions, to seek alliances with emerging third and minor parties at the state level. The only constraint on such alliances would be that there can be no alliance between the two major parties competing nationally even in a context where one or both is a third/minor party in a state. Conversely, third parties at the state level can be expected to be highly 'coalitionable', and therefore wooed by the two major parties at the state level (whichever they may be) since they can make the critical difference to electoral prospects, the only exception, perhaps, being if they are very thinly distributed and therefore do not seem worth offering a few/ some seats to in exchange for a pooling of votes in other seats.

Implications for Congress Attempts at Coalition-building

The major change in Election 2004 over 1999 has been that the Congress Party, which both resisted coalitions (the Pachmarhi Declaration of 1998) and which was inherently less "coalitionable" earlier, became a significant coalition builder in 2004. The Congress was considered inherently less "coalitionable" than the BJP

[6] For an account of the process of bipolarisation of state party systems in India since 1967, see Sridharan, "The Fragmentation of the Indian Party System", 475–503.

because the distribution of relative strength between the Congress and the BJP was such that in most of the states of the south and east the main contest was between the Congress and a regional or Left party, with the BJP being a third/minor party at best, while most of North India, Gujarat, and Maharashtra had direct contests between the BJP or BJP-led coalition and the Congress during the 1990s. Therefore, while the regional parties of the South and East (like the TDP, AIADMK/DMK, BJD or AGP, or Karnataka JD(U)/Lok Shakti) could find the BJP a useful ally against their main rival, the Congress could not coalesce with these regional parties or the Left parties since they were its main rivals in their states (except for states where the Congress itself was reduced to a third or worse position, such as in Tamil Nadu). The Congress, following this logic, could be an attractive coalition partner to first and second parties in states where it had been reduced to a third or fourth party status (e.g. Bihar, Tamil Nadu, potentially UP) or "coalitionable" where it faced a direct contest with the BJP/NDA and there was a third or fourth minor party present.

This does not mean that if these conditions obtain such coalitions will necessarily be formed. And likewise for the BJP under similar conditions where it is a first or second party facing the Congress with a third party available, or when it is a third or fourth party. These conditions should be viewed as merely necessary, not sufficient, for the formation of coalitions at the state level.

What is new is that the conditions for the Congress becoming "coalitionable" emerged in a number of major states for the first time. In 2004, one or other of the situations mentioned above came about in seven significant states – Maharashtra, Andhra Pradesh, Jharkhand, Jammu and Kashmir (J&K), Himachal Pradesh, Bihar, and Tamil Nadu (in the last two of which the same situation existed earlier). In Maharashtra, Andhra Pradesh, Jharkhand, and J&K, the Congress faced either the BJP (Jharkhand, Jammu region of J&K) or an NDA coalition in which the BJP was a partner, dominant (Maharashtra) or otherwise (Andhra Pradesh,

Kashmir, in which the National Conference was a potential post-poll NDA ally). In Bihar and Tamil Nadu, the Congress faced an NDA alliance in which the BJP was a junior partner.

In each of these states, this time there was a third force, either a party or coalition, with which the Congress could potentially ally against the BJP/NDA coalition. In Maharashtra, the NCP, already a coalition partner in the government, was a potential anti-NDA ally. The emergence of the TRS in Andhra presented the Congress with a coalition-building opportunity with an ally against the NDA. In Jharkhand, the JMM was a potential anti-NDA partner. In J&K, the PDP was a potential anti-NDA and anti-National Conference (a potential post-poll NDA ally) in all three regions of the state. In Bihar, the Congress, reduced to fourth party status, and already a coalition partner of the ruling RJD, was eminently "coalitionable" as a minor partner for the RJD. In Tamil Nadu too, as in the past, the Congress, reduced to third party status, was potentially "coalitionable" from the point of view of both the AIADMK and the DMK, this time going with the DMK-led alliance. And in Himachal Pradesh, the Congress negotiated the merger with itself of its breakaway faction of 1998, Sukh Ram's Himachal Vikas Congress, adding to its voter base.

Sequence of Major Events in Coalition Formation

The progress of alliance formation by the two principal coalitions unfolded as follows.[7] The NDA coalition continued with its existing constituents, except for the parties that left. Principally, these were the DMK, MDMK, and PMK in Tamil Nadu, the INLD in Haryana, and the National Conference in J&K. Ram Vilas Paswan's faction of the JD(U) had left in 2002 and renamed itself Lok Janshakti Party. In Tamil Nadu, the BJP decided to ally with

[7] Press reports from December 2003 to May 2004, too numerous to detail, for the dates and events in this section.

the AIADMK. In Assam, the AGP which had allied with the BJP in the 2001 assembly elections without success, but was not part of the NDA, did not join as the BJP decided to go it alone. Likewise, in Jharkhand the BJP decided to go it alone without possible partner JMM and existing NDA partner JD(U). In Haryana, the INLD broke with the NDA on 9 February. These decisions were partly a result of pressure to this effect from each of the respective BJP state units, and partly due to the INLD's and AGP's own decisions to go it alone. The significant addition to the NDA coalition were the rejoining of the BJP by Kalyan Singh on 3 February and the merger of his party with it in UP, and the joining of the BJP by the families of former chief ministers Bangarappa and Ramakrishna Hegde in Karnataka in early March. Two other smaller one-MP partners had also merged with the BJP – the MGR-AIADMK and Maneka Gandhi. While the existing NDA allies remained allies in principle, the actual allocation of seats took more time. It was only by 16 March that the BJP and the JD(U) hammered out a seat-sharing deal for all Bihar seats barring two, and the BJP decided to go it alone in Jharkhand. And only by 18 March did the TDP and the BJP reach a seat-sharing deal for Andhra, 33–9 for the Lok Sabha and 267–27 for the assembly. The process was smoother with the existing partner in Orissa (BJD), and in Punjab (Akali Dal), both vital for the BJP/NDA tally.

The Congress coalition-building strategy, the major story of this election, unfolded as follows. On 26 December 2003, Sonia Gandhi accepted that the would-be Congress-led coalition's partners would collectively decide on the leadership in the event of a victory. On 28 December, in Mumbai, she talked seriously for the first time of an anti-BJP alliance (although this was accepted in principle at the Shimla meeting in the summer of 2003). This was on the heels of the devastating defeat in the state assembly elections in Rajasthan, Madhya Pradesh, and Chhattisgarh in early December 2003. The importance of alliances and the damage that small parties could do was underlined by the fact that in the 2003 state assembly elections in Madhya Pradesh the BJP got only 3.5 per cent of the 9.2 per cent swing against the Congress, a larger chunk going to parties like the Samajwadi Party and the Gondwana Ganatantra Parishad, while in Chhattisgarh the vote shares of both the breakaway NCP led by V.C. Shukla (7 per cent) and the BSP (4.4 per cent) were more than the gap between Congress and BJP vote shares.

On 7 January the Congress set up a high-level team led by Sonia Gandhi to reach pre-poll alliances with secular parties. This approach was formally reinforced on 13 February when the Pranab Mukherjee report on the Congress defeat in the December 2003 state assembly elections in Rajasthan, Madhya Pradesh, and Chhattisgarh concluded that the Congress could win only with alliances.

On 3 January 2004 the DMK chief, Karunanidhi, who had in late 2003 left the NDA along with the MDMK and PMK, responded by talking of a DMK-Congress-Left alliance against the BJP and AIADMK. On 2 February the Congress accepted the 10 seats it was offered in Tamil Nadu by the DMK, resisted the allocation of Congress-held Pondicherry to the PMK, but eventually gave in. This was the only state-level alliance which was finalised, that is, including allocation of seats, before the 13th Lok Sabha was dissolved on 6 February. The last date for filing nominations was 23 April, over two and a half months away.

On 20 March, after over two months of negotiations, a day before the date of notification and just ten days before the last date for filing nominations for the first round of voting in the state, the Congress and the NCP reached a seat-sharing deal in Maharashtra along with minor allies, three RPI factions, and the JD(S). The Congress-NCP were to contest 26–18, leaving a seat each for the four smaller allies. The Congress and NCP were also allies in other states contesting a seat each in Goa, and contesting 25–1 in Gujarat. This process also led to the exit of P.A. Sangma from the NCP in late January.

On 20 January the Congress began wooing the newly formed Telangana Rashtra Samiti (TRS). On 24 March, the date of notification and just ten days before the last date for filing nominations for the first round of voting in the state, the Congress reached a deal with the TRS whereby it would contest 36 and the TRS 6 seats (out of 16 seats in Telangana) in Andhra Pradesh. The TRS would contest 37 of 107 assembly seats in the Telangana region.

In Bihar the significant development for the RJD-led alliance, that is, for the Congress-led alliance nationally, was that on 23 January Laloo Prasad Yadav's RJD and Ram Vilas Paswan's Lok Jan Shakti Party (LJSP) announced their alliance. Over two months later, on 27 March, three days after the date of notification and just four days before the last date for filing nominations for the first round of voting in the state, the final Bihar tie-up was announced in which the RJD would contest 26 seats, Paswan's LJSP 8, Congress 4, NCP 1, and CPM 1.

On 13 February the Congress began talks with the JMM in Jharkhand. On 21 March, three days before the date of notification and just ten days before the last date for filing nominations for the first round of voting in the state, the Congress and the JMM reached a deal in Jharkhand, but could not avoid "friendly" contests in Rajmahal and Koderma. It was to be a Congress-JMM- RJD-CPI alliance, with the JMM also contesting Mayurbhanj in Orissa, but not in alliance with the Congress there.

As early as 10 January the PDP and the Congress in J&K decided to ally in the coming elections. This eventually worked despite a partial clash wherein they had a "friendly" contest in one seat. In Kerala, the existing Congress-led UDF coalition finalised its seats deal by early March, three weeks before the last date for filing nominations.

In Karnataka, though there was some early talk of a coalition between the JD(S) and the Congress, this was shot down by sections of the state unit of the Congress, a disastrous decision in retrospect for the party. All attempts at a coalition in the crucial, largest state of UP failed, though the process continued tantalisingly until March. Following Kalyan Singh's return to the BJP in early February, the SP and Ajit Singh's RLD in UP finalised a 70–10 seat-sharing deal on 29 February. The Congress, despite keeping a negotiating process on with both the SP and the BSP, eventually failed to strike a deal. It did, however, give 3 seats to Paswan's LJSP and backed 3 independents in a minor alliance.

However, even after all seat-sharing arrangements were finalised, the coalition process continued in some important ways. On 2 May Paswan's LJSP withdrew its Haryana candidates in favour of the Congress just before the last date for withdrawals and the LJSP, RLD, NCP, and JD(S) asked their workers in Delhi to work for the Congress.

The Importance of Coalitions in Congress Victory

The statewise importance of coalitions can be gauged from the swing compared to 1999 for each coalition, computable from Table 1 (nationally), with Table 2 highlighting the importance of changes in alliance partners since 1999, and Table 3 giving a detailed state-by-state picture of alliances in 2004 compared to 1999. A statewise picture is vital for understanding 2004, particularly for the UPA coalition which did not exist in its present size in 1999 (though the increase/decrease in votes is a combination of the swing factor and coalitional aggregation of votes). It should be noted that even a negative swing against a party/coalition can still lead to an increase in seats if there is a greater negative swing against the other party/coalition. Conversely, a coalition pooling votes can reduce the adverse effect of a negative swing.

On the whole, coalitions (or merger in Himachal Pradesh) were critical for Congress victory in Tamil Nadu, Andhra Pradesh, Bihar, Jharkhand, Himachal Pradesh, and J&K. They were critical for Congress reduction of the margin of defeat/improvement of

Table 3. Party and Coalition Seats and Vote Shares (2004 over 1999)

State: Andhra Pradesh
Total Lok Sabha seats: 42
Turnout (2004): 69.9 per cent
Change in turnout as compared to 1999: +0.8 per cent

Party	*Seats Contested (2004)*	*Seats Won (2004)*	*Change since 1999*	*Vote (Per Cent) (2004)*	*Change since 1999 (Per Cent)*
Congress	34	29	+24	41.5	–1.3
TRS	23	5	+5	6.8	+6.8
CPI	1	1	+1	1.30	0
CPI (M)	1	1	+1	1.0	–0.4
TDP	33	5	–24	33.1	–6.8
BJP	9	0	–7	8.4	–1.5
MIM	2	1	0	1.2	–0.1

Note: The number of seats contested and the votes for the TRS include one independent candidate supported by the TRS. The Congress, the TRS, the CPI and the CPI(M) had an alliance in the 2004 Lok Sabha elections, though in many seats the candidates of the alliance partners contested against each other. The TRS did not exist in the 1999 Lok Sabha against each other. The TRS did not exist in the 1999 Lok Sabha elections. The TDP and the BJP had an alliance in the 1999 and the 2004 Lok Sabha elections.

State: Arunachal Pradesh
Total Lok Sabha seats: 2
Turnout (2004): 56.3 per cent
Change in turnout as compared to 1999: –15.9 per cent

Party	*Seats Contested (2004)*	*Seats Won (2004)*	*Change since 1999*	*Vote (Per Cent) (2004)*	*Change since 1999 (Per Cent)*
Congress	1	0	–2	10.0	–46.9
ARC	1	0	0	19.9	3.3
BJP	2	2	+2	53.9	+37.6

Note: The Congress and the ARC had an alliance in the 2004 Lok Sabha elections. In the 1999 Lok Sabha elections, the BJP and the ARC had an alliance.

Table 3 (*Contd.*)

State: Assam
Total Lok Sabha seats: 14
Turnout (2004): 69.1 per cent
Change in turnout as compared to 1999: –2.2 per cent

Party	*Seats Contested (2004)*	*Seats Won (2004)*	*Change since 1999*	*Vote (Per Cent) (2004)*	*Change since 1999 (Per Cent)*
Congress	14	9	–1	35.1	–3.3
AGP	12	2	+2	20.0	+8.1
BJP+	14	3	+1	30.8	+1.0

Note: The BJP + includes one seat contested and won by an independent candidate supported by the BJP and one seat contested by the BJP's ally, the JD (U). In the 1999 Lok Sabha elections, one seat was won by the same independent candidate, who was not supported by the BJP, and one by the CPI (ML)(L).

State: Bihar
Total Lok Sabha seats: 40
Turnout (2004): 57.9 per cent
Change in turnout as compared to 1999: –6.9 per cent

Party	*Seats Contested (2004)*	*Seats Won (2004)*	*Change since 1999*	*Vote (Per Cent) (2004)*	*Change since 1999 (Per Cent)*
Congress+	39	29	21	44.3	39
BJP+	40	11	–19	36.9	–6.4
Left Front	7	0	–1	1.9	–2.0

State: Chhattisgarh
Total Lok Sabha seats: 11
Turnout (2004): 52.1 per cent
Change in turnout as compared to 1999: –3.8 per cent

Party	*Seats Contested (2004)*	*Seats Won (2004)*	*Change since 1999*	*Vote (Per Cent) (2004)*	*Change since 1999 (Per Cent)*
Congress	11	1	–2	40.2	–3.2
BJP	11	10	+2	47.8	–0.1

Table 3 (*Contd.*)

State: Delhi
Total Lok Sabha seats: 7
Turnout (2004): 47.1 per cent
Change in turnout as compared to 1999: +3.6 per cent

Party	*Seats Contested (2004)*	*Seats Won (2004)*	*Change since 1999*	*Vote (Per Cent) (2004)*	*Change since 1999 (Per Cent)*
Congress	7	6	+6	54.8	+12.8
BJP	7	1	–6	40.7	–11.1

State: Goa
Total Lok Sabha seats: 2
Turnout (2004): 58.7 per cent
Change in turnout as compared to 1999: +13.6 per cent

Party	*Seats Contested (2004)*	*Seats Won (2004)*	*Change since 1999*	*Vote (Per Cent) (2004)*	*Change since 1999 (Per Cent)*
Congress	1	1	+1	29.8	–9.2
NCP	1	0	0	16.0	+12.2
BJP	2	1	–1	46.8	–4.7

Note: The Congress and the NCP had an alliance in the 2004 Lok Sabha elections. They did not have an alliance in the 1999 Lok Sabha elections.

State: Gujarat
Total Lok Sabha seats: 26
Turnout (2004): 45.2 per cent
Change in turnout as compared to 1999: –1.8 per cent

Party	*Seats Contested (2004)*	*Seats Won (2004)*	*Change since 1999*	*Vote (Per Cent) (2004)*	*Change since 1999 (Per Cent)*
Congress	25	12	+6	43.9	–1.5
NCP	1	0	0	1.2	+0.7
BJP	26	14	–6	47.4	–5.1

Note: The Congress and the NCP had an alliance in the 2004 Lok Sabha elections. They did not have an alliance in the 1999 Lok Sabha elections.

Table 3 (*Contd.*)

State: Haryana
Total Lok Sabha seats: 10
Turnout (2004): 65.7 per cent
Change in turnout as compared to 1999: +2 per cent

Party	*Seats Contested (2004)*	*Seats Won (2004)*	*Change since 1999*	*Vote (Per Cent) (2004)*	*Change since 1999 (Per Cent)*
Congress	10	9	+9	42.1	+7.2
BJP	10	1	–4	17.2	–12
INLD	10	0	–5	22.4	–6.3
HVP	9	0	0	6.3	+3.6

Note: In 1999 Lok Sabha elections, the BJP and the INLD had a pre-poll alliance. Both the allies had contested 5 seats each. In the 2004 Lok Sabha elections there was no alliance between any parties in the state."

State: Himachal Pradesh
Total Lok Sabha seats: 4
Turnout (2004): 59.7 per cent
Change in turnout as compared to 1999: +2.9 per cent

Party	*Seats Contested (2004)*	*Seats Won (2004)*	*Change since 1999*	*Vote (Per Cent) (2004)*	*Change since 1999 (Per Cent)*
Congress	4	3	+3	51.9	+12.4
BJP	4	1	–2	44.2	–2.02

Note: In the 1999 Lok Sabha elections, the BJP had an alliance with the HVC. In 1999, the HVC had won one seat and had secured 12.4 per cent votes. The change in votes since 1999 takes into account the votes secured by the BJP+HVC alliance in 1999. The HVC has since merged with the Congress.

Table 3 (*Contd.*)

State: Jammu and Kashmir
Total Lok Sabha seats: 6
Turnout (2004): 35.2 per cent
Change in turnout as compared to 1999: +2.9 per cent

Party	*Seats Contested (2004)*	*Seats Won (2004)*	*Change since 1999*	*Vote (Per Cent) (2004)*	*Change since 1999 (Per Cent)*
Congress+	4	3	+3	30.8	+12.98
PDP	3	1	+1	11.9	+11.9
National Conference	6	2	–2	22.0	–6.9
BJP	6	0	–2	23.0	–8.6

Note: The Congress and the PDP had an alliance in the 2004 Lok Sabha elections, though the two parties contested against each other in one constituency. The seats contested, seats won and the votes of Congress+ for the 2004 Lok Sabha elections include the figures for one independent supported by the Congress. Similarly, the change since 1999 for Congress+ takes into account the votes secured by one independent supported by the Congress in the 1999 Lok Sabha elections. The PDP candidates had contested as independent in the 1999 Lok Sabha election.

State: Jharkhand
Total Lok Sabha seats: 14
Turnout (2004): 55.6 per cent
Change in turnout as compared to 1999: +3.9 per cent

Party	*Seats Contested (2004)*	*Seats Won (2004)*	*Change since 1999*	*Vote (Per Cent) (2004)*	*Change since 1999 (Per Cent)*
Congress	9	6	+4	21.4	–2.4
JMM	5	4	+4	16.3	+6.8
RJD	2	2	1	3.5	–4.0
CPI	1	1	1	3.8	+1.2
BJP	14	1	–10	33.0	–12.5

Note: The Congress, the RJD, the JMM and the CPI had an alliance in the 2004 Lok Sabha elections, though the JMM and the Congress contested against each other in two constituencies. The Congress and the RJD had an alliance in the 1999 Lok Sabha elections though in two constituencies the candidates of the two parties contested against each other.

Table 3 (*Contd.*)

State: Karnataka
Total Lok Sabha seats: 28
Turnout (2004): 64.9 per cent
Change in turnout as compared to 1999: –2:7 per cent

Party	*Seats Contested (2004)*	*Seats Won (2004)*	*Change since 1999*	*Vote (Per Cent) (2004)*	*Change since 1999 (Per Cent)*
Congress	28	8	–10	36.8	–8.6
BJP	24	18	+11	34.8	+7.6
JD(U)	4	0	–3	1.9	–11.4
JD(S)	28	2	+2	20.5	+9.6

Note: The BJP and the JD(U) had an alliance in the 1999 and the 2004 Lok Sabha elections.

State: Kerala
Total Lok Sabha seats: 20
Turnout (2004): 71.5 per cent
Change in turnout as compared to 1999: +1.3 per cent

Party	*Seats Contested (2004)*	*Seats Won (2004)*	*Change since 1999*	*Vote (Per Cent) (2004)*	*Change since 1999 (Per Cent)*
UDF	20	1	–10	38.4	–8.6
LDF	20	18	+9	46.1	+2.4
BJP+	20	1	+1	12.0	+5.53

Note: The UDF in the 2004 Lok Sabha elections consisted of the Congress, the Muslim League and the Kerala Congress (Mani). The LDF consisted of the CPI(M), the CPI, the JD(S), the Kerala Congress and one LDFsupported independent. The BJP+ includes the BJP and its ally, the Indian Federal Democratic Party.

Table 3 (*Contd.*)

State: Madhya Pradesh
Total Lok Sabha seats: 29
Turnout (2004): 48.1 per cent
Change in turnout as compared to 1999: –6.4 per cent

Party	*Seats Contested (2004)*	*Seats Won (2004)*	*Change since 1999*	*Vote (Per Cent) (2004)*	*Change since 1999 (Per Cent)*
Congress	29	4	–4	34.0	–10.1
BJP	29	25	+4	48.1	+2.0

State: Maharashtra
Total Lok Sabha seats: 48
Turnout (2004): 54.4 per cent
Change in turnout as compared to 1999: –6.5 per cent

Party	*Seats Contested (2004)*	*Seats Won (2004)*	*Change since 1999*	*Vote (Per Cent) (2004)*	*Change since 1999 (Per Cent)*
Congress	26	13	+3	23.8	–5.9
NCP	18	9	+3	18.3	–3.27
RPI(A)	1	1	0	1.0	–0.5
RPI	1	0	0	0.4	–1.0
PRBP	1	0	0	0.7	+0.7
JD(S)	1	0	–1	0.6	–0.3
BJP	26	13	0	22.6	+1.4
Shiv Sena	22	12	–3	20.1	+3.2
PWP	3	0	–1	0.9	0
BBM	16	0	–1	1.3	–0.8

Note: The Congress, the NCP, the JD(S), the RPI(A), the RPI and the PRBP had an alliance in the 2004 Lok Sabha elections. The PRBP did not exist during the 1999 Lok Sabha elections. In the 1999 Lok Sabha elections, the Congress, the RPI, the BBM had an alliance. In the 1999 Lok Sabha elections, the NCP, the RPI(A), the JD(S), the SP, the PWP, the SPB had an alliance. The BJP and the Shiv Sena had an alliance in the 1999 and the 2004 Lok Sabha elections.

Table 3 (*Contd.*)

State: Manipur
Total Lok Sabha seats: 2
Turnout (2004): 67.4 per cent
Change in turnout as compared to 1999: +1.7 per cent

Party	*Seats Contested (2004)*	*Seats Won (2004)*	*Change since 1999*	*Vote (Per Cent) (2004)*	*Change since 1999 (Per Cent)*
Congress	1	1	1	14.88	–10.4
NCP	1	0	–1	10.37	–3.1
BJP	2	0	0	20.65	+19.7
MPP	1	0	7.4	0	–8.9

Note: The Congress and the NCP had an alliance in the 2004 Lok Sabha elections. One independent candidate won in the 2004 Lok Sabha elections. The MSCP had won one seat in the 1999 Lok Sabha elections. The party did not contest the 2004 Lok Sabha elections.

State: Meghalaya
Total Lok Sabha seats: 2
Turnout (2004): 52.7 per cent
Change in turnout as compared to 1999: –3.5 per cent

Party	*Seats Contested (2004)*	*Seats Won (2004)*	*Change since 1999*	*Vote (Per Cent) (2004)*	*Change since 1999 (Per Cent)*
Congress	2	1	0	45.6	+12.8
BJP	1	0	0	8.6	–0.9
TRMC	1	1	1	28.3	28.3

Note: In the 2004 Lok Sabha elections, the BJP and the TRMC had an alliance. The NCP had contested and won one seat in the 1999 Lok Sabha elections. The Meghalaya unit of the NCP merged with the TRMC before the 2004 Lok Sabha elections. Hence the TRMC has been treated as the successor party of the NCP in the state.

Table 3 (*Contd.*)

State: Mizoram
Total Lok Sabha seats: 1
Turnout (2004): 63.4 per cent
Change in turnout as compared to 1999: –1.9 per cent

Party	*Seats Contested (2004)*	*Seats Won (2004)*	*Change since 1999*	*Vote (Per Cent) (2004)*	*Change since 1999 (Per Cent)*
Independent (Congress)	1	0	0	45.7	45.7
MNF	1	1	0	52.5	52.5

Note: The MNF had not contested the 1999 Lok Sabha elections but had supported an independent candidate who won the seat. The votes secured by the candidate have not been taken into account for the information regarding change since 1999.

State: Nagaland
Total Lok Sabha seats: 1
Turnout (2004): 91.7 per cent
Change in turnout as compared to 1999: +15.5 per cent

Party	*Seats Contested (2004)*	*Seats Won (2004)*	*Change since 1999*	*Vote (Per Cent) (2004)*	*Change since 1999 (Per Cent)*
Congress	1	0	–1	25.8	–45.4
NPF	1	1	+1	73.1	+73.1

Note: The NPF did not exist during the 1999 Lok Sabha elections.

Table 3 (*Contd.*)

State: Orissa
Total Lok Sabha seats: 21
Turnout (2004): 66.0 per cent
Change in turnout as compared to 1999: +10.4 per cent

Party	*Seats Contested (2004)*	*Seats Won (2004)*	*Change since 1999*	*Vote (Per Cent) (2004)*	*Change since 1999 (Per Cent)*
Congress	21	2	0	40.4	+3.5
BJD	12	11	+1	30.0	–3.0
BJP	9	7	–2	19.3	–5.3
JMM	1	1	+1	1.5	–0.2

Note: The BJD and the BJP had an alliance in the 1999 and the 2004 Lok Sabha elections.

State: Punjab
Total Lok Sabha seats: 13
Turnout (2004): 61.6 per cent
Change in turnout as compared to 1999: +5.5 per cent

Party	*Seats Contested (2004)*	*Seats Won (2004)*	*Change since 1999*	*Vote (Per Cent) (2004)*	*Change since 1999 (Per Cent)*
Congess	11	2	–6	34.2	–4.2
CPI	1	0	–1	2.6	–1.1
Cpi (M)	1	0	0	1.8	–0.4
SAD	10	8	+6	34.3	+5.7
BJP	3	3	+2	10.5	+1.3
SAD (M)	6	0	–1	3.8	+0.4

Note: The Congress, the CPI and CPI (M) had an alliance in the 1999 and the 2004 Lok Sabha elections. The SAD and the BJP had an alliance in the 1999 and the 2004 Lok Sabha elections.

Table 3 (*Contd.*)

State: Chandigarh
Total Lok Sabha seats: 1
Turnout (2004): 50.9 per cent
Change in turnout as compared to 1999: +2.5 per cent

Party	*Seats Contested (2004)*	*Seats Won (2004)*	*Change since 1999*	*Vote (Per Cent) (2004)*	*Change since 1999 (Per Cent)*
Congress	1	1	0	52.0	+5.0
BJP	1	0	0	35.2	–9.8

State: Rajasthan
Total Lok Sabha seats: 25
Turnout (2004): 49.9 per cent
Change in turnout as compared to 1999: 4.0 per cent

Party	*Seats Contested (2004)*	*Seats Won (2004)*	*Change since 1999*	*Vote (Per Cent) (2004)*	*Change since 1999 (Per Cent)*
Congress	25	4	–5	41.4	–3.7
BJP	25	21	+5	49.0	+1.78

Note: The BJP had left one seat for its ally, the JD(U) in the 1999 Lok Sabha elections. The JD(U)'s votes in that constituency have been taken into account for calculating the change since 1999.

Table 3 (*Contd.*)

State: Sikkim
Total Lok Sabha seats: 1
Turnout (2004): 77.9 per cent
Change in turnout as compared to 1999: –3.8 per cent

Party	*Seats Contested (2004)*	*Seats Won (2004)*	*Change since 1999*	*Vote (Per Cent) (2004)*	*Change since 1999 (Per Cent)*
Congress	1	0	0	27.4	+22.6
SDF	1	1	0	69.8	+17.2
SSP	1	0	0	1.5	–40.7

State: Tamil Nadu
Total Lok Sabha seats: 39
Turnout (2004): 60.8 per cent
Change in turnout as compared to 1999: +2.8 per cent

Party	*Seats Contested (2004)*	*Seats Won (2004)*	*Change since 1999*	*Vote (Per Cent) (2004)*	*Change since 1999 (Per Cent)*
DMK	16	16	+4	24.6	+1.5
Congress	10	10	+8	14.4	+3.3
PMK	5	5	0	6.7	–1.5
MDMK	4	4	0	5.9	–0.1
CPI	2	2	+2	3.0	+0.4
CPI (M)	2	2	+1	2.9	+0.5
AIADMK	33	0	–10	29.8	+4.1
BJP	6	0	–4	5.1	–2.0

Note: The MGRADMK had won one seat in the 1999 Lok Sabha elections. The party did not contest the 2004 Lok Sabha elections. The DMK, the Congress, the MDMK, the PMK, the CPI and the CPI(M) had an alliance in the 2004 Lok Sabha elections. The AIADMK and the BJP had an alliance in the 2004 Lok Sabha elections. In the 1999 Lok Sabha elections, the DMK, the BJP, the MDMK, the PMK, the TRC and the MGRADMK had an alliance. In the 1999 Lok Sabha elections, the AIADMK, the Congress, the CPI and the CPI(M) had an alliance.

Table 3 (*Contd.*)

State: Pondicherry
Total Lok Sabha seats: 1
Turnout (2004): 76.0 per cent
Change in turnout as compared to 1999: +12.7 per cent

Party	*Seats Contested (2004)*	*Seats Won (2004)*	*Change since 1999*	*Vote (Per Cent) (2004)*	*Change since 1999 (Per Cent)*
PMK	1	1	+1	50.0	+18.3
BJP	1	0	0	35.7	+35.7

Note: The Congress had contested and won the seat in the 1999 Lok Sabha elections. The PMK had also contested the seat in the 1999 Lok Sabha election. However, in the 2004 elections, since the PMK and the Congress were part of the same alliance, the Congress had not contested the seat. In the 1999 Lok Sabha elections, the PMK and the BJP were in the same alliance. Since in the 2004 Lok Sabha elections, the PMK and the BJP had parted ways, the BJP contested this seat.

State: Tripura
Total Lok Sabha seats: 2
Turnout (2004): 66.9 per cent
Change in turnout as compared to 1999: –1.2 per cent

Party	*Seats Contested (2004)*	*Seats Won (2004)*	*Change since 1999*	*Vote (Per Cent) (2004)*	*Change since 1999 (Per Cent)*
Congress	2	0	0	14.3	+0.4
CPI(M)	2	2	0	68.8	+12.6

Table 3 (*Contd.*)

State: Uttar Pradesh
Total Lok Sabha seats: 80
Turnout (2004): 48.2 per cent
Change in turnout as compared to 1999: –5.5 per cent

Party	*Seats Contested (2004)*	*Seats Won (2004)*	*Change since 1999*	*Vote (Per Cent) (2004)*	*Change since 1999 (Per Cent)*
Congress	79	9	0	12.6	–0.92
BJP+	80	11	–14	23.0	–4.64
BSP	80	19	+5	24.7	+2.1
SP	68	35	+9	26.7	+1.7
RLD	10	3	+1	4.5	+1.9
SJP(R)	2	1	0	0.5	0
NLP	7	1	+1	0.6	+0.4

Note: One seat was won by an independent in the 2004 Lok Sabha elections. The Congress+ in the 2004 Lok Sabha elections includes the seats contested and votes secured by the Congress, the Lok Jan Shakti and Congress supported independents. The BJP+ in the 2004 Lok Sabha elections includes the BJP and the JD(U). The SP and the RLD had an alliance in the 2004 Lok Sabha elections. In the 1999 Lok Sabha elections, the Congress and the RLD had an alliance. In the 1999 Lok Sabha elections, the BJP+ includes the BJP, the JD(U), the Lok Tantrik Congress and one BJP-supported independent candidate.

State: Uttaranchal (later renamed Uttarakhand)
Total Lok Sabha seats: 5
Turnout (2004): 48.1 per cent
Change in turnout as compared to 1999: –1.8 per cent

Party	*Seats Contested (2004)*	*Seats Won (2004)*	*Change since 1999*	*Vote (Per Cent) (2004)*	*Change since 1999 (Per Cent)*
Congress	5	1	0	38.3	+0.2
BJP	5	3	–1	41.0	+1.4
SP	5	1	+1	7.9	+1.7

Table 3 (*Contd.*)

State: West Bengal
Total Lok Sabha seats: 42
Turnout (2004): 78.0%
Change in turnout as compared to 1999: +3.0 per cent

Party	*Seats Contested (2004)*	*Seats Won (2004)*	*Change since 1999*	*Vote (Per Cent) (2004)*	*Change since 1999 (Per Cent)*
Left Front	42	35	+6	50.8	+4.1
Congress	37	6	+3	14.6	+1.3
TRMC	29	1	–7	21.0	–5.0
BJP	13	0	–2	8.1	–3.0

Note: The Left Front in the 2004 Lok Sabha elections consisted of the CPI(M), the CPI, the RSP and the Forward Bloc.
Source: CSDS Data Unit.

position compared to 1999 in Maharashtra and Goa. The lack of a coalition of opposing forces was critical for the magnitude of the Congress victory and BJP defeat in Assam, Haryana, and Jharkhand (where an NDA coalition of not only the BJP and JD[U], but also potentially the JMM, was a possibility). Compared to 1999, the Congress lost only 1 seat in Assam, though its 35.1 per cent vote share was far less than the 50.8 per cent combined vote share of the BJP and the AGP, taken together. In Haryana, the Congress won 9 seats compared to none in 1999, with a vote share of 42.1 per cent compared to a combined vote share of the separately contesting BJP and INLD of 39.6 per cent. In Jharkhand, the BJP dropped from 14 to only 1 seat despite a vote share of 33 per cent compared to a Congress vote share of 21.4 per cent because the Congress-JMM-RJD-CPIalliance had a combined vote share of 44.5 per cent.

Conversely, the lack of a coalition with the JD(S), ironically a post-poll government partner, was critical for the Congress defeat in Karnataka. Coalitions were critical for NDA victories in Orissa and Punjab. As for the Left, coalitions were vital in West Bengal, Kerala, and Tripura, and in West Bengal a divided opposition greatly helped. For the Congress and Congress-led coalition, four large states in which coalitions were vital for victory (Tamil Nadu, Andhra Pradesh, Bihar, Jharkhand) contributed 114 out of 219 seats (52 per cent) for the UPA (excluding the Left although the CPM and the CPI or both were coalition partners at the state level in some of these states), or 48 out of 145 (33 per cent) for the Congress alone.

Major states in which coalitions' reduced defeat margins/improved positions since 1999 (Maharashtra, Gujarat) contributed 35 out of 219 seats (16 per cent) for the Congress-led alliance, or 17 seats more than in 1999 (the Congress-led alliance in 1999 was different; it did not include the NCP). States in which there was allied co-operation through non-contestation (Haryana, Delhi) contributed 15 seats, or 15 seats more than in 1999. Another way of looking at it is to view the situation in reverse. States in which victory was owed to the lack of an opposing coalition due to the BJP deciding to go it alone (Haryana, Assam, Jharkhand) contributed 30 seats, or 17 seats more than in 1999 to the Congress-led alliance (again different in 1999 in Jharkhand).

Conclusion

Coalitions have played a vital role in the unexpected Congress victory in 2004 in the ways outlined earlier, including in a negative sense, i.e. the lack of coalitions in the BJP's defeat in Haryana, Assam, and Jharkhand. Coalitions have also played a vital role for the BJP in states like Orissa, Punjab, and Maharashtra, and for the Left in its three traditional strongholds.

To what extent have the expectations derived from theory been met, i.e. to what extent has the Election 2004 coalition story been theory-confirming? The coalition experience of Election 2004 has been theory-confirming in the following ways:

(1) Coalitions have been largely opportunistic or office-seeking, formed primarily to aggregate votes regardless of program-

matic differences, following the imperatives of the SMSP electoral system. The best examples are that of the TRS, which differs on Telangana statehood; the NCP, which shelved its foreign origin reservations about Sonia Gandhi; the Left parties in various state-level alliances despite historic differences with the Congress primarily on economic policy; and parties like the DMK and its smaller allies, and the JMM, which had earlier had alliances with the BJP. Except for the Left parties, none of these would have been averse to doing a deal with the BJP. The BJP/NDA was either not interested or its offer was too niggardly. The last-minute character of most of these alliances reinforces this point.

(2) At the state level our prediction that the Congress is "coalitionable" only when it is either a third or fourth party, or where a third or fourth party emerges where the Congress is locked in competition with a BJP/NDA rival party or alliance, has been borne out. Each state-level Congress coalition in 2004 has been in one or the other of these situations.

How stable will the UPA alliance be? The first indications are that the odds are stacked against it, and it will need adroit political management to keep it stable. This is because, unlike the NDA, it is not only not a surplus majority coalition with redundant partners to give it a cushion but a minority coalition dependent on outside support, and that too from the Left parties, both of which have sharp differences on economic policy and are also the main political opponents of the Congress in West Bengal, Kerala, and Tripura. The first two states will have assembly elections two years into the UPA government, in May 2006. The challenge will be to reconcile contradictions at the state level with support to the Congress-led UPA at the national level, apart from the challenge of holding the UPA together.

Bibliography

Budge, Ian, and Hans Keman, *Parties and Democracy: Coalition Formation and Government Functioning in Twenty States* (Oxford: Oxford University Press, 1993), 10–19.

Laver, Michael, *Private Desires, Political Action: An Invitation to the Politics of Rational Choice* (London: Sage Publications, 1997), 137.

Laver, Michael, and Norman Schofield, *Multiparty Government: The Politics of Coalitions in Europe* (Ann Arbor, Michigan: University of Michigan Press, 1998), 25–6, 204–6.

Ramachandran, G., "Will There Be Inclusive Space and Depth?", *The Hindu*, 16 May 2004.

Sridharan, E., "The Fragmentation of the Indian Party System 1952–1999: Seven Competing Explanations", in Zoya Hasan, ed., *Parties and Party Politics in India* (New Delhi: Oxford University Press, 2002), 475–503.

Sridharan, E., "Principles, Power, and Coalition Politics in India: Lessons from Theory, Comparison and Recent History", in D.D. Khanna and Gert W. Kueck, eds, *Principles, Power and Politics* (New Delhi: Macmillan, 1999), 280–1.

Virmani, Arvind, "The Simple Economics of Election 2004", www.icrier.res.in.

5

Can Umbrella Parties Survive? The Decline of the Indian National Congress

Introduction

IN THIS PAPER we analyse the decline of the Indian National Congress Party (henceforth Congress Party or Congress) culminating in its catastrophic defeat in the 2014 Indian general election, registering its lowest-ever seat and vote shares.[1] We examine the longer-term trends in its gradual decline, punctuated by electoral recoveries beginning decades earlier, to identify the drivers of decline. We situate our analysis in theories of the relationships between political (including electoral) systems, social cleavages, and party systems to pose the question of whether Congress, and more generically the dominance of a Congress-type encompassing umbrella party, can survive the politicisation of social cleavages in a heterogeneous society and increasingly federal political system.

Political Systems, Social Heterogeneity, and Party Systems

There are, broadly speaking, two theories of the determinants of party systems – theories that view political systems (electoral rules,

[1] This paper is co-authored with Adnan Farooqui.

federalism, presidentialism) as the key determinants of party systems (the distribution of votes and seats), and theories that view social heterogeneity, or more specifically, the number of salient social cleavages as the key determinants.[2] The best-known political system theory, the electoral rules theory of party systems, postulates that the district magnitude (the number of representatives elected from each electoral district), ballot structure (choosing an individual candidate, party list or a mix of the two), and decision rule or electoral formula to convert votes into seats (proportional representation, simple plurality, variants of each) create varying disproportionalities between votes and seats, and hence, incentives for the coalescing, merging, or splitting of political parties which will be reflected in the number, relative weight, and ideological positioning of parties, hence, the party system.[3]

For the Indian and other first-past-the-post (single-member district, simple plurality or SMSP) systems, Duverger's law predicts that first-past-the-post systems tend towards two-party systems, a "law" that applies primarily to the district (constituency) level, which can get translated to the state/province level in a federal system or the national level in a British-type unitary system.[4]

Another variant of the political systemic theory of party systems is that federalism creates incentives to form state/province-level

[2] See Lipset and Rokkan (1967) for the classic statement of the social cleavage theory of party systems, and Bartolini and Mair (1990) for a modified version which argues essentially that social cleavages do not translate automatically into party systems but offer easy mobilisation opportunities. Much the same is argued by Kothari (1997: 58): "Those who complain of 'casteism in politics' are really looking for a sort of politics which has no basis in society . . . Politics is a competitive enterprise . . . and its process is one of identifying and manipulating existing and emerging allegiances in order to mobilise and consolidate positions . . .", thus making the social cleavage theory of party systems appear somehow natural. For works within the electoral rules theory of party systems, see Lijphart (1994), Taagepera and Shugart (1989), Grofman and Lijphart (1986), and for older classics Duverger (1963), and Rae (1967).

[3] Lijphart 1994: 10–21.

[4] Duverger 1963, 1986.

parties, that is, regional parties, and this is all the more so the greater the powers devolved to the regional level by the system since the fruits of victory at the regional level alone are considerable in terms of being able to make policies on issues which voters care about.[5] The more this is so, the less is the incentive for state-level parties to combine across state boundaries to form a federal party to contest national-level elections.[6] The alternative of forming coalitions instead of a unified federal party at the national level becomes a viable alternative in the event of no unified federal party getting a majority in parliament.[7]

Hence, Duverger's law would predict a two-party system at the national level under parliamentarism if federalism is weak and major policy powers are concentrated at the federal level, or alternatively, if federalism is strong, a range of state-level two-party systems, not necessarily of the same two parties as in the United States but one of multiple bipolarities resulting in a multi-party system nationally and hence a relatively fragmented parliament. A strong, decentralised federalism would also predict a multi-party system under parliamentarism.

The social cleavages theory of party systems argues that social heterogeneity would tend to produce a multi-party system reflecting that heterogeneity regardless of the electoral system. The classic statement of the social cleavages theory would argue that parties get formed around the salient cleavages in society (what cleavages are salient and why can vary in time and space).[8] For example, in ethnoculturally homogeneous industrialised societies, the class cleavage

[5] Chhibber 1999; Chhibber and Kollman 2004: chs 2 and 5.

[6] Chhibber 2005.

[7] Sridharan 2012.

[8] Lipset and Rokkan 1967. Of the four cleavages discussed by them in the context of European party systems, two, the centre–periphery cleavage and the state–church cleavage, were the product of "national revolutions". It is this tension between the core nation-builders and political, ethnic, or cultural peripheries, along with the secular and religious forces to some extent, that explains the emergence of the party system in post-Independence India. In the initial years, major tension between the centre and the periphery, and the

might be the most salient leading to a party system polarised between conservative and socialist/social- democratic/labour parties. Taagepera and Shugart predict that the number of relevant parties will be one more than the number of salient cleavages.[9] There is an unresolved debate on whether the pull of social heterogeneity will overcome the effects of electoral rules with Taagepera and Shugart holding that social heterogeneity will mean more effective parties whatever the electoral system, while Ordeshook and Shvetsova hold that Duverger's law will work even under social heterogeneity.[10] What emerges is that while Duverger's law predicts a two-party system, and in a federal system state-level two-party systems leading to a national multi-party system in the case of multiple bipolarities, Duverger's law along with federalism and social heterogeneity logically predicts multi-party systems organised around either regions or social groups such as those based on religion, caste, tribe, class, or language.

What is noteworthy is that *none* of the above theories predicts the dominance of an encompassing umbrella party like the Congress, which has ruled India in single-party majority governments from 1947 to 1989, except for 1977–9, and since 1989 as either a minority government (1991–6) or the lead party in a minority coalition, 2004–14.

Congress as an Umbrella Party

Where would one place Congress in a comprehensive party typology? Gunther and Diamond have "congress parties" as a specific category in their typology.[11] In a fivefold classification – elite, mass-based (ideological/socialist, ideological/nationalist, religious),

issue of secularism, was resolved within the Congress party. In that sense, the Congress-dominated party system was the outcome of the "national revolution/movement".

[9] Taagepera and Shugart 1989.

[10] Ordeshook and Shvetsova 1994.

[11] Gunther and Diamond 2001.

ethnicity-based (ethnic parties, congress parties), electoralist parties (catch-all, programmatic, personalist), movement parties (left-libertarian, post-industrial extreme right), all these being ideal types, they place congress parties as pluralistic, multi-ethnic parties which are coalitions of distinct ethnic, religious, and regional groups that contain conflict through sharing of power and resources among ethnic groups, gain votes through clientelistic loyalties and appeals to national integration, and have coalitional or federative organisation based on regional elites and local notables. Such a congress-type party can also be described as an umbrella party or an encompassing party, as we do in this paper, spanning cleavages of class, ethnicity (race, caste, religion, language), region, and political programme (moderate right, moderate left).

The other nearest type in their schema is the catch-all party that maximises electoral appeal through a broad aggregation of interests but has a weak party organisation, weak civil society linkages and is election-focused.[12] India's Congress in its first two decades, and Malaysia's Barisan Nasional (although this is a stable coalition but not a single party), and Nigeria's People's Democratic Party are described as the archetypes of congress parties. We take the position that the difference between an umbrella party and a catch-all party is that the former is more encompassing and includes contradictory social forces. Thus, the Congress in India includes both big business and the poor, upper castes and Scheduled Castes, as essential components of its support base, whereas a catch-all party is typically a class party in origin which seeks to reach out beyond its traditional base.

Comparatively speaking, the dominance of Congress as a congress-type party in a one-party-dominant system in India during its heyday was quite distinct from the dominance of other such parties in various countries in that in countries such as Tanzania, Nigeria, Kenya, and Mexico. Such dominance came to be associated with

[12] Kirchheimer 1966.

authoritarian rule, the only exception being the African National Congress (ANC) in post-apartheid South Africa. In most of these countries, there existed constitutional constraints on the formation as well as functioning of political parties which the ruling parties exploited to maintain their stranglehold. It is only very recently that most of these countries have made a transition from a semi-authoritarian "hegemonic" party system to democratic one-party dominant system or a multi-party system.[13] In Kenya and Tanzania there existed a constitutionally sanctioned one-party system. This continued right up to 1991 and 1992, respectively, when under sustained popular and political pressure the ruling parties Tanganyika African National Union (TANU)/Chama Cha Mapinduzi (CCM) in the case of Tanzania, and Kenyan African National Union (KANU), accepted the transition to a multi-party system. On the other hand, both in Nigeria in the 4th Republic under the People's Democratic Party (PDP), and Mexico under the International Revolutionary Party (PRI) the ruling congress-type party maintained its hold either legally through changes to the electoral laws to the disadvantage of opposition parties or through sheer manipulation and deceit. In the case of Nigeria, the PDP which came to power in 1999 ruled uninterruptedly right up to 2015 when the party was dislodged by the All Progressive Congress, an alliance of Nigeria's three biggest opposition parties.[14] In Mexico the PRI remained the pre-eminent party from 1929 to the early 1990s. The PRI's dominance was complete right up to the 1980s, with the divided opposition posing no serious threat. The situation only changed when the opposition parties of the right and the left emerged as serious opposition, which eventually led to the party losing its majority in both the houses of the national legislature in 1997. In 2000 after a continuous reign of seventy-one years, the PRI was dislodged from the presidency.[15]

[13] Spieb 2002: 7.
[14] Aleyomi 2013.
[15] Crespo 2004.

Thus, going by Sartori's category of one-party dominant system, we could argue that Tanzania, Nigeria, Mexico, and Kenya have had a dominant–authoritarian party system.[16] This holds true even for countries like Taiwan and Singapore where the principal parties, Kuomintong (KMT) and People's Action Party (PAP), respectively, displayed an authoritarian streak towards the opposition parties. This was distinct from the Malaysian case where the ruling Barisan Nasional is more of an alliance between the dominant party United Malay National Organisation (UMNO) and its allies. In all these cases, we see the eventual erosion of umbrella-party dominance. This is unlike India and South Africa where the dominance of an umbrella party endured under genuinely democratic conditions and a vibrant multi-party system. Thus, there have been very few durable congress-type parties in full-fledged democracies. How do they emerge and sustain themselves and can they survive the politicisation of social cleavages?

What Gunther and Diamond (2001) do not mention is the historical or path-dependent dimension of the formation of congress parties, particularly India's Congress. It emerged over six decades from 1885 to 1947 as an encompassing party in a very heterogeneous country because of its role as a mass party of the independence movement that sought to unite all Indians against British colonial rule, setting aside all other differences of class, ethnicity, religion, caste, language and region. Forged in this anti-colonial, independence movement context, it acquired its encompassing, multi-ethnic character and federative organisation which was grafted on the provincial structure of British India, and was not challenged by parties based on social cleavages, except for the Muslim League which went out of the political arena of independent India due to the partition of India. Hence, the dominance of Congress after independence for several decades was determined by a *specific colonial-historical trajectory that was quite different from the party system*

[16] Sartori 2005.

evolution of Western democracies. Other such dominant umbrella parties have also been the product of either independence movements or revolutions. To an extent, the evolution of Congress can be linked to Lipset and Rokkan's idea of a national revolution.

In the literature on Indian parties and party systems, Kothari has characterised Congress in its heyday, 1947–67, as an encompassing "party of consensus" surrounded by smaller and narrower-based "parties of pressure".[17] Lijphart (1996) later characterised Congress as a grand coalition of diverse interests because of which it, and the larger Indian political system, in which Congress was hegemonic, conduced to power-sharing (he went so far as to argue that India was a consociational democracy), and hence to the consolidation of democracy despite inconducive features such as social heterogeneity and poverty.

Chhibber and Petrocik (1990) argued that Congress was not an umbrella party at the state level; at that level, it was based on local social cleavages and particular social groups, varying state by state. Rather it was somewhat like the Democratic Party in the United States in that it was like a coalition of state-based parties that aggregated themselves into one party nationally to compete for the prize of national power. This was supported by later findings in the 1990s that the Congress' base by caste and class differed across states depending on whether it faced the right-wing Hindu-nationalist Bharatiya Janata Party (BJP) or the Left parties as its principal competitor.[18] However, aggregated nationally it fits the concept of a congress-type, encompassing umbrella party.

The Evolution of the Party System and the Rise of Competition for Congress

To understand the decline of Congress, we need to trace the evolution of the Indian party system through three major phases,

[17] Kothari 1970: 179.

[18] Heath and Yadav 1999; Yadav 2003.

1947–67, 1967–89 and 1989–2014. Duvergerian dynamics played themselves out in state after state over 1967–89, continuing after 1989 for both Lok Sabha and state assembly elections, leading to either a two-party system, or one party versus a coalition, or a two-coalition system, that is, bipolar party systems with the non-Congress opposition consolidating behind a particular party in each state (with exceptions like Uttar Pradesh).[19] However, this was one of multiple bipolarities – for example, Congress–Jana Sangh (precursor of BJP) in Rajasthan, Madhya Pradesh, Himachal Pradesh, and Delhi; Congress–Left in West Bengal, Kerala, and Tripura; Congress versus a regional party in Tamil Nadu (after 1972, two regional parties were the top two parties), Punjab, Jammu and Kashmir, and from the 1980s Andhra Pradesh and Assam; Congress versus fragments of the Janata Party in Haryana, Karnataka, and Odisha. What this implied was the possibility, in the event of an anti-Congress wave across states, of the victory of a motley collection of regional and other parties, which was what happened in 1989.

The fragmentation of the party system in the third (1989–2014) phase in particular reflects three mega-trends: the decline of Congress, the rise of BJP, and the rise and stable presence of regional parties. The net result of these Duvergerian dynamics was the bipolarisation of state party systems, but one of multiple bipolarities, leading to a fragmented Lok Sabha in which no single party obtained a majority in the seven consecutive elections from 1989 to 2009 until the BJP's narrow majority in 2014.

The Erosion of Congress Competitiveness

To put Congress' lowest-ever vote and seat shares of 2014 in some historical perspective, let us focus on some facts about the decline of Congress, nationally, and state- and constituency-wise.

[19] Chhibber and Murali 2006, and Sridharan 2002 for detailed accounts.

Loss of National Vote Share

Congress decline is the other side of the coin of the rise of other parties in the period since 1967, especially since 1989. The basic facts are as follows.[20] While the Congress suffered two setbacks in 1967 (when it slid to 40 per cent and a bare majority, losing power in eight of the then 16 major states), and in 1977 when it lost power for the first time to the Janata Party (the unified opposition), it was able to recover both times with big victories in 1971, 1980 and 1984 (Tables 1 and 2).

While up to the 1984 election Congress won majorities on the basis of pluralities of over 40 per cent of the vote, in 1989 it fell a fraction below 40 per cent for the first time (except for 1977) and since then declined further to as low as 25.8 per cent in 1998 recovering slightly in the next three elections but remaining under 30 per cent (Table 1). Compared to a majority mark of 273 seats it crossed 200 only twice (in 1991 and 2009) in the eight elections over 1989–2014, losing its status as the single-largest party in 1996, 1998, and 1999 despite a slightly higher vote share than the BJP due to the concentration of the BJP's votes in a smaller number of constituencies, mostly in north, central, and western India. The space vacated by Congress has been filled by BJP and a range of non-Left regional parties (the Left has remained relatively stagnant), with the non-Congress, non-BJP space being in the 44–53 per cent range over 1989–2014, though divided among a large number of parties. Post-1996, Congress remained below 30 per cent in vote share, the overall slide being from almost 40 per cent to 19 per cent over 1989–2014.

Competitiveness in States for General Elections

Given the Duvergerian dynamics that have been operating at the constituency and state levels from over 1967–89 and since then,

[20] All votes and seats data in this paper are from the Election Commission of India (www.eci.nic.in).

Table 1. Performance of Indian National Congress 1967–1984

	1967						1971					
State/Union territory	*TS*	*SC*	*SW*	*VS%*	*PV*	*CP third or worse*	*TS*	*SC*	*SW*	*VS%*	*PV*	*CP third or worse*
Andhra Pradesh	41	41	35	46.82	1	0	41	37	28	55.73	1	0
Arunachal Pradesh												0
Assam	14	14	10	45.84	1	0	14	13	13	56.98	1	0
Bihar	53	53	34	34.81	1	0	53	47	39	40.60	1	1
Goa	2	1	0	5.47	3	1	2	1	1	24.76	1	0
Gujarat	24	24	11	46.92	1	0	24	23	11	44.85	1	0
Haryana	9	9	7	44.06	1	0	9	9	7	52.56	1	0
Himachal Pradesh	6	6	6	48.35	1	0	4	4	4	75.79	1	0
Jammu & Kashmir	6	6	5	50.52	1	0	6	6	5	54.06	1	0
Mysore/ Karnataka	27	27	18	49.02	1	0	27	27	27	70.87	1	0
Kerala	19	19	1	36.15	1	1	19	7	6	19.75	2	0
Madhya Pradesh	37	37	24	40.78	1	0	37	36	21	45.60	1	0
Maharashtra	45	45	37	48.51	1	0	45	44	42	63.80	1	0
Manipur	2	2	0	32.68	1	0	2	2	2	30.02	1	0
Meghalaya												
Mizoram												
Nagaland	1	0	0	0	–		1	0	0	0	–	–
Orissa	20	20	6	33.33	1	0	20	19	15	38.46	1	0
Punjab	13	13	9	37.31	1	0	13	11	10	45.96	1	0
Rajasthan	23	22	10	39.95	1	0	23	23	14	50.35	1	0
Sikkim												
Madras/ Tamil	39	39	3	41.69	1	0	39	9	9	12.51	3	0
Tripura	2	2	2	58.25	1	0	2	2	0	36.30	2	0
Uttar Pradesh	85	85	47	33.44	1	6	85	78	73	48.54	1	0
West Bengal	40	40	14	39.69	1	1	40	31	13	28.20	2	0
Andaman & Nicobar Islands	1	1	1	52.57	1	0	1	1	1	61.48	1	0
Chandigarh	1	1	0	23.04	1	0	1	1	1	66.85	1	0
Dadra & Nagar Haveli	1	1	1	50.14	1	0	1	1	1	39.17	1	0
NCT of Delhi	7	7	1	38.79	2	0	7	7	7	39.17	1	0
Lakshadweep	1	NC	NC	NC	NC	NC	1	1	1	Single Contestant	0	0
Puducherry	1	1	1	39.83	1	0	1	1	1	66.27	1	0
Total	520	516	283	40.78	1	9	518	441	352	43.68	1	1

Table 1 (*Contd.*)

Table 1 (*Contd.*)

1977						1980						1984					
TS	*SC*	*SW*	*VS%*	*PV*	*CP third or worse*	*TS*	*SC*	*SW*	*V%*	*PV*	*CP third or worse*	*TS*	*SC*	*SW*	*V%*	*PV*	*CP third or worse*
												TS	*SC*	*SW*	*VS%*	*PV*	
42	42	41	57.36	1	0	42	42	41	56.24	1	0	42	42	6	40.81	2	0
2	2	1	41.25	1	0	2	2	2	44.13	1	0	2	2	2	43.22	1	0
14	14	10	50.56	1	0	14	2	2	51.01	1	0	14	13	4	23.43	1	4
54	54	0	22.90	1	5	54	54	30	36.44	1	7	54	54	48	51.84	1	1
2	2	1	39.98	1	0	2	1	0	12.19	3	0	2	2	2	46.21	1	0
26	26	10	46.92	2	0	26	26	25	54.84	1	0	26	26	24	53.24	1	0
10	9	0	17.95	2	1	10	10	5	32.55	1	2	10	10	10	54.95	1	0
4	4	0	38.58	2	0	4	4	4	52.08	1	0	4	4	4	67.58	1	0
6	3	3	16.37	2	0	6	1	1	18.68	1	0	6	4	3	30.23	2	0
28	28	26	56.80	1	0	28	28	27	56.25	1	0	28	28	24	51.63	1	0
20	11	11	29.13	1	0	20	11	5	26.32	1	0	20	13	13	33.27	1	0
40	38	1	32.47	2	0	40	39	35	47.20	1	0	40	40	40	57.08	1	0
48	47	20	47.02	1	0	48	48	39	53.30	1	0	48	47	43	51.24	1	1
2	2	2	45.31	1	0	2	2	1	22.99	1	0	2	2	2	34.95	1	0
2	2	1	35.92	1	0	2	1	1	74.31	1	0	2	2	2	62.42	1	0
1	1	0	37.07	1	0	1	NC	NC	NC	NC	NC						
1	1	0	48.32	2	0	1	NC	NC	NC	NC	NC	1	1	1	64.64	1	0
21	20	4	38.18	2	0	21	21	20	56.07	1	0	21	21	20	57.46	1	1
13	13	0	34.85	2	0	13	13	12	52.45	1	0	13	13	6	41.53	1	0
25	25	1	30.65	2	0	25	25	18	42.64	1	2	25	25	25	52.72	1	0
1	1	1	Single Contestant	1	NC	NC	NC	NC	NC	NC		1	1	0	25.84	1	0
39	15	14	22.27	2	0	39	22	20	31.62	1	0	39	26	25	40.5	1	0
2	2	1	39.74	1	0	2	2	0	22.61	2	1	2	2	0	45.61	1	0
85	85	0	24.99	2	0	85	85	51	35.9	1	9	85	85	83	53.03	1	0
42	34	3	29.37	3	0	42	41	4	36.51	2	0	42	42	16	48.16	1	0
1	1	1	58.45	1	0	1	1	1	53.2	1	0	1	1	1	52.85	1	0
1	1	1	28.37	2	0	1	1	1	49.65	1	0	1	1	1	66.02	1	0
1	1	1	46.93	1	0	1	1	1	61.89	1	0	1	1	0	40.31	1	0
7	7	0	30.15	2		7	7	6	50.4	1		7	7	7	68.72	1	0
1	1	1	58.59	1	0	1	1	0	3.85	3	1	1	1	1	54.47	1	0
1	NC	NC	NC	NC		1	1	1	66.45	1	0	1	1	1	58.86	1	0
542	492	154	34.52	2	6	542	492	353	42.69	1	22	541	517	414	49	1	7

Source: Election Commission of India, Statistical Report of Lok Sabha Elections, 1967–1984.
TS, total number of seats; SC, seats contested; SW, seats won; VS, vote share; PV, position by vote; CP, constituency position; NC, not contested.

Table 2. Performance of Indian National Congress 1989–2014

	1989					*1991*					*1996*					*1998*				
State/Union Territory	*TS*	*SC*	*SW*	*VS%*	*PV*	*TS*	*SC*	*SW*	*VS%*	*PV*	*TS*	*SC*	*SW*	*VS%*	*PV*	*TS*	*SC*	*SW*	*VS%*	*PV*
Andhra Pradesh	42	42	39	51	1	42	42	25	46	1	42	42	22	40	1	42	42	22	39	1
Arunachal	2	2	2	50	1	2	2	2	69	1	2	2	0	29	2	2	2	0	24	2
Assam	–	–	–	–		14	14	8	29	1	14	14	5	32	1	14	13	10	39	1
Bihar	54	54	4	28	2	54	51	1	24	2	54	54	2	13	4	54	21	5	7	5
Goa	2	2	1	47	1	2	2	2	58	1	2	2	0	35	1	2	2	2	32	1
Gujarat	26	26	3	37	1	26	16	5	29	2	26	26	10	39	2	26	25	7	37	2
Haryana	10	10	4	46	1	10	10	9	37	1	10	10	2	23	1	10	10	3	26	1
Himachal Pradesh	4	4	1	42	2	4	4	2	46	1	4	4	4	54	1	4	4	1	42	2
Jammu & Kashmir	6	3	2	39	1	–	–	–	–		6	6	4	28	1	6	6	1	19	3
Karnataka	28	28	27	49	1	28	28	23	42	1	28	28	5	31	2	28	28	9	36	1
Kerala	20	17	14	42	1	20	16	13	39	1	20	17	7	38	1	20	17	8	39	1
Madhya Pradesh	40	40	8	38	2	40	40	27	45	1	40	40	8	31	2	40	40	10	39	2
Maharashtra	48	48	28	45	1	48	48	38	48	1	48	48	15	35	1	48	41	33	44	1
Manipur	2	2	2	45	1	2	2	1	38	1	2	2	2	40	1	2	2	0	19	2
Meghalaya	2	2	2	55	1	2	2	2	57	1	2	2	1	54	1	2	2	2	48	1
Mizoram	1	1	1	49	1	1	1	1	38	1	1	1	1	43	1	1	1	0	35	2
Nagaland	1	1	1	60	1	1	1	0	44	1	1	1	1	62	1	1	1	1	87	1
Orissa	21	21	3	38	2	21	21	13	44	1	21	21	16	45	1	21	21	5	41	1
Punjab	13	13	2	27	2	13	13	12	49	1	13	13	2	35	1	13	8	0	26	2
Rajasthan	25	25	0	37	1	25	25	13	44	2	25	25	12	41	2	25	25	18	45	1
Sikkim	1	1	0	22	2	1					1				4	1	1	0	33	2
Tamil Nadu	39	28	27	40	1	39	28	28	43	1	39	29	0	18	3	39	35	0	5	7
Tripura	2	2	2	56	1	2	2	2	83	1	2	2	0	34	2	2	2	0	42	2
Uttar Pradesh	85	84	15	32	2	85	80	5	18	3	85	85	5	8	4	85	76	0	6	4
West Bengal	42	41	4	39	1	42	39	5	35	2	42	42	9	40	1	42	39	1	15	3
Chhattisgarh																				
Jharkhand																				
Uttarakhand																				
Andaman & & Nicobar islands	1	1	1	47	1	1	1	1	51	1	1	1	1	58	1	1	1	1	36	1
Chandigarh	1	1	0	40	2	1	1	1	36	1	1	1	0	30	2	1	1	0	39	2
Dadra & Nagar Haveli	1	1	0	29	2	1	1	1	62	1	1	1	1	56	1	1	1	0	4	3
Daman & Diu	1	1	0	38	1	1	1	0	22	2	1	1	1	51	1	1	1	0	2	3
NCT of Delhi	7	7	2	43	1	7	7	2	40	2	7	7	2	37	2	7	7	1	43	2
Lakshadweep	1	1	1	52	1	1	1	1	51	1	1	1	1	52	1	1	1	1	52	1
Puducherry	1	1	1	50	1	1	1	1	54	1	1	1	1	40	1	1	1	0	32	1
Total	529	510	197	40	1	537	500	244	36	1	543	529	140	29	1	543	477	141	26	1

Table 2 (*Contd.*)

Table 2 (*Contd.*)

1999					2004					2009					2014				
TS	*SC*	*SW*	*VS%*	*PV*	*TS*	*SC*	*SW*	*VS%*	*PV*	*TS*	*SC*	*SW*	*VS%*	*PV*	*TS*	*SC*	*SW*	*VS%*	*PV*
42	42	5	43	1	42	34	29	42	1	42	42	33	39	1	42	41	2	12	3
2	2	2	57	1	2	1	0	10	3	2	2	2	51	1	2	2	1	42	2
14	14	10	38	1	14	14	9	35	1	14	14	7	35	2	14	13	3	30	2
54	16	4	9	4	40	4	3	5	5	40	37	2	10	4	40	12	2	9	3
2	2	0	39	2	2	1	1	30	2	2	1	1	22	2	2	2	0	37	2
26	26	6	45	2	26	25	12	44	1	26	26	11	43	2	26	25	0	34	2
10	10	0	35	1	10	10	9	42	1	10	10	9	42	1	10	10	1	23	3
4	4	0	40	2	4	4	3	52	1	4	4	1	46	2	4	4	0	41	2
6	5	0	18	2	6	3	2	28	1	6	3	2	25	1	6	3	0	23	2
28	28	18	45	1	28	28	8	37	1	28	28	6	38	2	28	28	9	41	2
20	17	8	39	1	20	17	0	32	1	20	17	13	40	1	20	15	8	32	1
40	40	11	44	2	29	29	4	34	2	29	28	12	40	2	29	29	2	35	2
48	42	10	30	1	48	26	13	24	1	48	27	17	20	1	48	26	2	18	3
2	2	0	25	1	2	1	1	15	2	2	2	2	43	1	2	2	2	42	1
2	2	1	33	1	2	2	1	46	1	2	2	1	45	1	2	2	1	39	1
1					2					1	1	1	66	1	1	1	1	49	1
1	1	1	71	1	1	1	0	26	2	1	1	0	30	2	1	1	0	30	2
21	20	2	37	1	21	21	2	40	1	21	21	6	33	2	21	21	0	21	2
13	11	8	38	1	13	11	2	34	1	13	13	8	45	1	13	13	3	33	1
25	25	9	45	2	25	25	4	41	2	25	25	20	48	1	25	25	0	31	2
1	1	0	5	3	1	1	0	27	2	1	1	0	30	2	1	1	0	2	5
39	11	2	11	3	39	10	10	14	3	39	15	8	15	3	39	39	0	4	6
2	2	0	14	2	2	2	0	14	2	2	0	0	30.8	2	2	2	0	15	2
85	76	10	15	4	80	73	9	12	4	80	69	21	18	3	80	67	2	8	4
42	41	3	13	3	42	37	6	15	3	42	13	6	14	3	42	42	4	10	4
					11	11	1	40	2	11	11	1	37	2	11	11	1	20	2
					14	9	6	24	2	14	9	1	15	2	14	9	0	14	3
					5	5	1	38	2	5	5	5	43	1	5	5	0	34	1
1	1	0	43	1	1	1	1	56	1	1	1	0	432TaT		1	1	0	44	2
1	1	1	47	1	1	1	1	52	1	1	1	1	47	1	1	1	0	27	2
1	1	0	15	4	1	1	0	26	2	1	1	0	46	2	1	1	0	45	2
1	1	1	50	1	1	1	1	50	1	1	1	0	29	2	1	1	0	44	2
7	7	0	42	2	7	7	6	55	1	7	7	7	57	1	7	7	0	15	3
1	1	1	54	1	1	1	0	48	2	1	1	1	52	1	1	1	0	47	2
1	1	1	37	1	1	0	0	0	0	1	1	1	49	1	1	1	0	27	2
543	453	114	28	1	543	417	145	27	1	543	440	206	29	1	543	464	44	19	2

Source: Election Commission of India, Statistical Report of Lok Sabha Elections, 1989-2014.
TS, total number of seats; SC, seats contested; SW, seats won; VS, vote share; PV, position by vote share.

a party can be considered competitive in an SMSP system with bipolarised state party systems, that is, having a serious chance of winning and forming a government singly or in coalition if it is in the first or second position in vote share. If it is in the third or worse rank then it becomes *significantly* more difficult to win, although there have been exceptions such as seven cases, since 1989, of the BJP's rise from a third or worse position to top position by vote share, of which five were in the 2014 election (Uttar Pradesh in 1991 and 2014, Goa in 1998, and Bihar, Haryana, Jammu and Kashmir, Maharashtra, in 2014). Hence, we define *being competitive as being in one of the top two positions by vote share*. Looking at Congress decline in terms of competitiveness at the state and constituency level yields a more fleshed-out picture.

While in elections from 1967 to 1984 Congress slipped to third or worse in only three states for one election each, overwhelmingly retaining second place even where it lost, by contrast in the post-1989 period Congress has slipped to third or worse position in four major states – U.P., Bihar, West Bengal, and Tamil Nadu – that total 201 seats or 37 per cent of the seats in the Lok Sabha (Tables 1 and 2) for several elections. In the largest state of U.P., from second position in vote share in 1989, it fell to third in 1991, fourth in 1996, and remained at that except for a recovery to third place in 2009 (second in seats). In Bihar, it slipped from second in 1991 to fourth or worse from 1996. In Tamil Nadu, it slipped from first place (due to the then seat-sharing alliances) in 1991 to third in 1996 and remained at that or worse through to 2014. In West Bengal, following the breaking away of the Trinamool Congress in 1997, Congress slipped to third place in 1998 and finally to fourth in 2014. In the debacle of 2014, Congress slipped to third or worse position in as many as ten states (including the Union Territory of Delhi), that is, in addition to the four major states above, in Andhra Pradesh, Haryana, Jharkhand, Maharashtra, Sikkim, and Delhi, thus becoming uncompetitive in states that totalled 320 seats, or a majority of 59 per cent of Lok Sabha seats!

Competitiveness in State Assembly Elections

The pattern is roughly paralleled in Congress performance in state assembly elections (Table 3). In vote shares in state assemblies (held in varying years, mostly not coincident with Lok Sabha elections), Congress had become uncompetitive (third or worse) by the latest assembly elections in as many as nine states, including Delhi. Even in states where it remained among the top two in vote share, it lagged behind the leading party or coalition and has not been in power in some states for many years – Gujarat since 1995, Odisha since 1999, Madhya Pradesh and Chhattisgarh since 2003, Punjab since 2007, to name major states.

Palshikar (2015) divides the states into three categories – Congress states (Delhi, Haryana, Maharashtra, Manipur, Assam, Arunachal Pradesh, Meghalaya, and Mizoram), Congress-presence states (Himachal Pradesh, Punjab, Rajasthan, Gujarat, Goa, Karnataka, Kerala, Andhra Pradesh, Odisha, Madhya Pradesh, Chhattisgarh, Uttarakhand, Tripura, Nagaland, J&K), and non-Congress states (Tamil Nadu, U.P., Bihar, Jharkhand, West Bengal, Sikkim) (see Table 5). Of the Congress states, Delhi, Haryana, and Maharashtra could be considered to have moved to the Congress-presence category. We notice that non-Congress states add up to 216 Lok Sabha seats. If to this we add Congress-presence states in which Congress has not been in power for over a dozen years (Gujarat, Odisha, M.P., Chhattisgarh) we get a total of 303 seats, that is, Congress has become uncompetitive by this broader measure in states adding up to a substantial majority of seats.

Competitiveness at the Lok Sabha Constituency Level

From 1967 to 1984 Congress was third or worse in only as few as 45 constituencies over five elections, of which 22 were in 1980 (Table 1) but since 1989 has greatly declined from 28 constituencies in 1989 to 169 in 1998, recovering to only 84 in 2009, to

Table 3. Congress performance in the state assembly elections (1989–2014)

State/Union Territory	*TS*	*SC*	*SW*	*PS*	*VS*	*PV*	*TS*	*SC*	*SW*	*PS*	*VS*	*PV*	*TS*	*SC*	*SW*	*PS*	*VS*	*PV*	*TS*
				1989						1994						1999			
Andhra Pradesh	294	287	181	1	47	1	294	294	26	2	34	2	294	293	91	2	41	2	294
				1990						1995						1999			
Arunachal Pradesh	60	59	37	1	44	1	60	60	43	1	51	1	60	60	53	1	52	1	60
				1991						1996						2001			
Assam	126	125	66	1	29	1	122	122	34	2	31	1	126	126	71	1	40	1	126
				1990						1995						2000			
Bihar	324	323	71	2	25	2	324	320	29	3	16	2	324	324	23	4	11	3	243
				1989						1994						1999			
Goa	40	40	20	1	41	1	40	40	18	1	38	1	40	40	21	1	39	1	40
				1990						1995						1998			
Gujarat	182	181	33	3	31	1	182	181	45	2	33	2	182	179	53	2	35	2	182
				1991						1996						2000			
Haryana	90	90	51	1	34	1	90	90	9	4	21	4	90	90	21	2	31	1	90
				1990						1993						1998			
Himachal Pradesh	67	66	9	3	37	2	68	67	52	1	49	1	68	68	31	*	43	1	68
				1996						2002						2008			
Jammu & Kashmir	87	84	7	3	20	2	87	78	20	2	24	2	87	78	17	3	17	3	
				1989						1994						1999			
Karnataka	224	221	178	1	44	1	224	221	34	3	27	2	224	222	132	1	41	1	224
				1991						1996						2001			
Kerala	140	91	55	1	32	1	140	94	37	2	30	1	140	88	62	1	31	1	140
				1990						1993						1998			
Madhya Pradesh	320	318	56	2	33	2	320	318	174	1	41	1	320	316	172	1	41	1	230
				1990						1995						1999			
Maharashtra	288	276	141	1	38	1	288	286	80	1	31	1	288	249	75	1	27	1	288
				1990						1995						2000			
Manipur	54	54	24	1	34	1	60	60	22	1	29	1	60	47	11	2	18	1	60
				1993						1998						2003			
Meghalaya	60	60	24	1	35	1	60	59	25	1	35	1	60	60	22	1	30	1	60

Table 3 (*Contd.*)

Table 3 (*Contd.*)

SC	*SW*	*PS*	*VS*	*PV*	*TS*	*SC*	*SW*	*PS*	*VS*	*PV*	*TS*	*SC*	*SW*	*PS*	*VS*	*PV*	*TS*	*SC*	*SW*	*PS*	*VS*	*PV*
			2004					2009					2014									
234	185	1	39	1	294	294	156	1	37	1	175	173	0	0	3	3						
			2004					2009					2014									
60	34	1	44	1	60	60	42	1	52	1	60	60	42	1	50	1						
			2006					2011														
120	53	2	31	1	126	126	78	1	39	1												
			2005 (February)					2005 (October)					2010									
84	10	4	5	4	243	51	9	5	6	5	243	243	4	4	8	4						
			2002					2007					2012									
40	16	2	38	1	40	32	16	1	32	1	40	33	9	2	31	2						
			2002					2007					2012									
180	51	2	39	2	182	173	59	2	38	2	182	176	61	2	39	2						
			2005					2009					2014									
90	67	1	43	1	90	90	40	1	35	1	90	90	15	3	21	3						
			2003					2007					2012									
68	43	1	41	1	68	67	23	2	39	2	68	68	36	1	43	1						
			2014																			
			2004					2008					2013									
224	65	2	36	1	224	222	80	2	35	1	224	224	122	1	37	1						
			2006					2011														
77	24	2	24	2	140	81	38	2	26	2												
			2003					2008					2013									
229	38	2	32	3	230	228	71	2	33	2	230	229	58	2	36	2						
			2004					2009					2014									
157	69	1	21	1	288	170	82	1	21	1	288	287	42	3	18	3						
			2002					2007					2012									
58	20	1	26	1	60	59	30	1	34	1	60	60	42	1	42	1						
			2008					2013														
60	25	1	33	1	60	60	29	1	35	1												

Table 3 (*Contd.*)

Table 3 (*Contd.*)

State/Union Territory	*TS*	*SC*	*SW*	*PS*	*VS*	*PV*	*TS*	*SC*	*SW*	*PS*	*VS*	*PV*	*TS*	*SC*	*SW*	*PS*	*VS*	*PV*	*TS*
				1989						1993						1998			
Mizoram	40	34	23	1	35	1	40	28	16	1	33	2	40	40	6	2	30	1	40
				1989						1993						1998			
Nagaland	60	60	36	1	52	1	60	59	35	1	46	1	60	60	53	1	51	1	60
				1990						1995						2000			
Orissa	147	145	10	2	30	2	147	146	80	1	39	1	147	145	26	2	34	1	147
				1992						1997						2002			
Punjab	117	116	87	1	44	1	117	105	14	3	26	2	117	105	62	1	36	1	116
				1990						1993						1998			
Rajasthan	200	200	50	2	34	2	199	199	76	2	38	2	200	200	153	1	45	1	200
				1989						1994						1999			
Sikkim	32	31	0	2	18	2	32	31	2	3	15	3	32	31	0	0	4	3	32
				1989						1991						1996			
Tamil Nadu	234	214	26	3	20	3	234	65	60	2	15	3	234	64	0	0	6	4	234
				1993						1998						2003			
Tripura	60	46	10	2	33	2	60	45	13	2	33	2	60	42	13	2	33	2	60
				1989						1991						1993			
Uttar Pradesh	425	410	94	2	28	2	419	413	46	3	17	3	422	421	28	4	15	3	424
				1991						1996						2001			
West Bengal	294	284	43	2	35	2	294	288	82	2	40	1	294	60	26	3	8	3	294
				2003						2008						2013			
Chhattisgarh	90	90	37	2	37	2	90	87	38	2	40	2	90	90	39	2	40	2	
				2005						2009									
Jharkhand	81	41	9	3	12	3	81	61	14	3	16	2							
				2002						2007						2012			
Uttarakhand	70	70	36	1	27	1	69	69	21	2	30	2	70	70	32	1	34	1	
				1993						1998						2003			
NCT of Delhi	70	70	14	2	35	2	70	70	52	1	48	1	70	70	47	1	48	1	70
				1990						1991						1996			
Puducherry	30	17	11	1	25	1	30	19	15	1	30	1	30	20	9	1	25	1	30
				2014															
Telangana	119	113	21	2	25	2													

Table 3 (*Contd.*)

Table 3 (*Contd.*)

SC	*SW*	*PS*	*VS*	*PV*	*TS*	*SC*	*SW*	*PS*	*VS*	*PV*	*TS*	*SC*	*SW*	*PS*	*VS*	*PV*	*TS*	*SC*	*SW*	*PS*	*VS*	*PV*
	2003						2008						2013									
40	12	2	30	2	40	40	32	1	39	1	40	40	34	1	45	1						
	2003						2008						2013									
60	21	1	36	1	60	60	23	2	36	1	60	56	8	2	25	2						
	2004						2009						2014									
133	38	2	35	1	147	146	27	2	29	2	147	147	16	2	26	2						
	2007						2012															
116	44	2	41	1	117	117	46	2	40	2												
	2003						2008						2013									
200	56	2	36	2	200	200	96	1	37	1	200	200	21	2	33	2						
	2004						2009						2014									
28	1	2	26	2	32	32	0	0	28	2	32	32	0	0	1	3						
	2001						2006						2011									
14	7	5	3	7	234	48	34	3	8	3	234	63	5	5	9	3						
	2008						2013															
48	10	2	36	2	60	48	10	2	37	2												
	1996						2003						2007						2012			
126	33	4	8	4	403	402	25	4	9	4	403	393	22	4	9	4	403	355	28	4	12	4
	2006						2011															
262	21	3	15	3	294	66	42	2	9	3												
	2008						2013															
70	43	1	40	1	70	70	8	3	25	3												
	2001						2006						2011									
21	11	*	23	1	30	16	10	1	30	1	30	17	7	2	27	2						

Table 4. Number of seats where Indian National Congress constituency position has been third or worse (1989–2014)

State/Union Territory	*1989*	*1991*	*1996*	*1998*	*1999*	*2004*	*2009*	*2014*
Andhra Pradesh	1	1	2	5	1		1	27
Arunachal Pradesh				1				
Assam		1	2	1	1	2	2	2
Bihar	16	23	42	8	4		33	2
Goa								
Gujarat			2	1				
Haryana			2	2			1	4
Himachal Pradesh								
Jammu and Kashmir				3	4	1		1
Karnataka			7	2		2	3	
Kerala								
Madhya Pradesh	2		6	3		3		1
Maharashtra		2	6		13		1	
Manipur				2	1			
Meghalaya								
Mizoram								
Nagaland								
Orissa						1	1	10
Punjab	2		1	1				2
Rajasthan			2	1			2	3
Sikkim					1			1
Tamil Nadu			3	35	1			38
Tripura					2	1		
Uttar Pradesh	7	54	77	70	58	58	37	58
West Bengal				33	35	29	1	36
Chhattisgarh								
Jharkhand						2	2	2
Uttarakhand						1		
Andaman & Nicobar Islands								

Table 4 (*Contd.*)

Table 4 (*Contd.*)

State/Union Territory	*1989*	*1991*	*1996*	*1998*	*1999*	*2004*	*2009*	*2014*
Chandigarh								
Dadra & Nagar Haveli				1	1			
Daman & Diu		1						
NCT of Delhi								7
Lakshadweep								
Puducherry								
Total	28	82	152	169	122	100	84	194

Source: Election Commission of India, Statistical Report of Lok Sabha Elections, 1989–2014. CP, constituency position.

Table 5. Number of seats where the INC has not won since years 1989–1999

State/Union Territory	*1989*	*1991*	*1996*	*1998*	*1999*
Andhra Pradesh	1	1			
Arunachal Pradesh					
Assam		1			
Bihar	22	1			
Goa					
Gujarat	3			1	
Haryana					
Himachal Pradesh					
Jammu & Kashmir					
Karnataka		2		2	
Kerala	2				
Madhya Pradesh	5		2	1	
Maharashtra	2		3	1	6
Manipur					
Meghalaya					1
Mizoram					
Nagaland					

Table 5 (*Contd.*)

Table 5 (*Contd.*)

State/Union Territory	*1989*	*1991*	*1996*	*1998*	*1999*
Orissa	1		1	4	
Punjab	1				
Rajasthan	1				
Sikkim			1		
Tamil Nadu	5		14		
Tripura			2		
Uttar Pradesh	32		2		
West Bengal	14	12			
Chhattisgarh			2	1	
Jharkhand	5				
Uttarakhand	1				
Andaman & Nicobar Islands					
Chandigarh					
Dadra & Nagar Haveli				1	
Daman & Diu					
NCT of Delhi					
Lakshadweep					
Puducherry					
Total	95	17	27	11	7

Source: Authors own calculations based on Statistical Report of Lok Sabha Elections 1989–2014.

194 in 2014, marking a sharp erosion and pointing to a sharp contrast between the two periods (Table 4).

Looking at the situation since the elections of the 1990s (Table 5), despite recoveries in 2004 and 2009, Congress has not won 95 constituencies since 1989, another 17 since 1991, another 27 since 1996, another 11 since 1998 and another 7 since 1999, to mention only long-standing (since the end of the 1990s) lack of competitiveness.

Other than these constituencies there have been as many as 34 that Congress has won only once since 1989, 8 only once since 1991, 19 only once since 1996, 10 only once since 1998 and 6 only once since 1999, indicating a long-term erosion of competitiveness in the post-1989 period (Table 6). Part of this lack of competitiveness at the constituency level is because of slippage of support in the four major states mentioned above, part of it is due to splits in the party in West Bengal since 1997 and Maharashtra since 1999, followed most recently by Andhra Pradesh since 2012, all states which were Congress strongholds, and part of it due to decisions to hand over seats to allies like in Tamil Nadu and Bihar since the 1990s, later in Maharashtra and West Bengal, also an indication of lack of competitiveness and a process of ceding ground (Table 7).

Congress has lost competitiveness in constituencies even outside the four major states; Bihar, Tamil Nadu, West Bengal, and Uttar Pradesh; in which it has been decimated over the past quarter-century. In states other than these four, the Congress party had fallen to third or worse positions in 4 constituencies in 1989, 5 in 1991, 30 in 1996, 22 in 1998, 24 in 1999, 13 in 2004, 13 in 2009, and 60 in 2014. In 22 (of the total of 95) constituencies, other than in the above-mentioned four major states, the party has not won since 1989.

Partial Recoveries in 2004 and 2009

However, the decline of Congress has not been linear. Before the debacle of 2014, there were two important recoveries. The Congress won the 2004 elections in coalition, with 27 per cent votes and 145 seats, and won again, in coalition, improving its performance in 2009 with 28.6 per cent votes and 206 seats, and was in power for 10 years, 2004–14. These recoveries were on top of an improvement of vote share from 25.8 per cent in 1998 to 28.2 per cent in 1999 (though accompanied by a loss of seats). These recoveries also need explanation as part of the longer-term evolution of Congress.

It has been argued that the best explanation for the Congress' and its UPA coalition's very narrow victory (UPA won a fraction of a percentage point more than the BJP-led NDA) in 2004 was that

Table 6. Number of seats won by the INC only once since years 1989–1999

State/Union Territory	*1989*	*1991*	*1996*	*1998*	*1999*
Andhra Pradesh			5£	1©	1ħ
Arunachal Pradesh					
Assam					
Bihar	2X				
Goa					
Gujarat	4 €				
Haryana		1∞			
Himachal Pradesh					1·
Jammu & Kashmir				1¤	
Karnataka			7µ		
Kerala				2 °	
Madhya Pradesh	6#				
Maharashtra	3+		1π		3ŋ
Manipur					
Meghalaya					
Mizoram					
Nagaland					
Orissa	1$		4»		
Punjab			1æ		
Rajasthan					
Sikkim					
Tamil Nadu			4±		
Tripura					
Uttar Pradesh	12^				
West Bengal		4Σ			
Chhattisgarh				1g˘	
Jharkhand	5@		2e¨		
Uttarakhand	1!	3a			
Andaman & Nicobar Islands					1ŧ
Chandigarh					
Dadra & Nagar Haveli					
Daman & Diu					

Table 6 (*Contd.*)

Table 6 (*Contd.*)

State/Union Territory	*1989*	*1991*	*1996*	*1998*	*1999*
NCT of Delhi					
Lakshadweep					
Puducherry					
Total	34	8	19	10	6

Source: Authors own calculations based on Statistical Report of Lok Sabha Elections 1989–2014.

Notes: ×Nawada was won again in 2004; ERajkot, Porbandar and Junagadh were won again in 2009, and Amreli in 2004; #Ujjain, Mandsaur and Hoshangabad were won again in 2004, Rewa, Indore and Khajuraho in 1999; +Parbhani was won in 1998, Aurangabad in 1999 and Mumbai South Central in 2009; $Jajpur was won again in 1998; ^Aligarh, Mathura and Varanasi were won in 2004, Bareilly, Unnao, Sultanpur, Barabanki, Faizabad, Bahraich and Mahajganj were won again in 2009, Muzaffarnagar and Meerut were won in 1999; @Dhanbad, Singhbhum, Khunti and Lohardarga were won in 2004, Kodarma in 1999; !Garhwal was won in 1989; Warangal, 1Hisar was won again in 2004; Howrah, Srerampur and Tamluk were won again in 1996, Purulia in 2004; a Tehri Garhwal, Almora and Hardwar were won again in 2009; £Warangal, Srikakulam, Anakpali, Chittoor and Karimnagar were won in 2009; mBelgaum, Bagalkot, Shimoga, Hasan and Bangalore North were won again in 1999, Davnagere was won in 1998 and Chamrajnagar in 2009; pSatara was one again in 1998; +Nilgiris and Thenkasi were won again in 2004, Tiruchirapalli and Cuddalore in 2009; e¨Rajnandgaon and Raigarh were won in 1998; #Mahbubnagar was won in 2004; ¤Ladakh was won again in 2009; 8Iduki was won in 2009 and Kotayam in 1999; »Balasore and Sundargarh were won again in 2009, Sambalpur in 2004 and Dhenkanal in 1999; æGurdaspur was won again in 2009; gˇSarguja was won in 1999; Guntur was won again in 2004; l.Chota Udaipur was won again in 2004; ˛Dhule was won again in 2004 and Ramtek in 2009; tAndaman and Nicobar Islands were won again in 2004.

the Congress recognised its weakness in many states and went in for a pre-electoral coalition (Table 7) while the BJP went alone without a coalition in several states.[21] In other words, it was a victory

[21] Sridharan 2004; Wilkinson 2005; Yadav 2004.

Table 7. Ceding ground: Congress allies since 1991

Year	*Allies*
1989	Kerala Congress (M), Indian Union Muslim League
1991	All India Anna Dravida Munnetra Kazhagam, Indian Union Muslim League, Kerala Congress (M)
1996	Kerala Congress (M), Indian Union Muslim League
1998	Kerala Congress (M), Indian Union Muslim League
1999	All India Anna Dravida Munnetra Kazgham, Indian Union Muslim League, Kerala Congress (M), Rashtriya Janata Dal
2004	Nationalist Congress Party, Indian Union Muslim League, Pattali Makkal Katchi, Jharkhand Mukti Morcha, Telangana Rashtra Samiti, Lok Janshakti Party, Rashtriya Janata Dal, Jammu and Kashmir Peoples Democratic Party, Kerala Congress (M), Marumalarchi Dravida Munnetra Kazhagam, Dravida Munnetra Kazhgam
2009	Nationalist Congress Party, Indian Union Muslim League, Kerala Congress (M), Dravida Munnetra Kazhagam, Viduthalai Chiruthaigal Katchi, Jammu & Kashmir National Conference, All India Trinamool Congress, Jharkhand Mukti Morcha, Bodo People's Front, All India Majlis-e-Ittahadul Muslimeen.
2014	Bodo People's Front, Rashtriya Janata Dal, Nationalist Congress Party, Jammu & Kashmir National Conference, Jharkhand Mukti Morcha, Indian Union Muslim League, Socialist Janata Dal (Democratic), Revolutionary Socialist Party, Kerala Congress (Mani), People's Party of Punjab, Rashtriya Lok Dal, Mahan Dal.

Source: Authors' own compilation.

which in some ways was an admission of weakness.[22] Likewise, the Congress and UPA victory in 2009 owed more to *fortuna* (luck) than to *virtu* (prowess) according to Yadav and Palshikar (2009), a combination of a larger and more effective coalition than the eroded NDA, five years of record economic growth, and some social welfare measures that were made possible by the revenues from growth.

[22] Wilkinson 2005.

Decline in Congress Competitiveness: Possible Explanations

What are the possible causes of Congress decline as indicated by this erosion of competitiveness at the state level for both Lok Sabha and assembly elections, and at the Lok Sabha constituency level? We also need to take into account the Congress recoveries in 2004 and 2009; it was not a linear decline. The following explanations can be put forward.

General Explanations, 1967 Onwards

A generic and Rikerian explanation applying coalition theory to congress-type, encompassing, umbrella parties in general, conceiving of such parties as internal grand coalitions of interests, and assuming primarily office-seeking motivations and power as a fixed sum, or even with some upward flexibility, would imply that without the resources to keep all major interests satisfied a large umbrella party would be fated to disintegrate. This logic can be applied to the Congress from the late 1960s, particularly its inability to accommodate newly mobilised interests such as the intermediate caste, newly rich agrarian interests in North India after the Green Revolution. If the processes of internal democracy were undermined, such disintegration would be accelerated.

Following Sridharan (2002), the fragmentation of the national party system was due to Duvergerian dynamics at play since 1967 in a federal system with states with significant powers, and importantly, states which were distinct linguo-cultural units with their specific identities, which created incentives for mobilisation of single-state parties. These incentivised ethno-regional parties that reacted against the perceived insensitivity of the Congress to their demands; it also incentivised intermediate-caste agrarian parties in northern Indian states in response to upper-caste hegemony and the lack of internal democracy in Congress, particularly after the

1969 split, after which the Indira Gandhi-led Congress suspended the processes of internal elections and became a more centralised top-down party. The de-linking of national and state elections in a growing number of states since the early national election of 1971 also had the unintended consequence of furthering the prospects of regional parties which could take on Congress in state elections on state-level issues not overshadowed by a national election in which Congress had no polity-wide challengers and could project itself as the only party capable of leading the nation. These explanations can account for the gradual growth of a principal regional opposition party in state after state and a loose national opposition in the period of Congress hegemony before 1989, continuing since then, creating bipolar if not two-party systems in most states.

The Post-1989 Period

However, there are explanations for Congress decline – and for the rise of the BJP and some caste-based regional parties – that are specific to the post-1989 period. These can be divided into:

Organisational decay of Congress and the relative organisational vigour of the BJP: Chhibber, Jensenius, and Suryanarayan (2012) find that party organisation or the lack of it has a significant impact on the party system. Based on data from fifteen Indian states they find that the less parties are organised the more politicians have an incentive to defect. This would lead us to relate the lack of internal democracy and generally weak organisation of the Congress to its further decline by defection by politicians representing newly mobilised social constituencies to other parties or new parties. Manor (2007) and Hasan (2012) make the same point in a different way, emphasising the fact that the party now depends on government spending programmes as a substitute for a party organisation that can mobilise voter support as well as, related to the lack of organisation, the lack of a clear ideology or position on what Congress stands for. As Chandra (2000) put it: "The institutional decay of the Congress party over a period of time transformed the party system by gradually creating newer opportunities for the sections which the party had failed to accommodate over the years."[23]

Greater powers to the states in Indian federalism, linked to economic liberalisation and the rise of regional parties: Chhibber (2005), in an essay on the decline of the Congress (despite its victory in 2004), also emphasises the role of the changing nature of Indian federalism. He emphasises that compared to the 1980s state governments in India play a larger role in their economies compared to the Central government in the post-1991, post-liberalisation period with the end of central licensing of economic activity and states competing for domestic and foreign private investment in an increasingly private investment-driven economy. There were also other developments that made state governments more secure such as the prevalence of multi-party coalition governments since 1996 in which regional parties played a key role, and the Supreme Court's *Bommai* judgment (1994) which made it much more difficult to dismiss state governments and impose central rule under Art. 356. The result of these developments, for Congress, was that "party aggregation is more difficult to achieve when voters' preferences are mostly 'state'-based and candidates do not have to coordinate with politicians in other states."[24]

Sridharan (2012) makes a similar argument in that he argues that while the Indian system remains a power-sharing one among all significant groups, the nature of power-sharing has shifted in the post-1996 coalition era from one of power-sharing within an internally grand-coalitional party like Congress in its heyday to one of power sharing in a coalition of parties at the Centre, each party

[23] Chandra 2000: 52.

[24] Chhibber 2005: 53.

representing particularistic interests. This makes Congress simply less relevant to voters in achieving their objectives.

Furthermore, coalitions at the Centre since 1996 gave incentives for the rise of regional parties;[25] so does the absence of meaningful internal democracy within Congress, leading to the breakaway of significant parts or even the bulk of the state unit in major states like West Bengal (1997), Maharashtra (1999), and Andhra Pradesh (2012), with these new splinter parties enjoying the flexibility to participate in diverse central coalitions, in the process greatly weakening Congress and forcing it to rely even more on pre-electoral coalitions, sometimes with these same splinter parties.

New communal, caste and class dynamics since 1989: Since 1989, new communal, caste, and class dynamics that are often state-specific, with class dynamics related to caste and to economic liberalisation and growth, particularly the rise of the middle classes, including the seeming maturing of a "new social bloc" and the emergence of aspirational voting in 2014, having eroded the Congress base.

The major development for the Congress in the post-1990, post-Mandal era, compared to the 1980s is the rise of Hindu nationalist/anti-Muslim mobilisation by the BJP in the Ramjanmabhoomi/Ayodhya movement and the mobilisation by the Other Backward Classes (OBCs) (in effect, backward castes that are not Scheduled Castes), as well as later in the 1990s and 2000s, the rise of the Bahujan Samaj Party (BSP) with its principal support base of Scheduled Castes eating into the traditional Congress base.[26] The BJP was able to mobilise in several states of northern and western India, but most of all in U.P., its traditional support

[25] Wyatt 2002; Ziegfeld 2012.

[26] Heath and Yadav 1999; Yadav 1999, for the composition of the Congress voter base; Sridharan 2014a, 2014b, for the Congress and BJP bases in 2014; Varshney 2002: 60–86; Varshney 2014, for an overview of the BJP's ideology and politics.

among the upper castes from the late 1980s, partly due to Hindu anxieties arising from separatist movements in Punjab (1980s) and Kashmir (post-1989), and a sense that Congress was overly sympathetic to the Muslim minority, a fallout of the Shah Bano case (1986), as well as go beyond its traditional upper-caste support. The BJP was also able to mobilise, at least substantially because of the backlash to the Mandal decision to reserve 27 per cent of public sector jobs and college admissions for OBCs in 1990, the upper castes, particularly in North India, and thus eat into the Congress base.

The loss of Congress vote share since 1989 among various major segments of the electorate, according to CSDS/Lokniti post-election survey data, is shown in Table 8. As can be seen, from 1991 to 1999 the Congress vote share among Hindu upper castes plummeted steadily from 36 per cent to 16 per cent, recovering partially to 21 per cent and 26 per cent in 2004 and 2009, before plunging to 12 per cent in 2014. Among peasant proprietor castes, the support level of roughly a quarter of the group in 2004 and 2009, the only elections for which this was a separate category, plunged to 15 per cent in 2014. Among Hindu OBCs as a whole, support declined from 32 per cent in 1991 to 21 per cent in 1998, recovering partly to 27 per cent in 1999, 24 per cent in 2009, and plunging to 15 per cent in 2014. There has been somewhat of an erosion even among traditionally Congress voters (in most states) like the Scheduled Castes and Scheduled Tribes and even before the dips of 2014, the erosion among Scheduled Castes at least partly being due to the rise of the BSP in several states (in terms of vote share). Only among Muslims, at 38 per cent has the Congress support remained steady between 1991 and 2014.

In 2014, according to the CSDS National Election Survey, the BJP led Congress among upper-caste voters (54 per cent to 12 per cent), peasant proprietor castes (33 per cent to 15 per cent), upper OBCs (30 per cent to 15 per cent), lower OBCs (42 per cent to 16 per cent), Scheduled Castes (24 per cent to 19 per cent),

Table 8. Congress vote share among different social groups
Lok Sabha elections 1991–2014

Caste/community	*1991*	*1996*	*1998*	*1999*	*2004*	*2009*	*2014*
Hindu upper	36	27	20	16	21	26	12
Peasant proprietor					23	25	15
Hindu OBC	32	22	21	27	–	24	15
Upper OBC's					23	22	
Lower OBC's					23	27	
SC	39	32	27	32	28	27	19
ST	45	41	38	40	35	39	28
Muslim	38	34	43	50	37	38	38
Christian					39	28	29
Sikh					25	41	21

Source: National Election Study, various years, Centre for Study of Developing Societies, 1996–2014

Scheduled Tribes (38 per cent to 28 per cent), and among all four social classes though with a declining lead as one went down the ladder – upper (32 per cent to 17 per cent), middle (32 per cent to 20 per cent), lower (31 per cent to 19 per cent) and poor (24 per cent to 20 per cent). The BJP also led Congress both in rural areas (30 per cent to 19 per cent) and urban areas (33 per cent to 20 per cent).

What this reveals about the Congress base is that it has lost significant sections of its erstwhile base to the BJP and other, primarily caste-based, state parties, mainly in U.P. and Bihar, and become *less of an encompassing umbrella party* over the past two and a half decades. A rough calculation based on actual population shares and turnout taken together with group-wise Congress support estimates in Table 8 indicates that over half the Congress vote in 2014 came from Muslims, Scheduled Castes, and Scheduled Tribes.

Heath and Yadav (1999) and Yadav, Kumar, and Heath (1999) have outlined the profile of the Congress voter at the end of the decade (1990s) of the "second democratic upsurge" of higher turnout among the relatively deprived (lower castes and tribes, minorities, the poor and rural areas) as well as put forward a conception of the emerging BJP base as a loose "new social bloc"of upper and dominant castes including rising peasant castes, and of upper classes including the rising middle class, united by relative economic and social privilege.[27] The Congress profile over the 1990s had become increasingly dependent on minority, Scheduled Caste, Scheduled Tribe, rural, and poor voters while losing upper castes, OBCs, and the upper and middle classes to the BJP and other parties. The BJP's "new social bloc" seems to have come to fruition in 2014, a year in which as high as 49 per cent of the population self-identified as middle class,[28] and in which the BJP got more votes than Congress in all caste and religious groups except Muslims, even among the poor, the Scheduled Castes, and Scheduled Tribes.

Further buttressing the "new social bloc" argument is the emergence of what can be called aspirational voting, in which voters identify "upwardly" in class terms and vote accordingly. This is particularly so in the 2014 election, which we analyse below. The Congress plunged from 28.2 per cent to 19.3 per cent vote share, going below 20 per cent for the first time ever and no longer being the single largest party by votes, and to a derisory 44 seats, the first time it plunged below 100 seats.[29] The BJP's rise from 19 per cent to 31 per cent vote share as part of the NDA coalition's 38 per cent, and to a majority of 282 on its own, 336 with the NDA, was due to a regionally highly concentrated sweep in the entire Hindi belt of northern and central India and the western states of Gujarat, Maharashtra, and Goa, plus Karnataka in the South and Assam in the North-East. This was a more concentrated performance than earlier such performances in 1996, 1998, and 1999 when it won more seats than the Congress despite a smaller vote share precisely because its votes were geographically concentrated in

[27] Yadav *et al.* 1999.

[28] Kapur and Vaishnav 2015.

[29] For attempts at analysis, see Palshikar 2014 and 2015; Sridharan 2014a and 2014b.

the northern, central, and western states. As we noted earlier, the emergence of a principal opposition party in every state opens up the possibility of an anti-Congress sweep that benefits such opposition parties.

In 2014 it was the BJP that benefited from a combination of factors that kicked in after 2010 – economic slowdown and slow growth of jobs, persistent high inflation which neutralised the effects of populist welfare spending, and loss of legitimacy due to exposure of multiple corruption scandals to which Congress had no answer, the party split in Andhra, and exit of the Trinamool in West Bengal from the UPA coalition, and the party's organisational weakness and decay resulting in a weak mobilisation effort in the campaign.[30] By contrast, the BJP had corruption, inflation, and unemployment as weapons and a seemingly effective and inspiring leader in Modi, plus extremely effective organisational machinery. There also seemed to be a change of mood and expectations on the part of the electorate, with the Congress' populist, pro-poor message not working with a seemingly aspirational electorate that wanted more than anti-poverty slogans and programmes – for the first time according to the Lokniti/CSDS post-election survey, more of the poor, the Scheduled Castes, and Scheduled Tribes voted for the BJP than for the Congress, representing a significant downward expansion of the former's base.

The survey finding that 49 per cent of the population in 2014 self-identify as middle class,[31] contrary to estimates by economic, occupational and educational criteria,[32] makes sense only if a large part of the population is aspirational in that it identifies itself with higher social levels. Also, three CSDS/Lokniti post-election survey findings of 2014 that make sense only if the electorate is aspirational, are the responses to three questions on economic policy and conditions.

[30] Sridharan 2014b.

[31] Kapur and Vaishnav 2015.

[32] Kapur 2010.

First, more voters of each of the four classes including the poor said they strongly agreed or agreed that government should spend on infrastructure rather than on subsidies for the poor than strongly disagreed or disagreed, something that went counter to the redistributivist Congress line in the election campaign and was more in line with the "growth and jobs" Modi pitch.[33]

Second, in response to a question on the improvement or otherwise of the economic condition of India over the past five years,[34] 40 per cent said it was much better or better, and only 17 per cent said it was worse, seemingly indicating an endorsement of the ruling party that ran against the actual voting results. However, if one factors in 24 per cent who said it was the same and gives bad marks for a "same" response, that is, for an aspirational electorate "same" is stagnation and hence poor performance, this would fit better with the electoral result. The striking result of this table is that for three of the four classes (Rich, Lower, and Poor, except Middle), the responses Much Better and Better combined were much larger than the response Worse, but if one added the response Same to Worse it was larger than Much Better plus Better. If one makes the assumption that the electorate was aspirational and considered Same to be poor performance, the survey result fits the electoral outcome.

Third, in response to a question on the improvement or otherwise of the economic condition of "your household" over the past five years,[35] one gets exactly the same result as for Question 8 above, for the overall sample as well as for the Lower and Poor classes, again fitting the voting pattern by these classes (more voting for BJP than Congress) only if one assumes that Same is poor performance For the Rich and Middle Class, even adding Same to Worse left these responses smaller in percentage than Much Better plus Better. Given that these classes voted even more for BJP than for

[33] Responses to Question 23d of the CSDS National Election Survey 2014.
[34] Question 8, CSDS National Election Survey 2014.
[35] Question 16, CSDS National Election Survey 2014.

Congress, it would seem that these classes, other factors being equal, were even more aspirational and dissatisfied by their perceived improvement in household economic condition.

It would appear that Congress misread the mood of an increasingly impatient, aspirational middle class and young electorate in addition to other factors like corruption scandals, growth slowdown, and inflation.

In essence, since 1989 a centrist umbrella party like Congress could not compete in upping the ante in religion- and caste-based political mobilisations with parties that were explicitly Hindu nationalist (BJP), or caste-based like OBC parties or the BSP or some regional parties. In class terms, while the poor could also be mobilised by competing lower-caste parties, the middle classes that burgeoned with economic growth, which were disproportionately upper or dominant caste in composition, were mobilised by the appeal of Hindu nationalism or upper-caste resentment against reservations for the lower castes, primarily by the BJP. An aspirational electorate also means that poorer and disadvantaged groups might vote "upwardly" for the BJP's "new social bloc".

Taken together, these factors led to a steady erosion of the Congress base despite a limited recovery in vote share in 2004 and 2009, and electoral victories in those years that were heavily dependent on formation of pre-electoral and post-electoral coalitions which involved giving up turf, eroding its umbrella character, making it a party *more* dependent on some segments of its erstwhile broad bases, viz., minorities, Scheduled Castes and Scheduled Tribes, and the poor.

Can Congress Survive as an Umbrella Party? Or Has the Social Cleavages Theory of Party Systems Won Out?

Finally, this brings us back to the question of whether an umbrella party like Congress is viable in the long term once the pre- and post-Independence historical momentum that created its dominance peters out, particularly in the context of the continuing operation of the above factors, and particularly the growing and perhaps entrenched salience of regional identities, as well as varying state-level caste and religious cleavages. Is it possible to reconstruct an expanded umbrella party in the context of such cleavages? Or has the social cleavages theory of party systems won out? Or is the electorate evolving towards rewarding good governance and economic performance with identity politics around social cleavages assuming a back seat over time? Can Congress recover again as it did after 1967, and again after 1977, and rebuild a new social coalition around a new political economy, and win back the social segments it seems to have lost – the upper and dominant castes and middle classes – while retaining its remaining base among minorities, Scheduled Castes and Scheduled Tribes, and the poor? Can it build a sufficiently broad social coalition in a sufficient number of states to make it an umbrella party nationally, given the erosion of its competitiveness and even presence in a large number of states and constituencies over the past quarter of a century?

As Chhibber (2005) has argued, after 1967, particularly after the split of 1969, there was a centralisation of economic powers by Indira Gandhi as well as several political interventions in state governments, plus the centralisation of the Congress organisation, all of which helped to build support coalitions based on centralised dispensation of patronage to substitute for a vibrant, grass-roots-based organisation. This system helped maintain Congress as a coalition of state-based party units as well as recover support after the setback of 1967 and the defeat of 1977. However, this sort of centralisation is no longer possible after the deregulation of the economy from the early 1990s, after the bulk of investment in the economy is from private capital, both domestic and foreign, since that time, after the *Bommai* (1994) judgment made it far more difficult to dismiss state governments and impose President's Rule, and after the rise and consolidation of multi-state opposition parties like the BJP and powerful regional parties in a range of states since the 1990s. Most recently, the acceptance of the Fourteenth Finance Commission's recommendations for raising the states' share in the divisible pool of Central tax revenues from 32 per cent to 42 per cent will over time make states, and hence state-based parties including the state units of Congress (and BJP) more independent of the Central party leadership. Rebuilding a social base while being out of power and without tight control of state party units (which can defect as in West Bengal, Maharashtra, and Andhra) promises to be that much more difficult.

One ray of hope for the Congress is that the CSDS/Lokniti post-election survey of 2014 indicates fairly robustly that the secular consensus as regards the treatment of minorities seems to be intact. Large majorities of 58–68 per cent strongly agreed or agreed with the proposition that minorities should be treated equally and also with special provisions for minorities, while only about a sixth disagreed or strongly disagreed.[36] This seems to indicate that the BJP victory was not a victory for ideological Hindutva but for the promise of "better days" against the backdrop of economic slowdown, inflation, and corruption over 2011–14. The Congress' weak recoveries of 2004 and 2009 in which it did well among the upper castes, urban and rural middle class, and urban seats seems to indicate that a Congress recovery of lost social and geographical turf is possible under certain circumstances.

A broad centrist social coalition built around economic reforms for growth combined with targeted social expenditure within fiscal limits is a possibility, which is in fact what the Modi government appears to be attempting to build a broader BJP base. However, adopting such a strategy would need the Congress not to try to cast itself as only or mainly a pro-poor party (in an aspirational electorate in which 49 per cent self-identify as middle class, and those Below Poverty Line are a minority of the population) catering only to its post-2014 *remaining* base, but a broad-based growth-

[36] Sridharan 2014b.

cum-social justice party that does not upset the fine balance between growth-oriented policies and redistributive policies that seems to have been upset in the 2014 campaign and beyond.[37]

However, for such a makeover it will have to address the issues of internal democracy and organisational rebuilding along with a new political economy that balances growth and equity in a way that does not alienate the growing middle class, urban, and younger sections of the electorate whose weight will increase over time. The reorganisation and revival of the Congress party is indeed quite a difficult task, especially after the party's poor performance in the Lok Sabha elections and the subsequent assembly elections, but it is not necessarily impossible. Manor (2003) has argued that paradoxically it might be easier to attempt an organisational rejuvenation especially at the state level when the party is in opposition than when it is in power because when in power the state leaders have to contend with and resolve issues between different factions vying for their share in spoils of power. This further weakens the party organisation and simultaneously encourages factionalism.

To sum up, if the Congress cannot rebuild an encompassing coalition, as it arguably did in 2009, and recover *as an umbrella party*, there are two other possibilities – its disintegration and eventual demise by further splits and loss of social base, *or* its revival but as a broad, left-of-centre coalition of the disadvantaged, not an umbrella party, facing a broad, BJP-led, right-of-centre coalition. However, in the latter scenario, it would not be an umbrella party but a centre-left party, and the social cleavages theory of party systems would have won out.

Acknowledgements

The authors would like to acknowledge feedback on earlier drafts from Devesh Kapur, Matt Kavanagh, Jack Nagel, Wilfried

37 Ibid.

Swenden, Milan Vaishnav, and Ashutosh Varshney, and two anonymous referees.

Bibliography

Aleyomi, M.B. 2013. "Intra-party Conflicts in Nigeria: The Case Study of Peoples Democratic Party (PDP)," *Journal of Sustainable Development in Africa*, 15 (4), 281–96.

Bartolini, S., and P. Mair. 1990. *Identity, Competition and Electoral Availability: The Stabilisation of European Electorates, 1885–1985* (Cambridge: Cambridge University Press).

Chandra, K. 2000. "The Transformation of Ethnic Politics in India: The Decline of Congress and the Rise of the Bahujan Samaj Party in Hoshiarpur", *Journal of Asian Studies*, 59 (1), 26–61.

Chhibber, P.K. 1999. *Democracy Without Associations* (New Delhi: Vistaar).

Chhibber, P.K. 2005. "Party Decline in a Mature System: The Congress Party of India", *Taiwan Journal of Democracy*, 1 (1), 49–76.

Chhibber, P. K., F.R. Jensenius, and P. Suryanayaran. 2012. "Party Organization and Party Proliferation in India", *Party Politics*, 18 (1), 1–17.

Chhibber, P.K., and G. Murali. 2006. "Duvergerian Dynamics in the Indian States: Federalism and the Number of Parties in State Assembly Elections", *Party Politics*, 12 (1), 5–34.

Chhibber, P.K., and K. Kollman. 2004. *The Formation of National Party Systems: Federalism and Party Competition in Canada, Great Britain, India and the United States* (Princeton, NJ: Princeton University Press).

Chhibber, P.K., and J.R. Petrocik. 1990. "Social Cleavages, Elections and the Indian Party System", in R. Sisson and R. Roy, eds, *Diversity and Dominance in Indian Politics* (New Delhi: Sage), vol. 1.

Crespo, J.A. 2004. "The Party System and Governance in Mexico", *Policy Papers on the Americas*, 15 (2), 1–41.

Duverger, M. 1963. *Political Parties: Their Organisation and Activity in the Modern State* (New York, NY: Wiley).

Duverger, M. 1986. "Duverger's Law: Forty Years Later", in B. Grofman and A. Lijphart, *Electoral Laws and Their Political Consequences* (New York, NY: Agathon Press), 69–84.

Grofman, B., and A. Lijphart. 1986. *Electoral Laws and their Political Consequences* (New York, NY: Agathon Press).

Gunther, R., and L. Diamond. 2001. "Types and Functions of Parties", in L. Diamond and R. Gunther, eds, *Political Parties and Democracy* (Baltimore, MD: Johns Hopkins University Press), 3–39.

Hasan, Z. 2012. *Congress After Indira: Policy, Power, Political Change (1984–2009)* (New Delhi: Oxford University Press).

Heath, A., and Y. Yadav. 1999. "The United Colours of Congress: Social Profile of Congress Voters, 1996 and 1998", *Economic and Political Weekly*, 34, nos 34–5, 2518–28.

Kapur, D. 2010. "The Middle Class in India: A Social Formation or a Political Actor?" *Political Power and Social Theory*, 21, 215–40.

Kapur, D., and M. Vaishnav. 2012. "Being Middle Class in India", *The Hindu*, 10 January.

Kirchheimer, O. 1996. "The Transformation of the Western European Party Systems", in J. LaPalombara and M. Weiner, eds, *Political Parties and Political Development* (Princeton, NJ: Princeton University Press).

Kothari, R. 1970. *Politics in India* (Boston: Little, Brown).

Kothari, R. 1997. "Caste and Modern Politics", in S. Kaviraj, ed., *Politics in India* (Delhi: Oxford University Press), 57–70.

Lijphart, A. 1994. *Electoral Systems and Party Systems* (New York, NY: Oxford University Press.

Lijphart, A. 1996. "The Puzzle of Indian Democracy: A Consociational Interpretation", *American Political Science Review*, 90 (2), 258–68.

Lipset, S.M., and S. Rokkan. 1967. "Cleavage Structures, Party Systems, and Voter Alignments: An Introduction", in S.M. Lipset and S. Rokkan, eds, *Party Systems and Voter Alignments: Cross-National Perspectives* (London: The Free Press), 1–64.

Manor, J. 2003. "Organisational Renewal", *Seminar*, www.india-seminar.com/2003/526/526%20james%20manor.htm, accessed 28 November 2015.

Manor, J. 2007. *The Congress Party and the 'Great Transformation'*, http://www.columbia.edu/~sr793/doc/JManor.pdf, accessed 28 November 2015.

Ordeshook, P., and O. Shvetsova. 1994. "Ethnic Heterogeneity, District

Magnitude and the Number of Parties", *American Journal of Political Science*, 38 (1), 100–23.

Palshikar, S. 2014. "The Defeat of the Congress", *Economic and Political Weekly*, 49 (39), 57–63.

Palshikar, S. 2015. "Congress in the Times of the Post-Congress Era: Surviving Sans Politics", *Economic and Political Weekly*, 50 (19), 39–46.

Rae, D. 1967. *The Political Consequences of Electoral Laws* (New Haven: Yale University Press).

Sartori, G. 2005. *Parties and Party Systems: A Framework for Analysis* (Colchester: ECPR Press).

Spieb, C. 2002. *One-party-dominance in Changing Societies: The ANC and INC in Comparative Perspective* (Working Paper No. 10), http://archiv.ub.uni-heidelberg.de/volltextserver/4120/1/hpsacp10.pdf, accessed 9 November 2015.

Sridharan, E. 2002. "The Fragmentation of the Indian Party System 1952–1999: Seven Competing Explanations", in Z. Hasan, ed., *Parties and Party Politics in India* (New Delhi: Oxford University Press), 476–503.

Sridharan, E. 2004. "Electoral Coalitions in the 2004 General Elections: Theory and Evidence", *Economic and Political Weekly*, 39 (51), 5418–25.

Sridharan, E. 2012. "Coalitions and Democratic Deepening in India", in E. Sridharan, ed., *Coalition Politics and Democratic Consolidation in Asia* (New Delhi: Oxford University Press), 20–73.

Sridharan, E. 2014a. "Class Voting in the 2014 Lok Sabha Elections: The Growing Size and Importance of the Middle Classes", *Economic and Political Weekly*, 49 (39), 72–6.

Sridharan, E. 2014b. "India's Watershed Vote: Behind Modi's Victory", *Journal of Democracy*, 25 (4), 20–33.

Taagepera, R., and M. S. Shugart. 1989. *Seats and Votes* (New Haven: Yale University Press).

Varshney, A. 2002. *Ethnic Conflict and Civic Life: Hindus and Muslims in India* (New Haven: Yale University Press).

Varshney, A. 2014. "Hindu Nationalism in Power?" *Journal of Democracy*, 25 (4), 34–45.

Wilkinson, S.I. 2005. "Elections in India: Behind the Congress Comeback", *Journal of Democracy*, 16 (1), 153–67.

Wyatt, A. 2002. "The Federal Dimension of Party Politics in Tamil Nadu", *Indian Journal of Federal Studies*, 3 (2), 127–43.

Yadav, Y. 1999. "Electoral Politics in the Time of Change: India's Third Electoral System, 1989–99", *Economic and Political Weekly*, 35, nos 34–5, 2393–9.

Yadav, Y. 2003. "The New Congress Voter", *Seminar*, http:// www.india-seminar.com/2003/526/526%20yogendra%20yadav.htm, accessed 4 May 2016.

Yadav, Y. 2004. "The Elusive Mandate of 2004", *Economic and Political Weekly*, 39 (51), 5383–98.

Yadav, Y., S. Kumar, and O. Heath. 1999. "The BJP's New Social Bloc", *Frontline*, 16 (23), http://www.frontline.in/static/html/fl1623/16230310. htm, accessed 4 May 2016.

Yadav, Y., and S. Palshikar. 2009. "Between Fortuna and Virtu: Explaining the Congress' Ambiguous Victory in 2009", *Economic and Political Weekly*, 44 (39), 33–46.

Ziegfeld, A. 2012. "Coalition Government and Party System Change: Explaining the Rise of Regional Parties in India", *Comparative Politics*, 45 (1), 69–87.

6

Incumbency, Internal Processes, and Renomination in Indian Parties

Introduction

THIS PAPER EXAMINES a particular aspect of the internal dynamics of major Indian parties of varying types, namely the process of nominating candidates for the parliamentary elections to the lower house (Lok Sabha), which is directly elected from 543 single-member constituencies by the plurality rule (first-past-the-post) system.[1] The aim is to get a picture of the internal processes of various parties and relate them to the nomination outcomes, and see if this is related to party type, to whether there are institutionalised selection processes within parties, and to whether early elections make a difference. We compare the pattern of nominations in each election with the previous election over time in the light of our knowledge of the nomination processes gleaned from post-2009 interviews about the nominations processes in 2009 and 2004 with key party functionaries involved. We select for our study the two major national parties, the Indian National Congress (INC) and the Bharatiya Janata Party (BJP), and two other parties defined as national parties by the Election Commission of India (ECI), the Communist Party of India (Marxist) (CPI [M]) and the Bahujan Samaj Party (BSP), and the largest of what

[1] This paper is co-authored with Adnan Farooqui.

are defined as state parties by the ECI (and referred to in common parlance as regional parties, those that have significant vote shares in less than four states – in most cases effectively one state), the Samajwadi Party (SP). For the CPI (M), the BSP and the SP, we analyse their nomination processes only in their states of strength since they are marginal forces outside these states. Hence, we analyse the nominations of the CPI (M) in its three stronghold states of West Bengal, Kerala, and Tripura only, and those of the BSP and the SP in the state of Uttar Pradesh (U.P.) only.

Our research is informed by the normative importance of the intra-party nomination process in national situations in which, as William Cross has argued, either or both of representational and policy outcomes are determined by who gets to be nominated by major parties because this substantially determines who gets to be elected, i.e. the composition of the legislature and cabinet.[2] In the Indian case, nominations are very important for representational outcomes in a heterogeneous society and also, less definitively, for policy outcomes, the latter being more leadership-determined. This study has larger implications for predictable career paths for candidates within parties, entry barriers for new candidates, and in turn, whether there are incentives for working within existing parties as against moving to other parties or floating new parties.

Comparative Candidate Nomination Processes, and Internal Democracy

In this section, we review the comparative literature on internal democracy and candidate nomination processes in political parties in long-standing democracies. Broadly speaking, following Lars Bille, there are six types of nomination processes in political parties in Western European parliamentary democracies, ranging from completely top-down to completely bottom-up at the two

[2] Cross 2008.

extremes, with four intermediate levels of decentralisation or participation by the party rank-and-file, or in other words by levels of inclusiveness of the selectorate for nominations. These fall, from the most to the least centralised, into six broad categories.[3]

1. Candidate selection is completely controlled by the national party leadership.
2. Subnational party organs propose names but national leadership makes the final decision.
3. The national leadership provides a list of names from which the subnational party organs make the final selection.
4. Subnational party organs make nomination decisions, but need the final approval of national leaderships, and the latter can add or delete names according to various criteria.
5. Subnational party organs control the entire process and make the final decisions.
6. Nomination decisions are based on membership ballots, which are not the same as an open primary, but nevertheless the closest to grassroots participation.

In the context of the present project, the USA represents the decentralised extreme, that of party primaries for presidential and Congressional elections. However, it needs to be noted that these party primaries are conducted by state and local officials, publicly funded and under public law, not by party officials under party rules and with party funds. This system came into effect for presidential primaries from 1912 to 1968, running in parallel with the party convention, and since then has become the determinant of candidacy for public office.[4]

India lies near the other extreme in that most of its major parties are at the completely or near-completely top-down of the six types of party nomination processes, with the national party leadership having the final say. From interview data pertaining to

[3] The categorisation below paraphrases Bille 2001.

[4] See Aldrich 1995 and Epstein 1986 for the evolution of party organisation and primaries.

2009 and 2004, and the literature on Indian parties, we can classify the Congress, BJP and CPI (M) as being in the second most centralised category and the BSP and SP as in the most centralised top-down category.

Most European parties fall in between these extremes. In Bille's broad survey of party nomination rules and how they changed from 1960 to 1990 (covering as many as 57 parties in 1960 and 71 in 1990) in Western Europe, he found that the

> predominant candidate selection procedure in force around 1960, as well as that at the beginning of the 1990s, is the one in which the subnational party organisations control the process completely. Around 1960, and also around 1990, nearly half of all the parties applied this approach. In 1960, only Austria, Belgium, Ireland and the United Kingdom did not have any parties granting sub-national organs this influence. Around 1990, only Ireland and pre-1992 Italy were in this situation.[5]

Thus, he found that most of the parties fell in category (5). Furthermore,

> the second most widely used candidate selection method is the one that gives the right to decide on the subnational party organs, subject to the approval of the national party organisation. Around one-third of the parties belonged to this category in both 1960 and 1989. In sum, then, more than three-quarters of the parties have rules that give the subnational party organisations the power either to control the process completely or, at least, to have a major and substantial influence. The parties in question cover the whole ideological spectrum and they are present in all countries. There is thus no pattern regarding either party families or countries.[6]

Thus, three-quarters of the parties fell in categories (5) or (4), that is, in the relatively decentralised part of the range of types of nomination procedures.

[5] Ibid.: 367–8.

[6] Ibid.: 368.

Lastly, a move towards party primaries based on membership postal ballots, somewhat akin to US-style primaries but distinct from the latter in that they are conducted by party officials under party rules and limited to party members, has been in evidence, increasing from under one-fifth of the parties in 1960 to about a quarter in 1990, representing an increase in the selectorate for candidate nomination. It should be noted that these classifications are based on formal party rules and that informal mechanisms for greater leadership influence over the process can and do exist in many countries. However, the general trend has been towards larger and more inclusive selectorates and more influential sub-national party organs in this process.[7]

Party Types and Internal Democracy

Here it is relevant to mention that the literature tends to relate internal democracy to party type, and party types are supposed to have evolved in a certain sequence. Thus, Richard S. Katz and Peter Mair argue for an evolutionary sequence of party types, based on their relationship to civil societies and states in different stages of economic and social development, each with its typical internal organisation and pattern of functioning.[8] They argue that nineteenth-century clientelist parties of notables gave way to mass parties of the industrial working class, based on trade unions. In turn, these gave way in the post-World War II period of the rapid growth of the welfare state, the white-collar middle class and the post-industrial service economy, to Otto Kirchheimer's catchall party or electoral-professional party, and eventually the cartel parties, both of the moderate left and right, in the post-1970s period, closely integrated with the bureaucracies of a managerial state

[7] For such trends across a range of countries, see Bille 2001, LeDuc 2001, Hopkin 2001, and Rahat and Hazan 2001.

[8] Katz and Mair 1995.

deeply enmeshed in the economy, which Katz and Mair argue are adaptations of the mass parties to the rise of catchall parties.[9] They view the increase in internal decentralisation and democratisation of nomination processes over 1960–90 (expansion of selectorates) in the context of pressures to so democratise felt by catchall parties that were pitted against mass parties, and then felt by cartel parties against these and each other. The moves to democratise and decentralise were made to combat the phenomena of political apathy, low turnout and shrinking party membership by incentivising people by participation in party nomination processes.

However, this West European sequence ignores two important types of parties in India (out of three important types – catchall or Congress parties, ideological parties, and ethnic parties).[10] First, ideological parties of the Left and the Right, that is, the CPI (M) and its Left Front allies, and ideologically rightist parties like the Hindu nationalist BJP and the Shiv Sena in Maharashtra. Second, ethnic parties based on particular caste blocs like the BSP, based on the Scheduled Castes, and the SP, based on the Other Backward Classes (OBC), principally the Yadavs, the main OBC caste in the state of U.P. Both SP and BSP are based in U.P. and enjoy a considerable degree of support from the Muslim minority due to the latter's fear of the BJP. While catchall parties like the Congress might have to depend more on nominating candidates representing various social or ethnic groups to retain their allegiance, ethnic parties might have more autonomous leaderships due to strong ascriptive allegiances, and might try to construct majorities by striking coalition deals with other parties, delivering an ethnic bloc vote in return, akin to the consociational politics of ethnic elites described by Lijphart (1977). However, they could also try to expand the social base of their parties to construct majorities by

[9] See Kirchheimer 1966 for the catch-all party; Panebianco 1988 for the electoral-professional party; and Katz and Mair 1995 for the cartel party.

[10] For a detailed typology of political parties, see Gunther and Diamond 2001; for a typology applied to India, see Sridharan and Varshney 2001.

forming broader and more inclusive caste clusters. Likewise, ideological parties might also have more committed voter bases than catchall parties, somewhat akin to ethnic parties.

Election Nomination Processes in Indian Parties

Early studies of the process of nomination of candidates in the then dominant umbrella party, the Congress, in the 1950s and 1960s revealed the following patterns and evolution. Roy (1966, 1967a, 1967b) found that the party was still groping for a mechanism to stabilise the relationship between the different organisational levels of the party in selecting candidates in the 1957, 1962, and 1967 elections.[11] The process generally followed was that applications would be made at the local level, although it is not clear if they were largely made to the District Congress Committees (DCCs) or the Pradesh Election Committee (PEC). The PECs were to make decisions on nomination based on consultation with the DCCs given that the latter bore the burden of local mobilisation and campaigning. A PEC representative would attend the meetings of the DCCs that covered the relevant parliamentary constituencies. Analogously, the All India Congress Committee (AICC) would depute a representative to participate in the meetings of the PECs. However, while the Central Election Committee (CEC) was normally supposed to approve the decisions of the PECs, it reserved for itself the right to have the final say.

Roy found two contradictory tendencies: the tendency of centralisation of command and concentration of decision-making power into the hands of the higher-level organs growing out of the necessity to inject order and rationality into a process which is highly vulnerable to the pushes and pulls of parochial claims. Opposed to this is the tendency towards fragmentation of au-

[11] Roy 1966, 1967a, 1967b.

thority which reflects pressures from below for autonomy and power.[12]

In the 1962 election the selection process gave relatively greater weight to the lower levels of the hierarchy, including to the Mandal Congress Committees and the Panchayat Samitis, levels below the DCCs. In the 1967 election, the process became somewhat more centralised since intense competition for nominations at the local level, including newly mobilised caste groups, necessitated mediatory interventions by the CEC to resolve conflicts due to casteism, communalism, and localism. Candidates now applied directly to the PEC and while it was obligatory for them to consult the DCCs, the PEC became relatively more influential. The point to be noted here is that the tendency to centralisation of nominations is not just due to a unilateral centralising power drive by the top leadership but due to intense local-level factional rivalries rendering the DCCs and sometimes PECs dysfunctional and requiring and inviting mediation by the top.

Roy's account is supported by Palmer (1967) for the 1967 election. He found that

> For the Congress and for most other parties, mandal, district, state and national committees were involved in the selection procedure In general, but by no means universally, the recommendations of the subordinate committees on the State level were endorsed. These committees . . . in many cases (they) could not agree and therefore simply referred the selections to the national committees.[13]

He noted that non-Congress parties wait to see who the Congress candidate is before nominating their own candidates, a point also noted by Narain and Lal.[14] While the account of Narain and Lal is in general agreement with those of Roy and Palmer, the former are sceptical of finding a uniform pattern in the practice of

[12] Ibid.: 835.

[13] Palmer 1967.

[14] Ibid.: 280, and Narain and Lal 1969.

nominations, the latter being situationally determined, the key interaction being between the character of the party and the nature of the constituency, which they elaborate as being the nature of factionalism and bossism in the party at the local and state levels on the one hand, and the caste composition of the constituency on the other.[15]

Kochanek (1968) broadly agrees with the above authors but adds the important point that whatever the formal criteria, the criterion that carried greatest weight with the selection committee, whether DCC, PEC, or CEC, was the candidate's ability to win, and that this depended considerably on the social – caste and religious community – composition of the constituency, which was always factored in to the selection process.[16] He also adds that in the context of the 1967 election, which like the three earlier elections saw simultaneous parliamentary and state assembly elections, the state-level selection process, formally managed by the PECs, was dominated by chief ministers, and the latter's main concern was that the majority of assembly candidates should be constituted of their followers and should enable them to form a government. This led to non-accommodation of dissident factions in several states and large-scale defections and independent candidatures by dissident Congressmen for the first time. Thus, the concern with victory prospects, factionalism in the selection process, and caste and community were key factors in the selection process, going back to the 1950s and 1960s.

For the 2009 election and to some extent for 2004, we have the following detailed information from interviews with party functionaries, necessitated by the long gap in the literature after the 1970s.[17] In the case of the Congress, key functionaries were categorical that the elaborate bottom-up process described in the

[15] Narain and Lal 1969: 210–11.

[16] Kochanek 1968.

[17] There is very little work focusing on candidate renomination from the 1970s onwards. Hence the jump from the candidate nomination process from the 1970s to the 2009 election.

earlier literature became much more centralised after the Congress split of 1969 and the suspension of internal elections to the AICC from 1972, and that the restoration of the AICC elections since 1992 restored the balance only somewhat.[18]

The formal processes of candidate nomination in Indian parties in 2009 were as follows. In the Congress party, there was an elaborate system consisting of observers sent to each of the 543 Lok Sabha constituencies who prepare reports on potential candidates in their constituency for the DCC and the Pradesh (State) Congress Committee (PCC). The DCCs and PCCs give inputs to the State Election Committee (SEC) in each state, which s a panel of names listing the pros and cons and relevant details of each potential candidate to the AICC. The AICC appoints a screening committee for each state which consists of important party leaders, including a senior member of the Congress Working Committee, two senior leaders who do not belong to the state, the state PCC chief, and the state Congress Legislature Party leader. The screening committees prepare a docket listing the pros and cons and relevant details of each potential candidate and send these to the CEC of the party, the highest organ in the process, which makes the final decision. Although the process is supposed to begin and be completed early, well ahead of the election campaign, which begins just after the last date for withdrawal of nominations, a few days after the last date for nomination of candidates by parties, in actual practice the screening and nomination process begins late and drags on till the last moment. This is deliberate because early nomination is feared to lead to disappointed nominees either leaving the party or sabotaging the nominee's prospects. The process is one in which the central party organisation makes the final selection based on the dockets sent up by the SECs and centrally appointed screening committees for each state, although even at

[18] Confidential interviews, 31 August 2009 and 25 December 2010, respectively, with two Central ministers involved in the Congress nomination process, and likewise, 14 June 2012, with a former Central minister and chief minister involved in the process.

that level there are senior leaders for each state who do not belong to that state and hence are supposed to play the role of neutral arbiters.

In the BJP, there are just two formal levels of decision, the SEC and the CEC. The SEC is the final authority for municipal and local government-level elections in each state, with there being no need for names of potential candidates to be sent to the CEC. For state assembly and parliamentary elections, the SEC plays a recommendatory role, recommending names of candidates for each constituency but the CEC makes the final selection. Earlier, the CEC would usually accept the SEC's choices, with a few exceptions. However, in 2009 there was a significant change from 2004, part of an ongoing shift from the early 2000s, following the BJP's entrenchment in power nationally from its 1999 re-election. In 2009, unlike earlier, the SEC did not make a choice for each constituency and provide a list of preferences. It merely forwarded all the names to the CEC. And the CEC was itself sidelined by the formation of informal "core groups" for each state by the central leadership, which included certain key central leaders (Arun Jaitley, Sushma Swaraj, Venkaiah Naidu, Ananth Kumar) and selected state leaders. Some individuals were on the "core group" of two or more states and wielded enormous clout and functioned arbitrarily and with little knowledge of the grassroots realities in the states concerned.[19] Thus, the "core groups" made the final selection, in effect, which was rubber-stamped by the CEC after perfunctory debate on only a few seats. In 2009, the process started nine months before the election and was chaotic and degenerated into a centralised process.

If the CEC cannot agree on nominees for certain constituencies, the BJP president is empowered to make the decision. This

[19] Confidential interview, 4 January 2011, and follow-up telephonic interaction with a key BJP party functionary dealing with assessment of potential candidates, evaluation of party electoral prospects and observer for the election nomination process in some states.

was so not only in the 2009 national election but also in some state assembly elections before that. Unpublished surveys for internal consumption were commissioned by the party president, hiring three different polling firms of allegedly doubtful integrity, whose results were used to justify preconceived notions and certain selections.[20] Additionally, the extra-party Hindutva ideological "movement" organisation, the Rashtriya Swayamsevak Sangh (RSS), played an influential role in nominations in 2009 in some states (Madhya Pradesh [M.P.], Rajasthan, Chhattisgarh, and also in Delhi, Haryana, Assam, and Orissa), exerting pressure towards rewarding ideological loyalty over constituency-level victory prospects. The RSS functionaries on loan to the BJP party organisation (*sangathan mantris*) no longer perform the function of constituency-level assessment of a candidate's strengths that they used to in the pre-2000 period, but rather that of a lobby within the party for promoting ideological loyalists.

On the whole, there has been a shift within the BJP since 2000, and particularly since 2004, from field-oriented nomination and internal evaluation processes that assessed "merit", that is, victory prospects, from constituency-level feedback from grassroots workers to central party organisation-oriented nomination processes which rewarded those who had cultivated connections at this level. (This is further discussed in the second last paragraph of this section.) There has been a greater emphasis on caste as a factor in nominations, particularly in the states of U.P., Bihar, Rajasthan, and M.P., and in Delhi, Haryana, Assam, and Orissa, according to confidential interviews with key functionaries.[21]

In the CPI (M), we focus on the nomination processes in its

[20] Interview; this opinion of the polling firms was this functionary's opinion, which was critical of the party president.

[21] Confidential interview, 4 January 2011, and follow-up telephonic interaction with key BJP party functionary dealing with assessment of potential candidates, evaluation of party electoral prospects, and observers for the election nomination process in some states.

three stronghold states, West Bengal, Kerala, and Tripura.[22] In the CPI (M), the State Committee draws up the list of nominees for Lok Sabha candidates, which is cleared by the Politbureau of the Central Committee. However, this last step is basically a formality. It is the State Committee which essentially makes the nomination decision, particularly if some Central Committee members happen to be contesting from the state for the Lok Sabha. The (State) Committee Secretariat, which is the executive body of the State Committee, prepares a list of candidates after going through lists prepared in consultation with the District Committees (of the Party). Since parliamentary constituencies overlap districts, two District Secretariats might be consulted in cases of overlapping constituencies. The State Committee consists of about 80 members, of which 7–8 might be MPs and another 25–30 MLAs. This is the pattern in West Bengal, the numbers being smaller in Kerala and much smaller in Tripura. As of 2012, a two-term limit for MPs is proposed, and has already been introduced in Kerala.

On what basis are candidates selected? The CPI (M) being a cadre-based party of about one million members, the key criterion is having been active in party work in their area. Potential candidates will need to have gained recognition in their area of work in the party's mass organisations and fronts, for example among college teachers. There is some consideration given to caste/community, less so in West Bengal where caste politics is less important, more so in Kerala where caste and religion play a greater role in electoral politics. Also, in Kerala the vote share difference between the rival coalitions, the CPI (M)-led Left Democratic Front and the Congress-led United Democratic Front, being typically very narrow (1–2 per cent), there is a greater emphasis on wooing the floating vote, and hence, caste/community considerations are factored in to a greater extent. However, caste/community considerations play

[22] The account below is based on a detailed interview with Prakash Karat, General Secretary of the CPI (M), 29 October 2012.

a much smaller role in the CPI (M), according to the party, compared to other parties, the track record of candidates in party activity being much more important. Linked to this is the pattern of relatively high repetition of winners and candidates, particularly in West Bengal, in 2009 and 2004. Repeating the candidates in the same constituencies, which is a strong pattern, is also linked to recognition in local party work, and to the fact of coalition politics, in which seats are shared with smaller partner parties which have sub-state local bases from which candidates are repeated.

In contrast to the above three national parties, in which there are institutionalised internal processes of selection in which proposed nomination start from below and move upwards although the final decision is made by the national leaderships, the nomination processes in the SP and BSP are very tightly controlled by the top.[23] The process in the SP is a top-down one in which party president Mulayam Singh Yadav takes the final decision on all MP and MLA candidate nominations, although he does this in informal, not institutionalised, consultation and bargaining with other major party leaders. While there is a formal process in which each constituency unit of the party sends up 8–9 possible names, the SP being effectively a single-state party this process is constantly intervened in by Yadav and those close to him since he knows a very large number of local leaders of his party personally and is in constant touch with them. In the SP, nominations are again ultimately about victory prospects. However, also pertinent is a combination of caste and religion (to make various caste groups and the Muslim minority feel represented), and, though to a lesser extent than the BSP, about candidates who can bring resources to the party and at least partly fund their campaign – the SP did give

[23] When we speak of institutionalised processes, these need not necessarily be democratic. They can be controlled or guided processes. However, they are processes with stages nevertheless, and not arbitrary decisions or interventions by the top leadership.

candidates some campaign funds (Rs 5 million to a few tens of millions).[24] Caste matters not only in constituency-specific ways depending on the local demography but also has an effect on adjacent constituencies and on the state as a whole since party leadership resorts to "caste balancing" in which no caste is seen to be "over-represented' state-wise or in a region of the state to keep all segments of the social base of the party happy, while also trying to reach out to new social segments by offering nominations to candidates belonging to them. However, old loyalties and personal connections with Yadav, a veteran grass-roots political activist, also matter.[25]

In the BSP the nomination process is centrally about money and candidates are expected to "buy" their nominations by making contributions to the party, to be paid personally to the leader, Kumari Mayawati. The process begins with potential candidates approaching the district co-ordinators and mandal (covering 2–3 districts) co-ordinators, who are party functionaries, with initial payments for sending their names up to Mayawati. They then have to make direct payments to be considered for the nomination. In addition to money totalling anywhere between Rs 5 million and tens of millions to be paid for a nomination in various ways, including in purchase of campaign materials, as in the case of the SP caste balancing is a factor, and over and beyond this there was an attempt in 2009, beginning earlier in the U.P. assembly election of 2007 which the BSP won, at "social engineering", that is, at constructing a majority by giving nominations to persons from a wide range of castes, principally, upper castes, outside the party's usual social base of the Scheduled Castes.

There were some attempts before 2007 to forge a broader caste base for the BSP. Kanchan Chandra is of the view that the BSP has

[24] Interview with an editor and newspaper proprietor who was a BSP candidate in 2009 and who was earlier an SP member of parliament and knows both parties very well from the inside as a long-time associate of their top leaders, 15 February 2011; he is now again with the SP.

[25] Ibid.

always attempted to forge a broad social coalition and has attempted to reach out to the upper and backward castes since the early 1990s. This was done at first by building an alliance with the SP, BJP, and Congress, and later by appointing upper-caste office bearers and nominating a large number of upper-caste candidates. According to Chandra, though the groups included in the BSP's new social base might be same as the Congress, their terms of mobilisation are very different.[26] While the ticket distribution by the Congress party gave due consideration to caste identity, it did so quietly and kept it insulated from the identification of issues. Groups were targeted through patronage but rarely through the rhetoric of identity. In contrast, the BSP has done this through an open appeal to ethnic identity. While earlier, for the BSP, appeal to ethnic identity was restricted to Dalits, it now included its new social allies.[27]

Scholars like Sudha Pai have argued that failure of the BSP–SP alliance led to a change of strategy by the BSP in which it made a transition from a radical movement to a Dalit-based party with a primary aim of capturing state power.[28] In order to realise this goal, the party followed a strategy of widening its social base by giving tickets to non-Dalits and forming a coalition with the BJP. Though the party managed to broaden its base and increased its tally, by the latter 1990s the BSP had hit a ceiling and was in need of a new strategy to fulfil its goal of forming a government on its own. Pai argues that the BSP did so by keeping its Dalit base intact and seeking support from twice-born castes – Thakurs, Vaishyas, and notably Brahmins. It also avoided bickering over ticket distribution by not contesting a number of by-elections and boycotting local elections in 2006.[29]

Sohini Guha argues that a committed Dalit poor in U.P. is willing to vote for a BSP candidate irrespective of caste as she has

[26] Chandra 2007.

[27] Ibid.

[28] Pai 2009.

[29] Ibid.

faith in the BSP's overall commitment to their long-term socio-economic empowerment.[30] This is what makes them forgo patronage benefits in the short run and facilitates the BSP's nomination of candidates from Upper Castes, OBCs, and Muslims, groups that only vote for the BSP when the party fields a candidate from their own community. For her the BSP has been able to attract multiple social groups within its fold by promising and delivering patronage-based benefits to its non-"bahujan" voters while providing programmatic benefits to its core supporters.[31]

Christophe Jaffrelot carries forward the argument and states that the Dalits tend to vote for the BSP for both substantive and symbolic reasons. According to him, it would be wrong to classify the BSP as a Dalit party only on the basis of the social profile of its candidates. This is so because a large number of BSP candidates are from groups other than Dalits. Dalits vote for the BSP because its leader is a Dalit, but more so because, irrespective of the caste or social profile of its candidates, its agenda is "Pro-Dalit".[32]

From the literature, we can conclude that while there have been earlier attempts at "social engineering" by the BSP, the 2007 election was the first major electoral success of the strategy and it was based on a calculated nomination strategy that took caste into account. Overall, the BSP is the most centralised and top-down of all the parties we look at, with Mayawati tightly controlling the process and intervening at any stage.

Is there any general principle discernible in candidate selection across parties? The general criterion is "merit", a holistic judgement on current victory prospects taking all factors into consideration, and the general rule of thumb is "sitting-getting", in Indian political parlance, that is, incumbents get the nomination unless they are perceived to be no longer likely to win, for example if there are potentially damaging corruption or criminal charges against them, although this does not by itself rule them out.

30 Guha 2007.

31 Ibid.

32 Jaffrelot 2012.

Caste and (religious) community considerations are very important factors and are taken into consideration in assessing current victory prospects but there is no mechanical formula based on caste/community. Past performance, and hence, "sitting-getting", is also not an inviolable principle.

A further complication affecting renomination is the fact of coalition politics in which parties share seats in order to pool votes at the state level against the principal rival party or coalition. This entails not contesting in constituencies allotted by coalition agreement to one's coalition partner, and if such a seat happens to have been contested the last time by one's party, renomination of the candidate, even an incumbent, cannot happen. However, within both the major alliances, the Congress-led United Progressive Alliance (UPA) and the BJP-led National Democratic Alliance, both the number of seats allotted to each partner in a state and the particular seats allotted tend to be fairly rigid and allow of adjustments only within a narrow band.[33] There is no smoothly adjusting electoral market mechanism whereby a party can claim greater support on the basis of intervening assembly elections, for example, which leads to surrender of seats by a partner party. The only way to be able to contest significantly more seats is to break the coalition deal and go it alone, for example, as the Congress did in U.P. and Bihar in 2009. Therefore, while coalitional seat-sharing has some effect on renomination, it has only a rather limited effect.

Three Hypotheses on Party Type, Internal Processes, and Nominations

Before we present the Indian nomination data, we construct three hypotheses from our reviews of the comparative and Indian

[33] Interviews with party insiders in the Congress, BJP, SP, and BSP involved in the nomination process, including two current and two former Central ministers in both the Congress and the BJP, and with Prakash Karat, General Secretary of the CPI (M), 29 October 2012.

literature on party nominations, and from the interview material, against which we will later examine the nomination patterns. We will examine the following three hypotheses:

1. Early/snap elections, as in 1980, 1991, 1998, and 1999, or emergency/crisis elections as after Indira Gandhi's assassination in 1984, will result in high rate of renomination of incumbents and nominees because the MPs will not have finished even the major part of their terms and it will be more difficult for party leaderships, particularly if relatively new, to deny them nominations.
2. Ethnic (that is, caste- and/or religion-based) and ideological parties have a more loyal and committed, even if smaller, voter base, and therefore the leaderships of such parties have more leeway to drop incumbents without losing the support of their voters since such support is not for particular candidates representing particular interest groups. Catchall parties, on the other hand, depend on group representation and patronage for retaining their support base and hence should find it more difficult to drop incumbents.
3. Parties with institutionalised internal processes for nomination starting from below will find it more difficult to drop incumbents compared to parties with centralised, top-down selection processes. In the Indian context, parties that are most centralised by Bille's sixfold classification of centralised control of nominations, such as the BSP and SP, will find it easier to drop incumbents than more institutionalised parties which are at the second level of centralisation like the Congress, BJP and CPI (M).

The Nomination Data on Five Major Indian Parties

We consider the nomination of candidates for five major parties, the BJP, CPI (M), BSP, and SP, for the part of their existence that is relevant to such analysis, that is, when they are significant national parties or leading parties in their states. For the Congress, we consider the nomination data for the entire post-Independence period, focusing on renominations in each election compared to the previous election from the second general elections of 1957 until 2009; for the BJP, from the time of its emergence as a significant party, that is renominations from 1991 to 2009, and likewise for the CPI (M) which emerged as a regionally significant party from 1967, that is renominations from 1971 onwards. We consider CPI (M) only in its three stronghold states of West Bengal, Kerala, and Tripura. For the SP and the BSP, we focus on the 2004 and 2009 elections only for the state of U.P., for the period of their emergence as the two leading parties in the largest state, U.P., and with significance in national politics – their external support to the UPA-I government was crucial in not making the Left Front's support pivotal for its survival.

A point to note is that there was a delimitation of constituencies before the 2009 election. We consider, for the purposes of this paper, the same constituency to mean constituencies which retained the same name. This is a proxy for the boundaries having changed only a little. In India, 101 constituencies (19 per cent of constituencies) changed from 2004 to 2009 according to our definition of name change, that is, 101 constituencies (19 per cent of constituencies) in 2009 were not matched by any constituency of the same name in 2004. For the state of U.P., 11 out of 80 constituencies underwent a name change. As part of the delimitation process a small percentage of constituencies were unreserved or reserved for Scheduled Castes and Scheduled Tribes, which would have additionally affected renominations.

Congress

Taking the entire 1957–2009 period for the Congress (Table 1), the party has nominated 38 per cent (2611/6801) of its candi-

Table 1: INC, 1957–2009

Indicators	*1957*	*1962*	*1967*	*1971*	*1977*	*1980*
Renominated (by same party)/ nominated in previous election	174/ 479 (36%)	178/ 490 (36%)	144/ 488 (30%)	149/ 516 (29%)	221/ 441 (50%)	155/ 492 (32%)
Renominated (by same party) in same constituency/nominated in previous election	82/ 479 (17%)	108/ 490 (22%)	117/ 488 (24%)	142/ 516 (28%)	186/ 441 (42%)	139/ 492 (28%)
Renominated (by same party) in different constituency/ nominated in previous election	92/ 479 (19%)	70/490 (14%)	27/ 488 (6%)	7/516 (1%)	35/ 441 (8%)	16/ 492 (3%)
Renominated by different party/ nominated in previous election	7/479 (2%)	10/490 (2%)	12/ 488 (3%)	33/ 516 (6%)	13/ 441 (3%)	57/ 492 (12%)
Incumbents renominated/winners in previous election	168/ 364 (46%)	163/ 371 (44%)	129/ 361 (36%)	137/ 283 (48%)	215/ 352 (61%)	76/ 154 (49%)
Incumbents renominated in same constituency/winners in previous election	80/ 364 (22%)	102/ 371 (28%)	107/ 361 (30%)	132/ 283 (47%)	183/ 352 (53%)	68/ 154 (44%)
Renominated (by same party)/ contestants in the current election	174/ 490 (36%)	178/ 488 (37%)	144/ 516 (28%)	149/ 441 (34%)	221/ 492 (45%)	155/ 492 (32%)
Renominated (by same party) in same constituency/contestants in the current election	82/ 490 (17%)	108/ 488 (22%)	117/ 516 (23%)	142/ 441 (32%)	186/ 492 (38%)	139/ 492 (28%)
Incumbents renominated/ contestants in the current election	168/ 490 (34%)	163/ 488 (33%)	129/ 516 (25%)	137/ 441 (31%)	215/ 492 (44%)	76/ 492 (15%)
Incumbents renominated in same constituency/contestants in the current election	80/ 490 (17%)	102/ 488 (21%)	107/ 516 (21%)	132/ 441 (30%)	183/ 492 (37%)	68/ 492 (14%)

Table 6.1 (*Contd.*)

Table 1 (*Contd.*)

1984	*1989*	*1991*	*1996*	*1998*	*1999*	*2004*	*2009*	*Grand total*
218/492 (44%)	302/517 (58%)	253/510 (50%)	189/500 (38%)	158/529 (30%)	184/477 (39%)	137/453 (30%)	149/417 (36%)	2611/6801 (38%)
209/492 (42%)	297/517 (57%)	241/510 (47%)	181/500 (36%)	145/529 (27%)	164/477 (34%)	127/453 (28%)	112/417 (27%)	2250/6801 (33%)
9/492 (2%)	5/517 (1%)	12/510 (2%)	8/500 (2%)	13/529 (3%)	20/477 (4%)	10/453 (2%)	37/417 (9%)	361/6801 (5%)
11/492 (2%)	10/517 (2%)	11/510 (2%)	34/500 (7%)	25/529 (5%)	19/477 (4%)	14/453 (3%)	5/417 (1%)	256/6801 (4%)
208/353 (59%)	282/414 (68%)	159/244 (65%)	159/244 (65%)	98/140 (70%)	109/141 (77%)	73/114 (64%)	103/145 (71%)	2079/3680 (57%)
202/353 (58%)	278/414 (67%)	159/244 (65%)	156/244 (64%)	96/140 (69%)	102/141 (72%)	68/114 (60%)	81/145 (56%)	1814/3680 (49%)
218/517 (42%)	302/510 (59%)	253/500 (51%)	189/529 (36%)	158/477 (33%)	184/453 (41%)	137/417 (33%)	149/440 (34%)	2611/6762 (39%)
209/517 (40%)	297/510 (58%)	241/500 (48%)	181/529 (34%)	145/477 (30%)	164/453 (36%)	127/417 (31%)	112/440 (25%)	2250/6762 (33%)
208/517 (40%)	282/510 (55%)	159/500 (32%)	159/529 (30%)	98/477 (21%)	109/453 (24%)	73/417 (18%)	103/440 (23%)	2079/6762 (31%)
202/517 (39%)	278/510 (55%)	159/500 (32%)	156/529 (29%)	96/477 (20%)	102/453 (23%)	68/417 (16%)	81/440 (18%)	1814/6752 (27%)

Source: ECI Statistical Reports on General Elections 1952–2009.

dates of the preceding election. Looking at the data for the Congress from 1957–2009, we also conclude that the party has renominated a majority of its incumbents, hence largely adhering to the "sitting-getting" thumb rule, the total percentage of winners getting renominated being 57 per cent (2079/3680). However, what needs to be explained is the substantial 43 per cent of incumbents who were not renominated. This is too high to be explained by the triple factors of death, defection to another party, or retirement from politics from one election to the next. It clearly shows that the party nomination process drops incumbents and brings in fresh blood to a considerable extent.

In 1989 Congress was faced with a united opposition and a house divided, Rajiv Gandhi being weakened by the Bofors arms imports payoff allegations. Hence, the party repeated 68 per cent of its incumbents. From then on the party chose to repeat 65 per cent, 65 per cent, 70 per cent, and 77 per cent of the winning candidates in 1991, 1996, 1998, and 1999, respectively, climbing to historical highs by the end of the 1990s. This could be because of the two elections taking place in quick succession (1991 after 1989, and 1999 and 1998 soon after 1996) and the party going ahead with the incumbents rather than scouting around for fresh faces and risking dissidence within its ranks in the wake of three lost elections (1989, 1996, and 1998) which saw the party plunge to historic lows. In 2004 and 2009 the party repeated 64 per cent (73/114) and 71 per cent (103/145) of incumbents, respectively.

Comparing the data for the Congress between the time period 1952–2009 and 1991–2009 (Table 2) we see no significant difference in the percentage of contestants of previous elections getting renominated. What is interesting is the rise in number of incumbents getting renominated. For the two time periods 1957–2009 and 1991–2009, the respective percentages are 57 per cent and 68 per cent. What perhaps explains this is the decline in Congress fortunes in the early 1990s and the party finding it increasingly difficult to win elections and therefore relying on the incumbents.

Table 2. INC Aggregate 1952–2009 and 1991–2009

Indicators	*INC (1957–2009)*	*INC (1991–2009)*
Renominated (by same party)/ nominated in previous election	2611/6801 (38%)	1070/2886 (37%)
Renominated (by same party) in same constituency/nominated in previous election	2250/6801 (33%)	970/2886 (34%)
Renominated (by same party) in different constituency/nominated in previous election	361/6801 (5%)	100/2886 (4%)
Renominated by different party/ nominated in previous election	256/6801 (4%)	108/2886 (4%)
Incumbents renominated/winners in previous election	2079/3680 (57%)	701/1028 (68%)
Incumbents renominated in same constituency/winners in previous election	1814/3680 (49%)	662/1028 (64%)
Renominated (by same party)/ contestants in the current election	2611/6762 (39%)	1070/2816 (38%)
Renominated (by same party) in same constituency/contestants in the current election	2250/6762 (33%)	970/2816 (34%)
Incumbents renominated/contestants in the current election	2079/6762 (31%)	701/2816 (25%)
Incumbents renominated in same constituency/contestants in the current election	1814/6762 (27%)	662/2816 (24%)

Source: ECI Statistical Reports on General Elections 1952–2009.

Bharatiya Janata Party

The BJP renominated a substantial minority (43 per cent) of its candidates and a great majority (76 per cent) of its incumbents in elections from 1991 to 2009. In the elections held in 1991, 1998, and 1999 in particular, the BJP renominated a large number of incumbents (Table 3). Elections in 1991, 1998, and 1999 were close

Table 3. BJP (1991–2009)

Indicators	*1991*	*1996*	*1998*	*1999*	*2004*	*2009*	*Grand total*
Renominated (by same party)/ nominated in previous election	111/225 (49%)	144/468 (31%)	193/471 (41%)	223/388 (58%)	172/339 (47%)	125/364 (34%)	968/2255 (43%)
Renominated (by same party) in same constituency/ nominated in previous election	96/225 (43%)	136/468 (28%)	188/471 (40%)	212/388 (55%)	168/339 (50%)	86/364 (24%)	886/2255 (39%)
Renominated (by same party) in different constituency/ nominated in previous election	5/225 (2%)	8/468 (2%)	5/471 (1%)	11/388 (3%)	4/339 (1%)	39/364 (11%)	72/2255 (3%)
Renominated by different party/ nominated in previous election	2/225 (1%)	3/468 (1%)	6/471 (1%)	4/388 (1%)	11/339 (3%)	13/364 (4%)	39/2255 (2%)
Renominated in the same party (winning)/ nominated in previous election	68/85 (80%)	76/120 (63%)	143/161 (88%)	160/182 (84%)	139/182 (74%)	69/138 (38%)	655/868 (76%)
Renominated by same party in same constituency (winning)/ nominated in previous election	66/85 (78%)	75/120 (63%)	141/161 (88%)	153/182 (84%)	135/182 (74%)	52/138 (38%)	622/868 (72%)
Renominated (by same party)/ contestants in the current election	111/468 (24%)	144/471 (31%)	193/388 (50%)	223/339 (66%)	172/364 (47%)	125/433 (29%)	968/2463 (39%)
Renominated (by same party) in same constituency/ contestants in the current election	96/468 (21%)	136/471 (29%)	188/388 (49%)	212/339 (63%)	168/364 (46%)	86/433 (20%)	886//2463 (36%)
Renominated in same party (winning)/contestants in the current election	68/468 (15%)	75/471 (16%)	143/388 (37%)	160/339 (47%)	139/364 (38%)	69/433 (16%)	655//2463 (27%)

Table 3 (*Contd.*)

Table 3 (*Contd.*)

Indicators	*1991*	*1996*	*1998*	*1999*	*2004*	*2009*	*Grand total*
Renominated by same party in same constituency (winning)/ contestants in the current election	66/468 (14%)	75/471 (16%)	141/388 (36%)	153/339 (45%)	135/364 (37%)	52/433 (12%)	622//2463 (25%)

Source: ECI Statistical Reports on General Elections 1991–2009.

elections with very little gap between the successive elections in 1989 and 1991, 1996 and 1998, 1998 and 1999. Hence, it would have made sense for the party to avoid new faces and internal dissidence and continue with the incumbents. Current victory prospects of candidates were important criteria here and the underlying principle was "sitting-getting". However, what needs to be explained is the 24 per cent of incumbents who were not renominated over 1991–2009. This figure is too high to be explained by death, defection, or retirement from active politics from election to election. The BJP like the Congress drops incumbents and brings in fresh faces. A point to be kept in mind is that after 1996 the BJP was attempting to expand beyond its traditional upper-caste and urban voter base through what it called social engineering which implied bringing in nominees from newer segments of society.

Communist Party of India (Marxist)

Looking at the data for CPI (M) for the period 1971–2009 (Table 4), we discern that the CPI (M) is the only party which has consistently renominated a very high percentage of former candidates across parties, higher than the other parties. The party renominated a majority of its former candidates, 56 per cent (252/455), unlike the Congress and BJP, in the elections held from

Table 4. CPI (M) (1971–2009)

Indicators	*1971*	*1977*	*1980*	*1984*	*1989*
Renominated (by same party)/nominated in previous election	16/27 (59%)	19/51 (37%)	16/31 (52%)	29/41 (71%)	18/43 (42%)
Renominated (by same party) in same constituency/nominated in previous election	14/27 (52%)	16/51 (31%)	13/31 (42%)	26/41 (63%)	17/43 (40%)
Renominated (by same party) in different constituency/ nominated in previous election	2/27 (7%)	3/51 (6%)	1/31 (3%)	3/41 (7%)	1/43 (2%)
Renominated by different party/nominated in previous election	0/27 (0%)	0/51 (0%)	0/31 (0%)	0/41 (0%)	0/43 (0%)
Incumbents renominated/ winners in previous election	9/14 (64%)	16/24 (67%)	14/17 (82%)	27/37 (73%)	15/21 (71%)
Incumbents renominated in same constituency/winners in previous election	7/14 (50%)	13/24 (54%)	12/17 (71%)	24/37 (65%)	0/21 0
Renominated (by same party)/contestants in the current election	16/51 (31%)	19/31 (61%)	16/41 (39%)	29/43 (67%)	18/43 (42%)
Renominated (by same party) in same constituency/contestants in the current election	14/51 (28%)	16/31 (52%)	13/41 (32%)	26/43 (61%)	17/43 (40%)
Incumbents renominated/ contestants in the current election	9/51 (18%)	16/31 (52%)	14/41 (34%)	27/43 (63%)	15/43 (35%)
Incumbents renominated in same constituency/contestants in the current election	7/51 14%)	13/31 (42%)	12/41 (29%)	24/43 (56%)	0/43 (0%)

Table 4 (*Contd.*)

Table 4 (*Contd.*)

1991	*1996*	*1998*	*1999*	*2004*	*2009*	*Grand total*
29/43 (67%)	24/41 (59%)	25/42 (60%)	28/43 (65%)	27/46 (59%)	21/47 (45%)	252/ 455 (56%)
28/43 (65%)	22/41 (54%)	25/42 (60%)	28/43 (65%)	27/46 (59%)	19/47 (40%)	235/ 455 (52%)
0/43 (0%)	0/41 (0%)	0/42 (0%)	0/43 (0%)	0/46 (0%)	2/47 (4%)	12/455 (3%)
0/43 (0%)	0/41 (0%)	0/42 (0%)	0/43 (0%)	1/46 (2%)	0/47 (0%)	1/455 (2%)
24/29 (83%)	22/30 (73%)	23/30 (77%)	27/32 (84%)	25/31 (81%)	21/40 (53%)	221/ 305 (73%)
24/29 (83%)	22/30 (73%)	23/30 (77%)	27/32 (84%)	25/31 (81%)	19/40 (48%)	196/ 305 (64%)
29/41 (71%)	24/42 (57%)	25/43 (58%)	28/46 (61%)	27/47 (57%)	21/48 (44%)	252/ 476 (53%)
28/41 (68%)	22/42 (52%)	25/43 (58%)	28/46 (61%)	27/47 (57%)	19/48 (40%)	235/ 476 (49%)
24/41 (59%)	22/42 (52%)	23/43 (53%)	27/46 (59%)	25/47 (53%)	21/48 (44%)	221/ 476 (46%)
24/41 (59%)	22/42 (52%)	23/43 (53%)	27/46 (59%)	25/47 (53%)	19/48 (40%)	196/ 476 (41%)

Source: ECI Statistical Reports on General Elections 1967–2009.

1971. There has been only one instance, in 2004, where a former CPI (M) candidate has defected and contested on a different party ticket. The CPI (M) has renominated a large majority, 73 per cent (221/305), of its incumbents since 1971. These findings probably reflect the fact that the party has contested seats mostly from its three stronghold states of West Bengal, Kerala and Tripura, where it has either been in power for very long periods (West Bengal, 1977–2011, Tripura, 1993–2013) or alternated in power every term (Kerala since 1982). It would seem to make sense, in this context, to allow politicians the continuity to build political careers and also become the identifiable face of the party for the voters in the constituency.

Comparative Picture for the Congress, BJP, and CPI (M) in the post-Congress Hegemony Phase 1991–2009

The 1989 election marked the end of Congress hegemony in that the Congress plurality of votes no longer converted to a majority of seats, and since then all elections have resulted in hung parliaments and minority governments or coalition governments. Hence, it is useful to compare the three major national parties, Congress, BJP, and CPI (M) on renomination of candidates and incumbents since the 1991 election, the first after the 1989 watershed. We focus on the renomination of former candidates and of incumbents to see if any patterns are discernible and then try to explain those patterns. The patterns that emerge are as follows (from Table 5) for the Congress, BJP, and CPI (M) for the period 1991–2009.

Of the candidates nominated over the years 1991–2009, only the CPI (M) renominated a majority (59 per cent or 154/262) of its former candidates, the BJP 43 per cent (968/2255), and the Congress 37 per cent (1070/2886). The difference between the BJP and the Congress is marginal, primarily due to the decline in BJP fortunes in 2004 and 2009.

Table 5. Overall record for the Congress, BJP and CPI (M), 1991–2009

Indicators	*INC*	*BJP*	*CPM*
Renominated (by same party) nominated in previous election	1070/2886 (37%)	968/2255 (43%)	154/262 (59%)
Renominated (by same party) in same constituency/ nominated in previous election	970/2886 (34%)	886/2255 (39%)	149/262 (57%)
Renominated (by same in different constituency/ nominated in previous election	100/2886 (4%)	72/2255 (3%)	2/262 (1%)
Renominated by different party/ nominated in previous election	108/2886 (4%)	39/2255 (3%)	1/262 (0.4%)
Incumbents renominated/winners in previous election	701/1028 (68%)	655/868 (76%)	142/292 (74%)
Incumbents renominated in same constituency/ winners in previous election	662/1028 (64%)	622/868 (72%)	140/192 (73%)
Renominated (by same party)/contestants in the current election	1070/2816 (38%)	968/2463 (39%)	154/267 (58%)
Renominated (by same party) in same constituency/contestants in the current election	970/2816 (34%)	886/2463 (36%)	149/267 (56%)
Incumbents renominated/ contestants in the current election	701/2816 (25%)	655/2463 (27%)	142/267 (53%)
Incumbents renominated in same constituency/contestants in the current election	662/2816 (24%)	62/2463 (25%)	140/267 (52%)

Source: ECI Statistical Reports on General Elections 1989–2009.

Analysing the fate of the incumbents between 1991 and 2009, and hence the prevalence of the "sitting-getting" thumb rule or otherwise, we find that all three parties renominated a majority of their incumbents. The BJP renominated 76 per cent (655/868) of its incumbents, the CPI (M) 74 per cent (142/ 192) and the Congress 68 per cent (701/1028).

Viewing the renominations across parties from the perspective of the percentage of renominees in the total number of candidates nominated in a given election, we get the following picture. With the exception of the CPI (M) in several elections, and a few elections for other parties (Congress in 1989, BJP in 1999), only a minority of candidates in any election were candidates in the previous election, a result which holds even more strongly for incumbents (rows 7 and 9 for candidates and incumbents, respectively, in the tables).

Comparative Picture of the Five Parties Over the Last Two Elections 2004 and 2009

Comparing the five major parties that we analyse in the paper in the 2004 and 2009 elections can potentially yield useful insights into party behaviour on nominations. Comparing Congress, BJP, CPI (M), SP, and BSP for the years 2004 and 2009 (Tables 6 and 7 for the BSP and SP specifically, and Table 8 comparing all five parties) we discover the following patterns.

The Congress party renominated only 33 per cent (286/870) of its former candidates. For the BJP the figure was 42 per cent (297/703), for the CPI (M) 52 per cent (48/93) and for the SP and BSP, a relatively low 30 per cent (46/152) and very low 16 per cent (26/165), respectively. Clearly, with the exception of the CPI (M), the "sitting-getting" rule does not apply to candidates, least of all to the BSP and SP, in the last two elections.

Defections and nominations by other parties were much higher in the case of the SP in particular. As an indicator of politicians defecting to other parties before elections in search of nomination,

Table 6. BSP (2004–2009)

Indicators	*2004*	*2009*	Grand total
Renominated (by same party) nominated in previous election	14/85 (17%)	13/80 (16%)	27/165 (16%)
Renominated (by same party) in same constituency/ nominated in previous election	13/85 (15%)	8/80 (10%)	21/165 (13%)
Renominated (by same party) in different constituency/ nominated in previous election	1/85 (1%)	5/80 (6%)	6/165 (4%)
Renominated by different party/ nominated in previous election	3/85 (4%)	3/80 (4%)	6/165 (4%)
Incumbents renominated/ winners in previous election	6/14 (43%)	9/19 (47%)	15/33 (46%)
Incumbents renominated in same constituency/winners in previous election	6/14 (43%)	4/19 (21%)	10/33 (30%)
Renominated (by same party)/ contestants in the current election	14/80 (18%)	13/80 (16%)	27/160 (17%)
Renominated (by same party) in same constituency/ contestants in the current election	13/80 (16%)	8/80 (10%)	21/160 (13%)
Incumbents renominated/ contestants in the current election	6/80 (8%)	9/80 (11%)	15/160 (9%)
Incumbents renominated in same constituency/contestants in the current election	6/80 (8%)	4/80 (5%)	10/160 (6%)

Source: ECI Statistical Reports on General Elections 1999–2009.

Table 7. SP (2004–2009)

Indicators	*2004*	*2009*	*Grand total*
Renominated (by same party)/ nominated in previous election	28/84 (33%)	18/68 (27%)	46/152 (30%)
Renominated (by same party) in same constituency/nominated in previous election	28/84 (33%)	10/68 (15%)	38/152 (25%)
Renominated (by same party) in different constituency/nominated in previous election	0/84 (0)	8/68 (12%)	8/152 (5%)
Renominated by different party/ nominated in previous election	6/84 (7%)	10/68 (15%)	16/152 (11%)
Incumbents renominated/winners in previous election	15/26 (58%)	15/35 (43%)	30/61 (50%)
Incumbents renominated in same constituency/winners in previous election	15/26 (58%)	8/35 (23%)	23/61 (38%)
Renominated (by same party)/ contestants in the current election	28/68 (41%)	18/75 (24%)	46/143 (32%)
Renominated (by same party) in same constituency/contestants in the current election	28/68 (41%)	10/75 (13%)	38/143 (27%
Incumbents renominated/contestants in the current election	15/68 (22%)	15/75 (20%)	30/143 (21%)
Incumbents renominated in same constituency/contestants in the current election	15/68 (22%)	8/75 (11%)	23/143 (16%)

Source: ECI Statistical Reports on General Elections 1999–2009.

11 per cent (16/152) of SP candidates were nominated by some other party, and likewise 4 per cent (6/165) BSP candidates, 2 per cent Congress (19/870), 3 per cent (24/703) BJP candidates, and 1 per cent CPM (1/93). The SP's and BSP's former candidates for the years 2004 and 2009 nominated by other parties were in the SP's case, the BSP (11) and Congress (3), BJP (1), National Labour Party (1) and the BSP's case, the SP (2), Shiromani Akali Dal (1) and BJP (3).

Table 8: Aggregate for Congress, BJP, CPI (M), SP, and BSP 2004–2009

Indicators	*INC*	*BJP*	*CPM*	*SP*	*BSP*
Renominated (by same party)/nominated in previous election	286/870 (33%)	297/703 (42%)	48/93 (52%)	46/152 (30%)	27/165 (16%)
Renominated (by same party) in same constituency/ nominated in previous election	239/870 (28%)	254/703 (36%)	46/93 (50%)	38/152 (25%)	21/165 (13%)
Renominated (by same party) in different constituency/ nominated in previous election	47/870 (5%)	43/703 (6%)	2/93 (2%)	8/152 (5%)	6/165 (4%)
Renominated by different Party/ nominated in previous election	19/870 (2%)	24/703 (3%)	1/93 (1%)	16/152 (11%)	6/165 (4%)
Incumbents renominated/winners in previous election	180/259 (70%)	208/320 (65%)	46/71 (65%)	30/61 (49%)	15/33 (46%)
Incumbents renominated in same constituency/ winners in previous election	149/259 (58%)	187/320 (58%)	44/71 (62%)	23/61 (38%)	10/33 (30%)
Renominated (by same party)/ contestants in the current election	286/857 (33%)	297/797 (37%)	48/95 (51%)	46/143 (32%)	27/160 (17%)
Renominated (by same party) in same constituency/ contestants in the current election	239/857 (28%)	254/797 (32%)	46/95 (48%)	38/143 (27%)	21/160 (13%)
Incumbents renominated/ contestants in the current election	180/857 (21%)	208/797 (26%)	46/95 (48%)	30/143 (21%)	15/160 (9%)
Incumbents renominated in same constituency/contestants in the current election	149/857 (17%)	187/797 (24%)	44/95 (46%)	23/143 (16%)	10/160 (6%)

Renominations from the Same Constituencies and by the Same Parties?

Two other important findings from all the tables above, taken together, are as follows.

All parties, when they renominate either candidates or incumbents, tend to renominate them overwhelmingly from the same constituency (rows 2, 3, and 5 of the tables contain information on this). The only exception seems to be 2009 because the delimitation of constituencies, mentioned earlier, necessitated a certain degree of renomination from new constituencies, that is, those whose names were changed. Likewise, only a small percentage of politicians defected to and obtained nominations from other parties (row 4 of tables).

Renomination of Former Candidates and Incumbents

In conclusion, does the "sitting-getting" rule of thumb for candidate and incumbent renomination apply in general?

For candidates, the pattern is as follows. Overall, with the exception of the CPI (M) which renominated 56 per cent of candidates since 1971, the "sitting- getting" rule of thumb does not apply to any party except for occasional years when over 50 per cent were renominated (only 1989 for the Congress since 1957, and 1999 for the BJP since 1991). For the BSP the renomination rate was as low as 17 per cent. However, a substantial minority of candidates, on average, were renominated for the Congress (38 per cent), BJP (43 per cent) and SP (30 per cent) for the relevant periods, indicating that while the rule of thumb might be a starting point in the internal process, particularly for parties with institutionalised internal processes that start from the bottom, the actual criteria are the candidate's current victory prospects, and that applying this criterion the majority of losing former candidates tend to get eliminated at some stage in the internal processes described in the literature review.

For incumbents, the pattern is as follows. Overall, the Congress renominated 57 per cent of its incumbents over the 1957–2009 period, the post-Congress hegemony period of 1991–2009 seeing a rise to 68 per cent. In contrast, it renominated only a minority of incumbents in the first four elections in our dataset, 1957–71, falling to a low of 36 per cent in 1967. After 1977, it fell below 50 per cent only in 1980 (49 per cent). The BJP renominated a high overall 76 per cent of incumbents in the 1991–2009 period, the CPI (M) 73 per cent over 1971–2009, the SP 49 per cent, and the BSP 46 per cent over 2004–9. Clearly, the "sitting-getting" rule of thumb applies to nomination of incumbents, or at the very least is the starting point for the internal processes of parties, particularly for those that have relatively institutionalised selection processes that start from the bottom. However, since the percentage of incumbents dropped is also very considerable, and for the BSP and SP a majority, as was the case for the Congress up to 1971, the internal processes of parties also weed out incumbents for varying reasons including most probably, from interview material, because of the incumbent's current victory prospects look poor, and to accommodate new faces sometimes representing new sections of the electorate the parties want to woo.

How Do the Three Hypotheses Fare?

How do these patterns relate to our three hypotheses on party type, early/snap elections, institutionalisation of selection processes, and nominations?

The hypothesis about early/snap elections tending towards higher repetition of incumbents finds the following degree of support. There were five early elections, 1971, 1980, 1991, 1998, and 1999. The hypothesis gets support as far as the BJP is concerned in that its renomination of incumbents in the last three early elections (80 per cent, 89 per cent, and 88 per cent) is higher than its overall for the period (76 per cent). The hypothesis also gets support, although less strongly, for the CPI (M), whose renomination of incumbents in the last four early elections (82 per cent, 83 per cent, 77 per cent, 84 per cent) was above its overall for the period (73 per cent). The picture for the Congress is more mixed. The first two early elections were after the 1969 and 1978 splits in the Congress, which were also reflected in the lower than overall rate of renominations of candidates, as a significant number of former candidates and incumbents went to the breakaway factions or the Janata Party, respectively, after 1969 and 1977 and 1978. The rates of renomination in 1991, 1998, and 1999 (65 per cent, 70 per cent, and 77 per cent) were higher, however, than the overall 57 per cent for the entire period, and in the last two early elections higher than the 68 per cent overall figure for the post-1989 period. The post-assassination election of 1984 also saw a higher renomination percentage than all but one election until then, perhaps a new leader (Rajiv Gandhi) coming to power less than two months before the election not having the time or inclination to make changes in what was to an extent a plebiscitary election. Conversely, we might add, a weakened leadership in 1989, due to the Bofors allegations, also might have been constrained to renominate a large percentage of incumbents.

The hypothesis of ethnic or ideological parties that can take their voter base more or less for granted and hence being more autonomous in dropping candidates, finds support in the relatively low renomination rates for both incumbents and candidates by the caste- and community-based BSP and SP compared to the Congress, BJP, and CPI (M). However, if one looks at the ideological parties like the CPI (M) and BJP we find a relatively high rate of renomination of incumbents. For both, the relative stability of their core voter base has to be balanced against the more institutionalised process of selection that both parties have. Also, party leaderships, even if more autonomous due to assured core voters based on ideology and not on interest group representation and patronage, might not be inclined to drop their incumbents if they calculate that they are likely winners. For the BJP, we have to factor in the fact that of the six elections since 1991, three were early elections. Also, for the BJP we need to factor in the fact that in the post-1989 period, particularly after 1996, it was in the process of becoming a more catchall party that was consciously expanding beyond its traditional core voter base of the urban, upper castes, and middle classes.

Constituency instability in nominations, and other-party acceptance of defectors, are fairly low, indicated by nominations by the same party from another constituency, and other-party nominations of a particular party's candidate, both being under 5 per cent for the overall period of most parties. However, the ideological parties, BJP and CPI (M), show the least degree of defection or shuffling of constituencies. The larger point that emerges about relationship of incumbents to constituents is that there is a fairly strong relationship that is reflected in the low rate of reshuffling of constituencies in renominations.

The hypothesis of parties with more institutionalised and bottom-up internal processes for candidate selection finding it more difficult to drop incumbents finds support. The Congress, BJP, and especially CPI (M) have a significantly higher rate of renomination of incumbents, majorities in each case, compared to the BSP and SP which have dropped the majority of their incumbents in each of the two elections since they emerged as significant parties. However, this has also to be viewed against the background of party strategy in each of these elections. The BSP and SP have both attempted to broaden their base and incorporate new segments of the electorate in their stronghold state of U.P. over this period. This implies including members of such segments as candidates in at least some constituencies. In practice, this means reaching out to caste groups that would normally be outside the party's fold or making a catchall pitch that would attract votes. Outreach to new caste groups has been termed "social engineering" by the BJP and has been attempted by the BSP and SP. Such outreach dictates accommodative politics to newly mobilised groups or groups traditionally with other parties, which means giving them representation in nominations, which could also imply dropping incumbents in a large percentage of constituencies to include candidates who represent groups that are being wooed. The leadership of ideological or ethnic parties could, if they were so inclined, deny nomination to incumbents and former candidates without losing the support of their core voters. The larger point that comes out from the data and interviews about the relationship of candidates to party hierarchies (leaderships) is that the major Indian parties are leadership-dominated and find it possible to drop the majority of candidates of the past election.

Conclusion

This paper is a first cut at the relationship between incumbency, renomination, and internal processes in some major Indian parties. It is based on trying to relate the renomination data to three hypotheses related to election timing, party type, and internal processes based on the existing comparative and Indian party nomination literature and interview material. We have demonstrated support for the "sitting-getting" rule for incumbent renomination, though not for candidate renomination, and predominant support for the two hypotheses on early elections, and on institutionalised internal selection processes, tending to result in higher rates of repetition of incumbents, while yielding mixed support for the hypothesis that ethnic and ideological parties with assured voter bases can more easily drop incumbents. More definitive conclusions will require detailed interview material on nomination strategy for each election, something that is not possible given that some of the key players are no more, and even those that are still with us will not be able to recall the precise details of much earlier elections, even of the 1990s. However, a potentially fruitful direction for additional work is state-level patterns of renomination for both Lok Sabha and assembly elections, particularly for the past decade for which key actors might remember procedural details.

Acknowledgements

The anonymous referees and Carole Spary are thanked by the authors for their comments. The anonymous interviewees, who include two Central ministers and a former Central minister and chief minister, and leading party functionaries of the different parties, involved in the nomination process are also thanked. The support of the Center for the Advanced Study of India, University of Pennsylvania, at whose conference in Philadelphia in February 2011 an earlier version of this paper was presented is acknowledged.

Bibliography

Aldrich, J.W., *Why Parties? The Origin and Transformation of Political Parties in America* (Chicago: University of Chicago Press,1995).

Bille, L., "Democratizing a Democratic Procedure: Myth or Reality?", *Party Politics*, 7 (3), 2001, 363–80.

Chandra, K., "A Benign Rupture in UP Politics", *Indian Express*, 2007, retrieved 10 September 2013 from http://www.indianexpress.com/news/a-benign-rupture-in-uttar-pradesh/ 30668/0.

Cross, W., "Democratic Norms and Party Candidate Selection: Taking Contextual Factors into Account", *Party Politics*, 14 (5), 2008, 596–619.

Epstein, L.D., *Political Parties in the American Mold* (Madison: University of Wisconsin Press, 1986).

Guha, S. "'Asymmetric Representation' and the BSP in UP", *India Seminar*, 2007, retrieved 10 September 2013, from http://www.india-seminar.com/2007/571/571_sohini_guha.htm.

Gunther, R., and L. Diamond, "Types and Functions of Parties", in L. Diamond and R. Gunther, eds, *Political Parties and Democracy* (Baltimore: Johns Hopkins University Press, 2001), 3–39.

Hopkin, J., "Bringing the Members Back In? Democratizing Candidate Selection in Britain and Spain", *Party Politics*, 7 (3), 2001, 343–61.

Jaffrelot, C., "The Caste-based Mosaic of Indian Politics", *India Seminar*, 2012, retrieved 10 September 2013 from http://www.india-seminar.com/2012/633/633_christophe_jaffrelot.htm.

Katz, R. S., and P. Mair, "Changing Models of Party Organization and Party Democracy", *Party Politics*, 1 (1), 1995, 5–28.

Kirchheimer, O., "The Transformation of Western European Party Systems", in J. La Palombara and M. Weiner, eds, *Political Parties and Political Development* (Princeton: Princeton University Press, 1966), 177–200.

Kochanek, S.A., *The Congress Party of India: The Dynamics of One-party Democracy* (Princeton: Princeton University Press, 1968), 267–98.

LeDuc, L., "Democratizing Party Leadership Selection", *Party Politics*, 7 (3), 2001, 323–41.

Lijphart, A., *Democracy in Plural Societies: A Comparative Exploration* (New Haven: Yale University Press, 1977).

Narain, I., and M. Lal, "Election Politics in India: Notes Toward an Empirical Theory", *Asian Survey*, 9 (3), March 1969, 202–20.

Pai, S., "New Social Engineering Agenda of the Bahujan Samaj Party: Implications for State and National Politics", *South Asia: Journal of South Asian Studies*, 32 (3), 2009, 338–53.

Palmer, N.D., "India's Fourth General Election", *Asian Survey*, 7 (5), 275–91, May 1967, 280.

Panebianco, A., *Political Parties: Organization and Power* (Cambridge: Cambridge University Press, 1988).

Rahat, G., and R.Y. Hazan, "Candidate Selection Methods: An Analytical Framework", *Party Politics*, 7 (3), 2001, 297–322.

Roy, R., "Selection of Congress Candidates – I: The Formal Criteria", *Economic and Political Weekly*, 31 December 1966, 1 (20), 833–40.

Roy, R., "Selection of Congress Candidates II: Pressures and Counter-pressures", *Economic and Political Weekly*, 2 (1), 7 January 1967a, 17–24.

Roy, R., "Selection of Congress Candidates III: Claims and Counter-claims", *Economic and Political Weekly*, 2 (2), 14 January1967b, 61–76.

Sridharan, E., and A. Varshney, "Toward Moderate Pluralism: Political Parties in India", in L. Diamond and R. Gunther, eds, *Political Parties and Democracy* (Baltimore: Johns Hopkins University Press, 2001), 206–37.

7

Coalition Strategies and the BJP's Expansion, 1989–2004

Introduction

In this paper I attempt to analyse the expansion of the Bharatiya Janata Party (BJP) across states from 1989 to 2004 by coalition-building in India's federal parliamentary democracy with its single-member district, simple plurality (SMSP) electoral system. However, before the state-wise analysis it is necessary to outline the BJP's meteoric rise and geographical expansion from 1989 to 2004. In 1989 the BJP won 86 seats (out of 543 in the Lok Sabha or Lower House of parliament), up from two seats in 1984, and 11 per cent of the vote in an electoral alliance with the Janata Dal (JD)-led National Front (NF). Its vote share jumped to 20 per cent in 1991, taking it to 120 seats and second-party status, and in 1996 with the same vote share it jumped to 161 seats and first-party status. In 1998, it came to power leading a large, pre- and post-electoral coalition, with 25 per cent of the vote and 182 seats, repeating this feat with the same National Democratic Alliance (NDA) coalition of 24, mainly single state-based, small parties in 1999, getting 24 per cent of the vote and 182 seats again. From 1998 to 2004, it was in power nationally, leading a coalition, and this facilitated its coalition-making in the states because it was in a position to offer ministerial positions in the central (i.e. federal) government to potential regional party allies. This was perceived to be the case before the 2004 election too; all the opinion polls forecast an NDA victory of varying magnitude. It has also, from 1998 to 2004, been in a "dominant" position in that no other party, not even the second-ranking Congress, has been in a position to be the nucleus of an alternative coalition since it lacked the numbers and was the direct competitor of most other parties in their stronghold states.

The BJP, which in 1989 was a party whose influence was restricted to North India, spread geographically to the states of the west, south, and east, becoming one of the two leading parties for Lok Sabha elections in Gujarat, Maharashtra, Goa, Karnataka, and Assam, and able to win seats in coalition with other parties in Orissa, Andhra Pradesh (AP), West Bengal and Tamil Nadu.

The evolution of the party system in a way that permits the strategic exploitation of coalition opportunities is a major factor, I argue, in the BJP's expansion, in addition to the appeal of its Hindu nationalist ideology. The 1989–2004 period saw six parliamentary elections resulting in no single party getting a majority, that is, the emergence and ongoing evolution of a complex multi-party system in a federal polity, following the end of Congress party dominance. The increasingly multi-party character of the party system since 1989 is illustrated by the fact that the values of the Laakso–Taagepera index (N) (of the effective number of parties) by votes/seats were 4.80/4.35, 5.10/ 3.70, 7.11/5.83, 6.91/5.28, 6.74/5.87 and 7.6/6.5 in 1989, 1991, 1996, 1998, 1999, and 2004 respectively, whereas before 1989 the effective number of parties by seats exceeded three only once (3.16 in 1967) and the effective number of parties by votes exceeded five only once (5.19 in 1967).[1] I look at the BJP's coalition strategies in the post-1989 period within states for state and national elections, and across

[1] For the Laakso–Taagepera indices of the effective number of parties see *Journal of the Indian School of Political Economy*, XV/1–2 (Jan.–June 2003), Statistical Supplement, Tables 1.1–1.13, 293–30; for 2004, the index was calculated by the Centre for the Study of Developing Societies, New Delhi.

states for the national elections, and review the experience against the hypothesis put forward in the following section.

In that section, I derive from the literature on coalition politics a hypothesis about the BJP's strategy for expansion across states in a federal, parliamentary, SMSP (first past the post) system. In the section after that, I track coalition strategies in the expansion of the BJP across states since 1989. The final section concludes by comparing the findings with the hypothesis.

Perceived Pivotality and India's Federal, Parliamentary, SMSP System

In this section, I derive a hypothesis about the BJP's expansion strategy in India's federal, parliamentary, SMSP polity, post-1989. Following Laver and Schofield, there are two broad traditions of coalition studies – the game theoretic, formal rational choice tradition, and the "European politics" tradition of empirical studies of coalition politics informed by "empirical attempts to fit the experience of European coalition government to an inductive theory" from cross-country comparisons.[2] I broadly agree with the critique of game theoretic approaches as excessively schematic and parsimonious, missing out on vital details and the complexities of particular cases.[3] My approach is a soft rational choice approach that takes the deductive conclusions of game theoretic approaches as roughly indicative and assesses them against the realities of coalition politics in particular party systems.

The comparative and theoretical literature on coalitions has focused on post-election coalition formation, neglecting electoral coalitions.[4] Part of the reason for this is that coalition govern-

[2] See Laver and Schofield, *Multiparty Government*, for an account of the two traditions and page 8 for the quotation.

[3] Ibid., 14–35, 195–215.

[4] Note the relative absence of electoral coalitions in comprehensive works like ibid.; Budge and Keman, *Parties and Democracy;* and Dodd, *Coalitions in Parliamentary Government.*

ments are commonest in the proportional representation (PR) and mixed electoral systems of Europe and relatively rare in SMSP systems. In PR systems there is little incentive for electoral coalitions since small parties can get more or less proportionately represented in the legislature above a certain vote share, particularly in systems which have large district magnitudes and more proportional electoral formulae. In addition, post-election coalition formations can be modelled more easily since the numbers of seats of the various political parties are known unlike in the formation of electoral coalitions.

However, in SMSP (and some other systems like the Irish single transferable vote or Australian alternative vote) it has been recognised that there are strong incentives for electoral coalitions.[5] This is because in single-member districts a plurality of the vote is necessary for victory. This makes it imperative to aggregate votes to attain at least a plurality at the constituency level. Parties have an incentive to cast their net wide to try to encompass most sections of the electorate and also to form electoral coalitions with as many compatible parties as possible to aggregate votes. Electoral coalitions are formed by agreeing to share the seats contested by the coalescing parties in some ratio, so as to pool votes because a small addition of votes can hugely increase or alternatively decimate a party or coalition in terms of seats. What is relevant for my purpose is that in SMSP electoral systems, particularly for parties that cannot win on their own, there is a *strong incentive to add on coalition partners before elections under conditions of uncertainty about which party will win how many seats.* This is particularly so at the federal level where partners may be spatially compatible in that they do not contest in the same states, as in the Indian case where most of the smaller parties have a base only in one state. There is also an incentive to retain them in governments formed for long-term electoral prospects. These conclusions follow if one looks at the long-term electoral strategies of parties, extending

[5] Laver and Schofield, *Multiparty Government*, 25–6, 204–6.

coalition theory to "party competition as a whole, looking at the impact of elections on the politics of coalition and on future elections, as well as at the impact of the politics of coalitions on elections and future government formations."[6] Thus the SMSP system would tend to give incentives to politicians to form ideologically indiscriminate electoral coalitions, or even "seat adjustments", which are only partial, not true, coalitions in which parties contest each other in same constituencies while putting up common candidates in others.[7]

At the state level, too, there are strong incentives to form coalitions. In federal, parliamentary SMSP systems, national, i.e. substantially multi-state parties, which hope to form the government at the national level (henceforth centre, for India) but which have strong bases only in some states, would have an incentive to form coalitions with smaller parties which have bases in states where the major party is weak.[8] If the national party is a significant third party in a particular state its perceived pivotality for victory can make it – usually within the limits of ideological and programmatic compatibility but not always constrained by such limits – an attractive coalition partner to the first or second parties. This can enable it to leverage its pivotal character to strike coalition agreements in which it contests, and has a chance of winning, more seats than it would on its own. If this coalition strategy succeeds it can emerge progressively stronger in successive elections even in its weak states, thereby achieving expansion across states.

Thus, from the above theorising, the hypothesis about the coalition strategy for expansion of the BJP from 1989 to 2004 in India's federal, parliamentary, SMSP system that I will examine the validity of is: a multi-state but regionally concentrated party

[6] Laver, *Private Desires, Political Action,* 137.

[7] Sridharan, "Principles, Power and Coalition Politics in India", 280–1; Laver and Schofield, *Multiparty Government*, 25–6, 204–6.

[8] A national party in India is a party that has been recognised as a state party in four or more states by minimum seat and/or vote criteria.

like the BJP can *leverage expected vote shares in states where it is perceived to be a significant third party with a potentially "bridging" vote share*, i.e. its perceived pivotality for electoral victory helps it to form electoral coalitions with the first or second parties in the state in which it is allocated more seats to contest than in the previous election. This would be the path to incremental horizontal expansion across state boundaries in successive Lok Sabha and state assembly elections.

Before I proceed to analyse the BJP's expansion, an outline of the evolution of the party system and the nature of governments at the centre is necessary. While the Congress ruled from independence to 1989, except for 1977–9, based on winning a majority of seats with only a plurality of votes due to the fragmentation of the non-Congress votes, the party system at the state level was gradually bipolarised from 1967 onwards in more and more states. This was due to the bipolarising logic of Duverger's law extending from the constituency level to the state level. However, this process did not result in the same two parties in every state. What emerged were multiple bipolarities over 1967–89, that is, with different pairs of parties or coalitions in many or most states, which added up to a very fragmented and multi-party system nationally.[9] This is the case in the Indian party system. While most states have bipolar (two-party, two-coalition, or one party versus a coalition) party systems, the national party system, especially since 1996, is highly fragmented. The typical pattern of competition at the state level is bipolar with a small third party often present, which in Punjab, Haryana, and many states of the south and east was the BJP in the 1989–2004 period.

Coalition politics at the state level takes place against the backdrop of the power structure at the centre. For governments at the centre in a federal, parliamentary, SMSP system there would be an

[9] See Sridharan, "The Fragmentation of the Indian Party System", 475–503, for an account of the process of state-level bipolarisation and national-level fragmentation of the Indian party system.

incentive, under conditions of highly fragmented national party systems, to form surplus majority coalitions unlike the expectation of minimal winning coalitions of power maximisation theories of coalition formation.[10] Surplus majority coalitions take into the government parties not essential to a legislative majority.[11] This can be a political insurance policy so as to reduce the pivotal power

[10] There are two broad classes of theory relevant for our purposes. The first are power maximisation, and the second are policy-based theories of coalition formation and behaviour. Power maximisation theories, also called size principle theories, stress the maximisation of payoffs as the key factor in coalition formation, ignoring ideological and policy affinities, while policy-based theories consider such affinities vital. Power maximisation theories, accordingly, predict minimal winning coalitions, defined as a coalition in which each party is indispensable to the coalition's winning a simple majority of seats, because in such coalitions each coalition member's share of the payoff is maximised. Empirical evidence tends to support policy-based theories, and hence the importance of compatibility for coalition formation, and longevity. For power maximisation theories, see, for example, Riker, *The Theory of Political Coalitions*; Gamson, "A Theory of Coalition Formation", 373–82; and Dodd, *Coalitions in Parliamentary Government.* For policy-based theories, see for example, Axelrod, *Conflict of Interest*, and de Swaan, *Coalition Theories and Cabinet Formation.* For a critique of power maximisation theories, see Luebbert, "Coalition Theory and Government Formation in Multi-Party Democracies", 241. For more recent comprehensive comparative analyses of coalitions, see Laver and Schofield, *Multiparty Government*, and Budge and Keman, *Parties and Democracy.*

[11] Two types of non-minimal winning solutions to minority situations (in which no single party gets a majority) have been common – minority governments and surplus majority coalitions. Power maximisation theories treat these as deviations but once policy affinities are taken into account as central in coalition formation, and once parties' coalition strategies are conceived of in long-term electoral maximisation terms and not treated as episodic, these become explicable. 37 per cent of governments in minority situations in Europe during 1945–87 have been minority governments (including minority coalitions), and 24 per cent have been surplus majority coalitions, together exceeding the 39 per cent of minimal winning coalitions. See Laver and Schofield, *Multiparty Government*, 70–1, Tables 4.2 and 4.3, for the frequency of occurrence of minority and surplus majority coalitions.

of smaller parties, as in certain coalitions where parties to the left and right of the dominant coalition partner are kept on board for this reason.[12]

Surplus majority coalitions are also common in "dominated" party systems, that is, in party systems in which party leaders assume that no coalition is possible without a particular large party.[13] This indispensable "dominant" party then has an incentive to add coalition partners to protect itself against the threat of withdrawal of support. I would add that smaller parties would find that the only way to get a share of power is to coalesce with this "dominant" party, setting aside ideological differences. In a federal system in which this "dominant" party may not be a threat in a smaller party's state, the incentive is reinforced.

The NDA government of 1999–2004 was, for the first time at the centre, a surplus majority coalition in which there were redundant partners, so that the coalition would not lose its majority by the withdrawal of support by the largest partner party of the BJP, the Telugu Desam Party (TDP) (which opted out of participation in the government). This surplus majority character of the coalition, combined with the spatial compatibility of its partners, most having clearly demarcated state strongholds not overlapping with others, gave the NDA and its leading party, the BJP, an extraordinary stability despite being a 24-party coalition. It also gave the BJP exceptional bargaining power with actual and potential allies. Thus, an additional strategy that could be employed by the BJP during 1998–2004, was a coalition with state parties that offered them a share of ministerial positions at the centre in a would-be national coalition government led by the national party in return for seat-sharing arrangements for parliamentary seats from their stronghold states, in a context in which the leading national parties are expected to form coalition governments at the centre.

[12] Ibid., 82.

[13] Luebbert, *Comparative Democracy*, 72–80.

With these shifts in the party system and power structure at the centre as the backdrop we turn to a state-wise analysis of the BJP's expansion.

Leveraging Expected Vote Share? The BJP's Horizontal Expansion Across States Since 1989

In this section I trace the expansion of the BJP within north India in 1989–91, and its horizontal expansion from its stronghold states in the north to other states in the peninsula and east up to 2004, using pre-election coalitions both in Lok Sabha and state assembly elections. I cover the ten states of Maharashtra, Haryana, Punjab, Bihar, Orissa, West Bengal, Assam, Andhra Pradesh, Karnataka, and Tamil Nadu, all cases of the BJP's strategy for expansion using coalitions with varying degrees of success. I proceed state-wise and chronologically, zig-zagging between Lok Sabha and assembly elections for each state, looking at whether the deals struck on contesting seats enabled progressive expansion (see the state-wise tables for this zig-zag progress of coalitions in terms of seats contested, seats won and vote share, the coalescing or 'seat-adjusting" parties boxed in bold).

Uttar Pradesh, Rajasthan, Madhya Pradesh, and Gujarat

The BJP, which with its predecessor the Bharatiya Jana Sangh (BJS), had never exceeded 10 per cent of the vote or 35 seats nationally, except for 1977 when as a component of the Janata Party it won 99 of 295 seats won by the Janata Party, experienced a meteoric rise in seats from two in 1984 (7.4 per cent of votes) to 86 (out of 226 contested, 11 per cent of votes) in 1989. This was due to a combination of three factors – seat adjustments with the JD resulting in one-on-one contests against the Congress in most of the seats it contested in Uttar Pradesh (UP), Delhi, Rajasthan, Gujarat, Himachal Pradesh (HP) and Madhya Pradesh (MP), a sizeable swing in its favour with a regional concentration of this increase, and a greater number of seats contested.

What happened in the November 1989 Lok Sabha elections and February 1990 state assembly elections is of vital importance to the rise of the BJP and the JD (and the Left parties) and for the subsequent pattern of coalition politics.[14] While the BJP and the Left were not a part of the JD–TDP–DMK (Dravida Munnetra Kazhagam)–AGP (Asom Gana Parishad)–Congress (Socialist) NF coalition, seat adjustments between the JD and the BJP in north India and Gujarat and between the JD and the Left in Orissa were crucial for victory.

Seat adjustments, defined as agreements among parties to put up a common candidate and not compete with each other, along with an anti-incumbency wave, created an unfavourable situation for the Congress throughout the north, akin to 1977. The JD managed to negotiate as many as 184 out of a possible 205 seat adjustments with the BJP, particularly in U.P., Bihar, Haryana, Himachal Pradesh, M.P., Rajasthan and Gujarat.[15] Fickett defined (restrictively) an effective JD seat adjustment as an electoral contest in which the candidates of the two top parties, the JD and the Congress, polled 80 per cent or more of votes cast, no major opposition party contested and the JD candidate won. The JD had 89 effective seat adjustments or almost two-thirds of the 142 seats it won.[16] Of these 89, 25 were in U.P., 20 in Bihar, 11 in Gujarat, 6 in Haryana, 10 in Rajasthan, 2 in M.P., 3 in Maharashtra (all with the BJP), and 11 in Orissa (with the Left).

The BJP benefited as much or more from seat adjustments with the JD. Defining an effective BJP seat adjustment as an electoral

[14] See Heath, "Anatomy of BJP's Rise to Power", 2511–17, for a detailed analysis of the geographical spread of the BJP in the 1990s.

[15] Fickett, "The Janata Dal in the Ninth Indian General Election", 85.

[16] Ibid.

contest in which the candidates of the two top parties, the BJP and the Congress, polled 80 per cent or more of votes cast, no major opposition party contested and the BJP candidate won, the BJP had 55 effective seat adjustments accounting for more than 60 per cent of the 86 seats won.[17] The state-wise pattern was: 22 in MP, 11 in Rajasthan, 12 in Gujarat, 5 in Maharashtra, 4 in Delhi, and 1 in Bihar.

However, three points are worth noting. First, as Gould and Brass have separately pointed out, apart from seat adjustments there was a huge anti-incumbency wave that hurt the Congress, leading to a Congress defeat in many constituencies in which there were three- and four-cornered contests.[18] Second, Gould's and Brass' figures showing that the opposition parties did even better in the unadjusted seats could well reflect the fact that these were the pockets of overwhelming strength for either the JD or the BJP anyway, in which they did not need adjustments to win, adjustments being made in only those seats where there was a felt need by both parties.

Third, specific to the BJP and contrary to Brass's assessment of the greater importance of adjustments to the BJP in U.P., the BJP seems to have been less dependent on adjustments overall despite Fickett's figure of 55 of 86 seats won being due to adjustments. If one examines Fickett's breakdown of these seats state-wise, one notes that 37 of the 55 effective seat adjustments were in states (other than UP) where the BJP has had a strong independent base dating back to 1967 at least that was not dependent on the JD or its predecessors, that is, M.P., Rajasthan, Delhi. If one adds Gujarat to this list then 49 of 55 adjusted seats won were in BJP stronghold states. This would appear to indicate that the BJP was either overwhelmingly the senior partner in these adjustments or substantially independent of the JD contra the U.P. case as per Brass's data. The BJP has attempted to use coalitions or seat adjustments

[17] Ibid.

[18] Gould, "Patterns of Political Mobilization", 20; Brass, "Caste, Class and Community", 109–11.

to expand its base in 14 states for both Lok Sabha and assembly elections after 1989. In the February 1990 state assembly elections in Rajasthan, M.P., Himachal Pradesh and Gujarat, the BJP won a resounding victory in Himachal Pradesh with the BJP winning an absolute majority. In M.P., Rajasthan and Gujarat, the BJP won an absolute majority in MP, 85 of 200 seats in Rajasthan and 66 seats in Gujarat compared to 70 for the JD, in less tidy adjustments, much less complete than in the Lok Sabha elections. In old strongholds, Himachal Pradesh and M.P., the BJP formed single-party majority governments; in Rajasthan and Gujarat it formed coalition governments with the JD, with the chief ministership in the latter going to the JD. However, after the rupture between the BJP and the JD in November 1990, the BJP went its own way and has competed on its own against the Congress in these states since then. Thus, the BJP came to form state governments on its own for the first time ever in 1990, arriving as both a national and state-level political force, whereas earlier it had been a sub-state force.

From the above, we can conclude that the BJP was very successful in leveraging its pivotal status in electoral coalitions, hugely expanding its presence in these states.

Maharashtra

The BJP–Shiv Sena alliance has remained stable since the assembly elections of 1990 (Table 1).[19] The pattern has been one of a trade-off of Lok Sabha seats for assembly seats with the Shiv Sena contesting more assembly seats than the BJP and vice versa for Lok Sabha seats, complemented by a shared Hindu nationalist ideology. The BJP and Shiv Sena also ran a coalition government

[19] For election analyses of Maharashtra, see Katzenstein, *et al.*, "The Rebirth of the Shiv Sena", 257–86; Banerjee, "The Politics of Resentment", 233–48; Banerjee, "The 12th Lok Sabha Election"; Palshikar and Birmal, "Maharashtra: Fragmented Marathas Retain Power", 206–32; Palshikar and Deshpande, "Electoral Competition", 2409–22; CSDS Team and Palshikar, "'Split Factor' Decides the Outcome", 43–6.

Table 1. Elections in Maharashtra

		Lok Sabha				*Assembly*			
State	*Year*	*Party*	*Contested*	*Won*	*Vote %*	*Party*	*Contested*	*Won*	*Vote %*
Maharashtra	1989	INC	48	28	45.4				
		BJP	33	10	23.7				
		SS	3	1	1.2				
		JD- LED FRONT	50	6	18.1				
	1990					INC	276	141	38.2
						BJP	104	42	10.7
						SS	183	52	15.9
						JD- LED FRONT	301	38	17.2
	1991	INC	48	37	48.4				
		BJP	31	5	20.2				
		SS	17	4	9.4				
	1995					INC	286	80	31
						BJP	116	65	12.8
						SS	169	73	16.4
						IND	3196	45	26.7
						JD- LED FRONT	237	17	8.2
	1996	INC	48	15	34.8				
		BJP	25	18	21.8				
		SS	20	15	16.8				
		JD- LED FRONT	37	0	12.6				
	1998	INC	41	33	43.6				
		Minor Parties	7	4	6.7				
		BJP	25	4	22.5				
		SS	22	6	19.7				

Table 1 (*Contd.*)

Table 1 (*Contd.*)

State	Year	Lok Sabha Party	Contested	Won	Vote %	Assembly Party	Contested	Won	Vote %
	1999	INC	42	10	29.7	INC	249	75	27.2
		Minor Parties	6	1	3.5	Minor Parties	44	4	2.6
		NCP	38	6	21.6	NCP	223	58	22.6
		NCP Allies	15	3	4.4	NCP Allies	104	11	4.5
		BJP	26	13	21.2	BJP	117	56	14.5
		SS	22	15	16.9	SS	161	69	17.3
	2004	INC	26	13	23.8	INC	157	69	21.1
		CONG Allies	22	10	21	CONG Allies	8	6	1.3
		BJP	26	13	22.6	BJP	111	54	13.7
		SS	22	12	20.1	SS	163	62	20.0
						Others	14	3	1.5

Notes: 1. Electoral coalitions boxed in bold. Some coalitions are only partial seat adjustments.
2. The tables may not add up to 100% votes since some very small parties/independents not shown. Small parties clubbed as Others or Minor Parties.
3. INC ¼ Indian National Congress; BJP ¼ Bharatiya Janata Party; SS ¼ Shiv Sena; NCP ¼ Nationalist Congress Party; Other acronyms stand for minor parties.

Sources: See Journal of the Indian School of Political Economy, XV/1–2 (Jan–June 2003), Statistical Supplement, and the Election Commission of India website http://eci.gov.in/database_fs.htm; Press reports on coalitions"

from 1995–9 with the Sena as the senior partner. However, the balance has been shifting in favour of the Shiv Sena for Lok Sabha and BJP for assembly elections, especially since it has become clear since 1996 that in a situation in which neither major national party, the Congress, or the BJP could form a government on its own at the centre, regional parties both need to have and can have a substantial contingent in the Lok Sabha. The BJP's share of Lok Sabha seats contested has declined from 1991 to 2004, while it has been able to increase its share of assembly seats contested slightly, lower in 2004 than in 1999 but still higher than in 1990, while increasing its assembly vote share from 67 per cent to

83 per cent of the Sena's vote up to 1999, dropping again in 2004. The BJP and the Shiv Sena have both leveraged their status of being electorally pivotal for the other in state assembly and Lok Sabha elections, respectively.

Haryana

In Haryana (Table 2) the BJP has attempted to use coalitions to expand for both Lok Sabha and assembly elections.[20] In 1989, the BJP–JD 2–8 seat adjustment yielded 6 seats (39 per cent votes) for the JD and none (8.3 per cent votes) for the BJP. Contesting alone in the 1991 parliamentary and assembly elections the BJP improved its vote share to 10.2 per cent and 9.4 per cent respectively, but won no Lok Sabha seats and only 2 of 89 contested assembly seats. Subsequently, in the 1996 Lok Sabha and assembly elections the BJP leveraged this position with the Haryana Vikas Party (HVP) led by ex-Congressman Bansi Lal, to contest the Lok Sabha, BJP–HVP 6–4, and the assembly BJP–HVP 25 – 65, a classic trade-off of Lok Sabha for assembly seats between a national and a state party. It won 4 Lok Sabha (19.4 per cent votes) and 11 assembly seats (8.9 per cent votes) enabling a coalition government in Haryana in which it was a junior partner, an instance of incremental growth through coalitions. However, in the quick-succession Lok Sabha elections of 1998 and 1999, the BJP switched from the HVP as an ally to the INLD, as the alliance with the former did not yield results. The BJP–HVP contested 6–4 in 1998 and won only 1 seat each (BJP votes 18.9 per cent). The fall of the HVP state government due to the BJP switching support to the INLD took place before the 1999 elections and after the INLD came aboard the BJP-led coalition

[20] For Haryana elections in recent years, see Singh, "Social Cleavages and Political Alignments", 351–66; and Yadav and Heath, "A Split Verdict in Haryana", 49 – 51; for Punjab, see Kumar, "Electoral Politics in Punjab", 367–90, and "Punjab: Changing Political Agenda", 28–308.

Table 2. Elections in Haryana

State	Year	Lok Sabha Party	Contested	Won	Vote %	Assembly Party	Contested	Won	Vote %
Haryana	1989	INC	10	4	46.2				
		BJP	**2**	**0**	**8.3**				
		JD	**8**	**6**	**38.9**				
	1991	INC	10	9	37.2	INC	90	51	33.8
		BJP	10	0	10.2	BJP	89	2	9.4
		Others	11	1	17.8	Others	112	16	19.3
		SJP	10	0	25.4	SJP	88	16	22.0
	1996	INC	10	2	22.6	INC	90	9	20.8
		BJP	**6**	**4**	**19.4**	**BJP**	**25**	**11**	**8.9**
		HVP	**4**	**3**	**15.2**	**HVP**	**65**	**33**	**22.7**
		Others	24	0	27.9	Others	218	27	29.2
	1998	INC	10	3	26.0				
		BJP	**6**	**1**	**18.9**				
		HVP	**4**	**1**	**11.6**				
		Others	15	5	38.9				
	1999	INC	10	0	34.9				
		BJP	**5**	**5**	**29.2**				
		INLD	**5**	**5**	**28.7**				
		Others	5	0	4.7				
	2000					INC	90	21	31.2
						BJP	**29**	**6**	**8.9**
						INLD	**61**	**47**	**29.2**
						Others	165	3	11.4
	2004	INC	10	9	42.1				
		BJP	10	1	17.2				
		INLD	10	0	22.4				
		HVP	9	0	6.3				

Notes: 1. Electoral coalitions boxed in bold. Some coalitions are only partial seat adjustments.

2. The tables may not add up to 100% votes since some very small parties/independents not shown. Small parties clubbed as Others or Minor Parties.

3. INC = Indian National Congress; BJP = Bharatiya Janata Party; INLD = Indian National Lok Dal formerly HLD (R); HVP = Haryana Vikas Party; Other acronyms stand for minor parties.

Sources: As Table 1.

at the centre in March 1998. Subsequently, the BJP had to yield some ground, contesting the 1999 elections 5 – 5 with the INLD, which they won 5 – 5 with the BJP getting 29.2 per cent votes. In the 2000 state assembly elections, the BJP leveraged this to increase its share of seats contested to 29 – 61. However, it won only 6 seats with 8.9 per cent votes while the INLD got a majority on its own, winning 47 seats with 29.2 per cent votes, the alliance ensuring that it defeated the Congress despite the latter's higher 31.2 per cent votes. In 2004, the BJP went alone out of overconfidence and won only 1 out of 10 seats with 17.2 per cent votes. Haryana is, thus, a case of BJP growth since 1989 through shifting alliances with state parties on the basis, so far, of the BJP contesting a majority or at least half the Lok Sabha seats and an increasing minority of assembly seats but without notable success in expanding its seat and vote position in the latter contests.

Punjab

In Punjab (Table 3), the demographics of the state, with a small Sikh majority and a large Hindu minority concentrated in urban areas, make it imperative for the Sikh party, the Shiromani Akali Dal (SAD), to seek an alliance with a non-Congress party for the Hindu vote, to enable it to defeat the Congress. This has traditionally been either the BJP or its predecessor, the Jana Sangh, or the Left parties and, in the 1990s, the Bahujan Samaj Party (BSP). The BJP contested 9 of 13 Lok Sabha and 67 of 126 assembly seats in the low-turnout 1992 elections boycotted by the mainstream SAD. It won no parliamentary seats and only 6 assembly seats with 17 per cent votes in each. Subsequently, it contested the 1996 Lok Sabha elections alone, while the SAD allied with the BSP, 9 – 4 to win 8 – 3, the BJP winning no seats and getting only 6.5 per cent votes. In a shift of strategy by both the SAD and the BJP they contested the 1997 assembly elections as allies, contesting 92 – 22 out of 126 and winning 75 – 18 based on 38 per cent

Table 3. Elections in Punjab

State	Year	Lok Sabha Party	Contested	Won	Vote %	Assembly Party	Contested	Won	Vote %
Punjab	1989	INC	12	2	23.8				
		BJP	3	0	4.1				
		Others	11	1	11.3				
		SAD (M)	8	6	29.2				
	1992	INC	13	12	49.3	INC	115	87	43.7
		BJP	9	0	16.9	BJP	67	6	16.6
		Others	8	0	\6.8	Others	142	14	22.3
		SAD (M)	3	0	2.6	SAD	58	3	5.2
	1996	INC	13	2	35.1				
		BJP	6	0	6.5				
		SAD	**9**	**8**	**28.7**				
		BSP	**4**	**3**	**9.4**				
	1997					**INC**	**105**	**14**	**26.6**
						CPI	**15**	**2**	**3.0**
						BJP	**22**	**18**	**8.3**
						SAD	**92**	**75**	**37.6**
	1998	**INC**	**8**	**0**	**25.9**				
		Minor Parties	**5**	**0**	**16.1**				
		JD	**1**	**1**	**4.2**				
		BJP	**3**	**3**	**11.7**				
		SAD	**8**	**8**	**32.9**				
	1999	**INC**	**11**	**8**	**38.4**				
		Left	**2**	**1**	**5.9**				
		BJP	**3**	**1**	**9.2**				
		SAD	**9**	**2**	**28.6**				
		DBSM	**1**	**0**	**2.7**				
	2002					**INC**	**106**	**62**	**36.5**
						CPI	**11**	**2**	**2.2**
						BJP	**24**	**3**	**5.7**
						SAD	**90**	**41**	**30.5**
						DBS	**7**	**0**	**0.0**
	2004	**INC**	**11**	**2**	**34.2**				
		Left	**2**	**0**	**4.4**				
		BJP	**3**	**3**	**10.5**				
		SAD	**10**	**8**	**34.3**				

Notes: 1. Electoral coalitions boxed in bold. Some coalitions are only partial seat adjustments.
2. The tables may not add up to 100% votes since some very small parties/independents not shown. Small parties clubbed as Others or Minor Parties.
3. INC Indian National Congress; BJP Bharatiya Janata Party; SAD Shiromani Akali Dal; Other acronyms stand for minor parties.

Sources: As Table 1.

and 8 per cent of the vote. The SAD won a majority on its own but formed a surplus majority coalition with the BJP, lasting a full term. The alliance remained stable in the 1998 and 1999 Lok Sabha elections, with the SAD being part of the BJP-led coalition at the centre, and in the 2002 assembly elections. In 2002, it contested 90 – 24 with the SAD, marginally better than the terms of 1997, but slumped to 3 seats and 5.7 per cent votes in a defeat for the alliance. In the 2004 Lok Sabha elections the SAD–BJP combine contested all 11 seats, the BJP winning all 3 contested. The BJP has not been able to increase significantly the share of seats contested or votes. Punjab has been a case of attempting to leverage a pivotal third-party position without much success, playing the junior partner in both Lok Sabha and assembly alliances. This has been partly due to the greater incentive the SAD have in sending as large a contingent to parliament as possible, post-1998, and partly due to the limitations of the state's Hindu-minority demographics.

Bihar

Bihar is a state where the BJP grew successfully through coalitions up to 2000 to attain a dominant position in Lok Sabha elections and a strong challenger position in coalition in the assembly (Table 4).[21] As a result of the 1989 seat adjustments the BJP won 8 out of 24 contested seats, getting 12 per cent votes. Contesting largely alone in the assembly elections in 1990 it won 39 seats with 12 per cent votes. Contesting alone again it found it could not improve its position in the 1991 Lok Sabha and 1995 assembly elections. As a result of allying with the Samata Party,

[21] For election analyses of Bihar, see Prasad, "Bihar Elections 1999–2000", 332 – 50, and "Split the Votes" 129–58; Ojha and Kazmi, "Bi-polar Competition", 311–31; Kumar, "The Return of the RJD", 27–30, and "New Phase in Backward Caste Politics in Bihar", 2472–80; and CSDS Team, "Sharp Polarisation in Bihar", 36–8.

Table 4. Elections in Bihar

State	Year	Lok Sabha Party	Contested	Won	Vote %	Assembly Party	Contested	Won	Vote %
Bihar	1989	INC	54	4	28.1				
		BJP	24	8	11.7				
		JD	38	31	37.7				
		Others	24	8	12.5				
	1990					INC	323	71	24.7
						BJP	237	39	11.6
						JD	276	122	25.7
						Others	277	49	12.6
	1991	INC	52	1	24.2				
		BJP	51	5	15.9				
		JD-led Front	53	46	47.6				
	1995					INC	320	29	16.3
						BJP	315	41	13.0
						SAP	310	7	7.1
						JD	265	167	28.0
						CPI	61	26	5.8
						Others	424	33	9.7
	1996	INC	54	2	13.0				
		BJP	32	18	20.5				
		SAP	20	6	14.5				
		Others	71	26	40.0				
	1998	INC	21	5	7.4				
		RJD	37	17	26.3				
		Minor Parties	13	1	14.7				
		BJP	31	19	23.5				
		SAP	21	10	16.0				
		Others	53	1	12.8				
	1999	INC	16	4	8.8				
		RJD	36	7	28.3				
		CPM	2	1	1				
		BJP	29	23	23				
		JD(U)	23	18	20.8				
		Others	25	0	7.4				

Table 4 (*Contd.*)

Table 4 (*Contd.*)

		Lok Sabha				Assembly			
State	*Year*	*Party*	*Contested*	*Won*	*Vote %*	*Party*	*Contested*	*Won*	*Vote %*
	2000					RJD	292	124	28.2
						CPM	22	2	0.9
						BJP	167	66	14.5
						JD(U)	87	21	6.5
						SAP	120	34	8.8
						INC	319	24	11.1
						Others	592	28	11.4
	2004	INC	4	3	4.5				
		RJD	26	22	30.7				
		Minor Parties	9	4	9.2				
		BJP	16	5	14.6				
		JD(U)	24	6	22.4				

Notes: 1. Electoral coalitions boxed in bold. Some coalitions are only partial seat adjustments.
2. The tables may not add up to 100% votes since some very small parties/independents not shown. Small parties clubbed as Others or Minor Parties.
3. INC Indian National Congress; BJP Bharatiya Janata Party; JD Janata Dal; RJD Rashtriya Janata Dal; SAP Samata Party; JD(U) JD (United); Other acronyms stand for minor parties.

a breakaway faction of the JD, on a 32 – 20 basis it won 18 – 6 in 1996, its vote jumping to 20.5 per cent. The Samata remained its ally in 1998, contesting 31 – 21 that year, winning 19 – 10, and contesting 29 – 23 in 1999 (then called Janata Dal (United) or JD(U) due to a merger with another JD offshoot), winning 23 – 18, with 23 per cent votes for the BJP each time. In the 2000 assembly elections, the contested seats ratio was BJP–Samata–JD(U) (the latter two separated) 167 – 120 – 87 winning 66 – 34 – 21, with 15 per cent of votes going to the BJP. In the 2004 Lok Sabha elections in truncated (north) Bihar, the JD(U)–BJP contested 24 – 16, the latter slipping to junior partner status and losing to the RJD–Congress alliance, while losing to the Congress-led alliance in the new Jharkhand state (south Bihar) despite its single largest party status in votes, due to going it alone. The BJP–JD(U) alliance is one in which the BJP remained the senior partner for both Lok Sabha and assembly elections up to 2000 in united Bihar but remained critically dependent on the Samata and later Samata–JD(U) for their vote share. This is reflected in the growing share of the Samata even in Lok Sabha seat-sharing arrangements.

Orissa

Orissa is another clear case of growth through leveraging electorally pivotal status in coalitions both for Lok Sabha and assembly seats (Table 5).[22] The BJP contested elections without success until it formed a pre-election coalition with the Biju Janata Dal, the main state-level JD splinter group, in 1998, sharing the 21 Lok Sabha seats BJD–BJP 12 – 9 and winning them 9 – 7, its votes jumping to 21.2 per cent from 13.4 per cent in 1996, 7.9 per cent in the 1995 assembly elections, 9.5 per cent in 1991, 3.6 per cent in the 1990 assembly elections and 1.3 per cent in 1989. Thus it leveraged both its autonomous growth to a potentially "bridging" vote position in the state, and its potential ruling party status nationally, to strike a junior partner deal with the BJD for both levels of elections. In 1999, the BJD–BJP contested 12 – 9, winning 10 – 9, with the BJP getting 25 per cent of the votes. The same 4:3 ratio was maintained in the 2000 assembly elections at 84 – 62 despite the BJP getting 90 per cent of the BJD's number of seats in 1999, winning 68 – 38 with the BJP getting 18 per cent votes. In 2004, the BJD–BJP alliance maintained the same ratio of seats contested in both the Lok Sabha and assembly elections, winning both with the BJD emerging as the senior partner in both. Thus, the alliance has helped the BJP grow in seats and vote share for both Lok Sabha and assembly elections but has not yet helped it outgrow its junior partner status.

[22] For election analyses of Orissa, see Heath, "An Unequal Alliance in Orissa", 52–3; CSDS Team, "One-sided Contest", 44; and Roy, "Orissa: The Fall of the Congress Bastion", 235–64.

Table 5. Elections in Orissa

		Lok Sabha				Assembly			
State	*Year*	*Party*	*Contested*	*Won*	*Vote %*	*Party*	*Contested*	*Won*	*Vote %*
Orissa	1989	INC	21	3	38.4				
		BJP	6	0	1.3				
		JD	19	16	49.5				
		Left	2	2	6.6				
	1990					INC	145	10	29.8
						JD	139	123	53.7
						Left	12	6	3.8
						BJP	63	2	3.6
	1991	INC	21	13	44.0				
		BJP	21	0	9.5				
		JD	19	6	34.6				
		Left	2	2	5.1				
	1995					INC	146	80	39.1
						BJP	144	9	7.9
						JD	146	46	35.4
						Others	48	5	4.3
	1996	INC	21	16	44.9				
		BJP	20	0	13.4				
		JD	19	4	30.1				
	1998	INC	21	5	41.0				
		BJP	9	7	21.2				
		BJD	12	9	27.5				
	1999	INC	20	2	36.9				
		BJP	9	9	24.6				
		BJD	12	10	33.0				
	2000					INC	144	26	33.8
						BJP	62	38	18.2
						BJD	84	68	29.6
	2004	INC	21	2	40.4	INC	133	38	34.9
		BJP	9	7	19.3	BJP	63	32	17.1
		BJD	12	11	30.0	BJD	84	61	27.1

Notes: 1. Electoral coalitions boxed in bold. Some coalitions are only partial seat adjustments.
2. The tables may not add up to 100% votes since some very small parties/independents not shown. Small parties clubbed as Others or Minor Parties.
3. INC Indian National Congress; BJP Bharatiya Janata Party; BJD Biju Janata Dal; Other acronyms stand for minor parties.

Sources: As Table 1.

West Bengal

The BJP has tried to grow in West Bengal using coalitions but without much success (Table 6).[23] After contesting alone until 1996 without ever winning a seat or crossing the 12 per cent mark (1991 Lok Sabha) it allied with the breakaway Congress faction called the Trinamool Congress, a Bengal-based single-state party, in 1998 and 1999, contesting 29 – 14, Trinamool–BJP, in 1998, and winning 7 – 1 with 10.2 per cent votes, and contesting 28 – 13 or proportionately slightly more than its vote share relative to Trinamool in 1998, and winning 8 – 2, with 11.1 per cent votes in 1999. Though the Left Front won both elections in the state, the BJP won seats for the first time due to coalitions. In the 2001 assembly elections, the Trinamool abandoned the BJP to ally as a senior partner with the Congress. The BJP was reduced to no seats (226 contested) and 5.2 per cent votes. In 2004, the Trinamool–BJP contested 29 – 13 again but won only 1 and 0 seats, respectively, with the BJP getting only 8.1 per cent votes. The Bengal experiment in expansion through coalitions has had only very limited success to date.

Assam

The BJP grew steadily on its own steam throughout the post-1989 period, emerging as a small third party in 1991, with 2 seats and 9.6 per cent votes in the Lok Sabha, and 10 seats and 6.7 per cent votes in the assembly (Table 7).[24] In 1996 it increased its vote share to 16 per cent and 10.3 per cent in the Lok Sabha and assembly though dropping to 1 and 4 seats, respectively. However,

[23] For analyses of West Bengal elections, see Chaudhuri, "Regime Changes in West Bengal", 249–72; CSDS Team, "West Bengal: Limited Losses for the Left", 38–9; and Yadav and CSDS Team, "West Bengal: A Spectacular Show", 121–6.

[24] For analyses of Assam election, see Goswami, "Assam", 273–86; Baruah and Goswami, "Fractured Identities", 2492–501; and Yadav and CSDS Team, "Assam: On Predictable Lines", 127–9.

Table 6. Elections in West Bengal

		Lok Sabha				*Assembly*			
State	*Year*	*Party*	*Contested*	*Won*	*Vote %*	*Party*	*Contested*	*Won*	*Vote %*
West Bengal	1989	INC	41	4	41.5				
		BJP	19	0	1.7				
		Left	40	36	49.9				
	1991	INC	41	5	36.2	INC	284	43	35.1
		BJP	42	0	11.7	BJP	291	0	11.3
		Left	40	37	47.0	Left	282	242	47.5
	1996	INC	42	9	40.1	INC	288	82	39.5
		BJP	42	0	6.9	BJP	292	0	6.5
		Left	41	33	48.7	Left	286	202	48.6
	1998	INC	39	1	15.2				
		BJP	**14**	**1**	**10.2**				
		TRMC	**29**	**7**	**24.4**				
		Left	42	33	46.8				
	1999	INC	41	3	13.3				
		BJP	**13**	**2**	**11.1**				
		TRMC	**28**	**8**	**26.0**				
		Left	42	29	46.9				
	2001					**INC**	**60**	**26**	**8.0**
						Minor Parties	**231**	**60**	**31.3**
						BJP	266	0	5.2
						Left	291	199	49.1
	2004	Left	42	35	50.8				
		INC	37	6	14.6				
		BJP	**13**	**0**	**8.1**				
		TRMC	**29**	**1**	**21**				

Notes: 1. Electoral coalitions boxed in bold. Some coalitions are only partial seat adjustments.
2. The tables may not add up to 100% votes since some very small parties/independents not shown. Small parties clubbed as Others or Minor Parties.
3. INC Indian National Congress; BJP Bharatiya Janata Party; TRMC Trinamool Congress; Other acronyms stand for minor parties.

Sources: As Table 1.

Table 7. Elections in Assam

		Lok Sabha				*Assembly*			
State	*Year*	*Party*	*Contested*	*Won*	*Vote %*	*Party*	*Contested*	*Won*	*Vote %*
Assam	1984	INC	13	4	23.5				
		BJP	2	0	0.4				
		AGP	10	7	33.2				
		Others	21	1	21.4				
	1985					INC	125	25	23.2
						BJP	37	0	1.1
						AGP	111	65	35.0
						INC	124	66	29.2
						BJP	49	10	6.7
						AGP	120	19	17.9
						Others	283	16	19.7
	1991	INC	14	8	28.5				
		BJP	8	2	9.6				
		JD	6	0	5.2				
		Left	6	1	6.9				
		AGP	14	1	17.6				
	1996	INC	14	5	31.6	INC	126	36	30.7
		BHP	14	1	15.9	BJP	121	4	10.3
		AGP	11	5	27.2	AGP	99	61	30.1
		Minor Parties	6	2	8.4	Minor Parties	27	10	5.9
	1998	INC	13	10	39.0				
		UMF	1	1	4.3				
		BJP	14	1	24.5				
		AGP	10	0	12.7				
		Left	3	0	4.2				
	1999	INC	14	10	38.4				
		BJP	12	2	29.8				
		AGP	8	0	11.9				
		Minor Parties	4	0	4.1				
		CPI (ML)(L)	3	1	2.3				

Table 7 (*Contd.*)

Table 7 (*Contd.*)

State	Year	Party	*Lok Sabha* Contested	Won	Vote %	Party	*Assembly* Contested	Won	Vote %
	2001					BJP	46	8	9.3
						AGP	77	20	20.1
						ASDC (U)	5	2	1.1
						INC	126	70	39.7
						Others	104	3	5.5
	2004	INC	14	9	35.1				
		BJP	14	3	30.8				
		AGP	12	2	20				

Notes: 1. Electoral coalitions boxed in bold. Some coalitions are only partial seat adjustments.
2. The tables may not add up to 100% votes since some very small parties/independents not shown. Small parties clubbed as Others or Minor Parties.
3. INC = Indian National Congress; BJP = Bharatiya Janata Party; AGP = Assam Gana Parishad; Other acronyms stand for minor parties.

Sources: As Table 1.

in 1998 and 1999 it reaped the benefits of public disenchantment with the Asom Gana Parishad (AGP) state government, and its potential ruling party status at the centre, increasing its vote share clearly at the expense of the AGP, not Congress, to 24.5 per cent and 29.8 per cent respectively, emerging as the second party. In 2001 it went in for an unsuccessful coalition with the AGP for the assembly contesting BJP–AGP, 46 – 77, or more seats than its one-third of the AGP's votes in the 1996 assembly elections, a clear case of leveraging past vote share. However, the alliance lost to the Congress. In 2004, the BJP contested all 14 seats on its own, winning only 3, whereas if it had contested with the AGP it would have fared much better given that their combined votes were 15 per cent more than the Congress. Assam has been a case of largely autonomous, not coalition-derived, growth for the BJP.

Andhra Pradesh

The BJP emerged as a significant third party in 1991 with 9.6 per cent votes and 1 seat, slipping to 3 (280 contested) and 3.9 per cent votes in the 1994 assembly election (Table 8).[25] In 1996, it remained at a low 5.7 per cent votes and no seats. Following a coalition strategy since then, it first allied with the breakaway TDP faction, TDP (Lakshmi Parvathi), which had won 10.7 per cent votes in 1996. Gaining by almost perfect vote transfer from the TDP (LP) in 1998, it jumped to 18.3 per cent votes and 4 (of 38) seats. In 1999, it switched partners to form a coalition with the TDP, and contested 8 of 42 seats, leveraging its 1998 vote share almost exactly, and winning 7 seats and 9.9 per cent votes. In the assembly the TDP restricted the BJP to contesting 24 seats (TDP 269) and winning 12 with 3.7 per cent votes. In 2004, the TDP–BJP alliance contested the Lok Sabha 33 – 9 and assembly 267 – 27, that is on the same pattern as in 1999 with the BJP contesting 3 more seats, but was wiped out due to a strong swing in favour of the Congress-led alliance. The BJP has thus made some gains from its emergence on its own, especially in 1991, as a third party, but is restricted to a much more junior partnership by a relatively strong TDP, a situation more akin to Punjab than Maharashtra, Orissa or Assam.

Karnataka

In Karnataka the BJP built up its strength on its own in the early 1990s, jumping from 3.1 per cent in 1989 Lok Sabha and 4.1 per cent in 1989 assembly votes, to 29 per cent and second party status, winning 4 (of 28) seats in 1991 (Table 9).[26] In the 1994 assembly elections, it won 40 (of 223) seats with 17 per cent votes,

[25] For analyses of AP elections, see Srinivasulu, "Party Competition and Strategies of Mobilization", 141–66, and 210–34; Srinivasulu and Sarangi, "Political Realignments in Post-NTR Andhra Pradesh", 2449–58; CSDS Team and Suri, "A Triumph of Alliance Arithmetic", 48–50.

[26] For analyses of Karnataka elections, see Gould, "Political Self-Destruction in Karnataka, 1999", 94–140, and "The 12th General Election in Karnataka", 183–209; Shastri, "Twilight of Congress Hegemony", 2440–8; and CSDS Team and Shastri, "Congress (I) Dominates in all Regions", 46–8.

Table 8. Elections in Andhra Pradesh

		Lok Sabha				Assembly			
State	Year	Party	Contested	Won	Vote %	Party	Contested	Won	Vote %
Andhra Pradesh	1989	INC	42	39	51.6	INC	286	181	47.2
		BJP	2	0	2	TDP	243	74	36.8
		Minor Partes	6	0	6	BJP	12	5	1.8
		TDP	32	2	33.7	Left	34	14	5.1
	1991	INC	42	25	45.6				
		BJP	41	1	9.6				
		JD	2	0	0.5				
		Left	4	2	4.3				
		TDP	35	13	32.3				
	1994					INC	294	26	33.9
						TDP	251	216	44.2
						Left	37	34	6.4
						BJP	280	3	3.9
	1996	INC	42	22	39.7				
		BJP	39	0	5.7				
		TDP	36	16	32.6				
		Left	6	3	5.4				
		TDP (LP)	42	0	10.7				
	1998	INC	42	22	38.5				
		BJP	38	4	18.3				
		TDP(LP)	5	0	1.2				
		TDP	35	12	32.0				
		Left	6	2	5.5				
	1999	INC	42	5	42.8	INC	293	91	40.6
		BJP	8	7	9.9	BJP	24	12	3.7
		TDP	34	29	39.9	TDP	269	180	43.9

Table 8 (*Contd.*)

Table 8 (*Contd.*)

		Lok Sabha				*Assembly*			
State	*Year*	*Party*	*Contested*	*Won*	*Vote %*	*Party*	*Contested*	*Won*	*Vote %*
	2004	INC	34	29	41.5	INC	234	185	38.5
		TRS	23	5	6.8	TRS	54	26	6.8
		Left	2	2	2.3	Left	26	15	3.4
		BJP	9	0	8.4	BJP	27	2	2.7
		TDP	33	5	33.1	TDP	267	47	37.5

Notes: 1. Electoral coalitions boxed in bold. Some coalitions are only partial seat adjustments.
2. The tables may not add up to 100% votes since some very small parties/independents not shown. Small parties clubbed as Others or Minor Parties.
3. INC Indian National Congress; BJP Bharatiya Janata Party; TDP Telugu Desam Party; Other acronyms stand for minor parties.

Sources: As Table 1.

coming second in seats but third in votes due to a relatively spatially concentrated vote within the state. It slumped to third-party status in 1996 though winning 6 seats and an impressive 25 per cent votes. In 1998 and 1999, it adopted a coalition strategy, increasing its vote share slightly and its seats (considerably in 1998), by allying with Lok Shakti, a breakaway state-level JD faction. In 1998, BJP–Lok Shakti contested 18 – 10 and won 13 – 3; in 1999, the BJP–JD(U) (incorporating Lok Shakti) contested 19 – 10 (an imperfect adjustment) with the BJP contesting proportionately fewer seats than its relative vote share in 1998, and won 7 – 3 in an election in which the Congress won. In both elections the BJP won 27 per cent votes while contesting only two-thirds of the seats. In the 1999 assembly, the BJP–JD(U) contested 149 – 112 (again an imperfect adjustment) gaining 44 – 18 in an election won by the Congress, with the BJP jumping to 20.7 per cent, its highest in an assembly election. In 2004, the BJP–JD(U) contested the Lok Sabha 24 – 4 and the assembly 198 – 26, and won the Lok Sabha convincingly with the BJP getting 18 seats and 34.8 per cent votes. In the assembly, the BJP fared relatively less well, getting 79 seats and 28.3 per cent votes and

Table 9. Elections in Karnataka

		Lok Sabha				Assembly			
State	*Year*	*Party*	*Contested*	*Won*	*Vote %*	*Party*	*Contested*	*Won*	*Vote %*
Karnataka	1989	INC	28	27	48.9	INC	221	178	43.8
		BJP	6	0	3.1	JD	209	24	27.1
		JD	27	1	28.3	BJP	118	4	4.1
	1991	INC	28	23	42.1				
		BJP	28	4	28.8				
		JD	21	0	18.5				
	1994					INC	222	35	27.2
						BJP	223	40	17.0
						JD	220	114	33.2
	1996	INC	28	5	30.3				
		BJP	28	6	24.9				
		JD	27	16	34.9				
	1998	INC	28	9	36.2				
		BJP	**18**	**13**	**27.0**				
		LS	**10**	**3**	**11.5**				
		JD	28	3	21.7				
	1999	INC	28	18	45.4	INC	222	132	40.8
		BJP	**19**	**7**	**27.2**	**BJP**	**149**	**44**	**20.7**
		JD(U)	**10**	**3**	**13.3**	**JD(U)**	**112**	**18**	**13.5**
		JD(S)	27	0	10.9	JD(S)	203	10	10.4
	2004	INC	28	8	36.8	INC	224	65	35.3
		BJP	**24**	**18**	**34.8**	**BJP**	**198**	**79**	**28.3**
		JD(U)	**4**	**0**	**1.9**	**JD(U)**	**26**	**5**	**2.1**

Notes: 1. Electoral coalitions boxed in bold. Some coalitions are only partial seat adjustments.
2. The tables may not add up to 100% votes since some very small parties/independents not shown.
3. INC Indian National Congress; BJP = Bharatiya Janata Party; JD(U) = Janata Dal (United); JD(S) = Janata Dal (Secular); Other acronyms stand for minor parties.

Sources: As Table 1.

failed to form a government. Thus, the BJP has made significant gains from coalition-building on the base it had formed by its own distinctive appeal in the first half of the 1990s, to become the senior partner in both Lok Sabha and assembly elections in a state in which it was virtually non-existent in 1989.

Tamil Nadu

The BJP won its first-ever seats in Tamil Nadu in 1998 essentially by means of alliances (Table 10).[27] What is crucial is that it leveraged not its very small vote share in the state but its status as a potential ruling party (in coalition) at the centre to extract an allotment of Lok Sabha seats. In 1998, it allied with the All India Anna Dravida Munnetra Kazhagam (AIADMK), the erstwhile longtime ally of the Congress, plus four small state parties, to contest 5 seats and win 3 with 6.9 per cent votes. The same story was repeated in 1999, except that the BJP switched partners, now allying with the DMK and the four small parties, three of whom were the AIADMK's allies in 1998, to win 4 out of 6 contested seats with 7.1 per cent votes. In the 2001 assembly elections, the same alliance continued, with the BJP winning 4 (of 21) seats with 3.2 per cent votes in an election lost to the AIADMK-led alliance. In 2004, the DMK and its smaller allies left the NDA and allied with the Congress while the BJP chose to ally with the AIADMK as earlier as a minor partner contesting 6 of 39 seats. The DMK-led alliance won all the seats. In a state where the two leading parties are both state parties, the two major national parties being minor players, both become attractive as election allies to the state parties since they do not threaten their bases and can promise a share of power, if they win, in the coalition at the centre.

A final point I would like to make in this section is that the entire pattern outlined so far has been made possible by the

[27] For election analyses of Tamil Nadu, see Subramanian, "Beyond Ethnicity and Populism?", 50–93; Wyatt, "New Alignments in South Indian Politics", 733–53, and "The Federal Dimension of Party Politics in Tamil Nadu", 127–43; Yadav and CSDS Team, "Tamil Nadu: A Matter of Arithmetic", 113–17; and CSDS Team and Prasad, "No Major Shift in Popular Mood", 50–2.

Table 10. Elections in Tamil Nadu

		Lok Sabha				*Assembly*			
State	*Year*	*Party*	*Contested*	*Won*	*Vote %*	*Party*	*Contested*	*Won*	*Vote %*
Tamil Nadu	1989	INC	28	27	39.6	INC	217	26	20.2
		AIADMK	11	10	16.6	BJP	35	0	0.4
		BJP	3	0	0.3	DMK	203	151	33.3
		Left	6	1	5.7	AIADMK	199	27	21.3
		DMK	31	1	26.9				
	1991	INC	28	28	42.6	INC	65	60	15.2
		AIADMK	11	11	18.1	AIADMK	168	164	44.4
		BJP	15	0	1.6	DMK	176	2	22.5
		DMK	29	0	22.7	BJP	97	0	1.7
						Others	228	3	10.3
	1996	INC	29	0	18.3	INC	64	0	5.6
		AIADMK	10	2	7.8	AIADMK	168	4	21.5
		TMC	20	20	27.0	BJP	143	1	1.8
		DMK	18	17	25.8	DMK	182	173	42.1
		CPI	2	2	2.3	TMC	40	39	9.3
		BJP	37	0	2.9	BJP	143	1	1.8
		Others	38	0	6.4	DMK	182	173	42.1
						TMC	40	39	9.3
						Others	344	13	13.4
	1998	INC	35	0	4.8				
		TMC	20	3	20.2				
		DMK	17	5	20.1				
		CPI	2	1	2.5				
		BJP	5	3	6.9				
		AIADMK	22	18	25.9				
		Minor Parties	12	9	14.8				
	1999	INC	11	2	11.1				
		AIADMK	24	10	25.7				
		Left	4	1	5.0				
		BJP	6	4	7.1				
		DMK	19	12	23.1				
		Minor Parties	14	10	16.9				

Table 10 (*Contd.*)

Table 10 (*Contd.*)

State	Year	Lok Sabha Party	Contested	Won	Vote %	Assembly Party	Contested	Won	Vote %
	2001					INC	14	7	2.5
						AIADMK	141	132	31.5
						Minor Parties	79	56	16.1
						BJP	21	4	3.2
						DMK	183	31	30.9
						Minor Parties	26	0	3.9
	2004	INC	10	10	14.4				
		DMK	16	16	24.6				
		Minor Parties	13	13	18.5				
		BJP	6	0	5.1				
		AIADMK	33	0	29.8				

Notes: 1. Electoral coalitions boxed in bold. Some coalitions are only partial seat adjustments.
2. The tables may not add up to 100% votes since some very small parties/independents not shown. Small parties clubbed as Others or Minor Parties.
3. INC = Indian National Congress; BJP = Bharatiya Janata Party; AIADMK = All India Anna Dravida Munnetra Kazhagam; DMK = Dravida Munnetra Kazhagam; Other acronyms stand for minor parties.

Sources: As Table 1.

incentive structure for regional parties in the post-1989, especially post-1996, national and state party systems. Their primary coalition formation objectives have been two: (a) to capture or retain power in their state, and (b) in 1989–91, and since 1996, to carve out a parliamentary position that would allow them a share in the coalition expected to be formed at the centre, in a context in which the ruling party at the centre would fall very considerably short of a majority and have few or no seats from several states, thus requiring a number of coalition partners. These objectives, for regional parties, could be achieved by being a partner in government or an outside supporting party key to the government's majority, and would give them an incentive to make deals with the BJP in their states, particularly if it was a significant third party.

Conclusion: Coalition-Building and Growth Paths in a Federal, Parliamentary SMSP Polity

My hypothesis has been that a multi-state but regionally concentrated party like the BJP will leverage its expected vote share in states where it is perceived to be pivotal due to being a significant third party and (and able over 1998–2004 to offer a share of power at the centre) to form electoral and government coalitions to expand its bases in its weak states. I conclude that this hypothesis *is substantially confirmed*, that is, it is confirmed for many elections and in most states, particularly 1989 in U.P., Bihar, Rajasthan, Haryana, and Gujarat, since 1990 in Maharashtra, and after 1996 in Bihar, after 1997 in Punjab, and after 1998 in Orissa, Andhra Pradesh, Karnataka, and Tamil Nadu.

The victory of the Congress coalitions in several states (Bihar, Jharkhand, Andhra Pradesh, Tamil Nadu, Jammu and Kashmir) in the Lok Sabha elections of 2004 and in some state assemblies (Andhra Pradesh, Maharashtra) only further confirm the general point about state-level third parties, whichever they may be, being able to use their potential "bridging" vote share to form coalitions to expand. The Congress becomes "coalitionable", that is, attractive as a coalition partner either when it is a third or lesser party (e.g. in Bihar, Tamil Nadu) or where a third or lesser party exists in a situation where the two principal contestants in a state are the Congress and either the BJP or one of its NDA allies. This situation came about in 2004 in the Lok Sabha for the first time in a large number of states resulting in the Congress being able to form coalitions in such states, the outcome being helped by the BJP going it alone out of over-confidence in Haryana, Assam, and Jharkhand.

To sum up, the BJP's expansion path over 1989–2004 has proceeded in three overlapping stages. The first stage has been to acquire an electoral base in an area of concentration of support, usually sub-state pockets/regions consisting of several state assembly and some Lok Sabha constituencies, and win seats from these strongholds in assembly and parliamentary elections. This process began well before 1989 and has continued. The second step is to grow until the party emerges as the second party in the state (helped by the Duvergerian logic of bipolarisation of state party systems), and a credible challenger to, or displacing, the Congress party (as in Rajasthan, M.P., Himachal Pradesh, and Delhi, 1967–89, and Gujarat and most Hindi-speaking states except Haryana since 1989, in addition to coalition strategies in these states), succeeding in forming the state government and/or winning the majority of the state's Lok Sabha seats.

Third has been a coalition strategy, post-1989 and particularly post-1996, to expand into its weak states within the Hindi belt and Gujarat (1989–90), in the south and east (especially post-1996), which are vital if it is to hope to win power on its own. For this it has followed the strategy of leveraging its emerging third-party position in the southern and eastern states since 1989 (and north India and Gujarat in 1989) and forming electoral coalitions with the existing major state party (JD in UP, Bihar, Orissa, Haryana and Gujarat in 1989–90, TDP in Andhra Pradesh, JD in Karnataka, BJD in Orissa, AGP in Assam, SAD in Punjab, HVP/INLD in Haryana, Shiv Sena in Maharashtra, Samata Party in Bihar, in later years) for state as well as, especially, Lok Sabha elections as an increasingly powerful junior partner in electoral and governing coalitions, leveraging its expected "bridging" vote share. Over time, it hopes to grow by eating into the base of its coalition partner at the state level in both assembly and Lok Sabha elections, leveraging its cadre-based, organised character compared to the largely clientelistic and often personality-based regional parties. This strategy has been only partially and intermittently successful so far.

The BJP had a huge advantage in this incremental growth strategy through coalition-building for two reasons. First, it was faced with the Congress as its principal opponent in its strongholds in the north and Gujarat (except U.P. and Bihar), while the Congress faced the regional (including Left) parties in the states of the south and east into which the BJP seeks to emerge as a third and eventually second force. Therefore, the Congress was not "coalitionable" with the regional parties against the BJP, while for the BJP this was a possibility. In addition, since 1998, the BJP had been able to offer them a share of power at the centre. Second, the Congress is an umbrella party that can neither cede the status of representing a particular caste bloc or regional identity to a caste-based (e.g. BSP, Samajwadi Party in U.P.) or regional party, nor go too far in upping the ante in the politics of communal, caste or linguistic/regional polarisation, whereas other parties can and do play such games.

The basic driver of these coalitional strategies is the need for bridging votes to win a plurality, and hence the frantic search for electoral alliances or "seat adjustments" ignoring ideological incompatibilities except perhaps the most overarching one on secularism. The structure of coalitions is very much in a state of flux. It is still too early to say whether the system will stabilise into two broad, heterogeneous coalitions nationally, a BJP-led one and a Congress-led one. A great deal depends on the evolution of the saliency of cleavages, particularly the one the BJP wants to promote, Hindu–Muslim, and the advantages of cadre-based organisation versus caste and other ascriptive loyalties as mobilising devices.

Acknowledgements

I thank Katherine Adeney, Lawrence Saez, Douglas Verney and two anonymous referees for detailed comments on earlier drafts, Pramod Kumar, Suhas Palshikar and Sandhya Goswami for information on Punjab, Maharashtra and Assam, and Adnan Farooqui for research assistance. I thank the NETSAPPE group and the Ford Foundation for support of the project of which this paper is a part.

Bibliography

Banerjee, Sikata, "The Politics of Resentment: The Role of the BJP/Shiv Sena in Elections in Maharashtra", in Paul Wallace and Ramashray Roy, eds, *India's 1999 Elections and 20th Century Politics* (New Delhi: Sage, 2003).

Banerjee, Sikita, "The 12th Lok Sabha Election in Maharashtra: The Congress Alliance Defeats the BJP/Shiv Sena", in Ramashray Roy and Paul Wallace, eds, *Indian Politics and the 1998 Elections: Regionalism, Hindutva and State Politics* (New Delhi: Sage, 1999).

Baruah, A.K., and Sandhya Goswami, "Fractured Identities: Politics in a Multi-Ethnic State", *Economic and Political Weekly*, 21–28 Aug. 1999.

Brass, Paul, "Caste, Class and Community in the Ninth General Elections for the Lok Sabha in Uttar Pradesh", in Harold A. Gould and Sumit Ganguly, eds, *India Votes: Alliance Politics and Minority Governments in the Ninth and Tenth General Elections* (Boulder, CO: Westview Press, 1993).

Budge, Ian, and Hans Keman, *Parties and Democracy: Coalition Formation and Government Functioning in Twenty States* (Oxford: Oxford University Press, 1990).

Chaudhuri, Amiya K., "Regime Changes in West Bengal and the 1999 Parliamentary Elections", in Paul Wallace and Ramashray Roy, eds, *India's 1999 Elections and 20th Century Politics* (New Delhi: Sage, 2003).

CSDS Team and G. Koteswara Prasad, "No Major Shift in Popular Mood", *Frontline*, 19 Nov. 1999.

CSDS Team and K.C. Suri, "A Triumph of Alliance Arithmetic", *Frontline*, 19 Nov. 1999.

CSDS Team and Sandeep Shastri, "Congress (I) Dominates in all Regions", *Frontline*, 19 Nov. 1999.

CSDS Team and Suhas Palshikar, "'Split Factor' Decides the Outcome", *Frontline*, 19 Nov. 1999.

CSDS Team, "One-sided Contest", *Frontline*, 10 Dec. 1999.

CSDS Team, "Sharp Polarisation in Bihar", *Frontline*, 10 Dec. 1999.

CSDS Team, "West Bengal: Limited Losses for the Left", *Frontline*, 10 Dec. 1999.

De Swaan, Abram, *Coalition Theories and Cabinet Formation* (Amsterdam: Elsevier, 1973).

Dodd, Lawrence, *Coalitions in Parliamentary Government* (Princeton: Princeton University Press, 1976).

Fickett, Lewis P., "The Janata Dal in the Ninth Indian General Election of 1989 and Its Future Prospects", in Harold A. Gould and Sumit Ganguly, eds, *India Votes: Alliance Politics and Minority Governments in the Ninth and Tenth General Elections* (Boulder, CO: Westview Press, 1993).

Gamson, William A., "A Theory of Coalition Formation", *American Sociological Review*, vol. 26, no. 3 (June 1961).

Goswami, Sandhya, "Assam", in Paul Wallace and Ramashray Roy, eds, *India's 1999 Elections and 20th Century Politics* (New Delhi: Sage, 2003).

Gould, Harold A., "Patterns of Political Mobilization in the Parliamentary and Assembly Elections of 1989 and 1990", in Harold A. Gould and Sumit Ganguly, eds, *India Votes: Alliance Politics and Minority Governments in the Ninth and Tenth General Elections* (Boulder, CO: Westview Press, 1993).

Gould, Harold A., "Political Self-Destruction in Karnataka, 1999", in Paul Wallace and Ramashray Roy, eds, *India's 1999 Elections and 20th Century Politics* (New Delhi: Sage, 2003).

Gould, Harold A., "The 12th General Election in Karnataka: The BJP Achieves its Southern Beachhead", in Ramashray Roy and Paul Wallace, eds, *Indian Politics and the 1998 Elections: Regionalism, Hindutva and State Politics* (New Delhi: Sage, 1999).

Gregory M. Luebbert, *Comparative Democracy: Policy Making and Governing Coalitions in Europe and Israel* (New York: Columbia University Press, 1986).

Heath, Oliver, "An Unequal Alliance in Orissa", *Frontline*, 14 April 2000.

Heath, Oliver, "Anatomy of BJP's Rise to Power: Social, Regional and Political Expansion in 1990s", *Economic and Political Weekly*, 21–28 Aug. 1999.

Katzenstein, Mary Fainsod, Uday Singh Mehta, and Usha Thakkar, "The Rebirth of the Shiv Sena: The Symbiosis of Discursive and Organizational Power", in Zoya Hasan, ed., *Parties and Party Politics in India* (New Delhi: Oxford University Press, 2002).

Kumar, Pramod, "Electoral Politics in Punjab: From Autonomy to Secession", in Paul Wallace and Ramashray Roy, eds, *India's 1999 Elections and 20th Century Politics* (New Delhi: Sage, 2003).

Kumar, Pramod, "Punjab: Changing Political Agenda", in Ramashray Roy and Paul Wallace, eds, *Indian Politics and the 1998 Elections: Regionalism, Hindutva and State Politics* (New Delhi: Sage, 1999).

Kumar, Sanjay, "New Phase in Backward Caste Politics in Bihar: Janata Dal on the Decline", *Economic and Political Weekly*, 21–28 August 1999.

Kumar, Sanjay, "The Return of the RJD", *Frontline*, 31 March 2000.

Laver, Michael, and Norman Schofield, *Multiparty Government: The Politics of Coalition in Europe* (Ann Arbor, Michigan: University of Michigan Press, 1998).

Laver, Michael, *Private Desires, Political Action: An Invitation to the Politics of Rational Choice* (London: Sage Publications, 1997).

Luebbert, Gregory, "Coalition Theory and Government Formation in Multi-Party Democracies", *Comparative Politics*, Jan. 1983.

Ojha, A.K., and M.R. Kazmi, "Bi-polar Competition and the 13th Lok Sabha Elections in Bihar", in Paul Wallace and Ramashray Roy, eds, *India's 1999 Elections and 20th Century Politics* (New Delhi: Sage, 2003).

Palshikar, Suhas, and Nitin Birmal, "Maharashtra: Fragmented Marathas Retain Power", in Paul Wallace and Ramashray Roy, eds, *India's 1999 Elections and 20th Century Politics* (New Delhi: Sage, 2003).

Palshikar, Suhas, and Rajeshwari Deshpande, "Electoral Competition and Structures of Domination in Maharashtra", *Economic and Political Weekly*, 21–28 Aug. 1999.

Prasad, Binoy Shankar, "Bihar Elections 1999–2000, Business as Usual: Caste, Violence, Moribund Parties and Leadership", in Paul Wallace and Ramashray Roy, eds, *India's 1999 Elections and 20th Century Politics* (New Delhi: Sage, 2003).

Prasad, Binoy Shankar, "Split the Votes and Win the Election: An Analysis of the 12th Lok Sabha Election in Bihar", in Ramashray Roy and Paul Wallace, eds, *Indian Politics and the 1998 Elections: Regionalism, Hindutva and State Politics* (New Delhi: Sage, 1999).

Riker, William H., *The Theory of Political Coalitions* (New Haven: Yale University Press, 1962).

Roy, Ramashray, "Orissa: The Fall of the Congress Bastion", in Ramashray Roy and Paul Wallace, eds, *Indian Politics and the 1998 Elections: Regionalism, Hindutva and State Politics* (New Delhi: Sage, 1999).

Shastri, Sandeep, "Twilight of Congress Hegemony: Emergence of Bi-Polar Alliance System in Karnataka", *Economic and Political Weekly*, 21–28 Aug. 1999.

Singh, Ranbir, "Social Cleavages and Political Alignments in Haryana", in Paul Wallace and Ramashray Roy, eds, *India's 1999 Elections and 20th Century Politics* (New Delhi: Sage, 2003).

Sridharan, E., "Principles, Power and Coalition Politics in India: Lessons from Theory, Comparison and Recent History", in D.D. Khanna and Gert W. Kueck, eds, *Principles, Power and Politics* (Delhi: Macmillan, 1999).

Sridharan, E., "The Fragmentation of the Indian Party System, 1952–1999: Seven Competing Explanations", in Zoya Hasan, ed., *Parties and Party Politics in India* (New Delhi: Oxford University Press, 2002).

Srinivasulu, K., "Party Competition and Strategies of Mobilization", in Paul Wallace and Ramashray Roy, eds, *India's 1999 Elections and 20th Century Politics* (New Delhi: Sage, 2003).

Srinivasulu, K., and Prakash Sarangi, "Political Realignments in Post-NTR Andhra Pradesh", *Economic and Political Weekly*, 21–28 Aug. 1999.

Subramanian, Narendra, "Beyond Ethnicity and Populism? Changes and Continuities in Tamil Nadu's Electoral Map", in Paul Wallace and Ramashray Roy, eds, *India's 1999 Elections and 20th Century Politics* (New Delhi: Sage, 2003).

Wyatt, Andrew, "New Alignments in South Indian Politics: The 2001 Assembly Elections in Tamil Nadu", *Asian Survey*, XLII/5, Sept.–Oct. 2002.

Wyatt, Andrew, "The Federal Dimension of Party Politics in Tamil Nadu", *Indian Journal of Federal Studies*, 3/2, 2002.

Yadav, Yogendra, and CSDS Team, "Assam: On Predictable Lines", *Frontline*, 8 June 2001.

Yadav, Yogendra, and CSDS Team, "Tamil Nadu: A Matter of Arithmetic", *Frontline*, 8 June 2001.

Yadav, Yogendra, and CSDS Team, "West Bengal: A Spectacular Show", *Frontline*, 8 June 2001.

Yadav, Yogendra, and Oliver Heath, "A Split Verdict in Haryana", *Frontline*, 14 April 2000.

8

Coalition Congruence in India's Federal System

THIS PAPER ADDRESSES the issue of coalition congruence in federal democracies and asks the question of whether coalitions at the federal level and at the state/provincial level are congruent, that is, do coalitions at each level consist of the same parties, or at least, of parties that are not allied at one or another level to the opponents of their coalition partners? The paper puts forward two working hypotheses:

1. The more institutionalised the party system, the greater the congruence. Institutionalisation can be measured in various ways including duration as a proxy of durability. Congruence can also be measured in various ways but can be conveniently trichotomised into (a) full, 100 per cent congruence; (b) partial congruence, limited to core parties in a coalition; (c) absence of congruence.
2. The more federal/decentralised the system, the less the congruence. Here again it is possible to measure the degree of decentralisation in various ways.

The above conceptualisation – whether the same parties form the national and state-level coalitions – is a more restrictive and detailed conceptualisation which tends to suit the complexities of the Indian case. However, I also follow this book's template for conceptualising coalition congruence (or incongruence) so as to be comparable across countries, which is to compare the cabinets of India's prime ministers together with the composition of the cabinets of the state chief ministers as to the participating parties. Here, by "congruence" I don't mean the exact replication of the same coalition from national level, but at least no incongruence in the composition of the subnational cabinets. For instance, if a Party A and Party B are forming a coalition at the national level; with Parties C and D present in the opposition; a congruent cabinet at the subnational level would be a government: A; AB; B; C; D and CD. Therefore, an incongruent coalition at the subnational level would be a coalition formed by parties that, at the national level are apparently opposed, or vice versa. For instance, following the example above, the following coalitions would be incongruent—AC, AD, BC or BD. In this chapter, we first detail the congruence, full or partial, using the more restrictive earlier definition of sameness of coalitions, and then by the latter definition of cabinets being congruent if not actually incongruent.

Before discussing coalition congruence in India it is necessary to provide readers an outline of India's political system and social cleavages, parties, party system evolution and coalitions in the next few sections. In providing this background, I build on my earlier work.

The Political System and Major Social Cleavages

After independence India adopted a parliamentary and federal system of government with a bicameral parliament in which the Westminster-style executive is responsible to a directly elected lower house known as the Lok Sabha (Assembly of the People), a federal system with legislative powers divided between the national and state legislatures, with a strong centralising bias, an independent judiciary with the power of judicial review. Since 2014, India is divided into 29 states of very different sizes and seven federally administered Union territories. The states were reorganised on a linguistic basis after 1956 (except for Jammu and Kashmir, and the six northeastern border states). The electoral system is a single-member district, simple-plurality system (a "first-past-the-post" system). There have been 16 national elections since 1952 (the most recent one in 2014) and at least one election has been held every five years at the state level.[1]

India's politically salient social cleavages are those of religion, language, caste, tribe, class and the rural-urban divide. Hinduism is the majority religion, with its followers constituting 78 per cent of the population. Hindus are a majority in all states and union territories except seven (Arunachal Pradesh, Jammu and Kashmir, Lakshadweep, Meghalaya, Mizoram, Nagaland, and Punjab).[2] However, Hindus are internally divided by language, caste, and sect. Within each state, the Hindu population is traditionally (but unofficially) layered into five overarching caste categories – the Brahmins (priests), Kshatriyas (warriors), Vaishyas (merchants), Shudras (farmers, artisans), and the Dalits (formerly the untouchables). Caste is based historically on the traditional division of labour and is not a racial division but an endogamous group and therefore akin to ethnicity. The broad caste clusters are sub- divided into over 4000 actual castes (jatis) but the number in each state is different. Each state has a unique caste configuration in terms of both the specific endogamous jatis (which differ from state to state) and their relative population share. All states do not necessarily have the same jatis making it difficult to mobilise castes politically across states. The broad caste clusters are the upper castes (the Brahmins, Kshatriyas, and Vaishyas), who along with the so-called "dominant" castes or upper intermediate castes, are a minority of a rough sixth of the population nationally, the intermediate castes (Shudras),

[1] Jammu and Kashmir is only required to hold state assembly elections every six years.

[2] For all figures in this section except where specified otherwise the data are from: http://censusindia.gov.in/Census_Data_2001/India_at_glance/religion.aspx http://censusindia.gov.in/Census_Data_2001/India_at_glance/scst.aspx http://censusindia.gov.in/Census_Data_2001/Census_Data_Online/Language/Statement5.htm accessed on 5 July 2011.

and two constitutionally recognised groupings called Scheduled Castes (or ex-untouchables) and Scheduled Tribes (or aboriginal peoples).[3] To compensate the Scheduled Castes and Scheduled Tribes for the discrimination they have historically been subject to, quotas of 15 per cent and 7.5 per cent respectively in parliament, as well as in college admissions and public sector employment are provided for them. There tends to be a strong correlation between caste and class. The upper castes tend to constitute disproportionately the higher classes while the lower castes tend to constitute disproportionately the lowest classes.

The major religious minorities are Muslims (14.3 per cent), Christians (2.3 per cent), and Sikhs (1.9 per cent). There are also relatively small numbers of Buddhists (0.8 per cent), Jains (0.4 per cent), and Parsees (Zoroastrians). Muslims are in a majority only in Jammu and Kashmir. Less than 10 per cent of India's Muslims live in Muslim-majority areas.[4] Christians are in a majority only in Meghalaya, Mizoram, and Nagaland, while the great majority of the Christian population lives as a minority in other areas.

The Scheduled Castes (16.2 per cent) are distributed as a minority throughout the country. This is so even in constituencies reserved only for their candidates, making the non-Scheduled Caste vote decisive even in such constituencies. The Scheduled Tribes (8.2 per cent) are geographically relatively concentrated, enjoying majorities or near-majorities in many of their reserved constituencies. They are not, however, the majority in any state except Arunachal Pradesh, Meghalaya, Mizoram and Nagaland. The population in these states is less than 5 per cent of the Scheduled Tribe population.

The Constitution recognises 22 languages in India, of which Hindi enjoys a plurality of over 41 per cent. It is the language of nine of the twenty-nine states, including the largest, Uttar Pradesh.

[3] For the estimate of upper castes, including dominant castes, see Government of India (1980, Vol. I, Part I, p. 56).

[4] See Ansari (2006, Appendix, pp. 404–13) and Rudolph and Rudolph (1987), 196, Table 16, both for constituency estimates.

Bengali is the language of two states, West Bengal and Tripura, Telugu of two states, Andhra Pradesh and Telangana. The other major languages are each the official language of one state. India is 30 per cent urban and 70 per cent rural, although the proportion of people primarily dependent on agriculture is about 52 per cent, with a considerable non-agricultural population living in rural areas. However, by most international criteria, India is more urban than these figures would indicate. The proportion of the population below the official poverty line is 26 per cent although a recent new estimate operating with a different poverty line raises the level to 37 per cent.[5]

Relevant to our argument in this paper is the fact that in the coalition era of 1989 to the present, India's federal system has become more decentralized. Compared to the 1980s state governments in India play a larger role in their economies compared to the Central government in the post-1991, post-liberalisation period with the end of Central licensing of economic activity and states competing for domestic and foreign private investment in an increasingly private investment-driven economy. There were also other developments that made state governments more secure such as the prevalence of multi-party coalition governments since 1996 in which regional parties played a key role, and the Supreme Court's Bommai judgement (1994) which made it much more difficult to dismiss state governments and impose Central rule under Art. 356 on the grounds of constitutional breakdown.

Indian Party System

The Congress Party

The Indian National Congress (henceforth Congress party or simply Congress or INC) has ruled India for all but 14 years between 1947 and 2016 (from 2004 to 2014 it headed minority coalition governments).[6] With the exception of the 1977 election, it was

[5] Planning Commission, Government of India (2010).

[6] The account of the Congress in this section draws on several standard

the largest party of India for over four decades after independence. However, in the 1996, 1998 and 1999 elections, it lost its leading position to the BJP although remaining the single largest party by vote share in all elections until it lost this status in 2014 to the BJP. From 1989 to 2014 it declined from 39.6 per cent to 19.3 per cent in vote share.

Founded in 1885, the Congress grew from being a group of founding notables to a mass movement that included peasants and workers by the 1920s under the influence of Mahatma Gandhi's mass mobilisation. It was an umbrella movement and party for independence and tried to include all religious and linguistic groups, castes, classes and regions and encompassed ideological strands ranging from soft Hindu nationalism to radical socialism. As an independence movement it was gradualist and used non-violent methods under Gandhi's leadership, extracting concessions in the form of increasing degrees of self-rule from the British by successive rounds of pressure, the major constitutional changes to this effect being made in 1909, 1919 and 1935.

From the colonial period onwards, the Congress developed an encompassing and penetrative organisational machinery, organised on a provincial basis and dependent on local notables. In its internal functioning the Congress could be said to approximate a grand coalition of social and political forces, a multi-ethnic and multi-regional coalition, that was on balance ideologically centrist. The party was committed to democracy, secularism, minority rights, federalism, and a mixed economy.

Over the course of the 1960s, the party machine gradually disintegrated. In 1969, the party underwent a major split – between the faction led by then Prime Minister Indira Gandhi, and the leaders in control of the party organisation. Most of the party's office bearers in most states stayed with the organisational faction

---

works including Kothari (1970), Weiner (1967), Kochanek (1968), Sisson and Roy (1990), and Manor (1988).

leading to a crippling of the organisational capacities of the faction that emerged dominant, that of Mrs Gandhi. Mrs Gandhi used her personal charisma and populist appeals to win national elections, and defeat the organisational wing of the party in the 1971 elections, winning a thumping majority, trouncing the organisation wing. Her faction came to be considered the real Congress.

The decline of Congress over 1989–2016 has also been due to various newly assertive social groups deserting it for other or new parties. This actually began as early as the late 1960s, with the emerging prosperous peasant constituency in north India, largely belonging to the intermediate castes resenting the dominance of the "upper castes" in the Congress and moving to a range of other parties, primarily what were then called socialist parties.[7] This was followed in the 1989–2016 period by the upper castes and many intermediate castes moving towards the BJP, a large part of the Scheduled Castes and Muslims in north India towards other parties, and part of the Congress base moving towards regional parties in the south, west and east, leading to an erosion of the Congress base nationally.

The BJP and Other Parties

There are five other major categories of parties (although these groups of parties do not necessarily constitute coalitions). We classify them as:

1. Hindu nationalist parties [the Bharatiya Janata Party (BJP), and the Shiv Sena];
2. The communist parties, also termed the Left Front [including the Communist Party of India Marxist [CPI(M)] and the Communist Party of India (CPI), and the various CPI (Marxist-Leninist) splinters];
3. The agrarian/lower-caste populist parties [the Janata Party, the Janata Dal and its offshoots like the Samajwadi Party,

[7] Brass (1997).

Rashtriya Janata Dal, Rashtriya Lok Dal, Biju Janata Dal, Janata Dal (Secular), Janata Dal (United)]; and

4. Ethno-regional or ethnic parties based on particular regional linguistic groups or lower-caste blocs or tribes (in the northeastern states, in particular). Examples of such ethno-regional parties are the Dravida Munnetra Kazhagam (DMK) and the All India Anna Dravida Munnetra Kazhagam (AIADMK) of Tamil Nadu, the Shiromani Akali Dal of the Sikhs in Punjab, the National Conference and People's Democratic Party of Jammu and Kashmir, Asom Gana Parishad (AGP) of Assam, Telugu Desam Party (TDP) of Andhra Pradesh, the tribal Jharkhand Mukti Morcha of Jharkhand, and various small ethnic parties of the north-eastern rim states, and the Scheduled Caste-based Bahujan Samaj Party (BSP); and
5. Congress splinter parties, that is, regional parties formed by Congress leaders who have seceded from the parent party, for example, most prominently, the Nationalist Congress Party of Maharashtra and the Trinamool Congress of Bengal.

Most regional parties, and a large number of even smaller parties, are single-state parties and are officially termed state parties. In the last general election (2014), there were 6 national parties, 34 state parties, recognised by the Election Commission and over a hundred minor parties. Rather than demonstrating political fragmentation alone, these large numbers reflect the underlying diversity of India and the political mobilisation of groups that were hitherto not politically empowered.

The Evolution of the Party System: Fragmentation at the National Level Despite Bipolar Consolidation in the States[8]

India's party system evolution can be periodised as follows:

[8] This section draws heavily on Sridharan (2010).

Congress Hegemony 1952–1967

The first four general elections to the Lok Sabha, 1952, 1957, 1962, and 1967, coincided with elections to all the state assemblies. In the first three of these, the Congress party won an over two-thirds majority of seats in the Lok Sabha on the basis of only a plurality of votes of 44-8 per cent (Table 1). It also won a majority of seats in nearly all state assembly elections from 1952–62, again on the basis of mostly a plurality of votes against a fragmented opposition.

The Bipolarisation of State Party Systems 1967–1989

The 1967 election marks a break with the Congress winning only 283 seats on the basis of its lowest ever vote share until then (40.8 per cent) and losing power in 8 out of 16 states. The 1971 elections saw a restoration of a two-thirds Congress' majority in the Lok Sabha with 43.7 per cent votes and 352 seats. In the "exceptional" post-Emergency elections of 1977, the Congress faced a temporarily united opposition consisting of the Janata Party formed just before the elections, and having a seat adjustment with a Congress splinter group and the CPI-M, thus consisting of virtually the entire opposition. The Congress was trounced, plunging to its lowest-till-then vote and seat figures of 34.5 per cent and 154 seats respectively. The Janata Party won a majority (295 seats) on the basis of 41.3 per cent of the vote. This was a Congress-like victory in reverse, that is, a catchall umbrella party winning a seat majority on the basis of a vote plurality.

In 1980 another Congress restoration took place following the disintegration of the Janata Party, again a near two-thirds majority of 353 seats (out of 542) on the basis of a plurality of 42.7 per cent. The 1984 elections, another "exceptional" election, following the assassination of prime minister Indira Gandhi, saw the highest-ever Congress vote share (48.1 per cent) and 415 seats or a three-quarters majority. The 1989 elections marked another

Table 1. Vote and Seat Shares of Major Parties in National Elections, 1952–2014

	1952	*1957*	*1962*	*1967*	*1971*	*1977*	*1980*	*1984*
Total Seats	489	494	494	520	518	542	529	542
Indian National Congress (INC), (INCI) in 1980	364(479) 74.4% 45.0%	371(490) 75% 47.8%	361(488) 73% 44.7%	283(516) 54.4% 40.8%	352(441) 68% 43.7%	154(492) 28.4% 34.5%	353(492) 66.7% 42.7%	415(517) 76.6% 48.1%
Bharatiya Janata Party (BJP), (BLD) in 1977, (BJS) till 1971	3(94) 0.6% 3.1%	4(130) 0.8% 5.9%	14(196) 2.8% 6.4%	35(251) 6.7% 9.4%	22(160) 4.2% 7.4%	295(405) 54.4% 41.3%	–	2(229) 4% 7.4%
Janata Dal (United) (JDU) in 1999, (JD)1989-1998, (SWA) till 1971	–	–	18(173) 3.6% 7.9%	44(178) 8.5% 8.7%	8(56) 1.5% 3.1%	–	–	–
Communist Party of India	16(49) 3.3% 3.3%	27(110) 5.5% 8.9%	29(137) 5.9% 9.9%	23(106) 4.4% 5.0%	23(87) 4.4% 4.7%	7(91) 1.3% 2.8%	11(48) 1.8% 2.6%	6(66) 1.1% 2.7%
Communist Party of India Marxist (CPM)	–	–	–	19(62) 3.7% 4.4%	25(85) 4.8% 5.1%	22(53) 4.1& 4.3%	36(63) 7% 6.1%	22(64) 4.1% 5.7%
Lok Dal (LKD), (JPS) in 1980, (INCO) till 1977	–	–	–	–	16(238) 3.1% 10.4%	3(19) 0.6% 1.7%	41(294) 7.7% 9.4%	3(174) 6% 5.6%
Samajwadi Party (SP) in 1991, (JP) till 1989	–	–	–	–	–	–	31(432) 5.9% 19.0%	10(219) 1.8% 6.7%
Total Seats	489	494	494	520	518	542	529	542
Bahujan Samaj Party (BSP)	–	–	–	–	–	–	–	–

Table 1 (*Contd.*)

Table 1 (*Contd.*)

1989	*1991*	*1996*	*1998*	*1999*	*2004*	*2009*	*2014*
529	521	543	543	543	543	543	543
197(510)	232(492)	140(529)	141(474)	114(453)	145(414)	206(440)	44(464)
37.2%	45%	25.8%	26%	21%	26.7%	37.9%	8.1%
39.5%	36.5%	28.8%	25.9%	28.3%	26.4%	28.6%	19.5%
86(226)	120(468)	161(471)	179(384)	182(339)	138(264)	116(433)	282(428)
16.5%	23%	29.6%	33%	34%	25.4%	21.4%	51.9%
11.5%	20.1%	20.3%	25.5%	23.8%	22.2%	18.8%	31.3%
142(243)	59(307)	46(196)	6(190)	21(60)	8(33)	20(55)	2(93)
27%	11.3%	8.5%	1.1%	3.8%	1.5%	3.7%	0.36%
17.7%	11.8%	8.1%	3.2%	3.1%	1.9%	1.5%	1.1%
12(50)	14(42)	12(43)	9(58)	4(54)	9(33)	4(56)	1(67)
2.3%	2.7%	2.2%	1.6%	0.7%	1.6%	0.7%	0.18%
2.6%	2.5%	2.0%	1.8%	1.5%	1.8%	1.4%	0.8%
33(64)	35(60)	32(75)	32(71)	33(72)	43(69)	16(82)	9(93)
6.2%	6.7%	6%	5.9%	6.1%	7.9%	3.0%	1.65%
6.5%	6.2%	6.1%	5.2%	5.4%	5.7%	5.3%	3.3%
0(117)	0(78)	–	–	–	–	–	–
–	–						
0.2%	0.1%						
0(156)	5(345)	17(111)	20(164)	26(151)	36(237)	23(193)	5(197)
–	1%	3.1%	3.7%	4.8%	6.6%	4.3%	0.92%
1.0%	3.4%	3.3%	5.0%	3.8%	4.3%	3.4%	3.4%
529	521	543	543	543	543	543	543
–	–	11(117)	5(249)	14(225)	19(435)	21(500)	0(503)
		2%	0.9%	2.6%	3.5%	3.9%	–
		3.6%	4.7%	4.2%	5.3%	6.2%	4.2%

Table 1 (*Contd.*)

Table 1 (*Contd.*)

	1952	*1957*	*1962*	*1967*	*1971*	*1977*	*1980*	*1984*
Praja Socialist Party (PSP), (KMPP) in 1952	9(145) 1.8% 5.8%	19(189) 3.8% 10.4%	12(168) 2.4% 6.8%	13(109) 2.5% 3.1%	2(63) 0.4% 1.0%	–	–	–
Samyukta Socialist Party (SSP), (SOC) till 1962	12(254) 2.5% 10.6%	–	6(107) 1.2% 2.7%	23(122) 4.4% 4.9%	3(93) 0.6% 2.4%	–	–	–
Others	47 9.6% 16.5%	31 6.3% 7.6%	34 6.9% 10.5%	45 8.6% 10.0%	53 10.2% 13.8%	52 9.6% 9.9%	35 9.1% 8.5%	79 14.6% 10.0%
Independents	38 7.6% 15.9%	42 8.5% 19.4%	20 4% 11.1%	35 6.7% 13.7%	14 2.7% 8.4%	9 1.7% 5.5%	9 1.7% 6.4%	5 0.9% 8.1%

Table 1 (*Contd.*)

Table 1 (*Contd.*)

1989	1991	1996	1998	1999	2004	2009	2014
–	–	–	–	–	–	–	–
–	–	–	–	–	–	–	–
44	55	115	141	143	140	128	197
8.9%	11%	21.2%	26%	26.3%	25.8%	23.6%	36.27%
12.2%	12.1%	21.5%	26.3%	27.1%	28.6%	29.2%	34%
12	1	9	6	6	5	9	3
2.26%	0.2%	1.7%	1.1%	1.1%	0.9%	1.7%	0.55%
5.2%	3.9%	6.3%	2.4%	2.8%	4.3%	5.2%	2.4%

Notes: Elections were not held in 13 constituencies: 12 in Assam and 1 in Meghalaya Elections were not held in Assam (14 seats) Elections were not held in Jammu & Kashmir (6 seats) and Punjab (13 seats); 3 countermanded seats results excluded Figures in parentheses are seats contested, upper percentage is seat share, lower percentage is vote share Notes: *BLD* Bharatiy a Lok Dal, *BJS* Bharatiya Jana Sangh, *SWA* Swatantra Party, *INCU* Indian National Congress (Urs), *JPS* Janata Party Secular, INCO Indian National Congress (Organisation), *JP* Janata Party, *KMPP* Kisan Mazdoor Praja Party, *SOC* Socialist Party, *SJP* Samajwadi Janata Party Sources: David Butler, Ashok Lahiri and Prannoy Roy, *India Decides: Elections 1952–1995*. New Delhi: Books and Things, 1995; Election Commission of India, Statistical Report on General Elections, Vol. I (Ver. I) National and State Abstracts, for 1996, 1998, 1999; For 2004 and 2009, Election Commission of India website: www.eci.gov.in.

turning point with the Congress crashing to 39.5 per cent and 197 seats against an opposition electoral alliance consisting of seat adjustments, of the National Front coalition (of the Janata Dal and regional and minor parties) supported by the BJP and the Left parties that resulted in a large number of one-on-one contests with the Congress.

The post-1967 period also saw a very important de-linking of parliamentary and state assembly elections since 1971, and a suspension of organisational elections within the Congress from 1972 to 1992, hand in hand with the centralisation of power at the top of the party apparatus. It also saw the emergence of anti-Congress alliances, then of a principal opposition party to the Congress in state after state, in most states, representing a consolidation of the non-Congress space at the state level. The Index of Opposition Unity (IOU) showed an upward trend in state after state over 1967–89.[9] This is particularly so if one considers opposition coalitions – and first party plus its pre-electoral allies – as a single party for the purposes of the IOU. This bipolar consolidation was the key feature and driving force of the fragmentation of the national party system. However, these were not the same bipolarity like in the USA, or same two parties or coalitions in each state, but multiple bipolarities.

However, at the end of this 1967–89 period, just after the 1989 elections and the state assembly elections in early 1990, the Congress remained the leading party in more states (12) in terms of Lok Sabha seats and in terms of vote share (17) than any other, and remained one of the two leading parties in more states in terms of Lok Sabha seats (20) and vote share (24) than any other. In the state assemblies it remained the leading party in more states (9) and in terms of vote share (11) than any other, and one

[9] A measure of the fragmentation of the opposition space represented by the percentage share of the largest non-Congress (in today's terms, non-ruling party) vote in the total opposition vote. The higher the IOU the less fragmented the opposition space.

of the two leading parties in terms of vote share in more states (24, or all except Tamil Nadu) than any other. However, many of these were very small states, the Congress having lost U.P., Bihar, Orissa, and Haryana to the Janata Dal, Madhya Pradesh and Himachal Pradesh to the BJP, and Rajasthan and Gujarat to a Janata Dal-BJP coalition in both Lok Sabha and state assembly elections (except Haryana, which did not have assembly elections in 1989–90).

The Evolution of the Pattern of Fragmentation of the Party System 1989–2017

The 1989 election results were not just another repeat of broad-front anti-Congressism of the Janata Party kind, but signified a more far-reaching and seismic shift in the party system rooted in shifts in party organisational strength and support bases at the state level in increasing number of states, and in India's political economy and changing patterns of social mobilisation. The major trends of 1989–2016 are (1) the relative decline of the Congress and (2) the rise of the BJP and (3) regional or single state-based parties.[10]

Prior to 1989, the BJP and its predecessor the BJS, the political arm of the Rashtriya Swayamsevak Sangh (RSS), had never exceeded 10 per cent of the vote or 35 seats nationally, except in 1977 when as a component of the Janata Party it won 99 of 295 seats won by the Janata Party (more than the 86 seats it won in 1989). Its rise since then has been steady in terms of both vote and seat

[10] Regional party is something of a misnomer as it implies a party strong in two or more states in a region. All the regional parties, however, are single state-based parties except the Janata Dal (United), strong in Bihar and Karnataka, and the CPI (M), strong in West Bengal, Tripura and Kerala, if one considers them regional parties. These sets of states do not constitute recognisable regions. The JD(U) and the CPI (M) are really national parties with a limited geographical spread, the former being a rump of the once much larger Janata Dal.

shares. It experienced a meteoric rise in seats from a derisory 2 in 1984 (despite 7.4 per cent votes) to 86 (out of 226 contested, mostly in de facto alliance with the Janata Dal) in 1989 owing to the combination of three effects—seat adjustments with the Janata Dal resulting in one- to-one contests against the Congress in most of the seats it contested, an increase in contested seats and a sizeable and regionally concentrated swing in its favour.

In 1989–91, the BJP contested alone with a religiously polarising platform against the backdrop of the upper caste backlash against the National Front government's decision to implement the Mandal Commission recommendations for reservation of government jobs for backward classes defined in caste terms. Its vote share zoomed to 20.1 per cent, and it won 120 seats (of an unprecedented 468 contested), becoming the second largest party in terms of seats and votes.

The BJP came to form state governments on its own for the first time ever in 1990. It formed the government on its own in M.P. and H.P., and formed coalition governments with the Janata Dal in Rajasthan and Gujarat. The only time that it had dominated state governments earlier was when it was part of the Janata Party in 1977–79, during which period the Jana Sangh component of the Janata party dominated the government and occupied the chief minister's post in M.P., H.P. and Rajasthan. Thus the BJP arrived as a state-level political force, whereas earlier it had essentially been sub-state, thereby contributing to national party system fragmentation.

In 1991, with the external support of the 11-member AIADMK and some smaller allies the Congress was able to form a minority government dependent on abstention in confidence votes by a section of the opposition. It began adding to its numbers by splitting small parties such as the TDP in fractions of one-third or more (legal under the Anti-Defection law), and attained a majority on its own exactly halfway through its term (end-1993).

In 1996, its vote share declined still further to a then-historic low of 28.7 per cent, having been hit badly by the breaking away of the bulk of its Tamil Nadu unit and marginally by the breaking away of factions called the Congress (Tiwari) and the Madhya Pradesh Vikas Congress. For the first time, the Congress was overtaken as the single largest party, by the BJP, winning only 141 seats compared to the BJP's 161, although it remained the single largest party by vote share with 28.8 per cent compared to the BJP's 20.3 per cent.

In 1996, the BJP ran into the limits of contesting alone with a religiously polarising agenda. Despite being catapulted to its higher-ever seat tally of 161 seats, due to its more regionally concentrated vote, making it the largest party in the Lok Sabha and able to form the government for 12 days, its vote share remained stagnant at 20.3 per cent and it failed to win parliamentary support from enough other parties to form a minority or coalition government. Six states – U.P., M.P., Gujarat, Rajasthan, Bihar and Maharashtra–accounted for 143 of its 161 seats, with U.P. and M.P. alone accounting for almost half.

These results can be seen as a delayed reflection of the realignment of political forces that was represented by the results of the elections to the assemblies of 15 states between November 1993 and March 1995, which, by and large, represented major gains for the BJP, some regional parties like the TDP and Shiv Sena, and state-based parties such as the Samajwadi Party, the Samata Party and the BSP, while at best a holding operation for the Congress in some stronghold states such as H.P. and M.P.[11]

A United Front government consisting of 11 parties participating in government, including two parties represented only by Rajya Sabha (upper house) members, and three parties formally part of the United Front coalition but not participating in government, and supported from outside by the Congress, was formed in June 1996. The Congress withdrew support to Prime Minister

[11] Yadav (1996).

Deve Gowda in April 1997, but continued to support the UF government after his replacement as prime minister by I. K. Gujral, eventually withdrawing support to the UF in November 1997, precipitating fresh elections in February–March 1998.

In 1998, the BJP shelved its overt Hindu nationalist agenda to strike explicit or tacit alliances with a range of state-based parties, both regional parties and others, many of them earlier with the UF, a strategy that it consolidated after its victory.[12] The BJP strategy was certainly helped by the fact that the Congress had toppled the UF government and was the principal opponent of the constituents of the UF in several major states. This catapulted the BJP to power as it emerged once again as the single largest party (the Congress got only 141 seats) and led the single largest pre-election alliance.[13] A BJP-led 12-member minority coalition government consisting of 11 pre-election (including two independents and one from a one-Rajya Sabha MP party) and one post-election ally, and dependent on the support or abstention in confidence votes of at eight post-election allies and pre-election allies who opted out of the ministry, assumed power in March 1998.

In 1999, essentially the same BJP-led pre-election coalition fought the Congress- led coalition, the latter being a more tentative coalition with state-by-state agreements but no common national platform. The 21-party BJP-led alliance was formally christened the National Democratic Alliance (NDA). The Congress alliance was much smaller, the main difference being that the BJP was now allied to the DMK in Tamil Nadu while the Congress was allied to the AIADMK.

The NDA won a more decisive victory, getting 299 seats, with the BJP alone getting 182 as in 1998. With post-election adherents the number went up to 303 seats. The Congress got a lowest-ever

[12] For the BJP's use of coalitions as a strategy to expand its base across states, see Sridharan (2005).

[13] For details of the alliances, pre- and post-election in 1998, see Arora (2000).

111 seats, and only 134 with allies. However, in terms of vote share, the BJP alone declined to 23.8 per cent while the Congress rose to 28.4 per cent, remaining the single largest party. The NDA formed the government with the 29-member TDP and five other smaller pre-election allies opting to support it from outside.

In 2004, the incumbent BJP-led NDA coalition contested against the newly formed Congress-led coalition, called the United Progressive Alliance (UPA) after the election, and lost. The major change was that the Congress party became "coalitionable" in a significant way for the first time following a conscious decision to adopt a coalition strategy. The Congress-led alliance consisted of nineteen parties. This meant the addition of eight new allies – including the DMK-led alliance in Tamil Nadu – since the 1999 elections, and the dropping of two old allies. The Congress-led alliance won 222 seats and 36.53 per cent votes (or only a whisker ahead of the NDA in vote share) but 33 seats ahead. With the external support of the Left parties (61 seats) it gained a majority in the Lok Sabha and formed a government. The UPA also enjoyed the unilateral external support of two other significant parties (with whose support it could potentially retain a majority even if the Left withdrew), i.e., the Samajwadi Party (36 seats) and the Bahujan Samaj Party (BSP) (19 seats). The major difference between 2004 and earlier elections was the success of the Congress' coalitionability, which was critical to its universally unexpected victory.[14]

In 2009 the UPA coalition defeated the depleted NDA by a much greater margin with the Congress winning 206 seats on its own and 263 with its pre-electoral allies, of which, compared to 2004, it had lost the Left as a partial seat adjustment partner in Jharkhand, A.P. and Tamil Nadu, and lost the RJD, LJP, TRS, PMK, MDMK and PDP, but added the Trinamool Congress and the NC (Table 7). The NDA suffered major-ally depletion with the loss

[14] For details of the argument and figures, see Sridharan (2004).

of the TDP, BJD and the split in the Shiv Sena but added the AGP, TRS, and RLD. The Congress-led UPA formed a six-party government of the Congress, Trinamul Congress, DMK, NCP, NC, and Muslim League but excluded some pre-electoral [JMM, Bodoland People's Front, Kerala Congress (Mani)] and all post-electoral supporters who consisted of 9 parties and 3 independents totalling 59 MPs. This coalition resembled the NDA in that the legislative coalition including post-electoral allies constituted a considerable surplus majority and hence provided insurance against defection by any ally, rendering no ally pivotal, and also from the fact that the BJP numbers, down to 116, made it like the Congress during the NDA, in being too small to form a viable alternative coalition given that several parties like the Left, SP, RJD, TDP and BSP would not be prepared to ally with it due to differences on secularism and their need for religious minority votes.

In 2014, the NDA (see Table 2), consisting of the same parties except for the additional of the DMK in Tamil Nadu and a host of minor parties, defeated the UPA and formed a majority government which was an oversized coalition in which the BJP alone had a narrow majority of seats (52 per cent of the seats based on 31 per cent vote share, 38 per cent for the NDA).

Most states remained or became bipolar in the 1989–2016 period, except notably U.P. However, in a number of apparently bipolar or two-party states, if we look at vote shares we find the presence of a significant, often growing, third party which has a vote share in double digits but not yet large enough to win a significant number of seats. It is obviously cutting into the potential vote share of one or both of the two main parties or alliances in a way that makes it both a threat to either/both of the former as well as attractive as an ally of one to defeat the other. This is the case in states like Assam, Orissa, Goa, West Bengal, Manipur, Arunachal Pradesh.

This rising third party was the BJP in all of these states, and the BSP in Punjab, U.P. and in a small way, M.P. By emerging as a significant third party in vote share at the state level and hence,

Table 2. Congruence of Coalitions, State-wise, for the BJP alliances (1991–2016) in Lok Sabha and state assembly elections

General election year	*Alliance partners*	*States*	*Alliance partner in state (Lok Sabha)*	*Alliance partner in state (state assembly)*	*State assembly election year*
1991	Shiv Sena	Andhra Pradesh	–	–	1994
		Assam	–	–	1991
		Bihar	–	–	1995
		Haryana	–	–	1991
		Jharkhand	–	–	–
		Karnataka	–	–	1994
		Kerala	–	–	1991
		Maharashtra	Shiv Sena	Shiv Sena	1995
		Odisha	–	–	1995
		Punjab	–	–	1992
		Tamil Nadu	–	–	1991
		West Bengal	–	–	1991
1996	Samata Party, Shiv Sena, Haryana Vikas Party, Madhya Pradesh Vikas Congress, Jharkhand Shiromani Akali Dal	Andhra Pradesh		–	1999
		Assam	–	–	1996
		Bihar	Samata Party	Samata Party	2000
		Haryana	Haryana Vikas Party	Haryana Vikas Party	1996
		Jharkhand	–	–	–
		Karnataka	–	–	1999
		Kerala	–	–	1996
		Maharashtra	Shiv Sena	Shiv Sena	1999
		Odisha	–	–	2000
		Punjab	Shiromani Akali Dal	Shiromani Akali Dal	1997
		Tamil Nadu	–	–	1996
		West Bengal	–	–	1996
1998	AIADMK, Samata Party, Shiromani Akali Dal, All India Trinamool Congress, Shiv Sena, PMK, Lok Shakti, MDMK, Haryana Vikas Party,	Andhra Pradesh	NTRTDP		
		Assam			
		Bihar	Samata Party		
		Haryana	Haryana Vikas Party		
		Jharkhand	–		
		Karnataka	–		

Table 2 (*Contd.*)

Table 2 (*Contd.*)

General election year	*Alliance partners*	*States*	*Alliance partner in state (Lok Sabha)*	*Alliance partner in state (state assembly)*	*State assembly election year*
	Janata Party, NTRTDP, Mizo National Party Front, Biju Janata Dal	Kerala	–		
		Maharashtra	Shiv Sena		
		Odisha	Biju Janata Dal		
		Punjab	Shromani Akali Dal		
		Tami Nadu	AIADMK, MDMK, PMK		
		West Bengal	All India Trinamool Congress		
1999	Janata Dal (U), DMK, Samata Party, Biju Janata Dal, Shiromani Akali Dal, All India Trinamool Congress, Shiv Sena, PMK, Lok Shakti, MDMK, Indian National Lok Dal, Mizo National Front, Sikkim Democratic Front, MSCP, Telugu Desam Party, TRC, MGR Anna DMK	Andhra Pradesh	TDP	TDP	1999
		Assam	–	AGP	2001
		Bihar	JD(U)[a]	JD(U), Samata Party	2000
		Haryana	Indian National Lok Dal	Indian National Lok Dal	2000
		Jharkhand	–	–	–
		Karnataka	JD(U)a	JD(U)	1999
		Kerala	–	–	2001
		Maharashtra	Shiv Sena	Shiv Sena	1999
		Odisha	Biju Janata Dal	Biju Janata Dal	2000
		Punjab	Shiromani Akali Dal	Shiromani Akali Dal	2002
		Tamil Nadu	DMK and minor parties	DMK and minor parties	2001
		West Bengal	All India Trinamool Congress	–	2001
2004	Janata Dal (United), AIADMK, Telugu Desam Party, Biju Janata Dal,	Andhra Pradesh	TDP		2004
		Assam	–	–	2006
		Bihar	2005 a and b JD(U)	JDU	2005a 2005b

Table 2 (*Contd.*)

Table 2 (*Contd.*)

General election year	*Alliance partners*	*States*	*Alliance partner in state (Lok Sabha)*	*Alliance partner in state (state assembly)*	*State assembly election year*
	Shriomani Akali Dal, All India Trinamool Congress, Shiv Sena, Mizo National Front, IFDP, MSCP	Haryana	–	–	2005
		Jharkhand	–	JD(U)	2005
		Karnataka	–	–	2008
		Kerala	IFDP	IFDP merged with the BJP	2006
		Maharashtra	Shiv Sena	Shiv Sena	2004
		Odisha	Biju Janta Dal	Biju Janta Dal	2004
		Punjab	Shiromani Akali Dal	Shiromani Akali Dal	2007
		Tamil Nadu	AIADMK senior	–	2006
		West Bengal	All India Trinamool Congress	All India Trinamool Congress	2006
2009	Janata Dal (United), Shiv Sena, Indian National Lok Dal, Rashtriya Lok Dal, Asom Gana Parishad, Nagaland People's Front, Gorkha Janmukti Morcha, Uttarakhand Kranti Dal, Kamtapur Progressive Party, Ladakh Union Territory Front, Telangana Rashtra Samiti	Andhra Pradesh	TRS[b]	TRS[b]	2009
		Assam	Asom Gana Parishad, Rashtrawadi Sena	–	2011
		Bihar	JD(U)	JD(U)	2010
		Haryana	–	–	2009
		Jharkhand	JD(U)	JD(U)	2010
		Karnataka	–	–	2013
		Kerala	JD(U)	JD(U)	2011
		Maharashtra	Shiv Sena	Shiv Sena	2009
		Odisha	–	–	2009
		Punjab	Shiromani Akali Dal	Shiromani Akali Dal	2012
		Tamil Nadu	JD(U), Shiv Sena	–	2011
		West Bengal	Gorkhaland Jan Mukti Morcha, Kamtapur Progressive Party	GJM	2011

a – Samata Party and Lok Shakti fought under JD(U) symbol
b – TRS joined the BJP led NDA after the polling

both threatening to cut into the votes and seat prospects of either or both of the dominant parties, and hence creating incentives for the weaker of the two leading parties to ally with it, typically the regional party, since both the BJP, nationally, and the regional party in the state, face the Congress as their principal opponent.

Thus, a process of bipolar consolidation has been taking place in many states, but of multiple bipolarities (e.g. Congress-BJP, Congress-Left, Congress-Regional Party), contributing to fragmentation at the national level, contributing and directly or indirectly to potential bipolar consolidation of a Congress-led alliance versus BJP-led alliance, although both alliances are as yet unstable, marked by the exit and entry of smaller parties. Furthermore, both alliances are not perfect one-on-one seat adjustments but partial ones, in which the total seats contested by each alliance may exceed the total number of seats. For example, in 2009, the Congress alliances with its partners were explicitly limited to the partner's main state only, so that the latter were free to contest seats against the Congress in other states and did so, contributing to a larger effective number of parties by votes in 2009 despite the effective number of parties by seats shrinking. What this reflects is the drive by several smaller parties like the Samajwadi Party and the Nationalist Congress Party to expand their base horizontally across states, which brings into conflict with the Congress which needs to have as broadly multi-state a base as possible to be able to defend its status as the leading national party.

The Evolution of Coalition Governments in India[15]

The SMSP or first-past-the-post system strongly incentivises pre-electoral coalitions due to the imperative to win a plurality of

[15] For detailed accounts of coalition dynamics see Sridharan (2002, 2004), Ruparelia (2015), Diwakar (2017). This section draws heavily upon, with modifications, Sridharan (2010).

votes at the district level and in federal systems, at the state level.[16] Faced with an encompassing umbrella party this incentivised the fragmented and regionalised opposition parties from the late 1960s onwards to form both pre-electoral and post-electoral coalitions against the Congress party, a trend that continued into the 1970s and 1980s, including opposition party mergers, of which we give a brief historical account below.

The evolution of alliances in the Indian party system can be summarised as follows. The first phase of broad-front anti-Congressism in the 1960s and 1970s, was characterised by intra-state alliances. The component parties of the alliance, e.g., the Jana Sangh, Bharatiya Kranti Dal/Bharatiya Lok Dal, Socialists, Swatantra, Congress (O), had their state units, strongholds and interests in those states while having no ideological glue.

The second phase, again of broad-front anti-Congressism, was that of the Janata Party, which unified ideologically disparate non-Congress parties so as to have one- on-one contests aggregating votes at the constituency level so as to win. It reflected the imperative of aggregation, regardless of ideology, for victory. This also consisted of intra-state alliances of disparate parties within the overall umbrella of unification of those parties at the national level.

The National Front coalition, 1989–90, was a new departure in three senses. First, learning from the Janata Party experience, it did not try to unify very different parties but put together a coalition of distinct parties based on a common manifesto. Second, it brought in the explicitly regional parties like the DMK, TDP, and AGP, and the Left parties unlike the late 1960s/1970s experiments. Third, it also marked the beginning of inter-state alliances of parties or territorially compatible alliances where parties do not compete on each other's turf.

In 1996 a nine-party United Front (UF) minority coalition

[16] Golder 2006.

government, with another three (Left) parties formally part of the UF coalition but opting to support from outside, and also supported by the Congress, was formed. The UF was a territorial coalition but had a certain secular ideological mooring, ranged as it was against a hardline, perceivedly "anti-system" BJP. The Congress withdrew support in April 1997, forcing a change of prime minister, and then once again withdrew support in November 1997, precipitating early elections in February 1998.

All the coalitions since 1996 have been inter-state territorial, that is, federal coalitions. The period since 1991 has also seen the growth and sustenance of intra-state alliances based on ideology (like the BJP-Shiv Sena) and based on territorial compatibility of two kinds. This consists of intra-state alliances which are a reverse of the historical Congress-AIADMK (a regional party) kind in which the regional party allies with the state unit of the national party with the regional party getting the majority share of both Lok Sabha and assembly seats. The examples are the BJP-AIADMK-smaller parties in 1998 and 2004, the BJP-DMK-smaller parties in 1999, Congress-DMK-smaller parties in 2004, the BJP-TDP in 1999 and 2004, the BJP-Trinamool Congress in 1999 and 2004, BJP-BJD in Orissa in 1998, 1999 and 2004, BJP-Haryana Vikas Party in 1996 and 1998 and the BJP-INLD (Chautala) in 1999, and also RJD-Congress in 2004, and JD(U)-BJP in 2004.

Second, the reverse of this pattern, viz., an alliance between a minor state party and a national party in which the latter gets the lion's share of both Lok Sabha and assembly seats, the key being territorial compatibility in which the national party does not contest in the smaller regional party's intra-state strongholds. Examples are the BJP-Lok Shakti in Karnataka in 1998 and 1999, the BJP-Samata in Bihar over 1996–99, the BJP-HVC in H.P., and the Congress-JMM-smaller parties in 2004.

The clear emphasis of alliances since the nineties has been on territorial compatibility at the expense of ideological compatibility, particularly the BJP's alliances of 1998, 1999, 2004 and 2014, and the Congress alliances of 2004, 2009 and 2014, but even the UF coalition. However, the most important point to be noted is that in the whole history of alliances since the 1960s, with the exception of the Left Front limited to three states, alliances have been driven by the imperative to aggregate votes to win and not by ideology, programme or social cleavages except for overarching differences between the Congress and the BJP on secularism.[17]

Are Coalitions Congruent in India's Federal System?

Tables 2 and 3 are master tables of coalitions in India since 1991 comparing pre-electoral and government alliances for national elections and for the nearest (in time) state elections (since most such elections are not simultaneous). As mentioned earlier, there are strong incentives in India's SMSP system for pre-electoral coalitions, which lead to post-electoral government coalitions although pre-electoral allies can sometimes remain part of the legislative but not the executive coalition and some post-electoral allies can join the executive coalition.

We can take 1991 to be the beginning of the era of coalition politics in a sense since the Congress plurality did not translate into a majority of seats for the second consecutive time (1989 and 1991) and a non-Congress minority government was formed in 1989 and a Congress minority government in 1991. However, coalitions evolved after a period of flux through the 1990s until they took shape in the NDA coalition in 1998 and in the UPA coalition in 2004. But looking at congruence since 1991 is useful in that coalitions from this date contain the main parties that have been prominent in coalitions later.

The following patterns emerge from this historical record in Tables 2 and 3, and from Tables 4 and 5 which map out, party-wise, the

[17] For a detailed overview of state-level coalition politics in India, see Sridharan (1999, 2002, 2003). For a detailed state-wise analysis of the BJP's coalition strategies since 1989, see Sridharan (2005).

Table 3. Congruence of Coalitions, State-wise, for the INC Alliances (1991–2016) in Lok Sabha and State Assembly Elections

General election year	*Alliance partners*	*States*	*Alliance partner in state (Lok Sabha)*	*Alliance partner in state (state assembly)*	*State assembly election year*
1991	AIADMK, Kerala Congress (M)	Andhra			1994
		Assam			
		Bihar			1991
					1995
		Haryana			1991
		Jharkhand			–
		Karnataka			1994
		Kerala	Kerala Con- gress (M), IUML	Kerala Congress (M) IUML	1991
		Maharashtra			1995
		Odisha			1995
		Punjab			1992
		Tamil Nadu	AIADMK	AIADMK	1991
		West Bengal			1991
1996	AIADMK, Kerala Congress (M), IUML	Andhra Pradesh			1999
		Assam			1996
		Bihar			2000
		Haryana			1996
		Jharkhand			–
		Karnataka			1999
		Kerala	Kerala Congress (M), IUML	Kerala Congress (M), IUML	1996
		Maharashtra			1999
		Odisha			2000
		Punjab			1997
		Tamil Nadu	AIADMK	AIADMK	1996
		West Bengal			1996
1998	Rashtriya Janata Dal, RPI, IUML, Kerala Congress (M), Bahujan Samaj Party, Communist Party of India, MGRADMK,	Andhra Pradesh	–		
		Assam	–		
		Bihar	Rashtriya Janata Dal		
		Haryana	–		
		Jharkhand	–		
		Karnataka	–		

Table 3 (*Contd.*)

Table 3 (*Contd.*)

General election year	*Alliance partners*	*States*	*Alliance partner in state (Lok Sabha)*	*Alliance partner in state (state assembly)*	*State assembly election year*
	Samajwadi Party	Kerala	IUML, Kerala Congress (M)		
		Maharashtra	Samajwadi Party, RPI		
		Odisha	–		
		Punjab	Bahujan Samaj Party		
		Tamil Nadu	MGRADMK		
		West Bengal	–		
1999	RLD, All India Trinamool Congress, AIADMK, IUML, Kerala Congress (M), CPI, CPI(M), RPI, Marxist Coordination, Bharipa Bahujan Mahasangha	Andhra Pradesh	–	–	1999
		Assam	–	–	2001
		Bihar	RJD, CPI, MCC		2000
		Haryana	–	–	2000
		Jharkhand	–	–	–
		Karnataka	–	–	1999
		Kerala	Kerala Congress (M), IUML	Kerala Congress (M), IUML	2001
		Maharashtra	Bharipa Bahujan Mahasangha, RPI	–	1999
		Odisha	–	–	2000
		Punjab	CPI, CPI(M)	–	2002
		Tamil Nadu	AIADMK, CPI(M), CPI	AIADMK, CPI(M), CPI	2001
		West Bengal			2001
2004	RJD, DMK, NCP, PMK, TRS, LJP, JMM, MDMK, CPI(M), CPI, IUML, Kerala Congress (M), J&K PDP, RPI(A), JD(S), Arunachal Congress, RPI,	Andhra Pradesh	TRS, CPI(M)	CPI(M), TRS	2004
		Assam	–	–	2006
		Bihar	RJD, LJP, JMM	2005 a- no alliance; 2005-b RJD, NCP, CPI(M)	2005 a 2005 b
		Haryana	–	–	2005
		Jharkhand	RJD, LJP, JMM	JMM	2005

Table 3 (*Contd.*)

Table 3 (*Contd.*)

General election year	*Alliance partners*	*States*	*Alliance partner in state (Lok Sabha)*	*Alliance partner in state (state assembly)*	*State assembly election year*
	Peoples' Republican Party, Party for Democratic Socialism	Karnataka	–		2008
		Kerala	IUML, Kerala Congress (M)	IUML, Kerala Congress (M)	2006
		Maharashtra	NCP, RPI(A), JD(S), RPI, People's Republican Party	NCP	2004
		Odisha	–	–	2004
		Punjab	CPI, CPI(M)	–	2007
		Tamil Nadu	DMK, PMK, MDMK, CPI, CPI(M)	CPI(M), CPI PMK, DMK	2006
		West Bengal	Party for Democratic Socialism	Party for Democratic Socialism	2006
2009	All Indian Trinamool Congress, DMK, NCP, J&K NC, NCP, IUML, JMM, VCK, BPF, KC(M), RPI(A), RPI	Andhra Pradesh	–	–	2009
		Assam	BPF	–	2011
		Bihar	–	–	2010
		Haryana	–	–	2009
		Jharkhand	JMM	JVM	2010
		Karnataka	–	–	2013
		Kerala	IUML, KC(M)	IUML, KC(M)	2011
		Maharashtra	NCP, RPI, RPI(A)	NCP	2009
		Odisha	–	–	2009
		Punjab	–	–	2012
		Tamil Nadu	DMK, VCK	DMK, PMK, VCK	2011
		West Bengal	AITC	AITC	2011
2014	BPP, RJD, NCP, J&KNC, JMM, IUML, Socialist JD, RSP, KC(M), PPP, RLD, Mahan Dal	Andhra	CPI	–	2014
		Assam	BPP	–	2016
		Bihar	RJD, NCP	RJD, JD(U)	2015
		Haryana	–	–	2014
		Jharkhand	RJD, JMM	RJD, JD(U)	2014
		Karnataka	–	–	–
		Kerala	IUML, KC(M),	IUML,	2016

Table 3 (*Contd.*)

Table 3 (*Contd.*)

General election year	*Alliance partners*	*States*	*Alliance partner in state (Lok Sabha)*	*Alliance partner in state (state assembly)*	*State assembly election year*
			RSP, Socialist Janata Dal	KC(M)	
		Maharashtra	NCP	–	2014
		Odisha	–	–	2014
		Punjab	PPP		2017
		Tamil Nadu	–	DMK, IUML, Makkal DMK, Puthiya Thamizha-gam, MMK	2016
		West Bengal	–	CPI(M) led alliance	2016

allies of the BJP and Congress respectively; while Tables 2 and 3 give the actual historical record of pre-electoral (whether the coalition wins power or not) or government coalitions (in case the coalition wins power), Tables 4 and 5 list the parties which have been coalition partners, pre-electoral or in government (if the coalition wins power) of the BJP and Congress respectively, for Lok Sabha and state assembly elections and the duration of such alliances.

First, the two core parties, the BJP and the Congress, the nuclei respectively of the NDA and UPA coalitions have not allied in any election at the national or state level throughout this period.

Second, the overall pattern is one of partial congruence with the BJP leading the NDA coalition at the national level and the Congress the UPA coalition.

Third, however, due to the earlier described party system being one of regional parties based in only a single state each or at most two or three states in a very few cases (e.g. RJD in Bihar and Jharkhand), the two core parties typically have only one major coalition partner in each state in which they form a coalition (Kerala in

Table 4. BJP Allies (Pre-electoral/Government), Party-wise, 1991–2016

Party	*Lok Sabha*	*Assembly*	*Duration*
Shiv Sena	1991–2014	1995–2009 (not 2014)	23 years-stable
Akali Dal	1996–2014	1997–2017	20 years-stable
BSP		1995, 1997, 2002 Post-election	episodic, post-election
AGP	2009	2001, 2014	Episodic
Samata Party JD(U)	1996–2009	2000–2013	Broke Bihar government in 2013 semi-stable
INLD	1999, 1996	2000, 1996	Episodic
HVK	1998		
HJC	2014		
BJD	1998, 1999, 2004	2000, 2004	Episodic, both anti-Congress
TMC	1998, 1999, 2004	2006	Episodic
GJM	2009, 2014	2011, 2016	
TDP	1999, 2004, 2014	1999, 2014	Episodic
TRS	2009	2009	Episodic
DMK	1998, 1999,	2001	Episodic
AIADMK	2004		DMK government formation (1999–2004)

the UPA is an exception with the Congress having two longstanding partners in the IUML and the Kerala Congress (Mani), being parties based on the local Muslim and Christian minorities respectively). Therefore, the state-level coalition in both the UPA and the NDA are only partially congruent with the national UPA and NDA coalitions since most of the parties present in the national coalitions are not present in every state. The common presence is only the core party. However, as we shall see, for most states it is recurrently the same local partner who coalesces with the Congress or the BJP.

Fourth, this core party might even be a junior partner in the

Table 5. Congress Allies (Pre-electoral/government), Party-wise, 1991–2016

Party	*Lok Sabha*	*Assembly*	*Duration*
MUL	1991–2014	1991–2016	Stable
KCM	1991–2014	1991–2016	Stable
AIADMK	1991, 1996, 1999	2001	1991–1996, external support, trade off deal
DMK	2004, 2009	2006, 2011, 2016	2004–2013, UPA I&II coalition
NCP	2004, 2009, 2014	2004, 2009	Split away in 2014 assembly elections
TMC	2009	2011	Episodic, INC junior partner
RJD	1998, 1999, 2004, 2014	2005b, 2015	Episodic, INC junior partner
JMM	2004, 2009, 2014	2005	Episodic

coalition in the state as earlier mentioned, for state assembly (BJP and Shiv Sena in Maharashtra) or both national and state assembly elections (e.g., the BJP in Punjab, and the Congress-DMK alliance in Tamil Nadu, or Congress-RJD in Bihar) for example.

Fifth, in the NDA coalition there have been only two longstanding stable allies – the Shiromani Akali Dal (SAD) in Punjab, from 1996 to 2016 (currently they form a coalition government in Punjab), and the Shiv Sena in Maharashtra from 1991 to 2016 (currently they form a coalition government in Maharashtra although in 2014 for the state assembly election they contested separately after 24 years but formed a post-electoral coalition). Between 1991 and 2014, there was coalition congruence for national and state assembly elections for the BJP and Shiv Sena in Maharashtra except for contesting separately in 2014 due to the BJP not willing to play the role of a junior partner in the state assembly any more. Likewise, there was long standing coalition congruence for national and state assembly elections for the BJP and SAD in Punjab from 1996 to 2016. The glue that holds the NDA coalition together in Punjab and Maharashtra is that they have a common enemy, the Congress.

Sixth, for all the other major regional parties that have been allies of the BJP for one or more elections, or have formed post-electoral coalitions with the BJP (viz. BSP, TDP), the alliance can be described as episodic or at best semi-stable if it lasts two or three elections (e.g., JD (U) in Bihar). Thus alliances with parties such as the BSP in U.P., AGP in Assam, INLD, HVP and HJC in Haryana, BJD in Odisha, Trinamool Congress in West Bengal, TDP and TRS in Andhra Pradesh, DMK and AIADMK in Tamil Nadu can be described as episodic, with the JD(U) in Bihar being the closest to being stable.

Seventh, for the UPA coalition, the only stable longstanding partners of the Congress have been the IUML and the Kerala Congress (Mani) in Kerala. All other coalition partners – DMK and AIADMK in Tamil Nadu, Trinamool Congress in West Bengal, NCP in Maharashtra, RJD in Bihar and Jharkhand, and JMM in Jharkhand – have been episodic and have lasted only for one to three elections, the maximum being the RJD in Bihar and the NCP in Maharashtra (in 2014 however they contested separately for the state assembly). However, even in the case of the RJD congruence between national and state assembly elections has not been present during the entire alliance.

Eighth, the overall picture in a party system characterised by single-state regional parties and two major multi-state national parties since 1996, is one of only partial institutionalisation of coalitions and only partial congruence between state and national elections in the context of growing decentralisation of the federal system.

What are the Reasons for Such Outcomes?

First, there are strong incentives to form regional parties because Indian states enjoy substantial enough powers to make capture of power only at the state level an attractive enough prize.

Second, each state is an ethno-linguo-cultural entity with a specific caste and religion make-up and very often other strong regional specificities and regional identity that make it difficult for regional parties to spread across states with the exception of cadre-based ideological parties of the Right (Hindu-nationalist BJP) or Left (communist parties). In the Duvergerian process of the emergence of multiple bipolarities, there typically emerged a single main opponent to the Congress in almost each state with a minor third party seeking to emerge in the post-1989 phase which was either the BJP or a regional party which could be a splinter group of the Janata formations. Thus, at the state level for both national and state elections, coalitions consisted of a national party allied to the opponent of the other national party either as a senior or a junior partner.

Third, only a few of these alliances were of long duration because there is constant competition not only between coalition partners and their opponents but also within the coalition for social base and vote share, thus leading to tensions over allocation of seats to contest in pre-electoral coalitions and of ministerial portfolios in governments when formed.

Fourth, from the earlier three points, it logically follows that the pattern has been one of only partial congruence and partial institutionalisation of coalitions.

Comparable Congruence as Defined in This Volume

The foregoing detailed analysis of congruence and incongruence of pre-electoral and executive coalitions in India is necessary to understand the complexities of the Indian situation with regard to coalitions but might not lend itself to comparison across other federal countries. A simpler conceptualisation of congruence will make such comparison easier. To repeat what was said at the beginning of this chapter, this book's template for conceptualising coalition congruence (or incongruence) so as to be comparable across countries is to compare the cabinets of India's prime ministers together with those the composition of the cabinets of the State Chief Ministers' as to the participating parties. Here, by "congruence" I don't mean the exact replication of the same coalition from national level, but at least no incongruence in the composition of the subnational cabinets. For instance, if a Party A and Party B are forming a coalition at the national level; with Parties C and D present in the opposition; a congruent cabinet at the subnational would be a government: A; AB; B; C; D and CD. Therefore, an incongruent coalition at the subnational level would be a coalition formed by parties that, at the national level are apparently opposed, or vice versa. For instance, following the example above, the following coalitions would be incongruent – AC, AD, BC, or BD.

Using this conceptualisation we get the table (Table 6) for congruence during the coalition era of 1991–2014.

From the tables we can see that Indian coalitions are overwhelmingly congruent, in that they are not incongruent – parties opposed at the national cabinet level are not allied at the state cabinet level, and vice versa, with extremely few and very minor exceptions. There are only five cases of incongruence – in Manipur, Meghalaya, Delhi, Bihar, and Jammu and Kashmir – for specific elections, out of a total of 157 cases in all over the 1991–2014 national elections and the nearest (in time) state assembly elections, or 3.18 per cent incongruence.

Conclusion

The empirical record of the Indian case thus tends to confirm both hypotheses that we began with if we adopt the initial conceptualisation or full, partial or no congruence based on the sameness of the national and state pre-electoral coalitions and cabinets. Congruence between national and state coalitions is low and there is only partial congruence limited to the core parties. This is related

Table 6. Congruence of Indian Coalitions 1991–2014

Coalition	*State*	*State election year*	*Party/Parties in the state government*	*Types of government*	*Status*
1991					
INC, AIADMK, Kerala Congress (M)	Andhra Pradesh	1994	TDP	SPM	Congruent
	Arunachal Pradesh	1995	INC	SPM	Congruent
	Assam	1991	INC	SPM	Congruent
	Bihar	1995	JD	SPM	Congruent
	Delhi	1993	INC	SPM	Congruent
	Goa	1994	INC	SPMG	Congruent
	Gujarat	1995	BJP	SPM	Congruent
	Haryana	1991	INC	SPM	Congruent
	Himachal Pradesh	1993	INC	SPM	Congruent
	Karnataka	1994	JD	SPM	Congruent
	Kerala	1991	UDF	SMC	Congruent
	Madhya Pradesh	1993	INC	SPM	Congruent
	Maharashtra	1995	SS, BJP	SMC	Congruent
	Manipur	1995	INC, JLP	SMC	Congruent
	Meghalaya	1993	INC, IND	SMC	Congruent
	Mizoram	1993	INC, MJD	SMC	Congruent
	Nagaland	1993	INC	SPM	Congruent
	Odisha	1995	INC	SPM	Congruent
	Punjab	1992	INC	SPM	Congruent
	Puducherry	1991	INC	SPM	Congruent
	Rajasthan	1993	BJP, IND	SMC	Congruent
	Sikkim	1994	SDF	SPM	Congruent
	Tamil Nadu	1991	AIADMK	SPM	Congruent
	Tripura	1993	CPM Led	OC	Congruent
	Uttar Pradesh	1991	BJP	SPM	Congruent
	West Bengal	1991	CPM led	OC	Congruent

Notes: *INC* Indian National Congress, *BJP* Bhartiya Janata Party, *CPM* Communist Party of India Marxist, *AIADMK* All India Anna Dravida Munnetra Kazhagham, *MJD* Mizo Janata Dal, *SS* Shiv Sena, *SDF* Sikkim Democratic Front, *JLP* Joint Legislature Party, UDF INC led United Democratic Front, JD Janata Dal, TDP Telugu Desam Party.

Table 6 (*Contd.*)

Table 6 (*Contd.*)

Coalition	*State*	*State election year*	*Party/Parties in the state government*	*Types of government*	*Status*
1996					
JD, NC, TDP, AGP, TMC, AIICT, SP, DMK, MGP, CPI, CPM, RSP, AIFB	Andhra Pradesh	–			
	Arunachal Pradesh	–			
	Assam	1996	AGP	MC	Congruent
	Bihar	–			
	Delhi	–			
	Goa	–			
	Gujarat	–			
	Haryana	1996	BJP, HVP	C	Congruent
	Himachal Pradesh	–			
	Jammu & Kashmir	1996	NC	SPM	Congruent
	Karnataka	–			
	Kerala	1996	LDF	SMC	Congruent
	Madhya Pradesh	–			
	Maharashtra	–			
	Manipur	–			
	Meghalaya	–			
	Mizoram	–			
	Nagaland	–			
	Odisha	–			
	Punjab	1997	SAD, BJP	OC	Congruent
	Puducherry	1996	DMK	SPM	Congruent
	Rajasthan	–			
	Sikkim	–			
	Tamil Nadu	1996	DMK	SPM	Congruent
	Tripura	–			
	Uttar Pradesh	1996	BJP, BSP	C	Congruent
	West Bengal	1996	CPM led	OC	Congruent

Notes: *INC* Indian National Congress, *BJP* Bhartiya Janata Party, *CPM* Communist Party of India Marxist, *DMK* Dravida Munnetra Kazhagham, *UDF INC* led United Democratic Front, *JD* Janata Dal, *TDP* Telugu Desam Party, Shiromani Akali Dal, *LDF CPM* lead Left Democratic Front, *AIFB* All India Forward Block, *CPI* Communist Party of India, *NC* National Conference, *HVP* Haryana Vikas Party, *AIICT* All India Indira Congress Tiwari, *TMC* Tamil Manila Congress, *AGP* Asom Gana Parishad.

Table 6 (*Contd.*)

Table 6 (*Contd.*)

Coalition	*State*	*State election year*	*Party/Parties in the state government*	*Types of government*	*Status*
1998					
BJP, AIADMK, Samata Party, Shiromani Akali Dal, All India Trinamool Congress, Shiv Sena, PMK, Lok Shakti, MDMK, Haryana Vikas Party, Janata Party, NTRTDP, Mizo National Front, Biju Janata Dal	Andhra Pradesh	–			
	Arunachal Pradesh	–			
	Assam	–			
	Bihar	–			
	Delhi	1998	INC	SPM	Congruent
	Goa	1999	INC	SPM	Congruent
	Gujarat	1998	BJP	SPM	Congruent
	Haryana	–			
	Himachal Pradesh	1998	BJP, HVP, IND	C	Congruent
	Jammu & Kashmir	–			
	Karnataka	–			
	Kerala	–			
	Madhya Pradesh	1998	INC	SPM	Congruent
	Maharashtra	–			
	Manipur	–			
	Meghalaya	1998	INC, IND	MC	Congruent
	Mizoram	1998	MNF, MPC	C	Congruent
	Nagaland	1998	INC	SPM	Congruent
	Odisha	–			
	Punjab	–			
	Puducherry	–			
	Rajasthan	1998	INC	SPM	Congruent
	Sikkim	–			
	Tamil Nadu	–			
	Tripura	1998	CPM Led	OC	Congruent
	Uttar Pradesh	–			
	West Bengal	–			

Notes: *INC* Indian National Congress, *BJP* Bhartiya Janata Party, *CPM* Communist Party of India Marxist, *DMK* Dravida Munnetra Kazhagham, *NTRTDP NTR* Telugu Desam Party, Shiromani Akali Dal, *LDF* CPM lead Left Democratic Front, *HVP* Himachal Vikas Party, *AITC* All Indian Trinamool Congress, *MNF* Mizo National Front, *BJD* Biju Janata Dal, *MDMK* Marumalarchi Dravida Munnetra Kazhagham, *SAP* Samata Party, *LS* Lok Shakti, *PMK* Pattali Makkal Kachhi, *IND* Independent, *MPC* Mizoram People's Conference.

Table 6 (*Contd.*)

Table 6 (*Contd.*)

Coalition	*State*	*State election year*	*Party/Parties in the state government*	*Types of government*	*Status*
1999					
BJP, Janata	Andhra Pradesh	1999	TDP	SPM	Congruent
Dal (U), DMK,	Arunachal Pradesh	1999	AC	SPM	Congruent
Samata Party,	Assam	2001	INC	SPM	Congruent
Biju Janata Dal,	Bihar	2000a	a-Samata	a-MC	Congruent
Shiromani Akali			Party, BJP		
Dal, All India			IND		
Trinamool		2000b	b-RJD, INC,	b-MC	
Congress,			BSP, MCC		
Shiv Sena,			CPI, CPM		
PMK, Lok	Chhattisgarh	2003	BJP	SPM	Congruent
Shakti, MDMK,	Delhi	2003	INC	SPM	Congruent
Indian National	Goa	2002	BJP, MJP,	SMC	Congruent
Lok Dal, Mizo			IND		
National Front,	Gujarat	2002	BJP	SPM	Congruent
Sikkim	Haryana	2000	BJP, INLD	OC	Congruent
Democratic	Himachal Pradesh	2003	INC	SPM	Congruent
Front, MSCP,	Jammu & Kashmir	2002	PDF, INC,	C	Congruent
Telugu Desam			Panthers		
Party, TRC,			Party		
MGR Anna	Jharkhand	–			
DMK	Karnataka	1999	INC	SPM	Congruent
	Kerala	2001	UDF	SMC	Congruent
	Madhya Pradesh	2003	BJP	SPM	Congruent
	Maharashtra	1999	INC, NCP	SMC	Congruent
	Manipur	2000/	2000-	C	Incongruent
		2002	MSCP,		
			FPM, NCP,		
			MPP, RJD		
			JD(U), IND-	SMC	Congruent
			2002-INC		
	Meghalaya	2003	Meghalaya	MC	Congruent
			Democratic		
			Alliance		
	Mizoram	2003	MNF	SPM	Congruent
	Nagaland	2003	Democratic	SMC	Congruent
			Alliance		
	Odisha	2000	BJD, BJP	C	Congruent
	Punjab	2002	INC	SPM	Congruent

Table 6 (*Contd.*)

Table 6 (*Contd.*)

Coalition	*State*	*State election year*	*Party/Parties in the state government*	*Types of government*	*Status*
	Puducherry	2001	INC	SPM	Congruent
	Rajasthan	2003	BJP	SPM	Congruent
	Sikkim	1999	SDF	SPM	Congruent
	Tamil Nadu	2001	AIADMK	SPMG	Congruent
	Tripura	2003	CPM Led	OC	Congruent
	Uttar Pradesh	2002	BSP, BJP	C	Congruent
	Uttarakhand	2002	INC	SPM	Congruent
	West Bengal	2001	CPM led	SMC	Congruent

Notes: *INC* Indian National Congress, *BJP* Bhartiya Janata Party, *CPM* Communist Party of India Marxist, *DMK* Dravida Munnetra Kazhagham, *NTRTDP* Telugu Desam Party, Shiromani Akali Dal, *AITC* All Indian Trinamool Congress, *MNF* Mizo National Front, *BJD* Biju Janata Dal, *MDMK* Marumalarchi Dravida Munnetra Kazhagham, *SAP* Samata Party, *LS* Lok Shakti, *PMK* Pattali Makkal Kachhi, *IND* Independent, *MPC* Mizoram People's Conference, *SDF* Sikkim Democratic Front, *JD(U)* Janata Dal United, *MSCP* Manipur State Congress Party, *PDP* Jammu & Kashmir People's Democratic Party, *NCP* Nationalist Congress Party, *FPM* Federal Party of Manipur, *RJD* Rashtriya Janata Dal, MSCP Manipur State Congress Party, *MPP* Manipur People's Party, *INLD* Indian National Lok Dal.

RJD & NCP were not part of the ruling BJP led National Democratic Alliance. The two parties were NDA opponents in Bihar, and Maharashtra respectively.

Coalition	*State*	*State election year*	*Party/Parties in the state government*	*Types of government*	*Status*
2004					
INC, RJD,	Andhra Pradesh	2004	INC	SPM	Congruent
DMK, NCP,	Arunachal Pradesh	2004	INC	SPM	Congruent
PMK, TRS,	Assam	2006	INC	SPM	Congruent
LJP, JMM,	Bihar	2005	JDU, BJP	C	Congruent
MDMK,	Chhattisgarh	2008	BJP	SPM	Congruent
CPI(M),	Delhi	2008	INC	SPM	Congruent
CPI, IUML,	Goa	2007	INC, NCP,	SMC	Congruent
Kerala			MGP, IND		
Congress (M),	Gujarat	2007	BJP	SPM	Congruent
J&K PDP,	Haryana	2005	INC	SPM	Congruent
RPI(A),	Himachal Pradesh	2007	BJP	SPM	Congruent
JD(S),	Jammu & Kashmir	2008	NC, INC	C	Congruent

Table 6 (*Contd.*)

Table 6 (*Contd.*)

Coalition	*State*	*State election year*	*Party/Parties in the state government*	*Types of government*	*Status*
Arunachal Congress, RPI, Peoples' Republican Party, Party for Democratic Socialism	Jharkhand	2005	JMM(S), INC	MC	Congruent
	Karnataka	2004	INC, JD(S)	C	Congruent
		2008	BJP, IND	SMC	
	Madhya Pradesh	2008	BJP	SPM	Congruent
	Maharashtra	2004	INC, NCP	SMC	Congruent
	Manipur	2007	INC led	OC	Congruent
	Meghalaya	2008	MPA (Included NCP)[a]	SMC	Incongruent
	Mizoram	2008	INC	SPM	Congruent
	Nagaland	2008	Democratic Alliance	OC	Congruent
	Odisha	2004	BJD, BJP	C	Congruent
	Punjab	2007	SAD, BJP	C	Congruent
	Puducherry	2006	INC	SPM	Congruent
	Rajasthan	2008	INC	SPM	Congruent
	Sikkim	2004	SDF	SPM	Congruent
	Tamil Nadu	2006	DMK	SPMG	Congruent
	Tripura	2008	CPM Led	OC	Congruent
	Uttar Pradesh	2007	BSP	SPM	Congruent
	Uttarakhand	2007	BJP	SPM	Congruent
	West Bengal	2006	CPM led	OC	Congruent

Notes: *INC* Indian National Congress, *BJP* Bharatiya Janata Party, *CPM* Communist Party of India Marxist, *DMK* Dravida Munnetra Kazhagham, Shiromani Akali Dal, *AITC* All Indian Trinamool Congress, *BJD* Biju Janata Dal, *MDMK* Marumalarchi Dravida Munnetra Kazhagham, *SAP* Samata Party, *LS* Lok Shakti, *PMK* Pattali Makkal Kachhi, *IND* Independent, *SDF* Sikkim Democratic Front, *JD(U)* Janata Dal United, *PDP* Jammu & Kashmir People's Democratic Party, *NCP* Nationalist Congress Party, *FPMRJD* Rashtriya Janata Dal, *RPI(A)* Republic Party of India (Ambedkar), *JMM(S)* Jharkhand Mukti Morcha (Soren), *MGP* Maharashtrawadi Gomantak Party, *IUML* Indian Union Muslim League, *LJP* Lok Janshakti Party, *AC* Arunachal Congress, *TRS* Telangana Rashtra Samiti, *BSP* Bahujan Samaj Party.[a] MPA-Meghalaya Progressive Alliance included NCP, though NCP was part of UPA at the centre. NCP decided not to partner with INC.

Table 6 (*Contd.*)

Table 6 (*Contd.*)

Coalition	*State*	*State election year*	*Party/Parties in the state government*	*Types of government*	*Status*
2009					
All India Trinamool Congress, DMK, NCP, J&K NC, NCP, IUML, JMM, VCK, BPF, KC(M), RPI(A), RPI	Andhra Pradesh	2009	INC	SPM	Congruent
	Arunachal Pradesh	2009	INC	SPM	Congruent
	Assam	2011	INC	SPM	Congruent
	Bihar	2010	JDU, BJP	C	Congruent
	Chhattisgarh	2013	BJP	SPM	Congruent
	Delhi	2013	AAP, INC	C	Incongruent
	Goa	2012	BJP	SPM	Congruent
	Gujarat	2012	BJP	SPM	Congruent
	Haryana	2009	INC	SPM	Congruent
	Himachal Pradesh	2012	INC	SPM	Congruent
	Jammu & Kashmir	–			
	Jharkhand	2009	INC, JMM, IND	SMC	Congruent
	Karnataka	2013	INC	SPM	Congruent
	Kerala	2011	UDF	SMC	Congruent
	Madhya Pradesh	2013	BJP	SPM	Congruent
	Maharashtra	2009	INC, NCP	C	Congruent
	Manipur	2012	INC led	SMC	Congruent
	Meghalaya	2013	INC, IND	SMC	Congruent
	Mizoram	2013	INC	SPM	Congruent
	Nagaland	2013	Democratic Alliance	SMC	Congruent
	Odisha	2009	BJD	SPM	Congruent
	Punjab	2012	SAD, BJP	C	Congruent
	Puducherry	2011	AINRC, AIADMK	C	Congruent
	Rajasthan	2013	BJP	SPM	Congruent
	Sikkim	2009	SDF	SPM	Congruent
	Tamil Nadu	2011	AIADMK	SPM	Congruent
	Tripura	2013	CPM Led	OC	Congruent
	Uttar Pradesh	2012	SP	SPM	Congruent
	Uttarakhand	2012	INC led	SMC	Congruent
	West Bengal	2011	AITC	OC	Congruent

Notes: *INC* Indian National Congress, *BJP* Bhartiya Janata Party, *CPM* Communist Party of India Marxist, *DMK* Dravida Munnetra Kazhagham, Shiromani Akali Dal, *AITC* All Indian Trinamool Congress, *BJD* Biju Janata Dal, *MDMK* Marumalarchi Dravida

Table 6 (*Contd.*)

Table 6 (*Contd.*)

Coalition	*State*	*State election year*	*Party/Parties in the state government*	*Types of government*	*Status*

Munnetra Kazhagham, *SAP* Samata Party, *PMK* Pattali Makkal Kachhi, *IND* Independent, *SDF* Sikkim Democratic Front, *JD(U)* Janata Dal United, *NCP* Nationalist Congress Party, *RJD* Rashtriya Janata Dal, *RPI(A)* Republic Party of India (Ambedkar), *JMM(S)* Jharkhand Mukti Morcha (Soren), *MGP* Maharashtrawadi Gomantak Party, *IUML* Indian Union Muslim League, *LJP* Lok Janshakti Party, *AC* Arunachal Congress, *TRS* Telangana Rashtra Samiti, *BSP* Bahujan Samaj Party, *AIADMK* All India Dravida Munnetra Kazhagham, *AINRC* All India National Rajiv Congress, *BPF* Bodo Peoples Front, *VCK* Viduthalai Chiruthaigal Katchi, *RPI* Republican Party of India, *JKNC* Jammu Kashmir National Conference, *UDF INC* led United Democratic Front, *SP* Samajwadi Party.

INC and AAP fought against each other in a bitterly fought electoral contest. A hung verdict led to the formation of a single party minority government by AAP with the outside support of INC.

Coalition	*State*	*State election year*	*Party/Parties in the state government*	*Types of government*	*Status*
2014					
DMDK, PMK, MDMK, KMDK, Indhiya, Jananayaga Katchi, New Justice Party, Telugu Desam Party, Shiv Sena, Swabhiman Paksha, RPI(A), Swabhiman Paksha, Rashtriya Samaj Paksha, LJP, RLSP, Shiromani Akali Dal,	Andhra	2014	TDP & BJP	OC	Congruent
	Arunachal Pradesh	2014	INC	SPM	Congruent
	Assam	2016	BJP	SPM	Congruent
	Bihar	2015a	a-RJD, JDU, INC	SMC	a-Congurent
		2015b	b-BJP, LJP, JDU, RSLP	SMC	b-Incongruent
	Chhattisgarh	–			
	Delhi	2015			Congruent
	Goa	2017	BJP, MGP, GFP, IND	SMC	Congruent
	Gujarat	–			
	Haryana	2014	BJP	SPM	Congruent
	Himachal Pradesh	–			Congruent
	Jammu & Kashmir	2014	BJP, PDPb	C	Incongruent
	Jharkhand	2014	BJP	SPM	Congruent
	Karnataka	–			
	Kerala	2016	LDF	SMC	Congruent
	Madhya Pradesh	–			

Table 6 (*Contd.*)

Table 6 (*Contd.*)

Coalition	*State*	*State election year*	*Party/Parties in the state government*	*Types of government*	*Status*
Haryana Janhit Congress, Apna	Maharashtra	2014	BJP, Shiv Sena, IND	SMC	Congruent
Dal, RSP (B), Kerala	Manipur	2017	BJP, NPF, IND	SMC	Congruent
Congress (N),	Meghalaya	–			
All Indian NR	Mizoram	–			
Congress, NPP,	Nagaland	–			
MPP, NPF,	Odisha	2014	BJD	SPM	Congruent
UDF, GJM,	Punjab	2017	INC	SPM	Congruent
KPP, MGP,	Puducherry	2016	INC, DMK	C	Congruent
GVP, North	Rajasthan	–			
East Regional	Sikkim	2014	SDF	SPM	Congruent
Political Front	Tamil Nadu	2016	AIADMK	SPM	Congruent
	Telangana	2014	TRS	SPM	Congruent
	Tripura	–			
	Uttar Pradesh	2017	BJP	SPM	Congruent
	Uttarakhand	2017	BJP	SPM	Congruent
	West Bengal	2016	AITC	SPM	Congruent

Notes: *BJP* Bharatiya Janata Party, *INC* Indian National Congress, *RJD* Rashtriya Janata Dal, Aam Aadmi Party, *AITC* All India Trinamool Congress, *SS* Shiv Sena, *PDP* Jammu & Kashmir People's Democratic Party, *BJD* Biju Janata Dal, *AIADMK* All India Anna Dravida Munnetra Kazhagham, PMK Pattali Makkal Katchi, *MDMK* Marumalarchi Munnetra Kazhagham, *DMDK* Desiya Murpokku Dravida Kazhagham, *NPP* Nagaland Peoples Party, *NPF* Nagaland Peoples Front, *MGP* Maharashtrawadi Gomantak Party, *RLSP* Rashtriya Lok Samata Party, *LJP* Lok Janshakti Party, *GVP* Goa Vikas Party, *GFP* Goa Federal Party, *MPP* Manipur Peoples Party, *TDP* Telugu Desam Party, *TRS* Telangana Rashtra Samiti.

[a]JD(U) broke the alliance with RJD and INC in Bihar and decided to form a new government with the support of BJP. The BJP and JD(U) had contested the 2014 parliamentary elections and the 2015 assembly elections against each other.

[b]PDP and BJP had contested the 2014 parliamentary elections and assembly elections against each other. However, the two parties decided to come together and form the government together in Jammu & Kashmir after a hung verdict.

to the fact that the party system since 1989 is not institutionalised but in flux due to the jerky decline of Congress since 1989, with some recoveries like in 2004 and 2009, particularly since 1996, and that the political space consists of not only two major national parties but a host of single-state regional parties.

Congruence is also low due to the growing decentralisation of India's federal system over the period since 1989 in tandem with the growth of economic liberalisation removing many federal level regulatory powers that existed earlier like industrial and import licenses, and the growing presence of regional parties in national governing coalitions, besides the effective removal of emergency powers like the earlier use/misuse of Art. 356, and the growing decentraliation of federal fiscal relations. This development strengthens states vis-à-vis the federal government and strengthens regional parties when in power in their states in relations with the national party heading the national coalition government allowing regional parties to often set the terms of coalition agreements.

However, if we adopt the conceptualisation in the book's template, then congruence is extremely high in that there are only 3.18 per cent cases of incongruence over 1991–2014 of national and state cabinets for a particular national and nearest (in time) state assembly election, "contradicting" each other in having parties in a coalition at one level, state or national, that are opposed at another level, state or national. This is because, for a given national election and nearest-in-time state assembly election, the same regional parties tend to ally with one or another of the two major national parties, the Congress or the BJP, for both national elections and state elections. Hence, how we conceptualise congruence (or incongruence) is vital in arriving at a conclusion as to whether in India coalition congruence is high or not.

Bibliography

Ansari, I. A., *Political Representation of Muslims in India, 1952–2004* (New Delhi: Manak, 2006).

Arora, B., "Negotiating Differences: Federal Coalitions and National Cohesion", in F. Frankel, Z. Hasan, R. Bhargava, and B. Arora, eds, *Transforming India* (Delhi: Oxford University Press, 2000).

Brass, P., "The Politicisation of the Peasantry in a North Indian State", in S. Kaviraj, ed., *Politics in India* (New Delhi: Oxford University Press, 1997).

Butler, David, Ashok Lahiri, and Prannoy Roy, *India Decides: Elections 1952–1995* (New Delhi: Books and Things, 1995).

Diwakar, R., *Party System in India* (New Delhi: Oxford University Press, 2017).

Golder, S. N., "Pre-electoral Coalition Formation in Parliamentary Democracies", *British Journal of Political Science,* 36 (2), 2006, 193–212.

Government of India, *Census of India, 2011,* retrieved 5 July 2011 from http://censusindia.gov. in/Census_Data_2001/India_at_glance/religion.aspx,http://censusindia.gov.in/Census_ Data_2001/India_at_glance/scst.aspx, http://censusindia.gov.in/Census_Data_2001/Census_ Data_Online/Language/Statement5.htm.

Government of India, "Report of the Backward Classes Commission (Mandal Commission Report)", 1980.

Government of India, Planning Commission, "Report of the Expert Group on Methodology for Estimation of Poverty", 2010.

Government of India, Election Commission of India, *Statistical Report on General Elections, Vol. I (Ver. I)—National and State Abstracts,* for 1996, 1998, 1999; accessed from www.eci.gov.in.

Kochanek, S., *The Congress Party of India* (Princeton, NJ: Princeton University Press, 1968).

Kothari, R., *Politics in India* (New Delhi: Orient Longman, 1970).

Manor, J., "Parties and the Party System". in A. Kohli, ed., *India's Democracy* (Princeton: Princeton University Press, 1988).

Rudolph, L., and S. Rudolph, *In Pursuit of Lakshmi: The Political Economy of the Indian State* (Chicago: University of Chicago Press, 1987).

Ruparelia, S., *Divided We Govern: Coalition Politics in Modern India* (New Delhi: Oxford University Press, 2015).

Sisson, R., and R. Roy, *Diversity and Dominance in Indian Politics: Changing Bases of Congress Support,* vol. 1 (New Delhi: Sage, 1990).

Sridharan, E., "The Party System", in N.J. Gopal and P. Mehta, eds, *The Oxford Companion to Politics in India* (New Delhi: Oxford University Press, 2010), 119–29.

Sridharan, E., "Coalition Strategies and the BJP's Expansion, 1989-2004", *Commonwealth and Comparative Politics,* 43 (2), 2005, 194–221.

Sridharan, E., "Electoral Coalitions in the 2004 General Elections: Theory and Evidence", *Economic and Political Weekly,* 39 (51), 2004, 5418–25.

Sridharan, E., "Coalitions and Party Strategies in India's Parliamentary Federation", *Publius*, 33 (4), 2003, 135–52.

Sridharan, E., "The Fragmentation of the Indian Party System, 1952–1999: Seven Competing Explanations", in Z. Hasan, ed., *Parties and Party Politics in India* (New Delhi: Oxford University Press, 2002), 475–503.

Sridharan, E., "Principles, Power and Coalition Politics in India: Lessons from Theory, Comparison and Recent History", in D. Khanna and G. Kueck, eds, *Principles, Power and Politics* (New Delhi: Macmillan, 1999), 270–90.

Weiner, M., *Party Building in a New Nation* (Chicago: University of Chicago Press, 1967).

Yadav, Y., "Reconfiguration in Indian Politics: State Assembly Elections 1993–1995", *Economic and Political Weekly*, 31 (2-3), 1996, 95–104.

9

Why are Multi-party Minority Governments Viable in India? Theory and Comparison

Introduction: Two Questions

THIS PAPER IS AN attempt to compare the distribution of types of coalition and/or minority governments in India with those in long-standing democracies and explain India's apparent exceptionalism. The paper attempts, specifically, to explain the following, both of which make India an outlier in comparative terms: (i) Why have all but one of the non-single party majority governments, been minority governments, of which again all but two have been minority coalitions?[1] (ii) Why have the world's largest coalitions, consisting of 6–12 government parties, been formed in India since 1996?[2]

This paper is divided into the following sections. In the second section, which follows, I discuss the definitions and findings of the comparative literature on coalition and/or minority

[1] The early scholarly work on coalition politics in India focused on the coalition governments in the states from 1967 to 1974. For pioneering theoretically informed work, see Bueno de Mesquita (1975) and Mitra (1978). For more recent, theoretically informed, work analysing the post-1989 period, see Wyatt (1999), Sridharan (1999, 2003, 2004b, 2005), Nikolenyi (2002, 2004), Adeney and Saez (2005), and Macmillan (2005). For detailed accounts sensitive to the federal dimension and to history, see Arora (2000, 2002), Singh (2004a) and particularly, Chakrabarty (2005), for a comprehensive bibliography on coalition politics in India.

[2] I take into account the government formed after the 2009 elections for purposes of counting the number, types of, and number of parties in, governments.

governments. In the third, I profile the main parties and outline the history of coalition and/or minority governments in India. In the fourth, I look at the findings of the comparative literature on coalitions, and at India's minority governments in the light of theory, arguing that there are both general and India-specific rationales for the viability of multi-party minority coalitions. In the fifth, I detail the above two key regularities from the data which make India seem exceptional. In the sixth, I attempt to explain them. In the seventh, I conclude that Indian coalition behaviour fits rational-choice logic if one factors in the above general and India-specific rationales for minority governments.

Coalition and/or Minority Governments: Definitions

Before comparing India with other durable democracies in Tables 1 and 2, I begin with the following explanatory preface on definitions and their meaningfulness for party behaviour in India. My definition of government is comparable to the European data in Table 2, in that I use the Council of Ministers, that is, cabinet ministers and ministers of state (deputy/junior ministers), as equivalent to the term "cabinet" since in India both levels taken together constitute the political executive that is accountable to parliament. The Council of Ministers is also the locus for coalition formation since some small but crucial parties are accommodated at the minister of state level only.[3] I do not count parties which have not won a Lok Sabha (Lower House) seat but have a minister who is

[3] For example, in the two United Front governments of 1996–8, two small but electorally important parties at the state level, MGP and Congress (Tiwari), only had ministers of state; the same applied to Arunachal Congress and National Conference in the first and second Vajpayee governments, and to IUML in the Manmohan Singh government. The large and crucial ally, BJD, of Orissa state, had no cabinet minister in the Vajpayee government from early 2000 to its end in 2004.

a Rajya Sabha (Upper House) member since the latter do not participate in Lok Sabha votes of confidence or no-confidence.[4] Woldendorp *et al.* (1998), on whom I base Table 1, define a government as "any administration that is formed after an election and continues in the absence of: (a) a change of prime minister; (b) a change in the party composition of the cabinet; or (c) the resignation in an inter-election period followed by re-formation of the government with the same prime minister and party composition."[5]

Muller and Strom definitions,[6] on which Table 2 is based and which is also the basis for their Parliamentary Democracy Data Archive on coalition governments in Western Europe, use the following criteria for change of government: any election, any change in the identity of the prime minister or any change in the party composition of the cabinet, this being identical to Woldendorp *et al.* (1993), except for the latter's category (c) above not being a change of government for Muller and Strom.[7]

An alternative definition is to define governments by change of prime minister or fresh elections, *ignoring* the exit/addition of parties and independents if it does not lead to resignation of the prime minister. This also fits the legal definition in India, that is, it is considered the same government if the prime minister (and automatically, cabinet) do not resign. It also captures actual *political* behaviour better because governments after all view themselves and their options, constraints and incentives in coalition politics in terms of the existing constitutional rules and not in

[4] Three prime ministers, H.D. Deve Gowda, I.K. Gujral, and Manmohan Singh were/are Rajya Sabha members; this is constitutionally acceptable in India though the government is accountable to the Lok Sabha.

[5] Woldendorp *et al.* 1993: 5.

[6] Muller and Strom 2000/2003/2006: 13.

[7] I acknowledge use of the Parliamentary Democracy Data Archive, http://www.pol. umu.se/ccpd/Database.htm accessed on 15 May 2008, and Muller and Strom (2000/2003/2006).

Table 1. World Democracies: Type and Duration of Governments 1945–1995

Country	*SPM*	*MWC*	*SC*
Australia	9,6344,705	18,11,076,615	0, 0, 0
Austria	3,4232,1411	15,12,144,810	1,1420,1420
Belgium	3,139,464	23,14,817,644	5,1581,316
Canada	12,14,283,1190	0, 0, 0	0, 0, 0
Denmark	0, 0, 0	4,3226,807	0, 0, 0
Finland[a]	0, 0, 0	6,3044,507	20,10,953,548
France	0, 0, 0	6,1965,328	38,12,265,323
Germany	0, 0, 0	15,12,232,815	5,3513,1703
Iceland	0, 0, 0	18,15,772,876	1,1202,1202
Ireland	7,6026,861	4,4845,1211	0, 0, 0
Israel	0, 0, 0	15,4873,325	20,11,071,554
Italyb	0, 0, 0	3,944,315	28,10,191,364
Japan	23,12,593,548	1,373,373	6,2504,417
Luxembourg	0, 0, 0	15,17,706,1180	1,466,466
Netherlands	0, 0, 0	7,8400,1200	9,8476,942
New Zealand	23,18,813,818	2,464,232	0, 0, 0
Norway	6,5791,965	3,2880,960	0, 0, 0
Sweden	3,1478,493	5,3542,708	0, 0, 0
Switzerland	0, 0, 0	6,2185,364	45,16,436,365
UK	17,15,570,916	0, 0, 0	0, 0, 0
Total	106,86,522,816	166,120,488,726	179,80,078,447

Table 1 (*Contd.*)

Table 1 (*Contd.*)

SPMG	*MC*	*Caretaker*	*Total*
0, 0, 0	0, 0, 0	0, 0, 0	27,17,420,645
1,548,548	0, 0, 0	0, 0, 0	20,18,344,917
1,134,134	2,69,35	2,399,200	36,18,392,511
7,3333,476	0, 0, 0	0, 0, 0	19,17,616,927
14,7938,567	10,6689,669	0, 0, 0	28,17,853,638
4,1976,494	7,978,140	4,739,185	41,17,690,431
4,2340,585	5,1516,303	2,68,34	55,18,154,330
1,501,501	0, 0, 0	4,253,63	25,16,499,660
2,448,224	0, 0, 0	0, 0, 0	21,17,422,830
4,3488,872	4,2734,684	0, 0, 0	19,17,093,900
0,0,0	2,321,161	5,945,189	42,17,210,410
11,3139,285	8,2131,266	4,626,157	54,17,031,315
7,2336,334	2,325,163	0, 0, 0	39,18,131,465
0, 0, 0	0, 0, 0	0, 0, 0	16,18,172,1136
0, 0, 0	0,0, 0	4,706,177	20,17,582,879
0, 0, 0	0, 0, 0	0, 0, 0	25,19,277,771
10,7865,787	4,938,235	0, 0, 0	23,17,474,760
13,10,898,838	2,1603,802	0, 0, 0	23,17,521,762
0, 0, 0	0, 0, 0	0, 0, 0	51,18,621,365
1,227,227	0, 0, 0	0, 0, 0	18,15,797,878
80,45,171,565	46,17,304,376	25,3736,149	602,353,299,587

Notes: Caretaker (C), govt. formed is not interested to undertake any kind of serious policy-making; only minding the shop; MC, minority coalition; MWC, minimal winning coalition; SC (MP), surplus coalition (majority party); SC, surplus coalition; SC (NMP), surplus coalition (no majority party); SPM, single party majority govt; SPMG, single party minority government.

Source: Woldendorp *et al.* (1998). [a]The three numbers in each cell denote the number of governments, their total duration in days, and the average duration in days per government. The four X's referring to governments in the original table from which this table is derived which are not classified by type and hence omitted, total to 505 days, one of which lasted 347 days.

Table 2. Coalition Cabinets in Europe, 1945–1999

Country	*SPM*	*MWC*	*SC*
Austria	4, 5548, 1387	13, 10229, 787	3, 1626, 542
Belgium	3, 1393, 469	15, 10,638, 709	11, 4428, 402
Denmark	0, 0, 0	4, 3096, 774	0, 0, 0
Finland	0, 0, 0	6, 3117, 520	19, 10,476, 551
France	1, 611, 611	6, 4484, 747	8, 5611, 701
Germany	1, 442, 442	16, 14,520, 908	5, 2454, 491
Greece	6, 5309, 885	1, 92, 92	1, 141, 141
Iceland	0, 0, 0	16, 15,585, 974	4, 2850, 713
Ireland	6, 5657, 943	5, 5585, 1117	0, 0, 0
Italy	0, 0, 0	3, 1431, 477	21, 8974, 427
Luxemburg	0, 0, 0	14, 17,085, 1220	1, 472, 472
Netherlands	0, 0, 0	9, 9351, 1039	9, 7782, 865
Norway	6, 5775, 963	3, 2790, 930	0, 0, 0
Portugal	2, 2946, 1473	3, 1251, 417	3, 787, 262
Spain	2, 2489, 1245	0, 0, 0	0, 0, 0
Sweden	2, 735, 368	5, 3520, 704	0, 0, 0
UK	18, 18,430, 1024	0, 0, 0	0, 0, 0
Total	51, 49,335, 967	120, 102,774, 856	84, 45,601, 543

Table 2 (*Contd.*)

Table 2 (*Contd.*)

SPMG	*MC*	*Total*
1,537,537	0,0,0	21,17,940,854
2,141,71	1,47,47	32,16,647,520
14,7806,558	12,7890,658	30,18,792,626
4,1829,457	7,872,125	36,16,294,453
5,1804,361	2,1243,622	22,13,753,625
3,72,24	0, 0, 0	25,17,488,700
2,1309,655	0, 0, 0	10,6851,685
4,444,111	1,348,348	25,19,227,769
6,4878,813	4,2593,648	21,18,713,891
14,3044,217	9,3170,352	47,16,619,354
0, 0, 0	0, 0, 0	15,17,557,1170
0, 0, 0	3,319,106	21,17,452,831
12,9321,777	4,997,249	25,18,883,755
2,984,492	0, 0, 0	10,5968,597
5,4209,842	0, 0, 0	7,6698,957
16,13,450,841	2,1569,785	25,19,274,771
1,200,200	0, 0, 0	19,18,630,981
91,50,028,550	45,19,048,423	391,266,786,682

Notes: See notes to Table 1 for column heading acronyms. The three numbers in each cell denote the number of governments, their total duration in days, and the average duration in days per government. The cabinets in the database for which either the data is missing (code99999) or is not applicable (88888) or which are still continuing in office in 1999, are not included in the above table. It includes only the cabinets for which complete data is available.

Source: Parliamentary Democracy Data Archive, http://www.pol.umu.se/ccpd/Database.htm, accessed on 18 July 2008, and Muller and Strom (2000/2003/ 2006).

terms of scholarly classificatory categories. This definition helps to focus on the *manoeuvring* to remain in power, including adding coalition partners, negotiating outside support from other parties, and so forth. This focus is explanatorily important because it *has a bearing on the types, size and ideological diversity* of coalitions formed.[8] So I use this alternative definition in Tables 4 and 5 but also use, for comparative purposes the international data sets (Tables 1 and 2) based on Woldendorp *et al.* (1998) and Muller and Strom (2000/2003/2006), respectively, and use these standard definitions applied to the Indian case in Tables 3 and 6.[9] However, the comparative point made by Table 6 is that the exceptional nature of the size and distribution of types of coalition governments in India is *identical* whether one uses the Indian definition or the standard scholarly definitions of government. By both there is an exceptional prevalence of minority governments and within them, of minority coalitions since 1989, and since 1996, an exceptional prevalence of very large coalitions of 6–12 parties in government.

I define duration as in the notes to Table 4 from swearing-in to date of resignation, or notification of fresh elections in case of a government completing a full term, whichever occurs first, because there have been caretaker governments for several months after loss of confidence and formal resignation until the swearing-in of a new government after elections.[10] However, for comparability

[8] If one counts a change of government by the exit or entry of even one party or independent from/to a coalition, as per the standard definitions above, and given the large coalitions of 6–12 parties in the post-1996 period, then we get a very large number of separate governments, e.g. 11 for the NDA government of 1999-2004 (Table 6), from what is legally one government with the same prime minister. This *obscures* the *strategic* behaviour of the prime minister and leading party in such coalitions.

[9] In other words, one government by the alternative (Indian legal) definition could have two or more coalitions of parties by standard Woldendorp *et al.* (1998) and Muller and Strom (2000/2003/2006) definitions.

[10] This is almost identical to Muller and Strom (2000/2003/2006, 16, and Table 2) in which government duration is taken as up to the formal resignation

with Tables 1 and 2, in Tables 3 and 6, I follow Woldendorp *et al.* (1998), for definitions of duration (till the next swearing-in) as well as Muller and Strom (2000/2003/2006).[11]

On types of governments, I use the same categories as the above data sets (Woldendorp *et al.*, 1998; Muller and Strom, 2000/2003/2006), that is, single-party majority governments, single-party minority governments, minority coalitions, minimal winning coalitions, but I differentiate between surplus coalitions (no majority party), henceforth SC(NMP), and surplus coalitions (majority party) (Tables 4–6), not clubbing them together as surplus coalitions as in Woldendorp *et al.* (1998), except in Tables 1–3.[12]

---

date even if it continued in office until the next swearing-in, and *unlike* Woldendorp *et al.* (1993, 1998, and Table 1) which takes duration up to the next swearing-in. The rationale is that, *politically* speaking, the coalition has either lost the confidence of parliament, or in the case of notification of fresh elections, the Election Commission's restrictions on certain types of policy decisions become operative (to neutralise incumbency advantage and ensure a level playing field) and hence the government is not one with full powers. For example, the durations (Table 4) of the governments of Janata Party (Secular) in 1979–80, Samajwadi Janata Party in 1990–1, United Front (of Inder Gujral), 1997–8, look extremely extended by the criterion of the date of the next government's swearing-in, since they lost their majority several months before that. The Charan Singh government, 1979–80, lost the confidence of parliament and resigned in twenty-three days but it carried on as a caretaker government until the swearing in of the next government for over four times as long!

[11] I classify a government's status by what it began as (e.g. government that began as a minority government is classified as such even if it changed status to a majority government by merging defectors into the ruling party/ies, *so long as it does not add to the number of parties*, thereby remaining the same government even under standard international definitions. This is because it shows that a minority government can secure and extend its duration by change of status to majority status while remaining the same government by the Indian and international definitions. Some minority governments have survived by such means without any change in party composition (Congress 1991–6).

[12] At the national level (Table 4) there is only one surplus coalition (majority party). The literature tends to use the terms 'surplus majority coalition" (Laver and Schofield, 1990/1998) and "oversized coalitions" (Strom 1990;

Table 3. Indian Governments by International Definitions, 1947–2009

	SPM	*MWC*	*SC*
India govts (Woldendorp *et al.*)	10,14,337,1434	0, 0, 0	1,856,856
India govts (Muller and Strom)	13,13,845,1065	0, 0, 0	1,843,843

Table 3 (*Contd.*)

Table 3 (*Contd.*)

SPMG	*MC*	*Caretaker*	*Total*
2, 2014, 1007	19, 4680, 246	6, 455, 76	38, 22,342, 588
2, 1849, 925	22, 4445, 202	–	38, 20,982, 552

Notes: See notes to Table 1 for column heading acronyms. The three numbers in each cell denote the number of governments, their total duration in days, and the average duration in days per government. This table shows Indian governments from 1947 to 2009, excluding the government formed in 2009, according to the Woldendorp et al. (1993, 1998) definitions and the Muller and Strom (2000/2003/2006) definitions, for 1947–2009, derived from the relevant columns of Table 6. These rows were not inserted into Tables 1 and 2, but shown here as a separate table since the period is different and more up to date, which is important for the argument about coalitions in India. The caretaker governments are government nos 5, 7, 12, 14, 19 and 24 of Table 6.

Table 4. Coalition and Minority Governments (by Indian Definition of Government)

S. No.	*Coalition and/or minority governments (leading party or coalition)*	*Type of government*	*Number of partiesa*	*Date of swearing in*	*Date of resignation or notification of fresh elections*	*Number of days*
1.	Janata Party	SC(MP)[b]	2	24 March 1977	15 July 1979	843
2.	Janata Party (Secular)	MC	2	28 July 1979	20 August 1979	23
3.	Janata Dal-led National Front	MC	3	02 December 1989	7 November 1990	340
4.	Samajwadi Janata Party	SPMG	1	10 November 1990	6 March 1991	116
5.	Congress	SPMG[c]	1	21 June 1991*	27 March 1996	1741
6.	BJP-led coalition	MC	3	16 May 1996	28 May 1996	12
7.	UF under H.D. Deve Gowda	MC	9	1 June 1996	21 April 1997	324
8.	UF under I.K. Gujral	MC	10	21 April 1997	28 November 1997	221
9.	BJP-led coalition	MC	11	19 March 1998	17 April 1999	394
10.	NDA	MC	12	13 October 1999	29 February 2004	1599
11.	UPA I	MC	9	22 May 2004	2 March 2009	1745
12.	UPA II	MC	6	22 May 2009	–	–

Notes: See notes to Table 1 for type of government acronyms. I have placed surplus coalitions (majority party) and surplus coalition (no majority party) as separate categories of surplus coalitions (SCs). SC(MP)s are those in which a coalition government is formed by a party that enjoys a majority on its own while SC(NMP)s are majority coalition governments which have parties or independents not necessary for a majority but in which no single party has a majority. Alternative (Indian) definition of government: change of governments is defined by the change of prime minister. I ignore the exit of parties and independents if they do not lead to government termination due to resignation of the prime minister or notification for fresh elections. This fits the Indian legal definition of government. I count an independent as a separate member of a coalition. I classify a government's status by what it began as (e.g. government that began as a minority government is classified as such even if it changed status to a majority government by merging, losing defectors or coalition partners). This is because it shows that a minority government can secure and extend its duration by change of status to majority status while remaining the same government by the Indian definition. I calculate duration by calculating the number of days between the dates of swearing in and resignation of the prime minister or fresh notification of elections, whichever is earlier, including the former date and excluding the latter date, despite the government continuing until the next swearing in by the Indian legal definition, including its 'caretaker' phase.

Table 4 (*Contd.*)

Table 4 (*Contd.*)

Source: Asian Recorder, Keesing's Contemporary Archives, Data India. [a]I exclude parties that have a minister only from the Rajya Sabha (Upper House). [b]Janata Party government treated as a surplus coalition (majority party) due to the Akali Dal being a coalition partner. NDA, National Democractic Alliance led by BJP; UPA, United Progressive Alliance led by Congress. See notes to Table 5 for names and acronyms of parties. [c]Congress acquired a majority by merging defectors on 31 December 1993.

The Fragmentation of the Indian Party System and the Evolution of Coalition Governments

Before describing the evolution of coalition politics, I briefly profile the major Indian parties and distinguish between national and regional parties. Historically, the Indian National Congress (henceforth, Congress) dominated the landscape. It was the umbrella party of the independence movement and won seven of the eight post-independence elections from 1952 to 1984, and has ruled India for 52 of the 65 years since independence in 1947, winning majorities until 1989 (except in 1977) with pluralities of the vote of 40 per cent and above, against a fragmented opposition. Even since 1989 it has maintained a vote share plurality in all seven elections. The Congress is a secular party that subscribes to a linguistically and culturally pluralist notion of Indian nationhood. There are four other major categories of parties (each not necessarily constituting a coalition). I classify them as Hindu nationalist (the Bharatiya Janata Party, or BJP, and the Shiv Sena), the Communist

Volden and Carrubba, 2004) synonymously to mean what I call surplus coalitions (following Woldendorp *et al.*, 1998). I define, for the discussion on India, and for Tables 4–6, surplus coalitions (no majority party) more narrowly as coalition governments in which parties not necessary for a majority are in the government but in which the largest party does not have a majority on its own. I define surplus coalitions (majority party) as those coalition governments in which the largest party has a majority on its own and can, if it wished, form a single-party majority government. I define surplus coalitions as the total of these two categories (as used in Tables 1–3).

Table 5. Parties in Coalition Governments, Names and Numbers (by Indian Definition of Government)

Government	*Number of parties in ministry from Lok Sabha*	*Parties in ministry from Rajya Sabha*	*Post-electoral allies joining the ministry*	*Post-election/ split parties offering external support to the government*	*Pre-electoral coalition parties opting to give external support to the ministry*
Janata Party	JP, SAD (2)	–	–	–	–
Janata Party Secular	JP(S), AIADMK (2)	–	–	Congress	–
National Front	JD, TDP, Cong(S) (3)	DMK, AGP	–	–	BJP and the Left Parties supporting from outside
Samajwadi Janata Party	SJP(1)	Janata Party	–	Congress supporting from outside	–
Congress	Congress(1)	–	–	–	–
BJP	BJP, SHS, SAD (3)	–	–	–	–
UF under Deve Gowda	JD, TMC, SP, DMK, TDP, CPI, Cong(T), AGP, MGP (9)	Y.K. Alagh, B.S. Ramoowalia	CPI	CPI(M), RSP, AIFB Congress	–
UF under Inder Kumar Gujral	JD, TMC, SP, DMK, TDP, CPI, Cong(I), AGP, MGP (9)	NC, Y.K. Alagh, B.S. Ramoowalia	–	CPI(M), RSP, AIFB, Congress	–
BJP-led coalition	AC, BJP, SMT, BJD, PMK, SAD, SHS, AIADMK,	TRC	AC	NC, TDP, HLD(R), SDF MSCP, BSMC,	WBTC, HVP, MDMK, Ind (S.S. Kainth)

Table 5 (*Contd.*)

Table 5 (*Contd.*)

Government	*Number of parties in ministry from Lok Sabha*	*Parties in ministry from Rajya Sabha*	*Post-electoral allies joining the ministry*	*Post-election/ split parties offering external support to the government*	*Pre-electoral coalition parties opting to give external support to the ministry*
	LS, Inds (Buta Singh, Maneka Gandhi) (11)			Citizen Common Front, RJP (A.M. Singh)	
NDA	BJP, RLD, WBTC, SHS, SAD, JD(U), DMK, MDMK, NC, MSCP, Ind (Maneka Gandhi), PMK, BJD, IFDP (14)[b]	Ram Jethmalani	NC, RLD, IFDP	Independents (S.K. Bwismuthiary, Vanlalzawma)	TDP, INLD, SDF, HVC, ABLTC, MADMK[c]
UPA I	Congress, NCP, IUML, PMK, DMK, JMM, TRS, LJP, RJD (9)	–	–	Left Front, SP, BSP, AIMIM, SDF	JKPDP, MDMK, Kerala Congress
UPA II	Congress, WBTC, DMK, NCP, NC, IUML (6)	–	–	SP, BSP, RJD, JD(S), SDF, NPF, AUDF, JVM(P), BVA, Inds (M. Koda, S. Mandlik, G.H. Khan)	JMM, AIMIM, BPF, Kerala Congress, VCK

Notes: For alternative definitions see notes to Table 4. Parties in column 4 are included in column 2, but not parties/independents from column 2 which is there only for information. JP(S), Janata Party (Secular); SAD, Shiromani Akali Dal; JD, Janata Dal; DMK, Dravida Munnetra Kazhagam; TDP, Telugu Desam Party; AGP, Asom Gana Parishad; Cong(S), Congress (Socialist); SJP, Samajwadi Janata Party; BJP, Bharatiya Janata Party; SHS, Shiv Sena; TMC, Tamil Maanila Congress; SP, Samajwadi Party; CPI, Communist Party of India; CPI(M), Communist Party of India (Marxist); Cong (T), Congress (Tiwari); MGP, Maharashtrawadi Gomantak Party; NC, National Confer-

Table 5 (*Contd.*)

Table 5 (*Contd.*)

ence; RSP, Revolutionary Socialist Party; AIFB, All India Forward Bloc; AC, Arunachal Congress; SMT, Samata Party; BJD, Biju Janata Dal; PMK, Pattali Makkal Katchi; AIADMK, All India Anna Dravida Munnetra Kazhagam; MDMK, Marumalarchi Dravida Munnetra Kazhagam; NC, Jammu & Kashmir National Conference; MSCP, Manipur State Congress Party; TRC, Tamizhaga Rajiv Congress; HLD(R), Haryana Lok Dal (Rashtriya); SDF, Sikkim Democratic Front; BSMC, Bodoland State Movement Committee; BPF, Bodoland People's Front; RJP, Rashtriya Janata Party; HVP, Haryana Vikas Party; HVC, Himachal Vikas Congress; RLD, Rashtriya Lok Dal; WBTC, West Bengal Trinamul Congress; JD(U), Janata Dal (United); ABLTC, Akhil Bharatiya Loktantrik Congress; MADMK, MGR Anna Dravida Munnetra Kazhagam; IUML, Indian Union Muslim League; JMM, Jharkhand Mukti Morcha; TRS, Telangana Rashtra Samithi; LJP, Lok Janshakti Party; RJD, Rashtriya Janata Dal; BSP, Bahujan Samaj Party; JKPDP, Jammu & Kashmir People's Democratic Party; AIMIM, All India Majlis Ittehadul Muslimeen; IFDP, Indian Federal Democratic Party; NPF, Nagaland People's Front; AUDF, Assam United Democratic Front; JVM(P), Jharkhand Vikas Morcha (Prajatantrik); Bahujan Vikas Aghadi; VCK, Viduthalai Chiruthaigal Katchi.

Source: http://www.indian-elections.com/index.html, accessed on 1 May 2008; http://www.rediff.com/news/elec.htm, accessed on 1 May 2008. [a]Comprehensive seat adjustments without formal coalition. [b]Fourteen parties were part of the BJP-led NDA at various times but they were not there at the same time; the largest government was of 12 parties. [c]AC, TRC and two BSP splinter groups won no seats.

parties (the CPI(M), the CPI), the agrarian/lower-caste populist (the Janata Party, the Janata Dal and its off- shoots like the Samajwadi Party, Rashtriya Janata Dal, Rashtriya Lok Dal, Biju Janata Dal, Janata Dal (Secular), Janata Dal (United), etc.) and ethnic/ ethno-regional parties based on particular regional linguistic groups (DMK, AIADMK, SAD, TDP, AGP) or lower-caste blocs (BSP) or tribes (JMM) (Table 5, Notes, for acronyms used hereon). Except for the Congress, BJP and CPI (M), these are regional parties with a single-state stronghold.[13]

The first four general elections to the Lok Sabha (Lower House), in 1952, 1957, 1962, and 1967, coincided with elections

[13] Regional party is something of a misnomer as it implies a party strong in two or more states in a region. All the regional parties, however, are single state-based parties except the Janata Dal (United), strong in Bihar and Karnataka, and the CPI (M), strong in West Bengal, Tripura, and Kerala, if one considers them regional parties. These sets of states do not constitute recognisable regions. The JD (U) and the CPI (M) are really national parties with a limited geographical spread, the former being a rump of the once much larger Janata Dal.

to all the state assemblies. In the first three of these, the Congress party won two-thirds majorities in the Lok Sabha on the basis of only vote share pluralities of 44–48 per cent. It also won a majority of seats in nearly all state assembly elections from 1952–62, again on the basis of mostly a plurality of votes against a fragmented opposition. From 1967 onward, a consolidation of the non-Congress opposition took place, state-by-state, in tandem with such consolidation in state assembly elections leading to either two-party, one party versus a coalition, or two- coalition systems, i.e. bipolar systems. This bipolar consolidation was the key feature and driving force of the fragmentation of the national party system.[14] But this bipolar consolidation has been one of *multiple bipolarities* (e.g. Congress-BJP, Congress-Left, Congress-Regional Party, in different states), thereby contributing to fragmentation at the national level.

Duvergerian dynamics were the drivers of these multiple bipolarities. Duverger's law states that the first-past-the-post or single-member simple plurality (SMSP) system produces an imperative of consolidation of voters (and politicians) around a principal rival party to have a realistic chance of winning against a dominant party, thus leading to the elimination of third parties, or at least an alliance of other parties against a leading party.[15] While Duverger's law applies essentially at the constituency level, where strong local/state parties exist as in a federal polity like India's where the states are linguistic and cultural entities reflecting such social cleavages, and where the division of powers makes state-level power politically attractive enough to form single-state parties, Duvergerian dynamics can lead to two-party or bipolar state party

[14] For an account and explanation of the Duvergerian dynamic of bipolarisation at the district and state levels, see Chhibber and Murali (2006). For a view that Duverger's law does not apply at the district level, see Diwakar (2007); however, the latter's argument is consistent with state-level bipolar, if not two-party systems.

[15] See Duverger (1963) for the full argument.

Table 6: Coalitions by Prime Minister (by Woldendorp *et al.*, 1998; Muller & Strom, 2000/2003/2006, Definitions of Government and Duration)

S. No.	*Name of Prime Minister*	*Date of swearing in*	*Date of resignation or dissolution Lok Sabha or notification of elections whichever is earliest*	*Date of demitting office*
1.	Jawaharlal Nehru	15 August 1947	14 November 1951	13 May 1952
2.	Jawaharlal Nehru	13 May 1952	19 January 1957	17 April 1957
3.	Jawaharlal Nehru	17 April 1957	13 January 1962	1 April 1962
4.	Jawaharlal Nehru	1 April 1962		27 May 1964
5.	Gulzari Lal Nanda	27 May 1964		9 June 1964
6.	Lal Bahadur Shastri	9 June 1964		11 January 1966
7.	Gulzari Lal Nanda	11 January 1966		24 January 1966
8.	Indira Gandhi	24 January 1966	13 January 1967	13 March 1967
9.	Indira Gandhi	13 March 1967	27 December 1970	18 March 1971
10.	Indira Gandhi	18 March 1971	10 February 1977	24 March 1977
11.	Morarji Desai	24 March 1977	15 July 1979	28 July 1979
12.	Ch. Charan Singh	28 July 1979	20 August 1979	14 January 1980
13.	Indira Gandhi	14 January 1980		31 October 1984
14.	Rajiv Gandhi	31 October 1984	20 November 1984	31 December 1984
15.	Rajiv Gandhi	31 December 1984	23 October 1989	2 December 1989
16.	Vishwanath Pratap Singh	2 December 1989		10 November 1990
17.	Chandra Shekhar	10 November 1990	6 March 1991	21 June 1991
18.	P. V. Narasimha Rao	21 June 1991	19 March 1996	16 May 1996
19.	Atal Behari Vajpayee	16 May 1996	28 May 1996	1 June 1996
20.	H.D. Deve Gowda	1 June 1996		21 April 1997
21.	Inder Kumar Gujral	21 April 1997	28 November 1997	19 March 1998
22.	Atal Behari Vajpayee	19 March 1998		20 April 1998[a]
23.	Atal Behari Vajpayee	20 April 1998		14 April 1999[b]
24.	Atal Behari Vajpayee	14 April 1999	17 April 1999	13 October 1999
25.	Atal Behari Vajpayee	13 October 1999		5 February 2001[c]
26.	Atal Behari Vajpayee	5 February 2001		15 March 2001[d]
27.	Atal Behari Vajpayee	15 March 2001		22 July 2001[e]
28.	Atal Behari Vajpayee	22 July 2001		1 July 2002[f]

Table 6 (*Contd.*)

Table 6 (*Contd.*)

Number of parties in the government (Lok Sabha) only	*Type of government*	*Total number of days by Muller and Strom*	*Number of days by Woldendorp et. al.*	*Party or leading party and coalition*
1	SPM	1552	1733	Congress
1	SPM	1712	1800	Congress
1	SPM	1732	1810	Congress
1	SPM	787	787	Congress
1	SPM	13	13	Congress
1	SPM	581	581	Congress
1	SPM	13	13	Congress
1	SPM	353	413	Congress
1	SPM	1385	1466	Congress
1	SPM	2156	2198	Congress
2	SC(MP)	843	856	Janata Party
2	MC	23	170	Janata Party Secular
1	SPM	1752	1752	Congress
1	SPM	21	61	Congress
1	SPM	1788	1797	Congress
3	MC	343	343	Janata Dal-led NF
1	SPMG	116	223	Samajwadi Janata Party
1	SPMG	1733	1791	Congress
3	MC	12	16	BJP-led coalition
9	MC	109	109	Janata Dal-led UF
10	MC	221	332	Janata Dal-led UF
11	MC	32	32	BJP-led coalition
10	MC	359	359	BJP-led coalition
9	MC	3	182	BJP-led coalition
12	MC	479	479	BJP-led NDA
11	MC	38	38	BJP-led NDA
10	MC	129	129	BJP-led NDA
11	MC	344	344	BJP-led NDA

Table 6 (*Contd.*)

Table 6 (*Contd.*)

S. No.	*Name of Prime Minister*	*Date of swearing in*	*Date of resignation or dissolution Lok Sabha or notification of elections whichever is earliest*	*Date of demitting office*
29.	Atal Behari Vajpayee	1 July 2002		23 December 2002
30.	Atal Behari Vajpayee	23 December 2002		23 May 2003[h]
31.	Atal Behari Vajpayee	23 May 2003		8 September 2003[i]
32.	Atal Behari Vajpayee	8 September 2003		21 December 2003[j]
33.	Atal Behari Vajpayee	21 December 2003		30 December 2003[k]
34.	Atal Behari Vajpayee	30 December 2003		12 January 2004[l]
35.	Atal Behari Vajpayee	12 January 2004	29 February 2004	22 May 2004[m]
36.	Manmohan Singh	22 May 2004		24 July 2004[n]
37.	Manmohan Singh	24 July 2004		23 September 2006[o]
38.	Manmohan Singh	23 September 2006	2 March 2009	22 May 2009
39.	Manmohan Singh	22 May 2009	–	–

Notes: Dates of swearing-in include not only legal swearing in but also the start of a new government by Woldendorp *et al.* (1993, 1998) and Muller and Strom (2000/ 2003/2006) criteria, e.g. after the exit of a coalition partner. See notes to Table 1 for type of government acronyms. I follow the West European definition of Muller and Strom (2000/2003/2006) and the Parliamentary Democracy Data Archive (www.pol.umu.se/ccpd), and the cross-national definition of Woldendorp *et al.* (1998) and count a new cabinet only when (a) the party composition of the executive coalition changes (b) the prime minister changes (c) there is a general election. I further count independents as separate members of a coalition. I exclude parties which have a minister only from the Upper House. Due to the above reasons I do not classify the 1969 split in the Congress and formation of Congress(R) as leading to a separate government. This is so because there is no change of prime minister, no change of party composition and there is no general election. I do not count the addition of individual MPs to the ruling party as a change of government. For this reason P.V. Narasimha Rao's 1991 government is treated as an SPMG, even though there was a change of status and the government attained a majority in 1993. This was due to the independent MP's joining the Congress. I calculate the total duration (in days) of the government by both Wolderndorp et al. (1993, 1998) and Muller and Strom (2000/2003/2006). In the former case, I define it as the date of swearing in to the date of swearing in of the next government, and by Muller and Strom's definition, by the date of swearing in to the date of resignation or notification of fresh elections, or the change (a) above which does not involve resignation of the prime minister or an election. In each case I include the first date and exclude the second date mentioned in calculating duration.

Table 6 (*Contd.*)

Table 6 (*Contd.*)

Number of parties in the government (Lok Sabha) only	*Type of government*	*Total number of days by Muller and Strom*	*Number of days by Woldendorp et. al.*	*Party or leading party and coalition*
11	MC	175	175	BJP-led NDA
11	MC	151	151	BJP-led NDA
10	MC	108	108	BJP-led NDA
11	MC	104	104	BJP-led NDA
10	MC	9	9	BJP-led NDA
9	MC	13	13	BJP-led NDA
8	MC	48	131	BJP-led NDA
9	MC	63	63	Congress-led UPA
8	MC	791	791	Congress-led UPA
7	MC	891	972	Congress-led UPA
6	MC	–	–	Congress-led UPA

Source: Same as Table 5. [a]Buta Singh forced by A.B. Vajpayee to resign from the cabinet. [b]AIADMK ministers resigned from the Union Council of Ministers. [c]PMK quits NDA and the Union Council of Ministers. [d]Trinamool Congress quits NDA and the Union Council of Ministers. [e]RLD joins the NDA, Ajit Singh sworn in as the cabinet minister. [f]PMK rejoins the Union Council of Ministers, Maneka Gandhi (Ind) dropped from the Union Council of Ministers. She continues to support the government. [g]NC quits the Union Council of Ministers. [h]RLD quits the NDA and the Union Council of Ministers, and IFDP joins the Union Council of Ministers. [i]Trinamool Congress joins the NDA and the Union Council of Ministers. [j]DMK quits the NDA and the Union Council of Ministers. [k]MDMK quits the NDA and the Union Council of Ministers. [l]PMK quits the NDA and the Union Council of Ministers. [m]Prime Minister Vajpayee demits office. [n]Shibu Soren resigns from the cabinet following the arrest warrant issued against him; JMM continues to support the government. [o]TRS leaves the Union Council of Ministers and the UPA.

systems due to the consolidation of the state-level opposition to the principal party in a principal rival, whether a national or regional party, while simultaneously leading to a national multi-party system because the state- level two-party systems do not consist of the same two parties (Rae, 1971).[16]

The major trends of 1989–2009 are the relative decline of the Congress, the rise of the BJP, and the rise of regional parties. In 1989 the erosion of the Congress party's vote plurality to below 40 per cent led to a situation where this no longer converted to a seat majority. This process has resulted in an evolving party system in which no party has achieved a majority in the seven elections since 1989, necessitating minority and/or coalition governments. The national party system has become increasingly fragmented since 1989 while party systems at the state level have become bipartisan or bipolar, hence less fragmented, in more and more states. The fragmentation of the party system since 1989 is shown by the index of the effective number of parties (Table 7). There have been 12 cases of coalition and/or minority governments in India since independence (Tables 4 and 5) by my alternative criteria or 26 cases by standard criteria (Table 6), including all since 1989.

All the coalitions since 1996 have been inter-state territorial coalitions, that is, between parties based in different states. The period since 1991 has also seen intra-state alliances based on ideology (BJP–Shiv Sena) and based on territorial compatibility of three kinds. The first are intra-state alliances in which the regional party allies with a national party with the former getting most of both Lok Sabha and assembly seats.[17] Second, the reverse of

[16] See Sridharan (1997, 2002) for a detailed version of this argument for India.

[17] The examples are the BJP–AIADMK-smaller parties in 1998 and 2004, the BJP–DMK–smaller parties in 1999, Congress–DMK–smaller parties in 2004, the BJP–TDP in 1999 and 2004, the BJP–Trinamool Congress in 1999 and 2004, BJP–BJD in Orissa in 1998, 1999 and 2004, RJD–Congress in 2004, and JD(U)–BJP in 2004.

Table 7. Effective Number of Parties in Lower House Elections

S. No.	*Year*	*Effective number of parties (votes)*	*Effective number of parties (seats)*
1	1952	4.53	1.80
2	1957	3.98	1.76
3	1962	4.40	1.85
4	1967	5.19	3.16
5	1971	4.63	2.12
6	1977	3.40	2.63
7	1980	4.25	2.28
8	1984	3.99	1.69
9	1989	4.80	4.35
10	1991	5.10	3.70
11	1996	7.11	5.83
12	1998	6.91	5.28
13	1999	6.74	5.87
14	2004	7.60	6.50
15	2009	7.98	5.01

Source: See *Journal of the Indian School of Political Economy*, XV/1-2 (January–June 2003), Statistical Supplement, Tables 1.1–1.13, 293–307. For 2004, the index was calculated by the Centre for the Study of Developing Societies, New Delhi; for 2009 by the author.

this pattern, viz., an alliance between a minor state party and a national party in which the latter gets most of both Lok Sabha and assembly seats, the key being territorial compatibility in which the national party does not contest in its ally's intra-state strongholds.[18] Third, intra-state alliances in which the regional party contests fewer Lok Sabha seats and more assembly seats and its national party ally vice versa (BJP–Shiv Sena). The clear emphasis of coalitions has been on *territorial compatibility even at the expense of ideological compatibility*, particularly the BJP's alliances of 1998, 1999, and 2004, and the Congress alliances of 2004 and 2009,

[18] Examples are the BJP–Lok Shakti in Karnataka in 1998 and 1999, the BJP–Samata in Bihar over 1996–9, the BJP–HVC in HP, and the Congress–JMM–smaller parties in 2004.

but even the United Front (UF) coalition of 1996. Coalitions have been driven by the imperative to aggregate votes to win and not by ideological cleavages except for Congress–BJP and BJP–Left differences on secularism.[19]

Coalition Theory and India: Minority Coalitions Viable due to Institutional Features and Locked-in Supporters?

Of early theories of coalition formation, power maximisation or office-seeking theories predict minimal winning coalitions because in such coalitions each member's share of the payoff is maximised.[20] Early policy-based theories on the other hand, predict minimum connected winning coalitions,[21] i.e. coalitions that are composed of member parties adjacent on the ideological scale and, at least, not incompatible on major issues, and within this limiting condition, the minimum number of parties needed for a majority.

Neither set of these early theories predicts minority governments (which include minority coalitions) or surplus coalitions (with redundant partners, not necessary for a majority). However,

[19] For a detailed overview of state-level coalition politics in India, see Sridharan (1999, 2002, 2003, 2004a). For a detailed state-wise analysis of the BJP's coalition strategies since 1989, see Sridharan (2005). For a detailed analysis of the Congress" coalition strategies and their criticality in the 2004 elections, see Sridharan (2004b).

[20] For seminal theorising on coalitions see (for power maximisation theories) Riker (1962), Gamson (1961) and Dodd (1976), and (for policy-based theories) Axelrod (1970) and de Swaan (1973). For a survey of the evolution of theorising on coalition formation from office-seeking to policy-seeking assumptions and explanations see Budge and Keman (1990: 10–19) and Strom (1990: 29–37), and most recently Mitchell and Nyblade (2008). For more recent comprehensive analyses see Muller and Strom (2000/2003/2006), Laver and Schofield (1990/1998), Budge and Keman (1990), Strom (1990), Laver and Shepsle (1996).

[21] Axelrod 1970.

21 per cent of governments in 20 Western democracies over 1945–95, and 36 per cent of governments in 17 European democracies over 1945–99 have been minority governments, including the great majority of governments in Denmark, Norway, and Sweden, over 1945–95 (Tables 1 and 2). Minority coalitions have been 36 per cent (Table 1) or 33 per cent (Table 2) of all minority governments in stable democracies.

Later theorising argues that minority governments are signs of the largest party's strength and/or ideological centrality,[22] and policy acceptability.[23] Strom argues that minority governments form when the opposition can influence policy and that, "More than anything else it is the anticipation of future elections that predisposes party leaders to opt for minority governments."[24] Neo-institutional critics of early coalition theory point to the most viable government given country-specific institutional constraints, particularly the presence or absence of investiture votes.[25] SC (NMP)s are more likely when a vote of confidence is an investiture requirement, and minority governments when there are only votes of no-confidence.

Vital for understanding the dynamics of coalition governments in India are the distinctions between formal and substantive minority governments, and related to this, the relationship between executive and legislative coalitions, and pre-electoral and post-electoral coalitions. Following Strom, formal minority governments are those that have external support that was (i) negotiated prior to government formation *and* (ii) is explicit, comprehensive and more than short-term, *and* (iii) which makes a difference between minority and majority status.[26] Others are substantive

[22] Van Roozendaal 1992; Crombez 1996.

[23] Laver and Schofield 1990/1998: 68–9. See Muller *et al.* 2008: 19–25 for survey of the findings of research on the influence of structural, preference and institutional characteristics on the types of government formed.

[24] Strom 1990: 42–4 and 237.

[25] Bergman 1993; Strom *et al.* 1994.

[26] Strom 1990: 62.

minority governments that have to negotiate support from issue-to-issue. Formal minority governments can be like majority coalitions as Strom puts it: "if the commitment of these external supporters is just as strong as that of parties inside the government, then there would be no reason to expect minority governments to perform differently from majority coalitions."[27]

We can summarise this discussion and argue that minority governments can be considered to be solutions from the standpoints of both the party/ parties in the minority government and those in the opposition, in situations characterised by one or more of the following two features: (1) the minority government enjoys a near-majority and/or the opposition is ideologically divided, allowing it to survive and perhaps even be legislatively effective by being able to count on the support or abstention of varying parties in different confidence/no-confidence and legislative votes; (2) opposition parties can get policy payoffs since the minority government is vulnerable to pressure and calculating that participation will harm their future electoral prospects (incumbents tend to suffer at the next election, see Mitchell and Nyblade, 2008: 209), opt to forgo its short-term benefits while negotiating influence over policy as the price of support.[28] Under plurality-rule, unlike in European-style proportional representation (PR), a small vote swing can hugely increase or decimate a party, potentially either putting it in power or destroying its chances. This would tend to encourage minority government rather than majority coalitions because greater electoral volatility in seats also holds out the chance of an opposition party coming into power in the next election either on its own or in a coalition.

The Indian record since 1989 is that in only two (1999, 2009) of the seven elections did the ruling party or coalition get re-elected,

[27] Ibid.: 61.

[28] See Laver and Schofield 1990/1998: 66–81. Mitchell and Nyblade 2008: 232 support the above analysis of minority government formation in their recent and comprehensive survey of the determinants of government type.

and that a minority government was formed after each of these elections.[29] Additionally, a pivotal supporter can extract policy concessions.[30] Therefore, there is greater incentive for post- and even pre-electoral allies, with a longer time horizon to stay in the legislative coalition but out of the executive coalition, remain "untainted", and present themselves as credible alternatives in the next election.[31]

While the viability of minority governments, particularly after 1999, could have been enhanced by traditions of accommodative politics, and by learning from experiences, reflected in coalition management devices like a common minimum programme and a steering committee, the Indian system also has three features that incentivise either minority government formation and/or large and ideologically indiscriminate coalitions. They are as follows.

First, even when at the president's discretion, a vote of confidence is held in the event of a hung parliament, government parties have *only to show that the majority does not oppose them, rather than demonstrate a majority*, which facilitates minority governments by abstention of part of the opposition.

Second, as regards large and ideologically indiscriminate coalitions, an implication of the plurality-rule system's seat-vote

[29] It is also important to note that the BJP-led coalition re-elected in 1999 was not the same coalition as in 1998, switching and adding important partners. The right-wing BJP and the Left both supported the left-of-centre National Front government of 1989 from outside, the BJP coming to power later in 1998 and 1989. The Congress supported the Chandra Shekhar government in 1990, and formed a government after the 1991 elections. The AIADMK supported the Congress from outside in 1991 and became a part of the BJP-led government in 1998.

[30] Two prominent examples are those of the TDP supporting the NDA government of 1999–2004 from outside and extracting considerable allocations for its Andhra Pradesh state, and the Left Front supporting the Congress-led UPA government from 2004 to 2008 and extracting policy concessions on slowing down free market reforms.

[31] Macmillan 2005: 23–4 makes this point, in the Indian context, citing the NDA government, about parties wishing to remain "untainted" by remaining outside the executive.

disproportionality is that it would tend to give strong incentives to politicians to form pre-electoral coalitions.[32] National parties, that is, significantly multi-state parties like Congress and BJP, have to form pre-electoral coalitions with several regional parties (an India-specific feature of the party system) ignoring lesser ideological differences and also tacitly "ceding" territory, if they are to win enough seats to stand a fair chance of forming a government.[33] Both national and regional parties have strong incentives for such pre-electoral coalitions if they face a common opponent in parliamentary and/or state assembly elections. This has not been studied, to my knowledge, and makes the Indian case of very large coalition governments of 6–12 parties unique. Thus, Golder (2006: 195, fn. 10) admits that her data set of 237 pre-electoral coalitions in 292 elections in 20 democracies over 1946–98 includes *only two* cases (German and Australian) of coalitions between parties with different geographical bases of support.[34] Hence, the pattern of regional fragmentation into several single-state parties and the incentive for pre-electoral coalitions would tend to result in large pre-electoral coalitions and hence large, multi-party governments.

Third, I argue that there exists an India-specific feature of something like a "lock-in" effect incentivising minority governments because in a fragmented party system with a variety of regional parties, the formateur can be reasonably sure that external supporters, whether pre- or post-electoral, will not vote *against* its government in votes of no-confidence if: (a) such parties face the principal national opposition party and likely alternative formateur as their main rival in their stronghold state; and/or (b) if the principal national opposition party has basic ideological differences with them; and/or (c) the principal national opposition

[32] Laver and Schofield 1990/1998: 204–6; Clark and Golder 2006: 693; Golder 2006: 198.

[33] For the incentives of India's regional parties to coalesce with national parties, see Sridharan 2003: 135–52.

[34] Golder 2006: 195, fn. 10.

party's numbers and those of the parties with which it can possibly coalesce, that is, those that are not ideologically opposed and who are not their rivals at the state level, are too small to form an alternative coalition.

From this, I derive the following conclusion for the following reasons. I extend Strom's (1990) formal minority government concept to argue that the *legislative coalition formed in such cases, whether pre- or post-electoral, can be considered an SC (NMP)* in the Indian case if (1) no single external supporter is pivotal for a majority and (2) external supporting parties are bound to the leading party in the coalition by mutual electoral interdependencies at the state level due to having a common opponent that *makes it difficult for them to withdraw support without jeopardising a state-level pre-electoral alliance upon which their parliamentary and state assembly strength substantially depends* or (3) opening a window for an even less favoured party to form an alternative national coalition government; in the case of a major national party as supporter this would mean opening space for its major rival to form an alternative government. Such supporting parties can be considered to be *locked-in* to a great degree and hence a *minority coalition dependent on such supporters is actually like an SC (NMP)*. Such mutual electoral interdependencies are rooted in the electoral co-ordination incentives of the plurality-rule system, particularly in state-level contests between two well-matched parties in the presence of a significant minor party. In such party systems the addition of the votes of the third through an alliance in which the latter is allotted some seats to contest can make all the difference between victory and defeat in both Lok Sabha and state assembly elections. Hence, what matters is not so much the possibly small number of Lok Sabha seats of the allied regional party but its vote share, in its stronghold states, which is often crucial for the major coalition partner against a well-matched rival.[35]

[35] For details of the patterns of coalitions and hence of mutual electoral interdependencies at the state level since 1989, see Sridharan 2005.

To sum up, in addition to the two general circumstances favouring minority governments there are three India-specific institutional and party-systemic features favouring minority governments, and specifically, minority coalitions, and large, ideologically indiscriminate ones at that. These five circumstances, in the above order, can be listed as:

1. Near-majority for the formateur party and/or divided opposition.
2. External supporters stay out of government out of long-term electoral calculation in exchange for policy payoffs.
3. No majority needs to be demonstrated by government parties in votes of confidence at investiture.
4. Plurality-rule incentives for pre-electoral coalitions in the context of the fragmentation of the party system into one with several regional parties lead to large, pre-electoral coalitions.
5. Minority coalitions can resemble SC(NMP)s due to the substantially "locked-in" character of supporting parties in the legislative coalition due to state-level electoral interdependencies and national-level rivalries between major national parties.[36]

Two Key Regularities in the Data on Indian Coalition and/or Minority Governments

India diverges in two important ways from the international pattern of (i) the distribution of types of non-single party majority

[36] Manor 1995: 58 has made the point that some chief ministers find it useful to govern with a minority to discipline their own parties; an analogous incentive could apply to national minority governments. Adeney and Saez 2005: 5–6 cite Tsebelis' (2002) veto players argument that significant departures from the *status quo* are impossible when veto players are many and they have ideological differences, to argue that the stability of large coalitions like the NDA is not necessarily an aberration.

governments and (ii) the number of parties in coalition and/or minority governments – for both, see Tables 1 and 2 compared to Table 6 by standard Muller and Strom (2000/ 2003/2006) and Woldendorp *et al.* (1998) definitions and Tables 4 and 5 based on the Indian legal definition.[37]

First, there are *no* minimal winning coalitions, and one surplus coalition (majority party) while the rest are minority governments, of which all but two were minority coalitions, by both standard and Indian definitions. Eleven out of 12 non-single party majority governments, by the Indian definition, or 92 *per cent are minority governments* (Tables 4 and 5). By standard definitions (Table 6), there were 26 non-single party majority governments, of which 23 were minority coalitions, two single-party minority governments and one a surplus coalition (majority party), or 96 per cent minority governments compared to 26 per cent internationally. Not even Denmark, Norway, and Sweden have been so dominated by minority governments as a percentage of non-single party majority governments as India (96 per cent by standard definitions, Table 6), and no country has had so large a percentage of minority coalitions in minority governments (92 per cent by standard criteria, Table 6). If we compare India with other SMSP electoral system countries, UK, pre-1994 New Zealand and Canada, the common pattern has been domination by single-party majority governments, but India diverges from 1989, all governments since then being minority governments. If we compare India with federal countries then, unlike Australia, where all non-single party majority governments have been minimal winning coalitions and Canada where they have been single-party minority governments, all but two Indian minority governments have been minority coalitions. Federal Germany and Belgium,

[37] The figures in Tables 3–6 are from data collected from *Asian Recorder*, *Data India*, and *Keesing's Contemporary Archives* for the years concerned, and from contemporary newspaper reports for more minute details.

which use mixed-member and PR electoral formulas, have been dominated by minimal winning coalitions.[38]

Second, the period since 1996 has seen seven coalition governments formed (by Indian legal definition, Table 4), or 21 (by standard definitions, Table 6). The last six (or by standard definitions, 21) have been among the *world's largest coalitions;* 6–12 parties by both my alternative and standard definitions (Tables 4 and 6).[39] Why have such large coalitions been formed?

Explaining the Two Regularities

If one examines closely the minority situations (after elections or party splits) which have arisen in India in the light of the five circumstances (two general and three India-specific), listed earlier, that incentivise the formation of minority governments, including on all but two occasions, minority coalitions (Tables 4–6), we find that in each case several of the five circumstances apply.

In cases of short-lived governments like those of 1979 and 1990–1, when the Janata Party and the Janata Dal, respectively, split, the smaller faction that emerged sought to form a minority government with Congress support. The latter, in both cases, had no interest in being discredited in electoral terms by becoming a coalition partner in an inherently unstable arrangement which would make it dependent on a fickle faction of recent opponents. It refused to support the Janata Party (Secular) faction which had

[38] The Swiss case of near-total domination of surplus coalitions is also exceptional but that is not really comparable because the cabinet is not responsible to the legislature.

[39] The other largest cases being two of ten parties (one of which lasted three years) and one of nine parties in Israel, one of seven parties in Italy and of up to six parties in Belgium). Data from Woldendorp *et al.* 1998, and for Israel from http://www.knesset.gov.il/faction/eng/FactionGovernmenteng.asp and from Parliamentary Democracy Data Archive, http://www.pol.umu.se/ccpd/Database.htm, accessed on 28 May 2008; and Muller and Strom 2000/2003/2006.

to resign within three weeks, and kept the 54-MP SJP government going for a few months, buying time before withdrawing support at an appropriate moment and precipitating an election. In these two cases, splits in the ruling parties created short-lived minority governments.

In 1991, when the largest party, the Congress, managed only a plurality of 232 seats, 40 short of a majority, and faced an opposition divided sharply on secularism between the Hindu nationalist BJP (120 seats) and centre-left National Front and Left Front parties, it formed a single-party minority government since no majority needed to be demonstrated at investiture and manoeuvring from issue to issue was viable. In the vote of confidence, the Congress won 241 votes with 111 against (BJP) and 112 abstentions (by the Left and National Front).[40] The latter could be considered weakly locked-in because toppling the Congress would give space to their current major ideological opponent, the BJP. Circumstances 1, 3 and 5 making a minority government viable were present.

The formation of the seven other minority governments, all minority coalitions, the Janata Dal-led National Front of 1989 (supported separately by the BJP and the Left), two UF governments of 1996 and 1997 (both supported by the Congress and the CPI(M)), BJP-led coalitions 1998–9 and 1999–2004 (supported by the TDP), and the UPA I (supported by the Left) and UPA II, can also be explained by the presence of several of the five general or India-specific circumstances favouring minority governments. In all the following cases, it should be noted, the lack of the need to demonstrate a government parties' majority in the vote of confidence, made minority governments a viable option, there being no need to form majority coalitions. We outline below how the circumstances making minority government viable, applied in these seven cases.

[40] In 1996, the BJP-led government formed a 12-day minority coalition but could not muster the support to face a confidence vote and resigned.

In the NF, 1989–90 (146 seats), the secular Janata Dal (143 seats) did not share power with the BJP (85 seats), which would have also made it impossible for it to get Left support (52 seats), despite pre-electoral alliances with both, but took support separately from both the BJP and the Left, all wanting to keep the Congress out of power, building on the pre-electoral coalition in which the necessity of pooling anti-Congress votes in the Hindi-belt states, Gujarat, Maharashtra, and Orissa overcame ideological differences with the BJP and the Left. The BJP derived a policy payoff in not facing any obstacles to its anti-Muslim mobilisation campaign until it precipitated matters with a major Hindu nationalist mobilisation in late 1990.[41] Thus, the government was the result of a pre-electoral coalition, long-term calculations by supporting parties and policy payoffs to at least the BJP. Circumstances 2, 3, 4, and 5 making minority coalitions viable were present.

The UF I and UF II governments were, likewise, separately supported by both the Congress and the Left to keep the BJP out of power.[42] The UF had only 136 seats and the legislative coalition consisted of the Congress (141 seats) and the Left (40 seats), making the Congress pivotal. Taking the Congress in as a partner would not have been possible because of the need for Left support and vice-versa, due to the Congress-Left rivalry in West Bengal, Kerala, and Tripura, as well as due to the fact that the Congress was the principal rival of some UF state party partners like the TDP, TMC, DMK, and AGP. The government was the result of divisions in the non-government party space and long-term calculations by supporting parties to remain outside the government as well as the fact that the Congress and the Left could not possibly support a BJP-led alternative. The Congress, despite its pivotal position, and the Left were, therefore, weakly locked in until fresh elections were

[41] For an account of the NF government, see Chakrabarty 2005: 138–44, and in more detail, Jha 1993: 132–222.

[42] For details, see Chakrabarty 2005: 144, and Singh 2004b.

felt to be feasible. Circumstances 1, 2, 3, 4, and 5 making large minority coalitions viable were present.

In the BJP-led coalition of 1998–9, some parties (Shiv Sena, SMT, BJD, AIADMK) were pre-electoral allies, and the key post-electoral supporter, TDP, opted to support the BJP primarily because its state-level rival was the Congress.[43] The BJP-led executive coalition had only 243 seats while the legislative coalition had another 39 seats, making the 12-seat TDP pivotal. The latter opted for supporting the BJP from outside in 1998 and again in 1999 despite becoming a pre-electoral ally in the NDA, 1999–2004, to both weaken the Congress and not lose its minority Muslim voters by being in government with the Hindu nationalists, and won policy payoffs for its support with generous allocations for its state. The government was a result of a pre-electoral coalition and long-term calculation by the external supporters to remain outside in return for policy payoffs as well as the "locked-in" character of the TDP's external support, despite the latter's pivotal position, due to its principal opponent in its state being the Congress. Circumstances 2, 3, 4, and 5 making large minority coalitions viable were present.

The two BJP-led coalitions' ability to attract considerable post-electoral support as well as the relatively large number of pre-electoral allies opting for external support (Table 5) was due to policy payoffs combined with not wanting to be "tainted" by partnering the BJP in government as well as wanting to weaken their principal state-level rival, the Congress. In the NDA government, the fact that the Congress' numbers rendered it implausible as the nucleus of any alternative coalition, left the BJP as the only viable formateur, and hence contributed to "lock-in", and none of the supporters was pivotal. The NDA government was in effect an SC(NMP) rather than what it technically was, a minority coalition,

[43] For the BJP's coalition-building, see Sridharan 2005 for a state-wise account, and for events see Arora 2000, Singh 2004b, Chakrabarty 2005: 168–201, and Muralidharan 1999.

its executive coalition being 265 seats. This was because of the BJP's surplus majority *legislative* coalition (303 seats), with its pre-electoral allies who opted to be external supporters, the TDP, INLD, SDF, HVC, ABLTC, and MADMK, who were formally part of the NDA coalition and accepted its manifesto, the National Agenda for Governance. That none of the parties were pivotal, combined with the fact that the TDP (29 seats) and INLD (5 seats) at least, in their states of Andhra Pradesh and Haryana, were dependent on pre-electoral coalitions with the BJP to avoiding splitting of the vote against their common rival, the Congress party, meant that *they were "locked-in" to the BJP in a way that would make it very difficult for them to withdraw support without damaging their own electoral prospects.* Likewise, the BJD of Orissa, JD (U) of Bihar, SAD of Punjab, and Shiv Sena of Maharashtra, who were part of the executive coalition, were "locked-in" to the BJP by mutual electoral interdependence. So the argument of lock-in applies to the *executive* coalition too and therefore large coalitions can be stable! Circumstances 2, 3, 4, and 5 making large minority coalitions viable were present.

The UPA I, 2004–9, took the external support of the Left to form a government as both agreed on secularism and wanted to keep the BJP out but a Congress-Left coalition was considered unstable by both due to both state-level rivalry in West Bengal, Kerala and Tripura, and differences on economic liberalisation.[44] The Left's support of the Congress was due to its greater aversion to the BJP partly through its learning experience of the period since 1989, including the 1996–8 UF experience, as it became more amenable to tactical coalitions to keep out its least favoured party. The Left's policy payoff was that it was able to check economic liberalisation and influence foreign policy, as reflected in the Common Minimum Programme and in the first four years of the government, despite alternative sources of support offered ini-

[44] For events, see Ramakrishnan 2004.

tially by the SP and BSP which the Congress did not take up until its split with the Left in UPA I's final year, due to its reluctance to cede turf to these parties in the largest state of Uttar Pradesh (U.P.) with its 80 seats.[45] The UPA I, though a formal minority coalition (executive coalition 215 seats, legislative coalition 327 seats including Left, 59, SP, 36, and BSP, 19), thus also resembled an SC(NMP) because its legislative coalition included the Left, SP, and BSP, none being pivotal and none of which could afford to support the BJP on either ideological grounds or for fear of alienating the significant Muslim vote (18–25 per cent) in their stronghold states (U.P. for SP, BSP, West Bengal and Kerala for the Left) and hence could be considered "locked-in" barring exceptional circumstances of conflict with the Congress, not foreseeable at the outset.[46] Circumstances 2, 3, 4, and 5 making large minority coalitions viable were present.

The UPA II was like the NDA in reverse since the BJP's numbers (116) made it implausible as the nucleus of an alternative coalition. The executive coalition was 257 seats and the legislative coalition of supporting parties added another 61 seats including SP, 23, and BSP, 21, none being pivotal. Their ideological antipathy and state-level rivalry with the BJP and the lack of an alternative to a Congress-led coalition, led former electoral opponents like the SP, BSP, RJD, and JD(S) offering support to the Congress that was substantially of a "locked-in" character for reasons of being constrained from offering support to the BJP for reasons of the latter being a political opponent at the state level, and fear of loss of Muslim votes, besides standing for secularism in principle, thus making it more like an SC(NMP) than a minority coalition, with supporting parties having little alternative and

[45] For the Common Minimum Programme, see Athreya 2004.

[46] Such exceptional circumstances as the Congress–Left clash over the Indo–US nuclear deal were not foreseeable at government formation in 2004. Ending the BJP's hold on power was the top priority then for both Congress and the Left.

none being pivotal.[47] Circumstances 1, 3, 4, and 5 making minority coalitions viable were present.

Since 1996, the fragmentation of the party system, analysed earlier, resulted in both major national parties, Congress and BJP, getting 206 or less seats (majority mark, 273) in all elections since 1996, and under 150 seats in 2004, with the rest of parliament dominated by regional parties which did not exceed 46 seats (the leading party of the UF governments, 1996–8, the Janata Dal), or 36 seats (the SP in 2004), being typically under 20 seats, necessitating large, multi-party coalitions which still needed external support. Given the relative strengths of parties in the elections from 1996 to 2009, the minority coalitions needed 6–12 parties even to get within hailing distance of a majority and hence a semblance of stability.

The formation of each such minority coalition can be explained, as above, by the factors listed earlier that conduce to multi-party minority coalitions in which the formateur and many post- and even pre-electoral allies prefer such an arrangement. The SC(NMP) character of the legislative coalition of the NDA, UPA I, and UPA II was due to the *mutual electoral interdependence* of the formateur party and the leading supporting parties of this legislative coalition due to state-level electoral arithmetic. This gave the BJP in the NDA coalition and the Congress in UPA I, and in UPA II, the confidence that most of their external supporters were substantially "locked-in" in that they had little option to withdraw support, and even if they did, could at worst abstain but not join the coalition led by the other major party. The Left's least preferred party, nationally, on which it had differences on both secularism and economic policy, was the BJP. The SP, RJD, and even the BSP could not ally with the BJP because of their dependence

[47] It may be added that some regional parties like the BJD (Orissa) and INLD (Haryana) dropped the BJP as an ally before the 2009 election as they did not need it in their state or could not accommodate its demands and because it was not seen as a potential winner nationally.

on Muslim votes in UP and Bihar, and position on secularism, and in 2009 the same applied to the TDP and Trinamool Congress. Hence, the Congress can possibly have pre-electoral alliances with them or at least be sure of these parties as external supporters or abstainers in a vote of confidence. Likewise, the TDP, INLD, AGP, Shiv Sena, BJD, and SAD face the Congress as their principal state-level opponent and hence cannot ally with it but can possibly be pre-electoral allies of, or be depended on by, the BJP as external supporters or abstainers. For those parties that might opt to be external supporters of a Congress-led or BJP-led coalition, as the case may be, it pays to extract policy payoffs for their states while remaining external supporters, particularly if the formateur does not want to include them or if there is no alternative coalition possible.

Conclusion

From the explanations above, we can conclude that the apparently counterintuitive patterns in India, that do not seem to fit theory or comparative experience, actually *do fit* the rational choice expectations of behaviour if one takes into account the consequences of Indian political/electoral institutions such as the SMSP electoral system, federalism, multiple bipolarities in state party systems, several strong state parties, and the discretionary and plurality-rule vote of confidence.

The prevalence of minority governments, both minority coalitions and single-party minority governments, can be explained by the pattern of fragmentation of the national party system due to the operation of Duverger's law under federalism into a territorially compatible, multi-party system with numerous small regional parties with strong incentives for pre-electoral coalitions. This, when combined with ideological differences between parties on key issues like secularism and economic liberalisation, expectations of instability, and state-level rivalries that incentivise alliances of regional parties with either the BJP or the Congress, and which give the two national parties the confidence that *some* regional parties, are substantially "locked-in" by state-level electoral interdependencies and so will not support the other coalition, has made minority coalitions viable since 1996. These minority coalitions resemble SC(NMP)s due to this "locked-in" character of supporting parties. This argument holds even if one views minority governments and minority coalitions by the literature's standard definitions as in Table 6, which breaks up the NDA and UPA I governments into multiple governments. All, however, remain minority coalitions and hence need to be explained, and the above explanation of the viability of minority coalitions holds. It also gives support to both Strom's argument that some (formal) minority governments can be like majority coalitions,[48] and to neo-institutionalist arguments in the literature that explain minority governments due to their being the most viable given country-specific institutional constraints and incentives,[49] due to their reflecting, variously, case by case, one or more of the following – the largest party's strength and/or ideological centrality,[50] and policy acceptability.[51]

Acknowledgements

The author is grateful to the Institute of South Asian Studies, Singapore, and the Center for the Advanced Study of India, University of Pennsylvania, where earlier drafts were written, to Adnan Farooqui for research assistance, and to two anonymous referees for helpful comments. The author acknowledges the use of the Parliamentary Democracy Data Archive for Table 2.

[48] Strom 1990.
[49] Bergman 1993; Strom *et al.* 1994.
[50] van Roozendaal 1992; Crombez 1996.
[51] Laver and Schofield 1990/1998: 68–9; Strom 1990: 42–4.

Bibliography

Adeney, K., and L. Saez. 2005. "Introduction. Coalition Politics, Religious Nationalism and Public Policy: A Theoretical Examination", in K. Adeney and L. Saez, eds. *Coalition Politics and Hindu Nationalism* (London: Routledge), 3–12.

Arora, B. 2000. "Negotiating Differences: Federal Coalitions and National Cohesion," in Francine Frankel, Z. Hasan, R. Bhargava and B. Arora, eds. *Transforming India: Social and Political Dynamics of Democracy* (New Delhi: Oxford University Press), 176–206

Arora, B. 2002. "The Political Parties and the Party System: The Emergence of New Coalitions," in Z. Hasan, ed. *Parties and Party Politics in India* (New Delhi: Oxford University Press), 504–32.

Athreya, V. 2004. "A Step Forward", *Frontline*, 21 (12), 5–18 June.

Axelrod, R. 1970. *Conflict of Interest* (Chicago: Markham).

Bergman, T. 1993. "Formation Rules and Minority Governments", *European Journal of Political Research*, 23 (1), 55–66.

Budge, I., and H. Keman. 1990. *Parties and Democracy: Coalition Formation and Government Functioning in Twenty States* (Oxford: Oxford University Press).

Bueno de Mesquita, B. 1975. *Strategy, Risk and Personality in Coalition Politics: The Case of India* (Cambridge: Cambridge University Press).

Chakrabarty, B. 2005. *Forging Power: Coalition Politics in India* (New Delhi: Oxford University Press), 260–70.

Chhibber, P., and G. Murali. 2006. "Duvergerian Dynamics in Indian States", *Party Politics*, 12 (1), 5–34.

Clark, W. R., and M. Golder. 2006. "Rehabilitating Duverger's Theory: Testing the Mechanical and Strategic Modifying Effects of Duverger's Laws", *Comparative Political Studies*, 39 (6), 679–708.

Crombez, C. 1996. "Minority Governments, Minimum Winning Coalitions and Surplus Majorities in Parliamentary Systems", *European Journal of Political Research*, 29 (1), 1–29.

de Swaan, A. 1973. *Coalition Theories and Cabinet Formation* (Amsterdam: Elsevier).

Diwakar, R. 2007. "Duverger's Law and the Size of the Indian Party System", *Party Politics*, 13 (5), 539–61.

Dodd, L. 1976. *Coalitions in Parliamentary Government* (Princeton: Princeton University Press).

Duverger, M. 1963. *Political Parties: Their Organization and Activity in the Modern State* (New York: Wiley).

Gamson, W. 1961. "A Theory of Coalition Formation", *American Sociological Review*, 26 (3), 373–82.

Golder, S.N. 2006. "Pre-electoral Coalition Formation in Parliamentary Democracies", *British Journal of Political Science*, 36 (2), 193–212.

Jha, P.S. 1993. *In the Eye of the Cyclone: The Crisis in Indian Democracy* (New Delhi: Penguin Viking).

Laver, M., and N. Schofield. 1990/1998. *Multiparty Government: The Politics of Coalition in Europe* (Ann Arbor: University of Michigan Press).

Laver, M., and K. Shepsle. 1996. *Making and Breaking Governments: Cabinets and Legislatures in Parliamentary Democracies* (Cambridge: Cambridge University Press).

Macmillan, A. 2005. "The BJP Coalition: Partisanship and Power-sharing in Government", in K. Adeney and L. Saez, eds, *Coalition Politics and Hindu Nationalism* (London: Routledge), 13–36.

Manor, J. 1995. "India's Chief Ministers and the Problem of Governability", in P. Oldenburg, ed., *India Briefing: Staying the Course* (Armonk, NY: M. E. Sharpe).

Mitchell, P., and B. Nyblade. 2008. "Government Formation and Cabinet Type", in K. Strom, W.C. Muller, and T. Bergman, eds, *Cabinets and Coalition Bargaining: The Democratic Life Cycle in Western Europe* (Oxford: Oxford University Press), 201–36.

Mitra, S. 1978. *Governmental Instability in Indian States: West Bengal, Bihar, Uttar Pradesh and Punjab* (New Delhi: Ajanta Publications).

Muller, W.C., T. Bergman, and K. Strom. 2008. "Coalition Theory and Cabinet Governance: An Introduction", in K. Strom, W.C. Muller, and T. Bergman, eds, *Cabinets and Coalition Bargaining: The Democratic Life Cycle in Western Europe* (Oxford: Oxford University Press), 1–50.

Muller, W.C., and K. Strom. 2000/2003/2006. *Coalition Governments in Western Europe* (Oxford: Oxford University Press).

Muralidharan, S. 1999. "Vajpayee Again", *Frontline*, 16 (22), 23 October–5 November.

Nikolenyi, C. 2002. "Positive Political Theory and Politics in Contemporary India: An Application of a Positive Political Model in Non-western Polities", *Canadian Journal of Political Science*, 35 (4), 881–96.

Nikolenyi, C. 2004. "When the Central Player Fails: Constraints on Cabinet Formation in Contemporary India", *Canadian Journal of Political Science*, 37 (4), 395–418.

Ramakrishnan, V. 2004. "The Return of the Congress", *Frontline*, 21 (11), 22 May–4 June.

Riker, W.H. 1962. *The Theory of Political Coalitions* (New Haven: Yale University Press).

Rae, D.W. 1971. *The Political Consequences of Electoral Laws*, 2nd edn (New Haven: Yale University Press).

Singh, M.P. 2004a. "Theorising and Reforming Coalition Governance in India", in M.P. Singh and A. Mishra, eds, *Coalition Politics in India: Problems and Prospects* (New Delhi: Manohar), 21–42.

Singh, M.P. 2004b. "The National Front and United Front Coalition Governments: A Phase in Federalized Governance", in M.P. Singh and A. Mishra, eds, *Coalition Politics in India: Problems and Prospects* (New Delhi: Manohar), 75–100.

Sridharan, E. 1997. "Duverger's Law, Its Reformulations and the Evolution of the Indian Party System", IRIS India Working Paper No. 35, February, IRIS Center, University of Maryland.

Sridharan, E. 1999. "Principles, Power and Coalition Politics in India: Lessons from Theory, Comparison and Recent History", in D.D. Khanna and G.W. Kueck, eds, *Principles, Power and Politics* (New Delhi: Macmillan), 270–90.

Sridharan, E. 2002. "The Fragmentation of the Indian Party System, 1952–1999: Seven Competing Explanations", in Z. Hasan, ed., *Parties and Party Politics in India* (New Delhi: Oxford University Press), 475–503.

Sridharan, E. 2003. "Coalitions and Party Strategies in India's Parliamentary Federation", *Publius*, 33 (4), 135–52.

Sridharan, E. 2004a. "Unstable Parties and Unstable Alliances: Births, Splits, Mergers and Deaths", in M.P. Singh and A. Mishra, eds, *Coalition Politics in India: Problems and Prospects* (New Delhi: Manohar), 43–74.

Sridharan, E. 2004b. "Electoral Coalitions in the 2004 General Elections: Theory and Evidence", *Economic and Political Weekly*, 39 (51), 5418–25.

Sridharan, E. 2005. "Coalition Strategies and the BJP's Expansion, 1989–2004", *Commonwealth and Comparative Politics*, 43 (2), 194–221.

Strom, K. 1990. *Minority Government and Majority Rule* (Cambridge: Cambridge University Press).

Strom, K., I. Budge, and M.J. Laver 1994. "Constraints on Cabinet Formation in Parliamentary Democracies", *American Journal of Political Science*, 38 (2), 303–35.

Tsebelis, G. 2002. *Veto Players: How Political Institutions Work* (Princeton: Princeton University Press).

van Roozendaal, P. 1992. "The Effect of Central and Dominant Parties on Cabinet Composition and Durability", *Legislative Studies Quarterly*, 17 (1), 5–35.

Volden, C., and C.J. Carrubba. 2004. "The Formation of Oversized Coalitions in Parliamentary Democracies", *American Journal of Political Science*, 48 (3), 521–37.

Woldendorp, J., H. Keman, and I. Budge. 1993. "Political Data 1945–1990: Party Government in 20 Democracies", *European Journal of Political Research*, 24 (1), 1–119.

Woldendorp, J., H. Keman, and I. Budge. 1998. "Party Government in 20 Democracies: An Update (1990–1995)", *European Journal of Political Research*, 33 (1), 125–64.

Wyatt, A. 1999. "The Limitations on Coalition Politics in India: The Case of Electoral Alliances in Uttar Pradesh", *Commonwealth and Comparative Politics*, 37 (2), 1–21.

10

Political Finance in a Developing Democracy

The Case of India

INDIAN ELECTIONS ARE among the most contested polls in the world.[1] In fact, they are so competitive that candidates speak not of "contesting" elections, but of "fighting" them. In 2014 the size of the electorate was a gargantuan 834 million, out of which 554 million (66.4 per cent) voters cast their ballots on election day in favour of one of 8251 candidates representing 464 political parties.[2] While Indian elections have become increasingly free and fair over the past quarter century, the area of political finance remains decidedly murky; politicians spent an estimated $5 billion on the costs of campaigning during the 2014 general election, the vast majority of which was not publicly disclosed. Not surprisingly, political finance is widely perceived to be one of the foremost drivers of corruption in the world's largest democracy.[3] In this chapter, we survey the legal and regulatory history of political finance in India, situating it in the context of India's political economy.

We devote special attention to recent developments, including new election finance initiatives implemented by the Bharatiya Janata Party (BJP) government of Prime Minister Narendra Modi in

[1] This paper is co-authored with Milan Vaishnav.

[2] Gottipati and Singh 2014.

[3] Sridharan and Vaishnav 2016: 64–83.

2017. We also discuss possible areas of reform, including the regulation of political parties, which can lead to increased transparency and help the country break out of a corrupt equilibrium.[4]

The Political and Economic Context of Party Finance in India

Before getting into the details of India's political finance regime, it is worth taking stock of India's broader political and economic evolution. This evolution, after all, has had a direct bearing on how money in politics has been regulated (or not). Broadly speaking, the evolution of the Indian party system can be readily divided into three main phases.[5] The initial phase, which began with the first general election in 1952 and ended in 1967, was characterised by simultaneous Lok Sabha (lower house of parliament) and state assembly elections – both of which were dominated by the hegemonic Congress party. Drawing on a deep well of popular support flowing from its role in the Independence movement, Congress regularly won a majority, sometimes even a two-thirds majority, of parliamentary seats on the basis of a plurality of votes (typically ranging between 40 and 45 per cent).

This period of dominance came to an abrupt end in 1967, when the Congress lost assembly elections in half of India's then 16 major states. This widespread upheaval allowed opposition parties to consolidate, leading to a new phase in the party system that would last for more than two decades. Duvergerian – or two-party – dynamics played themselves out in both national and state assembly elections from 1967 to 1989, and this trend persisted even after 1989.[6] This pattern led to either a two-party (or two-coalition) system or a bipolar party system with the non-Congress

[4] In this chapter, we build on earlier work including Sridharan and Vaishnav 2016; Sridharan 2013: 43–70; Gowda and Sridharan 2012: 226–40; Sridharan 2006: 363–88; Sridharan and de Souza 2006: 15–36; Sridharan 1999: 229–54.

[5] Sridharan 2012: 314–43.

[6] In the field of political science, Duverger's law holds that plurality-rule

opposition consolidating behind a particular party (with a few exceptions, such as the state of Uttar Pradesh).[7] However, the precise configuration of the bipolarities varied considerably across time and space; for example, the competition was between the Congress–Jana Sangh (the precursor of the present-day BJP) in some states; Congress–Left in others; and Congress versus a regional party in yet others.[8]

In the third phase, bookended by the elections of 1989 and 2014, the party system fragmented considerably, due to three major trends: the decline of Congress, the rise of the BJP, and the rise of regional parties. The net result of these dynamics was a fractured Lok Sabha in which no single party obtained a majority in the seven consecutive elections from 1989 to 2009, until the BJP's narrow majority in 2014. With the pan-Indian resurgence of the BJP following the 2014 general election results, it is possible that India has entered a new, fourth phase. However, it is too early to deliver a conclusive verdict on that score.[9]

These political transitions occurred against the economic backdrop of a heavily regulated economy. After gaining independence, India adopted an import-substitution industrialisation strategy led by the public sector. Many industries were reserved for the public sector, nationalised, or forced to adhere to detailed state regulations concerning the set-up, expansion, and import of inputs – such as coal, petroleum, steel, and power. The government wielded myriad instruments of control over the private sector, including a vast thicket of mandatory licenses and permissions, a monopoly over most of the banking system, and significant

---

elections (such as India's first-past-the-post system) that are structured within single-member districts lead to the establishment of a two-party system. See Duverger 1954.

[7] For detailed accounts, see Chhibber and Murali 2006: 5–34; Sridharan 2002: 475–503.

[8] More accurately, these regional parties could be called state-based parties, as they were almost all based in a single state.

[9] Vaishnav and Smogard 2017.

leverage as a consumer. Economic liberalisation, beginning in the mid-1980s and picking up steam after 1991, has primarily taken the form of freer private sector entry into industries hitherto reserved for the public sector, combined with trade and foreign investment liberalisation. But, there are still overarching state regulations in many areas, as well as an undesirably high level of state control over most of the banking system. Discretionary state regulation pervades environmental clearances, land use, and natural resources – both at the central (federal) and state levels – even as the old system of industrial licensing is no more.[10]

The Evolution of India's Political Finance Regime

India's political finance regime has also evolved in three broad phases, broadly tracking the country's overall political and economic history. The first phase began in 1947 and ended around 1990, which saw the emergence and consolidation of a corrupt, opaque equilibrium. The second phase, 1990–2003, witnessed the early beginnings of reform.

The third phase, from 2003 to 2017, saw the emergence of greater transparency but very few – if any – structural changes. Given recent legislative changes introduced by the government of Prime Minister Narendra Modi in 2017, the overriding focus of reforms appears to be on curbing the use of cash at the expense of transparency. We elaborate below on the key developments of each of these phases.

The Emergence of a Corrupt Equilibrium: 1947–90

Internationally, we can identify four major features of political finance regulation: limits on expenditure, limits on contributions, public subsidy of elections and political parties, and reporting

[10] Chandra 2015: 46–58.

and disclosure requirements.[11] The evolution of political finance in India in these terms yields the following picture.

Under the 1951 Representation of the People Act (RPA), the foundational law that governs elections in India, there are strict limits on candidate spending. In terms of contributions, the then-dominant Congress party depended initially on membership dues, but rapidly shifted to private business as membership dues proved inadequate in keeping pace with the cost of increasingly competitive elections. This shift was encouraged by the fact that the government was heavily regulating businesses by licensing both capacity creation (and expansion) as well as imports. Businesses, therefore, gave money to parties and politicians in exchange for regulatory favours. This behaviour became rapidly institutionalised as part of the overarching, highly regulated, import-substituting industrialisation strategy that characterised India's economic management. In this climate, businesses evaded taxes and "donated" black money to political parties in exchange for policy or regulatory favours until engaging in such activities became an intrinsic part of running a business, rather than a choice.

During the decade of the 1960s, the first murmurs of political finance reform began to emerge as the broad contours of this new equilibrium became widely known. Indeed, the nexus between black money and political fundraising was mentioned as early as 1964, in the reports of the Santhanam Committee on Prevention of Corruption, and again in 1971, in the Wanchoo Direct Taxes Enquiry Committee.

A key turning point in the history of political finance in India occurred in 1969, when the Indira Gandhi-led Congress government banned corporate donations to political parties. Gandhi pushed the move because a weakened Congress faced a credible challenge from conservative forces on its right flank, especially after it sustained heavy electoral losses in 1967. Congress feared that

[11] For a comprehensive survey of political finance across the world, see Austin and Tjernstrom 2014.

the pro-business Swatantra Party, along with the Hindu nationalist Jana Sangh, would increasingly attract corporate donations, so banning the latter would deal a fierce blow to these rising challengers. However, Gandhi did not create any form of state funding or subsidy to political parties for elections to fill its place – a sharp contrast to the rise of public funding for parties in European democracies in the 1960s and 1970s.

The net result of this development was that, with company donations banned, there was no legal source of adequate finance for political parties. This inevitably meant a consolidation of the nexus between black money and politics. This tendency was reinforced by the policy shift from the late 1960s, engineered by Indira Gandhi, towards intensified government control of the economy. Beginning in 1969 and continuing through the first half of the 1970s, Gandhi tightened government control over the private sector, leading to a political economy of business financing ("donations") in exchange for regulatory and allocative favours. Newly imposed controls included the nationalisation of 14 major private banks in 1969; the Monopolies and Restrictive Trade Practices (MRTP) Act of 1969, which intensified regulation of big business; the Foreign Exchange Regulation Act (FERA) of 1973, which tightly controlled foreign investors; and the nationalisation of coal mining, petroleum, and general insurance in the early 1970s. In hindsight, the banning of company donations in 1969 – without adequately substituting for it with public funding – was a key moment in the path-dependent evolution of political finance because it strengthened ties between political parties and the black economy, while driving the funding of political campaigns further underground. The Congress, controlling most of the levers of power, stood to benefit in relative terms.

The next key development was the delinking of party and independent supporters' expenditure from candidate and candidate-authorised expenditure for the purpose of calculating a candidate's election spending. In other words, parties and independent supporters could spend unlimited funds on a political campaign without being subject to the strict limits on candidate expenditure. In 1974, the Supreme Court eliminated this loophole, ruling in *Kanwar Lal Gupta v. Amar Nath Chawla* that party spending on behalf of candidates would, in fact, be attributed to the candidate and, therefore, subject to the strict limits in place.[12] To circumvent this judgment, the government amended the RPA in 1975, introducing Explanation 1 to Section 77(1), which clearly stated that any spending by parties or independent supporters not authorised by the candidate would not count towards the spending limit. In effect, it removed any ceiling on party spending, rendering the candidate limit farcical. The end result was not surprising: the move touched off spending arms races in increasingly competitive elections.

The situation was altered slightly in 1979, when political parties were exempted from income and wealth taxes on the condition that they file annual tax returns.[13] Then, in 1985, Rajiv Gandhi's relatively liberalising (delicensing) and pro-business government relegalised company donations to political parties. Reversing Indira Gandhi's outright ban, the government amended the 1956 Companies Act to allow companies to donate up to 5 per cent of their average net profit over the prior three years, subject to board approval and declaration in their profit-and-loss accounts. However, there was no tax incentive for businesses to do so. In the end, the re-legalisation after a gap of 16 years did not succeed in bringing donations above the table. Not only were there few incentives for shedding anonymity, there were actually positive *disincentives*. For instance, a company that openly supported a particular party, even the ruling Congress, would alienate opposition parties that might be ruling in states where the company had business interests. By the mid-1980s, there was simply too much water under the bridge; the system of opaque donations to parties and politicians

[12] *Kanwar Lal Gupta v. Amar Nath Chawla & Ors* decided on 3 October 1974. Citations 1975 AIR (308), 1975 SCR (2) 269.

[13] These annual tax returns, like most other income tax returns, were not subject to public disclosure.

in exchange for regulatory favours had become too deeply entrenched in a highly state-controlled business environment.

The Beginnings of Reform, 1990–2003

The 1990s saw the beginning of a number of reform initiatives and proposals on political finance, emanating both from government and civil society. Minority governments, including minority coalitions and non-Congress parties, became more outspoken on the issue. Despite the increased chatter, many of the suggested changes never actually saw the light of day. And those that did operated at the margins, unable to fundamentally dislodge the corrupt equilibrium that prevailed.

The year 1996 saw two Supreme Court orders and one legislative change that had a bearing on the regulation of political finance. The first move occurred in January 1996, when the Supreme Court, in response to a public interest litigation (PIL) petition by the non-governmental organisation (NGO) Common Cause, ordered political parties to file their annual income tax and wealth tax returns. Although parties were required to file annual returns since being granted tax-exempt status in 1979, no party had regularly done so. The ruling broke new ground, although it had serious limits. Thanks to the court ruling, parties were compelled to file returns, but they were often doctored and remained under wraps until 2008.

In April 1996, just prior to the general election, the Supreme Court again issued a landmark decision on political finance by ordering the second major legislative change of the period. The court ruled that party expenditures would once more count towards candidate spending ceilings if parties did not file audited accounts of income and expenditure. In effect, problematic Explanation 1 would no longer exempt party expenditures from the spending limit if such accounts were not filed. This reinforced the earlier court order and led to parties filing their tax returns and, thus, reporting their incomes and expenditures. However, the ruling did not mandate these returns be subject to independent audit and, hence, they remained the handiwork of crafty party-appointed auditors.[14]

In 1998, the government introduced the first significant state subsidy for elections: free airtime on state-owned television and radio. The move built on the informal system in practice since the late 1970s, which had evolved with the consent of the ECI, parties, and government. The length of time each party had was based on a given time slab, with additional time based on past electoral performance for significant parties, which included seven national and 34 state parties. The same system was replicated at the state level for assembly elections.

In addition to these Supreme Court orders and legislative changes, there were a number of proposals for political party reforms in the 1990s. However, most of these reform blueprints went nowhere fast. We briefly mention them because they illustrate the fact that many prominent figures in Indian political life – from diverse quarters – recognised the knotty political finance predicament as far back as a quarter-century ago.

In 1990 the Janata Dal-led National Front government of V.P. Singh set up the Dinesh Goswami Committee on Electoral Reforms. The committee's report recommended limited public subsidy in the form of vehicle fuel (the main campaign expenditure then), but left Explanation 1 intact and recommended a ban on company donations. But, much like in 1969, the committee did not propose to substitute the loss of corporate donations with a system of public funding.

Indian industry also became increasingly concerned about the issue of political funding during the 1990s. This concern was a result of the economic reforms of 1991 – particularly trade and

[14] In addition, in July 1996, parliament amended the RPA to shorten the campaign period from 21 days to 14 days, thus potentially reducing the scale of campaign spending.

foreign direct investment (FDI) liberalisation – which increased foreign competition and eroded profit margins, at a time of mounting political demands on Indian companies. In response to the concerns of its member companies, the Confederation of Indian Industry (CII) set up a task force which recommended state funding of elections.[15]

Although the CII proposal did not gain traction, the government continued to dabble in this area by setting up new reform commissions. The 1996–8 United Front government set up the Indrajit Gupta Committee on State Funding of Elections. In its 1998 report, the Gupta Committee recommended only partial state funding, including free television and radio broadcasts on state-owned channels, vehicle fuel, paper, and other campaign paraphernalia, up to certain limits.[16] It also said that parties that failed to maintain audited accounts for the ECI or submit income tax returns should be denied state funding. Parties would be required to receive all donations above Rs 10,000 by cheque/bank draft, so that all significant donations could be traceable.[17]

In 1999 Lok Satta, an NGO founded by activist-cum-politician Jayaprakash Narayan, proposed the introduction of tax-deductible political contributions, both for companies that were not government contractors and for individuals. That same year, the 170th report of the Law Commission of India recommended deleting Explanation 1 and imposing minimum standards of transparency and internal democracy in parties as conditions for state

[15] The funds were to be raised either by a cess (earmarked tax) on excise duty or through contributions by industry to a fund pool managed by the ECI. The money would then be distributed to parties by a transparent formula, creating, in effect, an election tax on industry. It also recommended that company donations to parties be made tax-deductible, and that shareholder approval be required for such board decisions.

[16] On state funding, the committee recommended a separate election fund pool to which the central and state governments would together contribute Rs 6000 million annually (then $166 million) to enable partial state funding.

[17] The Gupta Committee also left Explanation 1 standing and said nothing specific about company donations.

funding of parties. In 2002 the National Commission to Review the Working of the Constitution also recommended dropping Explanation 1. However, it did recommend providing state funding only after a comprehensive reform of political parties to ensure internal democracy and transparency, which would include requiring candidates to disclose their assets and liabilities. None of these proposals were implemented with the exception of free airtime on state-owned television and radio channels.

From 2003 to 2017: Greater but Limited Transparency

The year 2003 marked the beginning of a series of significant, if still incomplete, steps forward in improving the transparency of political finance. The story of the first of these reforms dates back to November 2000, when the NGO Association for Democratic Reforms (ADR) filed a public interest petition demanding greater transparency on the backgrounds of aspirant candidates. The Delhi High Court responded by directing the ECI to collect and make public the criminal records, educational qualifications, and financial assets and liabilities of candidates (as well as their spouses and dependants). All parties resisted this move, but the judgment was reaffirmed, and the ECI issued an order making the above disclosures mandatory on 27 March 2003.

Arguably the most important legislative reform in campaign finance during this period was the Election and Other Related Laws (Amendment) Act passed in September 2003 by the BJP-led National Democratic Alliance (NDA) government. The law made corporate and individual donations to political parties 100 per cent tax-deductible under Sections 80 GGB and 80 GGC of the Income Tax Act respectively.[18] This created an incentive, for the first time, to contribute openly by cheque. The law also made it

[18] Company contributions remained subject to the ceiling of 5 per cent of average net profit over the prior three years under Section 293A of the Companies Act.

mandatory under Section 29C of the RPA for parties to list all donations received of Rs 20,000 and above to the ECI on an annual basis, with the names of the donors and amount received, thus introducing a limited degree of transparency.

The law also tried to close the loophole Explanation 1 opened up, by making it mandatory for candidates to report spending by parties and independent supporters towards their election, and stipulating that these expenditures would have to be counted for the purpose of the spending limit. However, the fine print undercut the larger stated objective. The law exempted the travel costs of the top leaders of recognised parties as well as party and independent supporters' spending on propagating the party's programme, as long as it did not favour any particular candidate. This last move, in particular, watered down the overall impact of the change.

The 2005 passage of the Right to Information Act (RTI), analogous to the Freedom of Information Act (FOIA) that operates in the United States, helped reshape the fight for greater transparency in India. Its impact on political funding, however, has been mixed. ADR used this new power to request that the Central Information Commission (CIC) make the income tax returns of political parties publicly available. Unsurprisingly, all parties resisted the demand, but in 2008 the CIC ruled in ADR's favour. This judgment forced political parties to publish their incomes and expenditures going back to 2004–5, thus providing a measure of transparency to party finances. This transparency is still incomplete, however, since the CIC did not insist on an independent or third-party audit, as recommended by the ECI.

The net effect of the candidate disclosure requirements introduced in 2003, the introduction of tax deductibility in the 2003 law, and the CIC's 2008 ruling under the RTI of 2005, is a modicum of transparency in party finance where there was virtually none before. However, these changes helped mainly on the margins. Parties still did not have to disclose the identities of donors if they were under the Rs 20,000 threshold. As it turns out, these anonymous donations constitute nearly 75 per cent of the income of six national parties.[19]

Despite the illusion of hyperactivity, the opaque political finance system, with roots in the 1969 decision to ban corporate donations without introducing an effective substitute, was still very much in place. Since 2013, there have been two noteworthy developments. First, in 2013, the Electoral Trusts Scheme allowed for the setting up of 100 per cent tax-exempt electoral trusts by companies, provided they disburse 95 per cent of their annual receipts (including surplus brought forward) to political parties. Also, under Section 182 of the Companies Act of 2013, the contribution limits for companies to parties was raised from 5 to 7.5 per cent of their average net profit over the prior three years.

The second notable development was the ECI's new transparency guidelines of August 2014, under which parties must identify all donors and amounts – with the exception of petty sums raised at rallies. However, these guidelines do not yet have the full force of law since, apart from the extraordinary step of derecognising a party's symbol, the ECI has no power to fine or deregister a party that violates the new guidelines.[20]

2017: A Possible Inflection Point

In 2017 parliament legislated several changes to the country's political finance regime – the first time since 2003 that political finance appeared on the national policy agenda. This was likely a direct result of the public debate that ensued in the wake of the government's November 2016 decision to abruptly invalidate or "demonetise" all high-value currency notes in circulation.

[19] Only a relatively small fraction of national party donations comes from identified donors and in specified amounts, a pattern that also holds true for state parties.

[20] S.K. Mendiratta (legal adviser to the ECI), in conversation with one of the authors, 5 November 2014.

In the immediate aftermath of the dramatic demonetisation announcement, many analysts pointed out that the manoeuvre alone was unlikely to have a sustained impact on India's black economy unless it was accompanied by complementary reforms in areas such as tax, administration, and regulation. For demonetisation to have a lasting impact, overhauling the regulation of political finance is arguably one of the most critical areas for future reform. Indeed, the government came under criticism for stating, on the one hand, that demonetisation would attack cronyism and corruption, while on the other hand failing to articulate any new measures especially designed to address political corruption. The outcry was initially sparked by a statement made by the union revenue secretary (later reiterated by the finance secretary) that deposits of newly invalid currency notes into the bank accounts of political parties would not attract tax scrutiny. In narrow legal terms, this statement was innocuous; under Section 13A of the Income Tax Act, political parties have long been exempt from paying tax, provided that they adequately maintain their books.

But the outcry that followed forced ministry officials and subsequently even Union Finance Minister Arun Jaitley to address the issue, stating, "The legal and taxation regime with regard to political parties remains absolutely what it has been in the last 15–20 years. There is not a single change that has been brought about nor is any change at the moment contemplated."[21] The government's position was less than credible; arguing that one is constrained by decades-old law rang hollow when it had just implemented a draconian measure such as demonetisation at a moment's notice.

In an unusual New Year's Eve address to the nation, Prime Minister Modi noted that the public had spoken and the time had come for the country to consider how best to cleanse the financing of politics. "Political parties, political leaders and electoral funding,

[21] *Times of India*, 18 December 2016.

figure prominently in any debate on corruption and black money. The time has now come that all political leaders and parties respect the feelings of the nation's honest citizens, and understand the anger of the people," Modi said. While the prime minister stopped short of articulating a blueprint or roadmap for reform, he urged that all parties and leaders give up their "holier than thou approach" to jointly discuss how to "free politics of black money and corruption."[22]

In principle, the government seemed to live up to its rhetoric and introduced several political finance reform measures in the 2017 Finance Bill. The core of the government's approach centred on three objectives – strengthening limits on cash giving, tightening income tax provisions, and introducing a new instrument known as "electoral bonds".[23] As with any new legislation, assessing their impact on political funding will depend on the quality of implementation and the details found in the fine print (which, in the case of electoral bonds, had yet to be issued at the time of writing). Nonetheless, we provide a preliminary analysis of the government's measures.[24]

Contributions

The first group of provisions strengthened limits on cash giving by changing the nature and limit of contributions to political parties. Under the status quo ante, no single anonymous contribution to political parties could exceed Rs 20,000. Any donation over this threshold required the individual or entity making the donation to disclose their identity. The changes enacted in the bill modified this in several ways. For starters, the act instituted a new Rs 2000 threshold for cash donations. Going forward, any donation above Rs 2000 must be transferred via cheque or digital payment (inter-

[22] *Indian Express*, 31 December 2016.

[23] Vaishnav and Brown 2017.

[24] Vaishnav 2017.

estingly, however, the act did not alter the Rs 20,000 limit for public disclosure). In addition, the act tied the new cash threshold to an individual rather than to any single contribution. This is an important detail because donors in the past regularly split their large contribution into many smaller donations (each below Rs 20,000) to avoid disclosure. This, of course, also allowed parties to obscure the identity of the vast majority of their donors.[25]

Under these new provisions in the Finance Act, anyone who donates more than Rs 2000 *in aggregate* will have to disclose their identity. The final adjustment requires that corporations make all contributions via check or digital payment, rather than cash. Shortly before the bill was to come up for a vote on the floor of the Lok Sabha, the government attached two further amendments to the Finance Bill with little advance notice. The first eliminated the cap on corporate giving (which previously stood at 7.5 per cent of a corporation's average net profits over the previous three years) while the second dropped the requirement that firms must declare their political contributions on their profit and loss statements.

The government's proposals to limit cash in politics are notable and consistent with demonetisation and the general move to curb the use of cash in the economy. Cash transactions, as many of the contributions in this book demonstrate, are rampant in electoral politics, difficult to observe and, therefore, hard to trace. Unfortunately, the government's measures do not provide adequate disincentives when it comes to cash. For instance, the government could have abolished cash contributions altogether, as opposed to simply placing a ceiling on cash donations at Rs 2000. Whenever an arbitrary limit is imposed (whether it is Rs 20,000 or Rs 2000), there is an incentive for those who want to game the system to report amounts just below the threshold. While it is technically illegal for any one individual to donate more than Rs 2000 without

[25] Interestingly, if donors choose the alternative route of electoral bonds that has been introduced (see section below), then disclosure of identities can be completely avoided.

disclosure, it is not clear what will stop parties from claiming they have received multiple small donations from anonymous individuals since they do not have to keep records of those who give less than the limit in any case.[26]

Perhaps the most surprising omission was to require the simplest and most obvious form of identification be linked to any cash donation of any size: the contributor's Aadhaar number. For a government so committed on leveraging Aadhaar in an ever-increasing number of government programmes, this was clearly deliberate. And for many in civil society who have pressed for greater transparency in electoral finance, their opposition to Aadhaar meant they could not press for it in this case.

Tax Scrutiny

Beyond altering the fine print around donations, the legislation also aimed to tighten provisions of the Income Tax (IT) Act as they relate to political parties. While political parties in India are tax-exempt, under prevailing law, political parties are required to keep updated financial accounts, maintain records of the names and addresses attached to large contributions, submit their accounts for audit, and file their income tax returns on an annual basis (in exchange for receiving tax-exempt status).[27] The Finance Act stipulated that these tax returns should be submitted within the time prescribed. Previously, many parties did not submit their tax

[26] As one politician remarked to one of the authors, the biggest winner of this reform will be chartered accountants, who will be able to demand bigger pay cheques in return for their expanded financial jugglery. Indeed, as one journalist noted, "Earlier, if a person had to give Rs 1 lakh in cash, they would make five receipts by breaking it up and keeping it under Rs 20,000. Now, they would have to make 50 receipts. It's a logistical nightmare but it still doesn't prevent the party from accepting cash donations." Meghnad 2017.

[27] In January 2017, the Supreme Court reconfirmed that the exception made to keep parties out of the tax net was one of executive determination, claiming that parties needed money to propagate their beliefs.

returns on an annual basis, while others failed to do so at all. This new provision ostensibly sought to close this loophole.

The lack of independent audit scrutiny and meaningful enforcement makes the new provision much better in theory than in practice. ADR has warned in the past that "there is a lack of frequent and complete scrutiny of financial disclosures of political parties" by tax authorities.[28] If tax officials do not scrutinise party accounts, it will make little difference if the documents are submitted on time or with substantial delay. Equally, there is no categorical schedule of penalties if parties fail to file their accounts "within the time prescribed". Indeed, under the Companies Act, all private companies in India must file tax returns within sixty days of their last annual general meeting, and there is a clear escalating schedule of financial and penal penalties the longer the delay in filing returns.[29] Clearly, the ramifications for the public if a political party fails to file returns in time are substantially greater than if a private firm fails to do so. Yet the bite of the law is much stronger on the latter compared to the former.

Electoral Bonds

The third and final innovation in the Finance Act is the introduction of a new instrument, the "electoral bond". At the time

[28] "Additional Views of ADR/NEW on Political Finance and the 255th Report of the Law Commission of India", Association for Democratic Reforms and National Election Watch, April 2015, accessed 6 June 2017, http://adrindia.org/sites/default/files/Additional_views_ADR-NEW_political_finance_255th_Law_commission_ECI.pdf.

[29] Under Section 92 (5) of the Companies Act, 2013, if a company fails to file its annual return, "the company shall be punishable with fine which shall not be less than fifty thousand rupees but which may extend to five lakh rupees *and every officer of the company who is in default shall be punishable with imprisonment for a term which may extend to six months* or with fine which shall not be less than fifty thousand rupees but which may extend to five lakh rupees, or with both" (emphasis added).

of writing, the government has not fully elaborated the details of how this bond would operate, but a few basic principles seem clear based on government documents and statements made by various finance ministry officials. Electoral bonds are time-limited bearer bonds that corporations can purchase from scheduled banks and subsequently transfer to a registered bank account of a political party. The fund flow would proceed entirely through the formal banking system, allowing for a step-by-step paper trail. However, the identity of the corporation purchasing the bond would not be publicly revealed (although, since the transaction is taking place via the banking system, regulators presumably would have access to this information). When the corporation deposits these bonds into a specially designated bank account of a registered party, the party would know who the donor is, but neither the party nor the corporation is required to disclose this information.

The upside to the new scheme is that corporations will now have a legitimate channel through which they can contribute funds to parties, as opposed to indulging in under-the-table transactions, while protecting their anonymity (which they greatly prize). But the upside is also the downside: transparency, as far as the public is concerned, is arguably the biggest victim; this is ironic considering the government explicitly framed the proposal under the heading of improving "transparency in political funding". Taking into account the elimination of the cap on corporate giving, the dropping of the requirement that firms disclose political giving on their financial statements, and the introduction of electoral bonds, "corporations can now legally give unlimited sums to political parties who, in turn, can accept unlimited sums of money – all without having to disclose a single rupee."[30] Advocates of the new changes rightly point out that there will be a digital paper trail (as there is with all banking transactions), but this trail will not be on public display, which means that electoral

[30] Vaishnav 2017.

bonds will not change the opaque status quo for the better in the foreseeable future.[31]

Net Assessment

The net effect of the recent changes in the rules could be an increased flow of funds to political parties by digital or cheque payments but absent disclosure of donor identities. Indeed, as the finance minister himself has said, part of the government's objective was to protect donor anonymity; the banks will know who bought electoral bonds but not to which party they were given. The question of who gave how much to which party will not be in public view. This is a far cry from transparency and disclosure of donor identities and amounts – standard in most developed democracies – but will boost (opaque) fund flow to parties over the next two years, something about which both parties and donors feel comfortable. We can expect an arms race in fundraising over the next two years before the 2019 election with the ruling party having an edge.

In the absence of public funding and/or increased tax deductibility, there is little incentive for donors to become more transparent. In fact, in a highly regulated political economy, there is no incentive to donate transparently to parties simply to support democracy without a *quid pro quo*. In a poor country with a regulated economy, there is a problem of donor self-interest that militates against the achievement of full transparency unless some system of adequate public funding is put in place. However, this system requires internal democracy and accountability in parties, something that most parties are loath to consider.

As of mid-2017, the push for further transparency of political

[31] To be clear, corporations have good reason for wanting to donate anonymously: given the discretionary authorities that are vested with the state, any firm that publicly donates funds to one political party fears retribution if a competing party comes to power.

parties and their finances remains stalled.[32] In June 2013 the CIC ruled that India's six national political parties (Congress, BJP, Communist Party of India [Marxist] [CPI(M)], Communist Party of India [CPI], Nationalist Congress Party [NCP], and Bahujan Samaj Party [BSP]) were "public entities" that should be subject to disclosures under the RTI Act, and repeated this in March 2015. However, these parties have consistently failed to comply and the CIC, lacking any coercive or punitive powers, has thrown up its hands. In May 2015 the Supreme Court, in reaction to the non-compliance of political parties to the repeated orders of the CIC to make disclosures under RTI, asked the six national parties and the central government to respond as to why they could not be more transparent. The central government, for its part, stated that the CIC had erroneously concluded that parties are public authorities. To the contrary, it argued, parties are not established under the Constitution or any law made by parliament, and that there is already transparency of their finances under the reporting requirements of the 1951 Income Tax Act and the RPA.

Political finance reform is ultimately a collective action problem among political parties and between parties and donors that requires the right alignment of incentives. And there are some positive examples of such collective action in the past. The Model Code of Conduct, a mutually agreed upon code among parties, that governs election campaigns is an example. What are the incentives to break out of a corrupt and opaque equilibrium that is the long-run path-dependent outcome of banning company donations without substituting them with state funding?

Any viable reform of political finance not only has to be in the public interest, but it must also serve the interests of existing political parties. Until 1989, when the one-party dominant era came

[32] For the information in this paragraph, see Rajagopal 2015.

to an end, the conditions for collective action did not exist because the Congress party had no incentive to constrain its superior fundraising potential. The changes to the party system that began in 1989 and led to the emergence of a multi-party system have arguably created some of the enabling conditions for collective action on political finance reform, including full transparency and possibly state funding too. However, we note that whether the solution is full transparency of donations and donor identities, or this combined with state funding of parties for elections or for general purposes, the key is some form of regulation of parties that requires internal democracy, transparency, and accountability; indeed, adoption of these principles should be made mandatory before any system of state funding is instituted. However, any such regulation of parties should also bear in mind that while they are performing public functions and overlap with the state when in power, they are ultimately private organisations representing citizen interests, and this character should not be destroyed by regulation.

From a broad comparative perspective, many aspects of India's political finance architecture are broadly shared: 40 per cent of countries (for which there is data) have limits on candidate spending;[33] 70 per cent of countries (including India) do not have any ceiling on spending by political parties. Likewise, another 40 per cent of countries have some form of limit on donations (although in 2017, India eliminated limits on corporate giving). Two-thirds of countries have direct public funding for parties and/or candidates. India and a collection of fragile democracies, including some Middle Eastern, African, and post-Soviet states, do not.

Taken as a whole, India's political finance system is heavily regulated on paper. In practice, however, loopholes and lax enforcement create a de facto laissez faire regime – especially when compared with developed democracies. India lacks any effective

[33] See Austin and Tjernstrom 2014 for the data cited in this paragraph.

ceiling on party spending, effective limits on donations, public funding (except for limited time on state-owned electronic media), and a practical system of reporting and disclosure. Clearly, despite steps in the direction of transparency and curbing the deployment of cash in politics, India has a very long way to go.

Bibliography

Austin, Reginald, and Maja Tjernstrom, eds. 2014. *Funding of Political Parties and Election Campaigns* (Stockholm: International IDEA).

Chandra, Kanchan. 2015. "The New Indian State: The Relocation of Patronage in the Post-Liberalisation Economy", *Economic and Political Weekly*, 50, no. 41, 10 October, 46–58.

Chhibber, Pradeep K., and Geetha Murali. 2006. "Duvergerian Dynamics in Indian States", *Party Politics*, 12, no. 1, 5–34.

Duverger, Maurice. 1954. *Political Parties: Their Organization and Activity in the Modern State* (New York: Wiley).

Gottipati, Sruthi, and Rajesh Kumar Singh. 2014. "India Set to Challenge U.S. for Election-Spending Record", *Reuters*, 9 March.

Gowda, M.V. Rajeev, and E. Sridharan. 2012. "Reforming India's Party Financing and Election Expenditure Laws", *Election Law Journal*, 11, no. 2, 226–40.

Indian Express. 2016. "Full Text: PM Narendra Modi New Year's Eve Address to the Nation", 31 December, retrieved 6 June 2017, http://indianexpress. com/article/india/full-text-pm-narendra-modi-new-years-eve-address-to- the-nation-4453587/.

Meghnad, S. 2017. "Why Jaitley's Political Funding Reforms Won't End Anonymous Donations", *The Wire*, 6 February, retrieved 6 June 2017, https://thewire.in/106262/ jaitley-political-funding-reforms-budget-anonymous-donations/.

Rajagopal, Krishnnadas. 2015. "Can't Bring Political Parties Under RTI, Centre Tells Supreme Court", *Hindu*, 24 August.

Sridharan, E. 1999. "Toward State Funding of Elections in India: A Comparative Perspective on Possible Options", *Journal of Policy Reform* 3, no. 3, 229–54.

Sridharan, E. 2002. "The Fragmentation of the Indian Party System 1952–1999: Seven Competing Explanations", in Zoya Hasan, ed.,

Parties and Party Politics in India (New Delhi: Oxford University Press), 475–503.

Sridharan, E. 2006. "Electoral Finance Reform: The Relevance of International Experience", in Vikram K. Chand, ed., *Reinventing Public Service Delivery in India: Selected Case Studies* (New Delhi: Sage), 363–88.

Sridharan, E. 2012. "Why are Multi-Party Minority Governments Viable in India? Theory and Comparison", *Commonwealth and Comparative Politics*, 50, no. 3, 314–43.

Sridharan, E. 2013. "Reforming Campaign Finance to Tackle Corruption in India: Possible Options from the International Experience", in Samuel Paul, ed., *Fighting Corruption* (New Delhi: Academic Foundation), 43–70.

Sridharan, E., and Milan Vaishnav. 2016. "India", in Pippa Norris and Andrea Abel van Es, eds, *Elections? Political Finance in Comparative Perspective* (New York: Oxford University Press), 64–83.

Sridharan, E., and Peter Ronald de Souza. 2006. "Introduction: The Evolution of Political Parties in India", in Peter Ronald de Souza and E. Sridharan, eds, *India's Political Parties* (New Delhi: Sage), 15–36.

Times of India. 2016. "No Plan to Reprint Entire Demonetised Amount, Says Arun Jaitley",18 December.

Vaishnav, Milan. 2017. "Finance Bill Makes Funding for Political Parties More Opaque Than Ever", *Hindustan Times*, 29 March.

Vaishnav, Milan, and Danielle Smogard. 2014. "A New Era in Indian Politics", Carnegie Endowment for International Peace, 10 June, retrieved 17 October 2017, http://carnegieendowment.org/2014/06/10/new-era-in-indian- politics-pub-55883.

Vaishnav, Milan, and Rebecca Brown. 2017. "Crafty Indian Politicians Can Game the New Political Funding Rules Even in Their Sleep", *Quartz*, 1 February, retrieved 6 June 2017, https://qz.com/900922/budget-2017-why-arun-jaitleys-new-rules-to-clean-up-indias-political-funding-simply-wont- work/.

Index

Note: Page numbers followed by 't' denote tables